THE
INCLUSION
PARADOX

2nd Edition

Praise for
The Inclusion Paradox
by Andrés T. Tapia

"Andrés Tapia has become one of the foremost thought leaders in the area of workplace diversity. His unique perspectives on inclusion have shifted the paradigm on how leaders now think about diversity."

—*John W. Rogers, Jr., Chairman and CEO, Ariel Investments*

"Andrés Tapia brings a unique combination of personal and professional experience to the subjects of cultural diversity and inclusion. His insights and approach can help a company strive toward achieving an inclusive environment in which a richly diverse global workforce can thrive."

—*Robert W. Lane, Chairman, Deere & Company*

"The Inclusion Paradox is a must-read for all who want to keep ahead of the forces of change. Andrés has focused his keen mind on the most critical issues that are creating global societal change today."

—*Carol Evans, CEO, Working Mother Media and Diversity Best Practices*

"An insightful and thoughtful analysis by an insightful and thoughtful leader in the field. Andrés captures the essence of the challenges facing global institutions in the 21st century and offers a path to success and sustainability."

—Gilbert F. Casellas, Vice President, Corporate Responsibility, Dell Inc. and former Chairman, U.S. Equal Employment Opportunity Commission

"Andrés Tapia has emerged as a rising star in business strategy. In *The Inclusion Paradox*, Tapia challenges us to call out our differences as a critical step to achieve inclusion. This book is a call to action. The megatrends are identified. The sustainable strategies are defined. The probing questions are outlined. Tapia equips the reader to lead change rather than be the victim of it. I recommend it to executives who are serious about being competitive by embracing and leveraging diversity."

—Gloria Castillo, President, Chicago United

"The Inclusion Paradox is a significant contribution to the field. Andrés's uncanny ability to weave together the unique tapestries of various cultural perspectives has helped to enlighten, inspire, educate and even transform our understanding of a topic that can often be complex and controversial."

—Mary-Frances Winters, CEO, The Winters Group

"Andrés is an insightful and provocative thought leader in diversity and inclusion. Based on his personal and professional experiences, he challenges the conventional approach. In clear and direct language, *The Inclusion Paradox* describes a new way to drive real results in your diversity and inclusion efforts."

—Jorge Figueredo, Executive Vice President, HR, McKesson Corporation

"In Andrés Tapia's new book, *The Inclusion Paradox*, Andrés masterfully examines American corporations' challenges with diversity. He astutely analyzes the difference between diversity and inclusion, and the importance of recognizing differences rather than minimizing them."

—Mellody Hobson, President, Ariel Investments

"This book takes a topic that can be perceived as feel-good liberalism and contextualizes it as crucial for even the most conservative business mind. Tapia explains how demographic, social, economic, and political forces have come together in a perfect storm that can drown and shred the best businesses, as we've already seen. He provides clear rationale, strategy, and practical steps for navigating the storm to penetrate new markets, grow existing ones, and attract and retain the best talent."

—*Dianne Hofner Saphiere, creator of the* Cultural Detective® *series, and Principal, Nipporica Associates, LLC*

"*The Inclusion Paradox* provides a provocative and shrewd perspective on global diversity. It provides a lucid picture of the globalized world and is a definitive handbook for business and diversity executives who want to succeed in shaping an inclusive work environment. The analysis provided in this book is illuminating, far reaching, and most importantly, absolutely correct. Tapia's book is notable for its emphasis on a global diversity perspective as a driving catalyst for economic growth in Corporate America."

—*Dr. Robert Rodriguez, author of* Latino Talent: Effective Strategies to Recruit, Retain and Develop Hispanic Professionals *and* Diversity Executive Magazine *columnist*

"*The Inclusion Paradox* provides a compelling, 21st century perspective towards an age-old question: How can the United States and our global community create a truly inclusive environment across the vast span of cultural differences? The solution, according to the author, is to engage the minds and hearts of all people through the constructive management of our differences. In order to do this effectively, intercultural competence is essential. Tapia provides needed information on why we need to rethink how inclusion operates in our workplaces and gives us personal stories that show how different cultural perspectives dramatically impact relationships in our families and organizations. The book also provides practical solutions. This book is, quite simply, required reading for leaders today."

—*Dr. Mitch Hammer, co-creator of the Intercultural Development Inventory (IDI), and CEO of Hammer Consulting*

"Today's educators shape tomorrow's quality citizens and corporate employees and executives. Andrés Tapia's expertise challenged us to rethink our priorities and practices as we strive to prepare our students for the 21st century. Andrés, an outstanding facilitator, is also a wonderful storyteller who immediately connects with others. While developing a warm, safe, and comfortable environment, he is capable of pushing participants to reflect on the challenging implications of an increasingly dynamic global reality. *The Inclusion Paradox* speaks directly to educators charged with preparing all students to succeed in a world where diversity must be, as he says — understood, embraced, and 'called out' so that crosscultural competence emerges as a result. It is a must-read for individuals seeking to foster equity and striving to achieve personal and systemic excellence."

—George V. Fornero, Superintendent of Schools,
Township High School District 113, Highland Park, Illinois

"Learning from and working with Andrés Tapia has been very impactful for me. While I have been involved with diversity and inclusion for many years as part of my HR role, and as part of my own personal passion around the power of respecting and valuing teamwork, I had a lot to learn about the way to optimize these principles in a global company. Andrés provided me with a world view and an appreciation for awareness of self and others that helped me in my quest to leverage diversity and inclusion on work teams. He has amazing insights and is able to probe deeply into the subconscious biases of individuals and organizations."

—Laurie S. Simpson, Director,
Global Team Enrichment & Diversity, Deere & Company

"Thanks to Andrés we now have a vehicle to open more paths into an authentic dialogue between artists and corporate audiences. Since the arts embrace diversity by allowing exploration and revelation of culture and self, it is an essential and necessary conversation for creating greater inclusion in organizations. And a word on Andrés' Latino background: like we have done in dance, in exploring and sharing our culture we create new insights that help all see each other in new ways."

—Eduardo Vilaro, founder of Luna Negra Dance Theater
and Artistic Director of Ballet Hispanico

"In his new book, Andrés Tapia leaves no stone unturned in addressing the thorny issues of diversity and inclusion, including how they've evolved and why corporations must and *can* do better in making them a more organic part of business in the 21st century. Tapia's advice is not only sound, but delivered with great intimacy and insight. That's because, given his Peruvian roots and successful rise in corporate America, diversity and inclusion are deeply personal matters — and have been for the almost decade I've known him as both a friend and a colleague. He has been a real pioneer in this area, talking about how to find the synergy between our gender, faith, sexual, age, and cultural differences long before it was fashionable, asking hard questions, offering contemplative answers, and advocating for an approach that goes beyond just forming committees and day-long diversity training."

—Jill Sherer Murray, Communications Practice Leader
with The Trion Group, and Author/Blogger of "Diary of a Writer in
Mid-Life Crisis" on WildRiverReview.com, Trion Group

"Andrés has skillfully translated his innovative views on inclusion and diversity into a set of practical approaches that form a valuable roadmap for change. This is definitely required reading for anyone who wants to take a leadership role in creating and driving an inclusive culture."

—Jeanne Mason, PhD., Corporate Vice President,
Human Resources, Baxter International Inc.

"The Inclusion Paradox is brilliant! The distinguished author, Andrés T.Tapia, has elevated the subject matter to bring meaning in a very unique way to it, as well as many, many associated terms. I find the book a wonderful read, both from an educational and entertainment point of view. His comprehension of 'The Power of Diversity Through the Arts' is so right and answers so many questions, as do other chapters. I congratulate Andrés for writing what could become a definitive treatise on the subject matter."

—Paul Freeman, Music Director,
Chicago Sinfonietta, Czech National Symphony Orchestra

Andrés T. Tapia

THE INCLUSION PARADOX

2nd Edition

The Obama Era and the Transformation of Global Diversity

THE INCLUSION PARADOX
2nd Edition
The Obama Era and the Transformation of Global Diversity

Copyright © 2013 by Andrés T. Tapia. All rights reserved.

No part of this book may be reproduced in any form or by any means, without written permission from the author, Andrés T. Tapia.

Blog: www.inclusionparadox.com
Web: www.diversitybestpractices.com
Twitter: @AndresTTapia

Library of Congress Control Number: 2013904412

ISBN–10: 0989098001
ISBN–13: 978-0-9890980-0-7

Printed in the United States of America

To Lori –

mi vida, who keeps it real

&

A Marisela –

m'hija quien vive y celebra la paradoja de las diferencias

One life
But we are not the same
We get to
Carry each other

One, U2

The Inclusion Paradox

2nd Edition

The Obama Era
and the Transformation
of Global Diversity

Contents

Contents

Contents

Contents

Author's Note
Introduction to the 2nd Edition

Regardless of one's own personal political preferences, the first time Barack Obama was elected president was historic. The second time marked actual culture change.

This, of course, doesn't mean that all welcome the change. But change has happened and so we must understand why and its implications. This is what inspired in me, a student and practitioner of culture change, to publish the first edition of this book, *The Inclusion Paradox: The Obama Era and the Transformation of Global Diversity*, a few years ago as the U.S.'s first Black president began his maiden term.

The election of Barack Obama was a defining moment that captured both metaphorically and literally the zeitgeist of the times. The moment has come to be known as the Obama Era, a period in history that was as much about the demographic changes in society that made possible the election of the United States' first Black president as about the man and leader himself whose own diverse biography would come to further define the early 21st Century.

That first election was certainly historic. It was a massive break through the color line. But it was too soon to tell if it was going to lead to being understood as being anything beyond a flash-in-the-pan stroke of luck due to an imploding economy so out of control that many millions were willing to take what for them was a what-the-hell bet of voting for the non-White person who could maybe magically save the nation. While the insurgency of the 2008 Obama election brought us to the tipping point of a new way of understanding a contemporary and diverse society, as the governing road got tougher and steeper, plenty of evidence mounted that Obama's historic election could end up being an outlier episode rather than a transformative era.

As there always is when societies are at a tipping point toward some sort of tectonic shift, powerful countervailing forces emerged to keep the tip from happening. True to form we saw this societal dynamic emerge through the fierce Tea Party phenomenon which led to major setbacks to the President's agenda in the midterm elections. Conventional wisdom settled in that this adventure wasn't lasting more than one term.

But for all the head winds the country's first Black president faced, the pundits and the opposition fell well short of their predictions. While theories abound of political strategy missteps, it's clear that the biggest oversight by one side, and the greatest asset of the other, was in how they responded to the shifting diversity demographics. A lesson that should not be lost on business leaders in relation to their talent and marketplace goals.

Diversity Is Leading to Permanent Policy Changes

Demographics is destiny. It affects the economy, the schoolhouse, the workplace, and the voting booth. The diverse demographic tsunami with its waves crashing against our electoral shores was a dramatic announcement that the long predicted diversity of the country had finally arrived. It was going to affect everything. The 2012 election only solidified this reality.

If diversity before the Obama Era had been about a Bill-Cosby-like-feel-goodism, the embrace of multicultural celebrations, and the paralysis of political correctness, then today's shifting demographics have implications that go far beyond sitcom TV shows and exotic cuisine. They head straight into public policy decisions about education, the healthcare system, the financial system, and the nation's tax structure that affects everyone's lives. There can be no denying that the massively shifting demographics have shifted the policy agenda.

Consider the following:

- Health care reform will end up insuring 32 million previously uninsured Americans – a disproportionate number of which (11 million) are people of color.
- For the first time a U.S. president supports gay marriage and the 20-year-old military policy of Don't Ask, Don't Tell gets repealed.
- Education reform with its signature Race to the Top program will disproportionately benefit kids of color as the focus is on failing schools, which are graduating less than 50 percent of African-American and Latino students.
- Financial reform had within its provisions the creation (for the first time ever) in the Federal Reserve System the Office for Minority and Women Inclusion in each of the Federal Reserve Banks. Not only does it call for greater diverse representation in its workforce and leadership, but for the Fed to also press the banks they regulate on their commitment to diversity.
- In 2012, nearly one million young undocumented Latinos living in the United States were offered a two-year reprieve from deportation under a presidential executive order.
- President Obama signs an Executive Order in 2011 establishing a coordinated government-wide initiative to promote diversity and inclusion in the federal workforce that, in his words, is intended "to develop and implement a more comprehensive, integrated, and strategic focus on diversity and inclusion as a key component of their human resources strategies."
- Secretary of Defense Leon Panetta in January 2013 lifts the ban on women serving in combat roles thus removing one of the greatest obstacles to career advancement for women in the military.

But still, was the 2008 election and the four years that followed just going to end up being an episodic blip, or instead be the first surge of a rising and lasting tidal wave of change?

The results of the 2012 election provide the answer. The changes due to the demographic shifts are here to stay. Barack Hussein Obama swept back into office with the following diverse votes: 90 percent of Blacks, 70 percent of Asians, 70 percent of Latinos, 65 percent of voters under 40, and 55 percent of the female vote. The cultural markers here are that, yes, there are now enough "minority" voters that have come together to become majorities and tip the balance once again in the election of the president of the United States.

This is why Obama's second election – and the various state referenda on gay marriage as well as the election of the first out lesbian U.S. senator, and the election of the greatest number ever of women to Congress – ended up being a thunder clap announcing that true culture change had arrived.

While many will disagree, even vehemently, with the merits or values behind the culture changes, for better or for worse, the point has fully tipped. Its myriad implications for the economy, education, energy, immigration, and individual and collective responsibilities – while still happening in fits and starts – are irreversible.

To keep driving the point further that this embrace of diversity will continue in Obama's second term, both symbolically and literally, his second Inaugural ceremony featured the first ever Latina Supreme Court Justice administering the vice president's oath of office, the first Black female to give the invocation, the first Latino, who is also openly gay, to recite an Inaugural poem.

And in substance, the first Black president was the first ever to refer to Gay Rights in an Inaugural speech and spoke up for the equal rights for women and the citizenship rights for the millions of undocumented Latino immigrants. He tied it all together in a stunning statement when referring to the Civil Rights legacy that ran "through Seneca Falls and Selma and Stonewall."

This is an upside-down time. If before in the diversity field we singularly focused on how minorities or those traditionally on the margins of society were affected by or were at the mercy of the choices of the majority, we now see this emerging New Mainstream bending the arc of history as they challenge the rules of engagement for those who have traditionally held power.

This, of course, does not mean that the actual solutions are obvious or that they won't require vigorous debate of how best to address. But when African-Americans, Latinos, Asians, LGBT, youth, and single women decide the election for president for a second time, the agenda has been set by these voters for what needs to be addressed for the United States.

People on both sides of the political and philosophical divide agree that they want the United States to remain economically competitive in a world where change – demographically, economically, politically, technologically – is happening at warp speed. What they don't agree on is how best to do this. But one thing is clear: those who have traditionally been marginalized and whose voices were either not heard or dismissed, given their sheer numbers, cannot be ignored any longer.

And here's where I pivot to the implications to business. The hyper-diversity of the workforce and the marketplace are completely upending long-held beliefs and practices in human resources, marketing, and product development.

Since the publication of the first edition I have moved from the position of Chief Diversity Officer at Hewitt Associates to the post of President of Diversity Best Practices. Then as now, I've had the opportunity to serve as an executive diversity and inclusion consultant to the C-suite of dozens of Fortune 500 companies. I have stood in front of thousands of leaders and employees around the world from companies such as John Deere, Marriott, McKesson, Baxter, United Airlines, IBM, Discover, and dozens more including multinationals from India, China, South Korea, and various European countries.

These experiences allow me to say even more confidently that the ideas and solutions presented here are not just theoretical or hopeful. They work. And not just for corporations, but also for not-for-profits, government institutions, schools, law enforcement agencies, and healthcare organizations.

Many of today's problems are legacy outcomes – the results of policies and philosophies that have little to do with today's realities. So the way out is through divergent thinking, through the ability to see our issues in new ways never seen before. The best way to do this? Tap an unprecedented diversity to bust through calcified, narrow-vision traditional thinking. 'Cuz same old will continue to mold.

The mold buster is indeed the diversity that too many still fear. If unleashed, leveraged, and managed well, diversity and inclusion can lead the way to breakthrough creativity and innovation. Here's how one of the poster children of the new economy, Indian-born, Ivy-league-educated, U.S.-based CNN political scientist and commentator, Fareed Zakaria, sees the U.S. as narrated on his show *GPS* right after Obama's reelection: "edgy, experimental, open-minded – and brilliantly diverse."

And here's how the namesake of the Obama Era sees it as stated in his reelection acceptance speech in Chicago on election night in 2012: "I believe we can keep the promise of our founders, the idea that if you're willing to work hard, it doesn't matter who you are or where you come from or what you look like or where you love. It doesn't matter whether you're Black or White or Hispanic or Asian or Native American or young or old or rich or poor, able, disabled, gay or straight, you can make it here in America if you're willing to try."

The work of diversity and inclusion has never been more important or relevant. Many already see it and are reaping and spreading its benefits, but too many still don't. This is why we still have work to do.

As you open up this 2nd edition with its updated facts, figures, and up-to-date current event references, I believe more than ever that diversity and inclusion hold the keys to strengthening our organizations, our markets, our economies, our families, our relationships, and our nations.

What is required to move forward are influential, well-informed, committed, and passionate leaders like you.

¡Adelante! (onward)

Andrés T. Tapia
Chicago, November 2012

Foreword

By Carol Evans
CEO, Working Mother Media and Diversity Best Practices

As the CEO of Working Mother Media and Diversity Best Practices, I've spent the majority of my career steeped in the issues surrounding diversity and inclusion. The advancement of women, the vast diversity of the workplace, and the issues affecting working families are matters that rightfully concern the most progressive executives and their companies. The way in which we address those topics indicate how our companies will thrive in the marketplace, and essentially, represent make or break issues for organizations around the globe.

But the outcomes are bigger, grander, and more important than just what occurs on the shop floor, in the cubicle farm, or in the executive suite — because those issues touch our families and societies as a whole. I arrived at my beliefs both as a corporate executive and as a working mother. Although my children are now adults, my advocacy for working families, diversity and inclusion, and the advancement of women and men of all races and ethnicities remains undiminished.

The crux of the matter is that diversity and inclusion is about leveraging all the skills, talents, and perspectives that employees bring to work. It's about finding and nurturing the best talent and fundamentally changing the way we view the workforce and the individuals who shape it.

Throughout the years, I've had the privilege and opportunity to speak with thousands of women and men of all ages and races about their experiences at work. As you can imagine, with such great diversity of people comes an even greater assortment of perspectives and opinions. Yet, a common theme continued to run through those discussions: these women and men want to succeed at work and they want their employers to value their multifaceted multidimensionality — they want to bring their whole selves to the workplace. They also want to be able to offer their whole selves at home, to be available — physically and emotionally present — to their families, friends, and communities. They want and need to be enabled by organizations that allow them to flex their day, their week, their year, and their entire career. In essence, they seek workplaces that support their ambitions both inside and outside their organization's physical and virtual walls.

Every fiber of my being believes that diversity and inclusion is the right thing to do. We must open the gates of opportunity to millions of employees who have been denied real chances for career fulfillment and advancement because of their sex, race, orientation, looks, dress, different abilities, and cultural heritage.

But it's also right for business. The most profitable businesses, research from the National Association for Female Executives (NAFE) and Catalyst has shown, also have the greatest gender and racial diversity in their leadership and executive ranks. The laws of probability prove over and over that companies drawing from a greater number of talent pools obtain the greater share of top-notch talent.

And it's not only a diverse workforce; it's also a diverse marketplace out there. Companies that design, develop, and market products and services that meet the needs of the dramatically shifting consumer base will win. And those that don't will be gone.

These are the reasons why I acquired Diversity Best Practices in 2006. While much of my work up to that point had been focused on the advancement of women and work-life issues, the launch of our Multicultural Women's initiative in 2002 taught me about the additional challenges they faced due to their skin color, accents, or cultural backgrounds. I realized our portfolio of services — and knowledge — at Working Mother was incomplete. Diversity Best Practices, with its wide reach embracing the full spectrum of diversity issues was the perfect organization to extend our work. As we grew the scope of Diversity Best Practices from services to leadership I knew we needed a visionary leader to take the helm of this organization. I found that person in Andrés.

In the world of diversity and inclusion, Andrés Tapia is a true standout. In the press release announcing him as the new President of Diversity Best Practices we quoted one of our Diversity Best Practices members who called him a diversity rock star — which he certainly is!

I first met Andrés when he was Chief Diversity Officer at Hewitt and an active member participant in Diversity Best Practices. I came to appreciate the innovative and novel approaches he brought to our events. The more I heard him speak and read his thought-provoking views about diversity around the world, the more I realized that his insights offered us a way to re-imagine how our workplaces, our societies, and our world can operate.

Since taking the helm of Diversity Best Practices in early 2011, Andrés has helped us imagine and work together toward a new social order — one where everyone's abilities, perspectives, and values are harnessed for the individual and collective good both in the workplace and in the marketplace. Andrés' approach encourages us to include everyone: people with disabilities, women, people of color, LGBT, veterans, Millennials, people of faith, seniors, White males, blue collar, white collar, and pink collar, introverts — the list goes on.

While a philosopher and thinker Andrés is fundamentally a man of action. I have witnessed first-hand how he transforms his ideas into actionable strategies, solutions, and programs. He has brought the same effectiveness he showed when he led Hewitt's diversity efforts to Diversity Best Practices, much to my delight and that of our members.

This has included taking our think tank work to a transformative level where the best practices advocacy and collection we have always been known for are invigorated by the next practices thinking Andrés is always urging us to create.

Through his thought leadership and the work of our consulting team, he is helping members and clients create first-in-class diversity strategies and develop innovative solutions for culture change. Andrés' work in looking at employee healthcare benefits and long-term retirement savings through a diversity lens and the central role social media must play in the work of diversity practitioners are just two examples of how he pushes our members and clients to look beyond best practices to emerging needs and issues.

In this second edition of *The Inclusion Paradox: The Obama Era and the Transformation of Global Diversity*, Andrés provides updated data and weaves in current events that have taken place since the book was published in 2009.

Readers will gain a clear understanding of how CEOs, businesses, human resource and affinity group leaders in the most influential business, not-for-profit, and government organizations — many of whom are our Diversity Best Practices members — have collectively been moving the work forward in ways that are relevant, contemporary, effective, and exciting.

The arguments of Andrés' book not only hold; they were strengthened by the meta global and U.S. trends unfolding these past four years. Anyone hearing President Obama's second Inaugural Address will recognize that the premise of this book has become even more relevant than the day it was first published.

As the global economy blurs boundaries of nations across the world's largest economies from India to China, from the United States to Brazil, and as work and supply chains flow from South America, the Arab states, the Pacific Rim, Europe, and Africa, we desperately need voices to guide the work of the relevance of diversity and inclusion to this business revolution we are all in.

Andrés is one such voice. As you read his words here and, if you have a chance, get to hear him speak, you will not only be glad you did, but you will be charged and inspired to continue to make a difference in this great work that our organizations need us to lead.

Carol Evans
New York City

Introduction

It turns out that the warm, let's-all-just-get-along connotations of inclusion are misleading. Achieving true inclusion is hard — very hard. It's harder, in fact, than achieving awareness, tolerance, and sensitivity. It's harder than diversity itself. Ironically, at the same time, it's actually become easier and more hip to talk about diversity and inclusion. Around the world, corporations, not-for-profits, educational institutions, police departments, governments, and the military are catching on that the workforce is changing in dramatic, unstoppable ways. After years of ignoring the swelling demographic tsunami, finally they grasp that these changes raise myriad implications for how organizations hire, manage, develop, promote, and reward their workers in ways that will motivate them to stay and do their best.

Over the past decade, think tanks, boutique consultancies, magazines, and books have showcased stories of winning strategies and programs. Conferences are abuzz with high-voltage diversity energy, while across organizations, an array of initiatives — from mentoring and diversity training to diversity councils and affinity groups — sprout up like mushrooms in the forest after a rainstorm. Stories abound of CEOs making brave statements, of innovative strategies and programs that helped crack the glass ceiling, and of members of traditionally marginalized groups landing on career platforms and performing to their full potential. All this has resulted in organizations becoming more diverse overall.

Such accomplishments give us plenty to celebrate, if only for a moment. After a generation of diversity work, organizations increasingly worry that — despite their success at bringing diversity in the door — even the most diligently executed initiatives will not be enough to shatter the glass, concrete, bamboo, tortilla, and rainbow ceilings. Despite years of incremental progress, truly meaningful break-throughs remain elusive, with managerial and leadership ranks falling *far short* of reflecting what should be the most diverse workforce in the history of civilization. Increasingly, top-of-the-house leaders realize if they don't get this right, if they fail to tap into the ranks of diverse talent around them, organizations face weakened financials at best, and extinction at worst.

As a leader in the diversity and inclusion space and consultant to many multinational organizations, I've witnessed firsthand how employers across the United States, Canada, India, China, Latin America, and Europe — even those who have heartily embraced diversity — were caught off guard by the implications of an increasingly diverse workforce. As they seek to portray themselves as being open to a workforce that *looks* different, they have done little to adjust to a workforce that *thinks* different. Such thinking leads to different behaviors, which, in turn, further churn up the usual organizational undercurrents.

Consider the complexities of the following scenarios: White females managing African-American males, who in turn manage White males, Latina women, and immigrant- and U.S.-born Asians — all of whom are charged with delivering profitability for an enterprise statistically still run by White males. Then there are Indians managing teams in the United States, Argentineans shaping the global financial system of a U.S.-based multinational, and Muslims making global real estate decisions from their offices in Dubai.

These workforce shifts take place amidst massive global demographic, political, and economic changes, where trends in each of these arenas accelerate those in another. The election of Barack Obama was a defining moment that captured both metaphorically and literally the zeitgeist of the times.

The Obama Era is about a period in history where various factors including massively shifting demographics made possible the election of America's first Black president. It's also about how Obama's historic election and now his reelection will further define the early 21st Century. The period will redefine the United

States' role in this era and its evolving identity. The Obama Era carries with it profound cultural implications, both in the United States and globally, that will affect not only personal, group, and institutional relationships, but also how we go about doing our work strategically and day-to-day. Among the populations most significantly impacted will be the emerging workforce. An increasingly multi-cultural workforce requires a deeper cultural understanding from many different angles — not only what cultures are in the mix, but what individuals believe, how they act, and why they act that way.

The Inclusion Paradox: The Obama Era and the Transformation of Global Diversity explores the impact of the Obama phenomenon from a cultural, rather than political, perspective. Sure, there are myriad political observations to be made on blue state/red state shifts and in the many legitimate yet contentious policy debates swirling in Washington. But whether our views align more with the Tea Party, the Occupy Wall Street crowd, or is uncategorized regardless of how such matters end up getting hashed out politically, there's an undeniable, transformative story unfolding that includes all of us globally. Whatever one's political preferences or passions, we're all unwitting players in this culture-change drama.

In the context of extensive consulting and speaking, I have identified eight cultural implications that I believe are hallmarks of the Obama Era. I believed these to be true at the start of the Obama Era and after four years of testing, believe that they have held to continue to be true.

- Inclusion is a transformative force.
- Whatever we do has global impact.
- Diversity and inclusion requires intentionality.
- We'll experience a renaissance of values-driven decision making.
- We must have a heightened focus on results.
- The bottom-up is as important as the top-down.
- Both/and trumps either/or.
- True diversity and inclusion requires calling out our differences, not minimizing them.

Let's explore them in more detail, using Obama's words, legislative achievements, and executive actions to frame the discussion:

Inclusion Is a Transformative Force*

"If there's anyone out there who still doubts that America is a place where all things are possible; who still wonders if the dream of our founders is alive in our time; who still questions the power of our democracy, tonight is your answer. It's the answer told by lines that stretched around schools and churches in numbers this nation has never seen, by people who waited three hours and four hours, many for the very first time in their lives, that their voice could be that difference. It's the answer spoken by young and old, rich and poor, Democrat and Republican, black, white, Latino, Asian, Native American, gay, straight, disabled, and not disabled."
– President-elect Barack Obama's Acceptance Speech in Grant Park, Chicago, November 4, 2008.

Changing demographics have radically transformed the workplace. Massive immigration and aging populations have significantly changed the face of the American workforce. More generations are in the workforce than ever before, forcing organizations to deal with and benefit from the differing perspectives of Traditionalists, Boomers, Gen Xers, and Millennials. At the same time, women and racial/ethnic minorities account for a rapidly growing portion of the workforce, with some even reaching the upper echelon of their organizations. Xerox, eBay, Yahoo, HP, Kraft, and Pepsi all have strong women CEOs, while McDonald's, Kodak, BJ's Wholesale Club, and MasterCard have African-American, Latino, Asian, and Indian chief executives.

It's no coincidence that we're seeing these demographic trends. A generation ago, women and minorities were achieving breakthroughs in the arenas of sports and entertainment. Today, gender and color glass ceilings are cracking in the

---

* Since that historic night President Obama has continued to speak about before about the transformative force of diversity:. *"An America that doesn't simply tolerate people of different backgrounds and beliefs, but an America where we are enriched by our diversity. An America where we treat one another with respect and with dignity, remembering that here in the United States there is no "'them'" or "'us;'" it's just us. An America where our fundamental freedoms and inalienable rights are not simply preserved, but continually renewed and refreshed ... Put simply, we must be the America that goes forward as one family, like generations before us, pulling together in times of trial, staying true to our core values and emerging even stronger. This is who we are and this is who we must always be".* – President Obama's remarks during Iftar Dinner, August 10, 2011.
And
"For we know that our patchwork heritage is a strength, not a weakness. We are a nation of Christians and Muslims, Jews and Hindus - and non-believers. We are shaped by every language and culture, drawn from every end of this Earth; and because we have tasted the bitter swill of civil war and segregation, and emerged from that dark chapter stronger and more united, we cannot help but believe that the old hatreds shall someday pass; that the lines of tribe shall soon dissolve; that as the world grows smaller, our common humanity shall reveal itself; and that America must play its role in ushering in a new era of peace." – President Obama's Inaugural Address, January 20, 2009.

arenas of power. With this new talent come new styles of leadership, new business strategies, and corporate policies, along with new approaches to creating more inclusive environments.

When there are more people who "look like me" up the succession path, more employees can hope that they, too, have a chance to succeed. Just over 15 years ago, Linda DeLavallade, an African-American diversity practitioner at Allstate, was working for a major bank. She was told she could not aspire to a certain role "because we only have one Black man and one Black woman in the executive recruiting organization at a time." This meant she had to wait until the Black woman who currently occupied the position resigned.

In the wake of Obama's 2008 and 2012 elections, Linda reflected on how different corporate America feels now, compared to that time at the bank. "I've received quite a bit of support in recent years from the diverse teams I've been on," she says. "Not only have I seen greater opportunity, but the teams I'm on and the leaders of those teams have supported me by letting me be me and not force fitting me into a certain mold."

Whatever We Do has Global Impact

"We have taken these positions because we believe that freedom and self-determination are not unique to one culture. These are not simply American values or Western values — they are universal values. And even as there will be huge challenges to come with a transition to democracy, I am convinced that ultimately government of the people, by the people, and for the people is more likely to bring about the stability, prosperity, and individual opportunity that serve as a basis for peace in our world. So let us remember that this is a season of progress. For the first time in decades, Tunisians, Egyptians and Libyans voted for new leaders in elections that were credible, competitive, and fair. This democratic spirit has not been restricted to the Arab world. Over the past year, we've seen peaceful transitions of power in Malawi and Senegal, and a new President in Somalia. In Burma, a President has freed political prisoners and opened a closed society, a courageous dissident has been elected to parliament, and people look forward to further reform. Around the globe, people are making their voices heard, insisting on their innate dignity, and the right to determine their future." – President Obama's Remarks to the U.N. General Assembly, September 25, 2012.[1]

5

The U.S. election was followed with deep, vested interest by people in capitals, towns, and hamlets outside the United States with the understanding that the choice made in both Novembers in 2008 and 2012 would have an impact not only for Americans, but for people around the world. From the get-go, Barack Obama got this as he framed it in his 2008 Acceptance Speech: "To all those watching tonight from beyond our shores, from parliaments and palaces to those who are huddled around radios in the forgotten corners of our world — our stories are singular, but our destiny is shared." Similarly, choices made at multinational corporate headquarters in London, Stuttgart, Paris, New York, Chicago, and Los Angeles have great impact on the far-flung parts of their companies.

In a world where happenings in Washington, Delhi, Beijing, London, and Dubai have instant impact everywhere, the challenges facing President Obama are in some ways similar for business leaders. Our words, decisions, and actions have immediate impact on employees' commitment and enthusiasm and, by extension, on the quality of their work. "This challenges us as diversity leaders to step it up and come up with transformative ways of doing things," says Deb Taylor, former director of global diversity at Deere & Company.

Pauline Kiejman, a global human resources consultant who is a French citizen working in the United Kingdom, viewed the dawn of the Obama Era in light of its effects on global diversity: "Obama's election simply gave me hope. In a gloomy economic climate, watching the world celebrate this election together was truly uplifting. It made me feel there's hope for the values of diversity, for real change in how we interact with each other. As I looked around me in our London office, I thought about how diverse we are as a team — from Australians to Indians, Swedes, French, English, Scots, Irish, and Americans — and I hoped this could go even further in the future."

Diversity and Inclusion Requires Intentionality

"To realize more fully the goal of using the talents of all segments of society, the Federal Government must continue to challenge itself to enhance its ability to recruit, hire, promote, and retain a more diverse workforce. Further, the Federal Government must create a culture that encourages collaboration, flexibility, and fairness to enable individuals to participate to their full potential.... By this order, I am directing executive departments and agencies to develop and implement a

more comprehensive, integrated, and strategic focus on diversity and inclusion as a key component of their human resources strategies. This approach should include a continuing effort to identify and adopt best practices, implemented in an integrated manner, to promote diversity and remove barriers to equal employment opportunity, consistent with merit system principles and applicable law." – President Obama, Executive Order 13583 — Establishing a Coordinated Government-wide Initiative to Promote Diversity and Inclusion in the Federal Workforce, August 18, 2011.

True inclusion begins with a deliberate proclamation, but it can't end there. It must then be followed by relentless intentionality at every level of the organization. When I first met Russ Fradin at the start of his tenure as Hewitt's CEO a few years ago, he told me about his commitment to diversity, stressing that he was not so much for talking about it than doing it. "As I create my leadership team, I plan to have a diverse executive council," he said matter-of-factly.

Sure enough, his intentionality surfaced when four of his nine direct reports were women and two were people of color. "Hewitt has a proud legacy of inclusion that is part of what makes us a special company," he said then. "Our strong and longstanding commitment to creating a diverse workforce is not only the right thing to do, but it's good for business." He added pragmatically that Hewitt's clients spanned the majority of the Fortune 500 — "a diverse set of companies with a diverse set of employees. We find that reflecting this same diversity in our own workforce allows us to approach our work from multiple perspectives."

Many other CEOs have led with this point of view. "If we're to succeed in today's very competitive environment, which requires us to have the best talent from as many different diverse pools as possible, we need to treat diversity with the same focus and dedication as we have put into our company hallmarks such as quality," says Bob Lane, Deere & Company's former chairman and CEO.

Sodexo's chief diversity officer Rohini Anand reflects further on what this means in terms of changing the way organizations operate in the Obama Era: "It might mean reframing how work is getting done. It's a new day in many ways, and I think that we're seeing a new generation, a generation of folks who have not necessarily seen the hardships of the civil rights era. I think we know that there's a lot more work to be done, but we need to reframe how that's done. And think about new strategies to get there."

We'll Experience a Renaissance of Values-Driven Decision Making*

"We the people declare today that the most evident of truth that all of us are created equal — is the star that guides us still; just as it guided our forebears through Seneca Falls and Selma and Stonewall; just as it guided all those men and women, sung and unsung, who left footprints along this great mall, to hear a preacher say that we cannot walk alone; to hear a King proclaim that our individual freedom is inextricably bound to the freedom of every soul on Earth. It is now our generation's task to carry on what those pioneers began, for our journey is not complete until our wives, our mothers and daughters can earn a living equal to their efforts. Our journey is not complete until our gay brothers and sisters are treated like anyone else under the law, for if we are truly created equal, then surely the love we commit to one another must be equal, as well. … Our journey is not complete until we find a better way to welcome the striving, hopeful immigrants who still see America as a land of opportunity, until bright young students and engineers are enlisted in our workforce rather than expelled from our country." – President Obama, 2nd Inaugural Speech, January 21, 2013.

The publishing world always keeps one ear to the ground, listening for upcoming trends in the public discourse — and what will make for a bestseller, of course. Much of the current buzz is about a "renaissance for values-driven decision making." In other words, making decisions by paying attention to how we make them and how we treat others.

Recently, a CEO prefaced a presentation regarding some tough decisions around cost management by saying, "Speaking from my heart … " He went on to explain how his leadership team had considered the tight economy and how difficult it would be for laid-off workers to find jobs. As a result, the company chose to offer voluntary reduced hours and unpaid sabbaticals, so employees would be able to keep their jobs and full-time healthcare benefits.

---

* Here the President continues the oft-repeated theme regarding the common bonds Americans share, and which represents his deeply felt value that were are each others' keepers. *"There are mothers and fathers who will lie awake after their children fall asleep and wonder how they'll make the mortgage, or pay their doctor's bills, or save enough for college. There is new energy to harness and new jobs to be created; new schools to build and threats to meet and alliances to repair. The road ahead will be long. Our climb will be steep…but America — I have never been more hopeful than I am tonight that we'll get there. I promise you — we as a people will get there. So let us summon a new spirit of patriotism; of service and responsibility where each of us resolves to pitch in and work harder and look after not only ourselves, but each other."* — President-elect Barack Obama's 2008 Acceptance Speech.

During the global financial crisis that began in 2008, Pricewaterhouse-Coopers pledged to lay off people only as a last resort and instead asked every employee to take responsibility for making hard cost-reduction decisions within their spheres of influence. Other companies made similar choices. As Pauline Kiejman observes, "As we work with leaders, part of the message now, more than ever, is the need for them to speak from the heart and rather than draw on people's worst fears, draw from their best hopes."

We Must Have a Heightened Focus on Results*

"I feel confident in being able to say that every one of the agencies in this government has been focused on how do they improve, get smarter, get better, get faster, become more focused on delivering good value to the end user." – President Obama's remarks before the President's Council on Jobs and Competitiveness, January 17, 2012.

The Obama administration faces huge challenges in terms of the economy, the environment, terrorism, health care, and retirement. Every organization faces some of these same issues, albeit on a smaller scale. How do we come out stronger following a worldwide recession? How do we harness our know-how — our core knowledge and skills — to help our customers, clients, and constituents better address these huge challenges and still remain viable and financially strong?

Diversity and inclusion must not merely inspire, it must also contribute tangibly to business and organizational objectives. "Clearly in these tough economic times, heightened focus on results applies to diversity and inclusion as well. It's not immune from the need to deliver results," says Sodexo's Anand. "We have to focus on the bottom line. And yes, in addition to contributing to profits, the work must lead to tangible and visible improvement to a company's representation and culture of inclusion. Results must positively impact on our clients' and customers' quality of life."

In 2008, Robert Parkinson, chairman and CEO at Baxter International Inc., launched the 75-year-old company's sustainability philosophy and strategy. His approach is typical of an emerging mindset that puts its stake in the powerful

---

* The President, like business leaders everywhere, is assessed on his results. Diversity is no exception to this political and business reality. *"America, we have come so far. We have seen so much. But there's so much more to do. So tonight, let us ask ourselves — if our children should live to see the next century; if my daughters should be so lucky to live as long as Ann Nixon Cooper [the 106-year-old voter he referred to earlier in the speech], what change will they see? What progress will we have made?"* — President-elect Barack Obama's 2008 Acceptance Speech.

combination of both a results- and values-driven orientation. Here's how Parkinson framed it on Baxter's Web site:

"No global corporation can afford not to act responsibly in today's marketplace. Baxter's approach to sustainability reflects the quality of our management, our people, and our company culture. It also reflects the responsibility and accountability we must demonstrate to remain a global leader in our industry. We also see sustainability as a way to attract and retain talent and make Baxter a rewarding place to work and develop. Ultimately, we believe our efforts in sustainability enhance shareholder value by making Baxter a more competitive company in an increasingly challenging business environment. Our efforts to bring lifesaving therapies to countries where many people still go untreated for conditions such as hemophilia, kidney disease, and others are not altruistic. It's our business. But the goal is similar to other elements of sustainability — to save and sustain lives. It's this higher purpose that binds everyone at Baxter together as a company and as global citizens."[2] In his presentations to employees, Parkinson also emphasizes diversity and inclusion's role in creating a sustainable and profitable culture.

The Bottom-up Is as Important as the Top-down

"And above all, I will ask you to join in the work of remaking this nation the only way it's been done in America for 221 years — block by block, brick by brick, calloused hand by calloused hand. What began 21 months ago in the depths of winter must not end on this autumn night. This victory alone is not the change we seek — it's only the chance for us to make that change. And that cannot happen if we go back to the way things were. It cannot happen without you." – President-elect Barack Obama's 2008 Acceptance Speech.

For the diverse crowd of 250,000 in Chicago's Grant Park on Election Night, the emotion of the night went beyond history-in-the-making or even beyond a partisan victory. What seemed to come from deep in the hearts of homemakers, professionals, janitors, executives, massage therapists, hip hop teenagers, actors, homeless people, college students, retirees, able-bodied and disabled people, and gay and straight people was the visceral sense that this moment wouldn't have been possible without each group and each individual having actively chosen to participate. The consensus analysis of the 2012 election result was that this was even more critical the second time around.

McKesson's chief diversity officer Daina Chiu shared with her company's top 200 leaders the following posting someone had made on her Facebook page the night of the election: "Rosa sat so Martin could walk. Martin walked so Barack could run. Barack ran so our children could fly." The culture's sense is that we're all part of making this happen.

Obama grounded his inclusion philosophy in the American national motto of "Out of the many, one" *("E Pluribus Unum")*. Empowerment is much more than a state of mind. In the case of Obama's election, it yielded a tangible historic result. When traditionally marginalized individuals are given an opportunity to have their voices heard and their talents showcased, the potential which is revealed will make what seemed impossible, possible — not just for them, but for the world around them.

There's a lesson here for organizations seeking diversity breakthroughs. Baxter's former vice president of diversity Don Wilson explains, "As much as we look to our leaders to set the course, no matter how right the path may be, it means nothing unless all of us, regardless of our role or pay band, find our place to contribute and step into it."

Both/And Trumps Either/Or

"For it's precisely the pursuit of ideological purity, the rigid orthodoxy, and the sheer predictability of our current political debate that keeps us from finding new ways to meet the challenges we face as a country. It's what keeps us locked in 'either-or' thinking: the notion that we can have only big government or no government; the assumptions that we must either tolerate 46 million without health insurance or embrace socialized medicine.... What's needed is a broad majority of Americans — Democrats, Republicans, and independents of goodwill who are reengaged in the project of national renewal and who see their own self-interest inextricably linked to the interests of others... I imagine they are waiting for a politics with the maturity to balance idealism and realism, to distinguish between what can and cannot be compromised, to admit the possibility that the other side might sometimes have a point. They don't always understand the arguments between right and left, conservative and liberal, but they recognize the difference between dogma and common sense, responsibility and irresponsibility, between those things that last and those that are fleeting." – From *The Audacity of Hope: Thoughts on Reclaiming the American Dream* by Barack Obama, 2006, Crown Publishers.

Through this new mindset, Obama has attempted to chart a course to move the discourse from either/or to both/and possibilities. Admittedly this has proven significantly more difficult that anyone had imagined but even in the midst of the historic polarization, there's still an angling for a historic bipartisan "Grand Bargain" where both Democrat and Republican competing priorities on spending, taxing, and investment are hashed out. The only way out of polarized either/or debates and thinking is both/and.

While his realm is in politics — trying new ways of addressing foreign policy, abortion, gay civil rights, health care — this also creates new possibilities in organizations. "There's speed, quality, and low cost," the workplace adage says, "but you can only have two out of the three." Today's upside-down, fast-paced world is rejecting this either/or choice. The times demand solutions that can deliver all three.

Both/and allows us to celebrate individual accomplishments, while still reveling in being our brothers' and sisters' keepers. Or to celebrate a working woman for her accomplishments as a mother *and* her success as a senior executive of a leading corporation. Or to create a more inclusive definition of diversity that goes beyond race and gender, but that still addresses the unfinished business of under-representation in management and leadership. Or that moving forward the work of diversity does not entail doing it at the expense of the White male, but rather including him in it in ways that he also benefits.

True Diversity and Inclusion Requires Calling Out Our Differences, not Minimizing Them

Here's Obama on race:

"For the African-American *community, that path means embracing the burdens of our past without becoming victims of our past. It means continuing to insist on a full measure of justice in every aspect of American life. But it also means binding our particular grievances — for better health care, and better schools, and better jobs — to the larger aspirations of all Americans — the white woman struggling to break the glass ceiling, the white man who's been laid off, the immigrant trying to feed his family. And it means taking full responsibility for our own lives — by demanding more from our fathers, and spending more time with our children, and reading to them, and teaching them that while they may face challenges and discrimination in their own lives, they must never succumb to despair or cynicism;*

they must always believe that they can write their own destiny … In the white community, *the path to a more perfect union means acknowledging that what ails the African-American community does not just exist in the minds of black people; that the legacy of discrimination — and current incidents of discrimination, while less overt than in the past — are real and must be addressed. Not just with words, but with deeds — by investing in our schools and our communities; by enforcing our civil rights laws and ensuring fairness in our criminal justice system; by providing this generation with ladders of opportunity that were unavailable for previous generations. It requires all Americans to realize that your dreams do not have to come at the expense of my dreams; that investing in the health, welfare, and education of black and brown and white children will ultimately help all of America prosper."* – Senator Barack Obama's "A Perfect Union" speech, March 18, 2008.

Here's Obama on sexual orientation:

"No longer will our country be denied the service of thousands of patriotic Americans who were forced to leave the military — regardless of their skills, no matter their bravery or their zeal, no matter their years of exemplary performance — because they happen to be gay. No longer will tens of thousands of Americans in uniform be asked to live a lie, or look over their shoulder, in order to serve the country that they love. As Admiral Mike Mullen has said, 'Our people sacrifice a lot for their country, including their lives. None of them should have to sacrifice their integrity as well.' …Finally, I want to speak directly to the gay men and women currently serving in our military. For a long time your service has demanded a particular kind of sacrifice. You've been asked to carry the added burden of secrecy and isolation. And all the while, you've put your lives on the line for the freedoms and privileges of citizenship that are not fully granted to you. You're not the first to have carried this burden, for while today marks the end of a particular struggle that has lasted almost two decades, this is a moment more than two centuries in the making." – President Obama's remarks at the signing of the repeal of the Don't Ask, Don't Tell Act, December 22, 2010.

In the Obama Era, effectively calling out differences matters more than ever — not just in our interpersonal relationships, but in product design, development, and marketing. Pharmaceuticals, for example, are realizing they need to call out differences in their clinical trials because the bodies and chemical levels of homogenous male participants respond differently than women's bodies and that the physiological response of African-Americans to certain medicines may be different than that of Africans or Latinos. Likewise, BASF, the German chemical company, had a breakthrough on behalf of its client Adidas, when it tuned into the reality that Asian feet are different from Western feet. That explained why Adidas running shoes were not selling well in Asia. As soon as the company redesigned the shoes to the realities of Asian feet, sales took off.

The same applies to people. For people to more fully be included in their work organizations, we must get better at constructively calling out the differences among the talent in our midst. This, in turn, will help us shape programs and opportunities that entice the best talent to come work for us and then to do their best work and thrive. More than ever, organizations must build platforms that give voice to their diverse populations, which are still highly concentrated in the lower rungs of our organizations.

"The Obama election taught us that we need to recognize and tap into the various different constituencies and their unique needs and points of view," says Edie Fraser, a diversity pioneer and currently managing director of Diversified Search Odgers Berndtson. "So, it's very clear that the active participation of women, Hispanics, LGBT, and so many others in the electoral process — there's recognition that in order to win you've got to include diversity and inclusion in terms of volunteers, money, and votes. And so you've got to have the policies that call out and address the unique needs of various different groups."

This quote of then Senator Barack Obama from his seminal speech on race, "A Perfect Union" delivered at Constitution Center in Philadelphia, Pennsylvania on March 18, 2008 captures the diversity and inclusion ethos of the Obama Era: *"I believe deeply that we cannot solve the challenges of our time unless we solve them together — unless we perfect our union by understanding that we may have different stories, but we hold common hopes; that we may not look the same and we may not have come from the same place, but we all want to move in the same direction — towards a better future for our children and our grandchildren."*

What Is the Inclusion Paradox?

This brings us to the concept of the Inclusion Paradox, which will be used throughout the book to explore the various cultural dimensions of the Obama Era.

Before we can define the paradox, however, we must first distinguish between diversity and inclusion. These terms are often bandied about as synonyms. While they relate to the same ultimate goal, they are in no way synonymous. In *The*

Inclusion Paradox, I offer a differentiated view of these two terms — one that has resonated with clients in diverse industries and different countries.

Diversity is the mix. Inclusion is making the mix work.^{TM}

Many diversity best practices have focused on bringing those who are different in the door. Many of these efforts have been quite successful, and companies have achieved diversity — the mix. But in many places, the mix is not working well. We end up with *diversity without inclusion.* Here, diversity's promise — that greater diversity leads to greater innovation and profitability — dies.

Our inclusion deficiencies show up in higher turnover rates for people of color across the board, and for women in certain companies and industries. The non-budging nature of the different ceilings (glass, concrete, bamboo, tortilla, and rainbow) attests to the fact that inclusion has fallen short of its promise.

Without inclusion, advancement becomes difficult. Good management and leadership skills often are not recognized when they are manifested differently than the organization's mainstream. And, rather than leading to new ways of doing things, "different" ends up being defined as poor performance.

How do we achieve both diversity and inclusion? *For starters, we must challenge the longstanding "best practice" belief that to achieve inclusion we need to minimize differences.* Differences based on gender, race/ethnicity, nationality, faith, income, education, sexual orientation, physical abilities, military experience, and other dimensions are too ingrained, too hard-wired into what makes us *us* and shapes our thinking. Trying to submerge these for the sake of a definition of inclusion rooted in sameness is unrealistic.

Rather than minimizing differences, we need to call them out constructively. Calling out differences has significant implications for workforce policies and programs. "The diversification of the workforce means that the term 'average employee' will soon fade away," says Andy Hiles, benefits thought leader at McKinsey. "Workforce polices and programs designed to support the 'average employee' increasingly miss the mark in meeting employees' needs and desires."

Calling out differences unleashes the true creative contributions of diverse perspectives that play off each other and lead to better work relationships, greater innovation, and profitability that benefit individuals, teams, and organizations. *This is what I refer to as the Inclusion Paradox.*

And throughout, the Obama Era will be the canvas against which we'll explore how to apply the Inclusion Paradox.

A Three-Step Approach to Mastering the Inclusion Paradox

The foundation for creating true inclusion lies in organizations and individuals who can manage these called-out differences. They must possess a bundle of skills, referred to as *crosscultural competence* which entails three fundamental steps for navigating the Inclusion Paradox. Because the levels of awareness are interdependent and sequential, we must master these sequential steps:

1. **It's all about me.** Know who you are and what you believe. What is the foundation for those beliefs? How do you put those beliefs into action? How do others perceive you and your actions?
2. **It's all about them.** Know how others are different. What do you see in others? Why do they act as they do? How are their beliefs reflected in their actions?
3. **It's all about us.** Know how to navigate the gap. Since you can't know everything about everyone, how can you bridge the gap between what you know and don't know about others? When is an issue personal, cultural, or something else? How do you make sure that what you said is actually what is heard? How do you resolve cultural differences to arrive at mutually satisfying solutions?

These three steps, coupled with the eight Obama Era implications, will help equip you for the lifelong journey of mutually transforming yourself, the people around you, and the organizations of which you are a part. Becoming culturally competent is an essential skill in our global, multicultural, multigenerational diverse world. Those who master it will be best positioned to thrive in this transformative time.

Site Map for Book

I wrote this book from the perspective of a get-it-done, strategy-focused, corporate officer. It's geared toward stimulating paradigm shift thinking to achieve diversity and inclusion breakthrough in the workplace. At the same time, it is not a book about best practices and not intended as a detailed roadmap for change.

Every workplace is unique. What works for some may not work for others. Rather, *The Inclusion Paradox* looks beyond best practices and gets readers to open themselves to new ways of thinking about both common and vexing challenges. In *The Inclusion Paradox*, I share stories as well as strategic steps that individuals, teams, and organizations can take to create true inclusion.

The Inclusion Paradox is divided into five major sections:

— Part 1: The Urgency of Inclusion
— Part 2: Calling Out Differences in Relationships
— Part 3: Calling Out Differences in Groups
— Part 4: Calling Out Differences in Organizations
— Conclusion: Inclusion Threats and Opportunities

There's a logical build from the first to the last section, but the chapters within are written topically. For the most part, therefore, they stand on their own and can be read in any sequence based on what interests you the most.

Part 1: The Urgency of Inclusion

The *emerging workforce* is more diverse, virtual, autonomous, and empowered, yet smaller and less skilled. In this section, I lay out the business case for addressing the major global forces — demographics, technology, longer life spans, financial risk management by corporations and government — that necessitate a fundamentally different approach to the workplace. While drastic changes will be needed to engage and harness the energy of this emerging workforce, the Inclusion Paradox focuses on the need to create more powerfully inclusive environments.

Part 2: Calling Out Differences in Relationships

Workplace clashes are *inevitable*. The seemingly minor mismatches and mutual judging of those who are different contribute to underlying tensions between people. When these differences are minimized, rather than called out, "going along to get along" often leads to greater conflict and frustration, rather than resolution. This section focuses on ways to create profitable interpersonal relationships in the workplace. It touches on the various ways in which we're different — gender, race/ethnicity, nationality, sexual orientation, and ability — and how this plays out in relationships between people who are working together to get the job done.

Part 3: Calling Out Differences in Groups

This section explores the challenges and opportunities related to today's multicultural, diverse teams. It examines the sociological characteristics of diverse groups, as defined by gender, race/ethnicity, nationality, sexual orientation, age, and ability — and how these play themselves out in intergroup interactions. By calling out differences and managing them effectively, organizations can achieve true inclusion and successful group relationships, which in turn leads to more profitable products and services.

Part 4: Calling Out Differences in Organizations

Organizations have a compelling story to tell. This section showcases those that have effectively, legally, and profitably taken into account differences in how they execute human resources programs such as recruiting, performance management, benefits, leadership development, succession planning, and employee engagement. By calling out differences, organizations can better evaluate the effectiveness of their corporate communications and training, thus motivating employees to make informed decisions about their benefits.

Conclusion: Inclusion Threats and Opportunities

The book ends on a note of hope. While the threats of the new world order are evident, so are the possibilities for an exponential explosion of creativity, innovation, and life-improving products and services birthed through the union of diversity and inclusion. Embracing the mix and knowing how to make it work will give us the power to create an alternative, uplifting, and creative vision.

On a more immediate note, this book's message is that corporations, not-for-profits, government, law enforcement, and the military will have to attract and retain the best talent from multiple labor pools if they are to survive the talent war. The key to attraction lies in creating truly inclusive environments. Don't be fooled by how soft and effortless that sounds. Inclusion is one of the hardest things to achieve.

"This is our moment. This is our time," Obama proclaimed as he closed his 2008 acceptance speech. In a world where rules are changing at a dizzying rate and we find ourselves facing unparalleled and simultaneous threats and opportunities, the question of the moment is this: In the urgency of now, in your life and in your work, what new possibilities do you see? *The Inclusion Paradox* is meant to help you answer this question. ♀

PART 1:
THE URGENCY
OF INCLUSION

The Urgency of Inclusion

Context is everything. Words, actions, gestures. Policies, pronouncements, punditry. Their impact — or lack of it — is given life by the ground on which the seed falls. In Part 1, I delve deeper into the overture of themes sounded in the book's introduction. What are the specific trends shaping the Obama Era? How are these trends shaping today's and tomorrow's emerging workforce? What implications do they have on diversity and inclusion? And what does it all mean for each of us, both personally and in the work that we do?

In the pages that follow, I present a holistic view of how today's environment — steeped in economic crisis, unstoppable globalization, and wildly escalating diversity — has upped the ante and created both greater peril and greater opportunity for organizations and individuals.

No country is an island. The interconnections among us and among our countries and institutions are inextricable. Much like the Chaos Theory posits that the flutter of a butterfly's wings can trigger a chain reaction, potentially leading to hurricanes and other natural disasters, the flutter of decisions made in the boardroom can lead to massive job losses or gains anywhere in the world. Financial decisions made on Wall Street sweep through Main Streets from London to Lhasa. A misinterpreted gesture can result in the loss of a multimillion dollar deal. A misplaced word can ruin a relationship for a lifetime.

Before we get into specific strategies for addressing implications of the mix and making it work, we must understand the context in which we live and work. It doesn't matter if you're a small, independently owned and operated mom and pop or a major multinational. Nor does it matter if you're a chief executive, a manager, or an entry-level employee. Context affects everyone regardless of size, geographic location, or position. To make smart decisions, we must be grounded in context.

At the same time, the global context needs to be, well, contextualized to each individual country or specific diversity and inclusion issue. Granted, there is demographic change worldwide, but how it manifests itself could be very different.

Organizations must tune in to these differences when formulating their inclusion strategies or they run the risk of seeing their efforts backfire, resulting in employee turnover and alienation. They must factor in challenges other countries might face that are unique to their own demographics and may not always parallel those of the United States.

The Inclusion Paradox requires that we not only acknowledge the differences among us, but learn to navigate those differences to make the mix work. To meet the challenge of difference, to navigate the paradox of inclusion, we need the foundational skill of crosscultural competence. It's not a skill that comes naturally, but it can be learned.

So join me as we take a closer look at today's context and examine crosscultural competence, a critical capability which will be essential for successfully navigating the Obama Era and beyond. ♀

1

Chapter 1

An Upside-Down World

The world is not flat — it's upside-down.

An African-American is President of the United States; minorities are the majority in many places; to be young is to be more experienced in a high-tech world; to be a woman is to be rising in opportunities. Economic instability rocks the most advanced economies, and Dubai is now a capital of innovation. Financial behemoths on Wall Street in New York and in The City in London either disappeared overnight a la Lehman Brothers, been swallowed up by others, or been hammered with charges of wrongdoing.

Meanwhile what had at one time been called the "Third World" which was beset by violence, dictatorships, and dysfunctional economies are now bursting with economic booms. By the beginning of 2009, $2 trillion in oil monies alone transferred from Wall Street and The City to the capitals of oil-producing nations such as Saudi Arabia, Venezuela, and Russia.[1] And the global consultancy McKinsey & Company estimates that oil-producing Gulf nations will receive $3.5 trillion by 2020.[2] China will be surpassing the United States as the largest economy in the world by 2016.[3] Brazil and India are economic powerhouses. Even the small are becoming mighty. Peru's economy will have grown 7 to 9 percent in 2013 continuing its streak as one of the fastest growing economies in the world even as developed countries went into economic freefall during the Great Global Recession.

All of these economic double-takes, plus China holding about 9 percent of U.S. Treasury securities[4] (making it the nation's largest creditor), temporary and contingent workers expected to be about 50 percent of the workforce by 2020[5], and a new U.S. president rising with a power base in the grassroots and not in Washington, clearly indicate that an old economic and political order is being dismantled, and a new one is coming together.

Daily, even hourly, we feel the relentless aftershocks of changes at work — in our retirement portfolios, in municipal budgets, in therapy sessions. Myriad questions remain about where we'll land, but we can't help feeling in our bones that changes of historic proportions are transforming the economic, political, and social landscapes. Even the weather's topsy turvy behavior has both real and metaphorical messages to it.

That leaves us with the following question: Will the work of diversity and inclusion be washed away amidst the swelling riptides of this global financial tsunami?

We have many reasons to worry. Many diversity and inclusion best-practice "givens" once seemed as solid as Lehman Brothers, AIG, and a soaring Dow Jones Industrials Stock Index. Now, they, too, are poised to disappear. But rather than a total wipe out, the breakdown of the old financial order and the rise of the new will mean greater, not lesser, urgency for diversity and inclusion.

In this time of reckoning for so many industries and institutions, we must take stock of diversity and inclusion work. One thing is for sure: Conventional diversity and inclusion wisdom will no longer be sufficient, as the new financial and political order demands new thinking and a wrenching self-examination of how our work gets done.

In the midst of the 2008 financial market meltdown, a European senior leader for a large investment firm was called to an urgent meeting in London, sponsored by one of the organization's Chinese leaders. The European leader recalls, "There we were in the meeting and he was telling us — a dozen white male Europeans in the financial capital of Europe — what economic sectors to invest in, which ones to get out of. I realized right there and then that my world had changed overnight." Sharing the story with a group of diversity and inclusion leaders, Ernst & Young's chief diversity officer at the time, Pierre Hurstel, summed up the significance of the encounter as follows: "Money is moving faster than our business, and diversity and inclusion processes, structures, ideas, and beliefs, can't keep up with. Diversity and inclusion needs to be rethought in the context of the restructuring of the financial system."

Changes in business and the economy are not just about the squeeze being placed on diversity and inclusion budgets. They are about the urgent need to offer relevant and compelling answers to the huge economic challenges organizations face. Before we wrestle with how best to provide value through diversity and inclusion, we need to ground ourselves in the current, yet rapidly changing, context of this work.

Tectonic shifts caused by global demographic, economic, sociopolitical, and technological megatrends are shaping an emerging workforce unprecedented in how it moves and behaves. Changes in birth rates, retirement trends, and job requirements are reducing the size of the workforce and creating significant skill shortages, while eased trade barriers, telecommunications advances, and the knowledge economy are producing a highly global and virtual workforce. At the same time, loosened cultural norms about who can do what work, higher minority birth rates, and relaxed migration barriers are creating a thoroughly diverse workforce. This coupled with the knowledge economy, social media technologies, and a new kind of employment contract are giving rise to the most autonomous, empowered group of workers ever.

The emerging workforce is indeed vastly diverse. But there is much more to it than that. Other characteristics must be taken into account if we're to shape high-impact strategies and programs for making the most of this talent.

Before delving into the specifics of this workforce, let's first explore five megatrends that are turning the global workplace and workforce upside-down:*

- Political and Economic Volatility
- Multifaceted, Unprecedented Diversity
- Fewer Government and Corporate Guarantees
- Rapidly Evolving, Game-Changing Technology
- Multilayered Globalization

---

* Note: This chapter draws substantially from the research and insights of Hewitt Associates' Robert Gandossy, Tina Kao, and Elissa Tucker. Much of this content originally was published in various Hewitt books and white papers, including "Next Generation Talent Management – Insights on How Workforce Trends Are Changing the Face of Talent Management" by Elissa Tucker, Tina Kao, and Nidhi Verma, 2005, and *Workforce Wake-Up Call: Your Workforce is Changing, Are You?* By Robert Gandossy, Elissa Tucker, and Nidhi Verma, 2006.

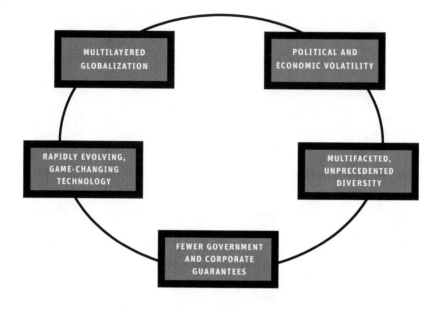

Megatrend #1 — Economic and Political Volatility

Life Is Less Predictable

Having grown up in a Latin American country — where we survived a 12-year dictatorship along with press censorship, states of emergency, and dusk-to-dawn curfews and where the booms of car bombs jarred us from sleep in the middle of the night — my mother's home country of the United States seemed like a bastion of stability and security. In this upside-down world, however, that is no longer the case. Terrorists struck in Oklahoma City and New York City; a presidential election result was contested all the way to the Supreme Court; natural disasters have decimated New Orleans and parts of New Jersey and New York City. As if that wasn't enough, California — one of the world's ten largest economies — is now on the brink of insolvency. The United States right now is not exactly a bastion of security.

Volatility is everywhere. In Latin America, elections lurch from right to left and back again. Political polarizations split countries or pit country against country. In recent years, we've witnessed unscheduled changes in government and suppression in the Philippines, Thailand, Nepal, and Tibet. The Republics of the former Soviet Union have armed themselves against attempts to bring them back into the fold; the Middle East boils over with myriad political fissures as the Arab

Spring has moved to a stage of great ferocity and uncharted waters of the way forward; and several African countries still contend with genocide and famine. Meanwhile, global terrorism and global warming inject greater instability. By their very nature, both the human and nature made acts of devastation surprise us, with no part of the world safe as terrorists have targeted Bali, Madrid, Baghdad, London, Islamabad, and Mumbai and cyclone, hurricanes, earthquakes, and tsunamis have hit Japan, Thailand, New York and New Jersey with unprecedented fury. Who knows where will be next?

With non-stop, instantaneous coverage of these events feeding our apprehension that anything can change at any time in any place, it's no wonder our safety, health, retirement, and jobs are thrown into question in an instant.

Megatrend #2 — Multifaceted, Unprecedented Diversity

We Are More Different

Suddenly, it seems the global demographic tsunami is upon us. While it is certainly reaching its peak, it has been coming for some time now.

Across Europe, the aging and declining population is becoming more racially and ethnically diverse due to the swelling influx and higher birth rates of immigrants from Africa and the Middle East. In Germany, nearly 20 percent of babies are born to immigrants from North African, Middle Eastern, and/or Muslim families.[6] By 2025, Muslims are expected to be nearly 10 percent of Europe.[7] In Latin America, meanwhile, regional migration is creating new labor force dynamics as Peruvians show up in Chile, Brazilians in Argentina, and Bolivians in Paraguay.

In the United States, the 2010 Census report confirms the Latino population is not only continuing to grow in the traditional bastions of California, Texas, and Illinois, but will comprise nearly one-third of the United States by July 1, 2050.[8] Statues of the Virgin de Guadalupe, the patron saint of Mexico, are even starting to show up in traditionally homogenous Connecticut, Kansas, and Washington State.

Such demographic shifts create implications for employers and workers. Small and large companies are grappling with the implications of multicultural work teams. In 2012, nearly 70 percent of the U.S. workforce was comprised of women and minorities,[9] while Europe's only population growth currently comes from Middle Eastern and North African migrants.[10] Clearly, Europeans can no longer ignore the racial and ethnic tensions that surround them.

Obama's election helped bring some of these tensions to the fore not just in the United States but around the world. French Blacks, for example, live in a society that philosophically seeks not to call attention to racial/ethnic differences. Nonetheless, the election attracted attention to their economic and social plight.[11] These kinds of status quo-changing demographics strain existing organizational and governmental programs that were built around the needs of a more homogenous workforce.

With rising demographic numbers comes greater economic and political power. Muslims in England can resolve their disputes through a sharia court.[12] Women around the world are exerting greater influence.[13] In Europe, for example, women now represent half the workforce and are a driving force behind government efforts for gender pay equity.

In the United States, in 2008 Latino voters tipped New Mexico, Nevada, and Colorado toward Obama, delivering those states' first Democratic victory in several elections.[14] By the 2012 election, Latinos in those battleground states and others, like North Carolina, Wisconsin, Virginia, and Ohio also voted decisively for Obama.[15] The Latino influence was so decisive in the 2012 election that both Democrats and Republicans acknowledge Latinos have permanently changed the political landscape and electoral equations.[16] Obama's second term will most likely see the limbo status of 12 million undocumented Latino immigrants resolved positively for them.

And on the list goes. The Lilly Ledbetter Act guaranteeing equal pay for women. The repeal of Don't Ask, Don't Tell in the U.S. Military, which now protects those who are LGBT. The massive focus on the growth and strengthening of community colleges to make higher education more affordable.

One doesn't have to agree with the particular policies to see that demographics is having a major impact on policies. A generation ago, gender and color barriers were broken most often in the fields of sports and entertainment. Today, it's happening in the power arenas of business and politics. It's been said that demographics is destiny. Indeed, Obama's elections signal the cresting of a demographic tsunami is having a tangible impact on every area of society

Megatrend #3 — Fewer Government and Corporate Guarantees

We Are More on Our Own

Everywhere we turn, someone is taking something away. Companies are freezing corporate pensions, not-for-profit pension payouts are continually being reduced,[17] and retiree medical insurance is being grandfathered out. While the United States traditionally has had more of a fend-for-yourself mentality, it still has provided an extensive safety net. That net is shrinking, however, in every state and with each congressional budget. Financial planners are telling us not to count on Social Security when planning for retirement because no one knows if Social Security will be solvent by the time many are ready to golf nine-to-five.

Corporations face a massive rise in benefit costs just as they're struggling against the headwinds of aggressively managing operating costs. Municipalities, school districts, and airlines are cutting back on services and making customers pay for each "perk," such as in-flight meals or baggage checking. One airline even began charging for using the in-flight restroom![18]

To face their economic challenges, companies have begun moving from a paradigm of "corporate benefactor" to one of personal responsibility — first by asking employees to cover a greater slice of their health care coverage costs, and more recently by putting nearly the entire retirement savings burden on employees. While they're willing to match savings up to a point — typically 4 to 6 percent of what employees put into it — organizations will do so only if the employee participates. During this economic crisis, some employers are even pulling back from this promise. This is particularly alarming in light of the fact that average contributions will not be enough to cover employees' true retirement needs.

While financial advisors have recommended saving enough to cover roughly 80 percent of our current costs in retirement, Hewitt's projections in 2009 suggested a more accurate figure being somewhere around 130 percent. This is because people are living longer and future health care costs will be chewing up a larger-than-planned percentage of their retirement income.[19] This presents quite a different picture from when companies provided full pensions that covered all retirement costs for loyal, lifelong employees.

Of course, that's when the concept of cradle-to-grave employment was still alive and well. Lifelong employment is no longer in the realm of reality. Not only are we not guaranteed a job will last our lifetime, the job itself is not guaranteed to stay in the country as offshoring continues to be a fact of life. Employees nowadays are free agents and are treated as such, owning responsibility for their own benefits planning, development, and career management.

This fend-for-yourself trend is being challenged in the Obama Era and the philosophical debate this is engendering is at the heart of what is turning into a hyper-polarized decade in the political realm. Candidate Obama spoke against the culture of "fend for yourself," frequently declaring his belief that we are each other's keepers. This philosophy is, in part, what feeds the expectation that the U.S. government needs to address the uninsured status of millions; needs to grant tax breaks to companies who keep jobs here rather than sending them overseas; and needs to continue the wave of interventions to keep the auto companies from going bankrupt or preventing families from losing their homes.

Love it or hate it, how much is government responsible for the well being of its citizens is one of the major debates of this time. But regardless of how things end up regarding the particulars of different political debates, there will be no going back to the days when a state or company adopted a parental role, providing for our needs more fully. The Obama Era belief that we should not be left to fend for ourselves is still tempered with the conviction that citizens must act with personal responsibility to take care of their own needs and those of their family.

Put simply, the time of generous benefits is gone.

Megatrend #4 — Rapidly Evolving, Game-changing Technology

Anytime, Anyplace, Anything

Providing a global platform on which work could be shared, the Internet was the first modern technological inflection point. Now, we've moved on to broadband wireless, which allows workers to untether themselves from the workplace. This newfound flexibility comes not just from being able to connect with any other worker or source of information, but to ever-larger items. The size of attachments no longer matters. Time lags are absent. It's now possible to have seamless communication between any two locations — with no delay. Still, two things have stood in the way of fully untethering the workforce: cost and policy. The cost issue is being resolved as prices for networked broadband wireless computing come down as network upgrades are implemented. In the policy arena, corporations are struggling to keep control as young workers bring their own devices to work and simply want to be able to connect them to the enterprise's network to do their work.

With broadband wireless, you can be at the airport, home, cabin, taxi, beach, or yes, even the office, and still do your work. It also makes it possible for far-flung teams to work together as if in the same location — though no one has yet solved the half-day time zone differences that guarantee meetings at midnight and dawn for half of the participants. Work can be digitally disseminated across the globe — Europeans can pass data to Argentineans to crunch, those numbers are then picked up by Indians for analysis and distributed globally for interpretation. As the number of employees working offshore grows, so will employee power in those locations. Already, Indian and Polish back offices demand front-office accountability and decision making. With power shifts and cultural differences across borders, global diversity tension buzzes through billions of bits and bytes, pulsating through transatlantic fiber-optic cables and Wi-Fi networks.

While Web 1.0 was primarily about content aggregation, Web 2.0 or the interactive Web, which is social media, is about two-way communication that generates new content. It allows for the "wisdom of crowds" to be scalable out to millions. In the Obama Era, this inflection point will speed action supporting the belief that bottom-up is just as important as top-down. No longer will government decision making be confined to Washington and the corridors of Congress.

Leveraging social networking, the Obama Administration seeks out Web-savvy citizens who can be mobilized to influence legislation, speak up on policy, and empower themselves to participate in the innovation these times require. Obama connects via BlackBerry, his supporters via mybarackobama.com, and all interested citizens via whitehouse.gov.[20] Leveraging the power of this social media was at the strategic heart of both of his electoral victories.

President John F. Kennedy's challenge of "a man on the moon within ten years" was met by technology elites in the hallowed halls of NASA. The Obama Era equivalent, to "be energy independent within ten years," will be achieved both by top-down efforts but also by the masses. Equipped with broadband wireless and social networking tools, technology whizzes in basements, dorms, cafes, corporate cubicles, and garages will drive the energy revolution from the bottom-up at the same time it's being driven top-down. In fact, the United States in now on track to be energy independent by 2020.[21]

Technology serves to amplify diverse voices so they can be better heard above the din, not just in the political sphere but increasingly within companies as well.

Megatrend #5 — Globilization

We Are the World

It was once said that when the United States sneezed, the rest of the world would catch pneumonia. In an upside-down world, no country can make a move without affecting other nations. Any country or region can sneeze and spread pneumonia everywhere else — including the United States.

Our financial markets are linked. Our labor supply chain is linked. Our technologies are linked. Our ability to access products and services is linked. One look at the world's roller-coaster stock market indices proves we're completely and intrinsically linked. Asian markets wake to respond to the previous day's financial happenings in Europe, and Americans respond to what happened overnight in Asia.

Jobs, too, are rapidly moving around the globe. Since 2005, some 2.6 million manufacturing jobs have moved overseas. Analysts predict that in the next 15 years, American employers will transfer 3.3 million white-collar jobs and $136 billion in wages to places like India, China, and Russia. Developing countries could be on the receiving end of about 25 percent or 30 to 40 million American offshored jobs, according to Dr. Alan Binder, who served on President Clinton's Council of Economic Advisors.[22] What's more, the International Labor Organization (ILO) World Employment Report (2001) predicts that only 3 percent of the 460 million new job seekers in the next ten years will hail from Europe and North America, while 75 percent will come from Asia.[23]

This trend actually has begun to slow — although it won't reverse — due to instability in parts of India and elsewhere, rising wages in emerging markets, declining wages or even wage depression in the United States, high cost of transportation, and Obama Administration policies aimed at rewarding companies that keep or bring back jobs to the United States.

Indeed, some companies are bringing jobs back stateside, as offshoring is beginning to lose its cachet – politically, socially, and economically. As many as 3 million manufacturing jobs could return to the United States within the next five years, according to the Boston Consulting Group.[24] But even this reverse trend is disruptive since it once again forces a wholesale rewiring of labor strategies and policies.

Characteristics of the Emerging Workforce

These megatrends have implications not only for economics, politics, and society, but also for an emerging workforce whose characteristics are very different from those of the late 20th Century. Not only does it differ in what it looks like, but also in the challenges it faces and how it gets its work done. Today's workforce is:

- Smaller and less skilled
- Highly global and virtual
- Vastly diverse
- Burdened with multilayered responsibilities
- Autonomous and empowered

While the "diverse" characteristic comes as no surprise, it cannot be the only focus of a successful diversity and inclusion strategy. Such efforts will be incomplete if they don't account for all the major dimensions of the emerging workforce. Let's explore each one in detail.

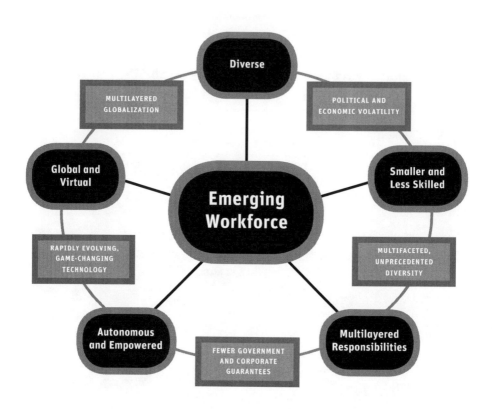

Workforce Trend #1 – Smaller and Less Skilled

Smaller

We can't predict the short-term impact of the current economic challenges, yet long-term demographic trends still show that, given current population growth, a certain number of workers will be needed to deliver the products and services the population needs. Despite the deep recession of 2008–09, most experts anticipate a continuing talent shortage, primarily due to the vast number of Baby Boomers who are retiring, leaving behind far too many jobs for the much smaller Generation X to fill. When the decline of Boomer workers hits bottom, member nations of the Organization for Economic Co-operation and Development (OECD) will have experienced a combined reduction of 65 million people from the workforce.[25] At the same time, those countries with increasingly restrictive immigration policies may be unwittingly undermining their ability to meet their talent needs. To remain viable, organizations will need to nurture and surface talent in all labor pools. This is one of the key business cases for diversity.

Less Skilled

As the Millennials fully enter the workforce, there will be enough of them to make up for the dearth of middle-aged and mature workers though the time between the enormous wave of Boomer retirees and Millennials having gained enough experience will be painful. Gen Xers, who are in-between the Boomers and the Millennials, are limited in how much of the gap they can fill simply due to their size which is half that of Boomers.

While they have the numbers, not enough Millennials will possess the skills and experience demanded by the Digital Economy. According to the United States Department of Labor, U.S.-based employers will need more than 30 million new college-educated workers in the next ten years, yet only 23 million young adults will graduate from college.[26] Changes in how much education, and specifically, what fields Millennials may choose to pursue, mean these workers could be woefully unprepared to contribute meaningfully to the workforce of the 21st Century.

Consider the engineering talent crisis. Technology and utility companies are seeing waves of experienced, knowledge-rich Baby Boomers activate their pensions and retire. Yet looking at the pipeline of current college students pursuing engineering degrees, it's clear these industries will not find enough replacement workers in the coming decade. Even more worrisome, according to Ron Glover, vice president of global workforce diversity for IBM, "the process to produce an engineer with the capabilities we need really starts at kindergarten and goes right through high school. Because if you don't get the kids in sufficient quantity getting the fundamental math and science curricula that they need at that point, you have no chance of producing enough people with the skill sets at the end of the university pipeline. And everything that we saw starting in 2008 around what was in the pipeline in the United States, caused us to be pretty alarmed."

Jobs for scientists and engineers are expected to increase at twice the rate for overall jobs between 2004 and 2014, according to the National Science Foundation.[27] That means companies fueled by these specialized skills must tap nontraditional engineering labor pools, such as women, minorities, immigrants, and expatriates, to try to meet their need. So far, they are falling short.

It's not just engineers and scientists either. Industrialized nations are experiencing acute shortages of nurses and other highly skilled professionals. And developing countries are short on accountants, lawyers, and business administrators. In Peru, for example, unprecedented decentralization by the federal government has put more tax revenues under the control of the departamentos (provinces). Yet ambitious plans for long-needed sustainable irrigation, potable water, electricity, and manufacturing projects remain unaddressed. Despite finally overcoming more than 200 years of limited access to tax revenues, these provinces simply don't have enough people with the requisite skills to make plans for spending the money as intended.[28] Due to this talent gap, in 2012 they left over 30 percent of their infrastructure budgets unspent.[29]

It's not just book-learning or new technical skills that are needed in the new economic order. Technological breakthroughs are creating new products at warp speed. Rapidly changing local and global politics and economics affect everything from the price of oil to the Dow Jones Index to immunization plans. Companies will continue to restructure, re-engineer, de-layer, off- and on-shore work. The competencies of problem-solving, adaptability, flexibility, learning agility, and innovation are more critical than ever. Unfortunately, these competencies are in short supply. From the C-suite to the shop floor, the most valuable workers will be those who solve never-before-seen problems and flex, bob, and weave with the constantly evolving marketplace.

Workforce Trend #2 – An Increasingly Global and Virtual Workforce

Global

As technology and economic reform enables increasing global reach, traditional geographic workplace boundaries crumble fast. Without those boundaries, a truly global job market is rising. No longer are workers limited to marketing their skills solely within one country or region. They can market themselves to organizations anywhere in the world.

Mobility and migration are on the rise, with workers far less likely to remain in one physical location throughout their careers. Over the past 40 years, global migration of less-skilled and highly skilled workers has doubled.[30] Among developed nations, the United States is by far the biggest recipient of labor inflows, but other nations are also increasing their share of migrant labor as talent shortages heighten.[31]

And what about the jobs these workers follow?

Increasingly, the jobs themselves are being relocated to places that best match company needs in terms of labor, skills, costs, and capacity. Low-cost communication technologies and rising education levels in developing nations make it not only possible, but financially attractive to move jobs across the globe. A 2005 Hewitt survey found that 45 percent of participant companies were either currently offshore or considering offshoring jobs in the next three years.[32] This intention came to pass and we all have felt the repercussions by either losing jobs or seeing many lose theirs. Jobs in IT, call center support, HR, finance, and accounting have primarily gone to countries in the Asia-Pacific region, which boast large populations of college-educated workers along with low labor and operational costs. And as talent in those markets gets tapped out and their wages rise, the global economy is finding more talent in Latin America, Eastern Europe, and Southeast Asia.[33] And more recently in Africa.

In the Obama Era, President Obama has been trying to balance the paradox of wanting to protect American jobs with acknowledging and even capitalizing on an exceptionally mobile global workforce and his belief in free trade. In addition to the trends mentioned above, the key may also lie in finding ways to make it attractive for emerging markets to offshore certain work to the United States. While wages are higher (even if they've stagnated in the United States they're still significantly higher compared to other countries), the services and innovation American workers could offer those markets, given their edge in university education and innovation, could be pivotal.

Before policies were enacted to discourage offshoring, this trend showed no signs of slowing. The number and types of jobs offshored and the nations to which they're offshored had been broadening. Jobs outsourced globally have become increasingly sophisticated.[34] Some estimate that up to 25 percent of American jobs are susceptible to offshoring.[35] Consider IBM's example. The technology giant eliminated 4,000 jobs and let laid-off workers take jobs in another country if they were willing to work on local terms and conditions.[36] Already, half of IBM's workforce is located outside the United States.[37]

While global offshoring is mostly an American trend — three-fourths of off-shored jobs originate in the United States — other nations are expected to adopt the practice.[38] As offshoring increased, so, too, have concerns about its negative impact on the workforce. Not surprisingly, global outsourcing reportedly has boosted worker stress and competition and diminished worker engagement in the countries doing the offshoring. However, these concerns won't stop the trend as long as global offshoring is equated with significantly enhanced competitive advantage.

Global Musical Chairs: Labor Migration

A *New York Times* article a few years ago[39] explored Romania's severe talent shortage, which surfaced when the European Union eased labor migration laws. At that time, talent-hungry Spain capitalized on the situation by enticing Romanian workers into its borders. To plug this talent hole, Romania began flying in Chinese workers. China, in turn, started importing workers from Africa to make up for its loss. (Times have turned and Spain's boom metamorphed into Spain's bust and in the decade of the 2010s is seeing a brain drain of its most talented to newly booming areas particularly in Latin America.)

Peruvians are in Chile. Brazilians are in Argentina. Americans are going to India — not on expat assignments or to visit the Taj Mahal, but to get hired for the very jobs that were offshored there.[40] So, while labor migration benefits many recipient countries, it creates a vicious circle in that those countries that are exporting their labor force are in turn discovering that their own resources are being diminished by this process.

Canada's Alberta province is the canary in the talent-shortage mine. Alberta's labor shortage is so severe, McDonald's must pay $15 an hour to keep its workers. Stores close at 4 p.m. because there's no one to mind the shop. This storyline extends from the St. Lawrence Seaway to the Pacific Ocean. Check out this stomach-in-your-throat precipitous drop: In the last 25 years of the 20th Century, the Canadian labor force grew by 226,000 per year. During the first decade of the 21st Century, it only grew by 123,000. By 2010, it grew a measly 42,000. By 2016, growth will have been near zero.[41]

The result is a zero-sum game. One country's — or province's, state's, city's, or company's — gain is another's loss.

Highly Virtual Workforce

The definitions of "coworker" and of being "at work" are changing as workers connect via the latest communication technologies. Across the world and across industries, workers are "freed" from their desks and relieved of their traditional nine-to-five schedules. Growing use of wireless phones, high-speed broadband connections, and smart phones is redefining the concepts of "workplace" and "workday."

No longer is a fixed physical location a requirement for work. Instead, workers are laboring from their cars, at client sites, in hotel rooms, at home, and even while on vacation. A recent survey of senior executives found a "significant upsurge in remote working."[42] According to a report by the Conference Board, the number of remote workers in the United States has nearly doubled and more than tripled for some professions, such as insurance underwriters and records clerks.[43]

Workers now can work at any time. A growing number of workers are on call all the time. Multitasking like never before, they seamlessly switch back and forth between their work lives and their personal lives. They may respond to e-mails while waiting at the dentist's office and log back in to work after the kids are in bed. For some workers, this capability brings a new level of work-life synchronization and satisfaction. For others, it's fostering unhealthy workaholic tendencies. According to a February 2009 USA Today survey, 65 percent of workers can't go more than an hour without checking their e-mail. A McKinsey study found that workers spend about 27 days a year checking and responding to e-mail, which spills over into time at home. The study also found that laptops and smart phones have extended the workday to about 12 hours (7 a.m. to 7 p.m.) as employees keep close tabs on their e-mail.[44]

Together, virtual coworking and the virtual workspace are creating an "always on" workforce that sees no limits to jobs.[45] Many workers are simply afraid to slow down, afraid to disconnect for fear of losing job security in an increasingly competitive, global labor market. Unfortunately, the consequences of an "always on" workforce can be dire — leading to "lousy employees: tired, depressed, mistake-prone, resentful, and eventually burned out."[46] On the upside, workers have more flexibility to take care of their work, home, and other personal demands. In fact, some studies[47] indicate many workers view this flexibility as the ultimate perk.

With the ubiquitous availability of broadband wireless Internet and social networking, the tools are there, and capital investments are being made to keep up. The emerging workforce is pressing for a shift in mind-set and a change in pol-icy. (For more, see Chapter 14, "Work-Life Flexibility: The Mother of All Battles.")

To truly grasp how much technology has driven our ability to connect and make things happen, one need only look to the Obama campaign's unprecedented use of social networking to mobilize a seamless, virtual volunteer force — one better organized and more powerful than anything preceding it.

On the "Get Involved" page of the "Obama for President," Web site, sup-porters in *any* part of the country were able to choose a project, such as Women Calling Women in Ohio or Latinos Calling Latinos in Nevada. With the click of a mouse, a phone list of registered voters in the selected state, with the defined demographic profile, popped up on the screen. Alongside the list was a script for the volunteer to follow. Depending on the campaign, the goal varied, with volunteers filling out appropriate details about each call recipient on a form they submitted electronically.

The forms — filled out by tens of thousands of volunteers working from whatever location and using their own phones — were converted into actionable lists for the Obama team's field offices. These scrubbed lists then guided a door-to-door campaign effort. Thus, volunteers didn't waste their time knocking on doors where the voter no longer lived. This helped increase the efficiency of the persuasion campaigns by avoiding voters who were already dead set on voting for John McCain in 2008 and Mitt Romney in 2012 — or Obama. (After all, you don't want to waste time preaching to the choir.) Instead, volunteers zeroed in on leaning voters and undecideds — the swing voters who ultimately decided the election. This was unprecedented micro-targeting.

How can we harness these same technologies to achieve similar results for our organizations? What can companies accomplish if they truly untether their workforces and outsource certain types of work to the multitudes? The technology is now in place. The switch is ready to be flipped.

Cisco, the digital networking company, is using its untethered workforce to stress-test its virtual network of Web, high-definition video, and social media. By using it real-time, employees provide ongoing, continuous input regarding the way they use the tools. This data instantly becomes part of Cisco's real stories sales pitch and feeds their ravenously hungry technology backbone and design teams, which eagerly seek ways to differentiate Cisco from competitors. "As life and work get mashed together, we want to create 'anywhere computing,' where what employees experience at home or work is the same," says Lance Perry, at the time Cisco's Vice President of IT Customer Strategy and Success.

Procter & Gamble has been creating a virtual workforce of 120,000 self-selected innovators from more than 175 countries who are not even on the company payroll. In addition to its legendary R&D group, the company now taps into the entire world by posting technology challenges — such as how to print a message on a Pringle potato chip — to its Web site. Winners receive cash rewards if their ideas work out. "As of 2006, the company was deriving 35 percent of its ideas from outsiders," write the authors of *We Are Smarter Than Me: How to Unleash the Power of Crowds in Your Business.*[48]

Workforce Trend #3 – A Vastly Diverse Workforce

We now are experiencing the most diverse workforce ever in terms of age, gender, and ethnicity and life pursuits. Workers are entering the workforce earlier and staying longer. As many as four generations are in the workforce at once. In the United States, growing consumerism, coupled with the rising cost of education, is motivating more teenagers to enter the workforce. Labor force participation of American youth (16 and 24 years old) is roughly 63 percent,[49] and a similar trend has been noted in Europe.[50]

As workers enter the workforce at increasingly younger ages, older workers are bucking the tradition of retiring at 65. Motivated by longer life expectancies, changing cultural expectations, shrunken retirement savings accounts, and the availability of knowledge and service work, they're working longer. In the United States, workers are staying on the job for an average of 15 years beyond age 55[51] and more people age 50 to 79 are going back to work to fulfill financial needs due to the troubled economy, stalled retirement plans, or simply to stay active.[52] Going forward, 80 percent of U.S. Baby Boomers expect to keep working past 65.[53] Outside the United States, older workers aren't employed to such an extent, but that, too, is expected to change.

With so many generations in the workforce at one time, workers are finding themselves the brunt of stereotypes and discrimination. In the United Kingdom, age discrimination now tops the region's list of claims. And in the United States, age discrimination claims rose nearly 24 percent (from 19,000 to 23,000) between 2007 and 2011.[54]

Age represents only one diversity element. Motivated by loosened cultural norms and economic necessity, large numbers of women have entered the workforce in recent decades. Women now represent 40 percent of the global workforce, according to the ILO. Today, 70 percent of women in the developed world and 60 percent in the developing world are engaged in paid employment.[55] In the United States, women are expected to make up 48 percent of the workforce by 2015.[56] In Organisation for Economic Co-operation and Development (OECD) nations[57] — which includes most European countries, the United States, and Mexico — female labor force participation rates are also expected to rise.

As more females enter the workforce, men and women are increasingly choosing occupations previously dominated by the opposite gender. Today, women participate in all industries, professions, and job levels. They are asking for combat roles in the military, life saving roles in firefighting squads, climbing poles for utility companies, filling half of the enrollment in law, medical, and MBA programs. In the meantime, given the decimation of manufacturing jobs that have been traditionally held by men, the guys are increasingly taking on what were traditionally female roles, becoming librarians, secretaries, nannies, preschool teachers, nurses, paralegals, and typists. Unfortunately, many men in historically female roles report high levels of stress and discrimination,[58] while 56 percent of women believe their job opportunities are not equal to those of men.[59]

Race and ethnicity increase the mix. Migration levels and high birth rates are boosting the proportion of ethnic minorities in the developed world. Since 1975, global migration has doubled.[60] Since 1970, U.S. migration has tripled.[61] In 2010, about one in ten people in the developed world was a migrant[62], and an estimated 214 million people are living in a country different from their birthplace.[63]

These population trends are global:

- In **Japan,** 20 percent of the population is age 65 or older. By 2055, that number will be 40 percent.[64] Increasingly, companies are rehiring retirees to fill gaps. Meanwhile, only 10 percent of managerial positions are held by women, compared to 43 percent in the United States.[65]
- In **China,** more than 100 million people are age 65 or older.[66]
- In **Britain,** 70 percent of population growth is driven by migration, but the population overall is declining.[67]

- In **Chile**, immigration has doubled over the past decade, reaching 185,000 people, despite its small population. Only 47 percent[68] of women work, compared with 52 percent in the rest of Latin America.[69]
- In **Argentina**, the number of undocumented workers stands at 750,000, while two million Argentineans (7 percent of the population) have some form of disability. The percentage of retirees for every 100 citizens will increase from 18 percent in 2000 to 32 percent by 2050.[70]

Yet another trend is more diversity in lifestyles or life patterns. Fewer workers are following life's traditional path — first education, then work and family, followed by leisure. Instead, they're mixing and matching stages in personalized sequences.[71]

Current organizational structures and processes are calcified into forms that support a far more homogenous workforce. Stress fractures are beginning to appear as the emerging workforce pushes against these rigid processes.

Workforce Trend #4 — An Autonomous and Empowered Workforce

The more governments and corporations push the burden for retirement planning, healthcare coverage, and career development to employees, the more these individuals are going to equip themselves to play the game. Along comes Salary.com, giving them the ability to see if their salary measures up to others doing similar jobs. Along comes LinkedIn, making résumés and personal profiles accessible to multitudes just two degrees of separation away. Along comes Facebook, and friendships are rediscovered, created, and nurtured without time and space barriers.

Increasingly, workers are taking responsibility for the direction and substance of their professional lives. Recognizing they have job- or profession-specific expertise their managers do not have, knowledge workers are becoming the logical decision makers in their organizations. Using the Internet and intranets, these workers access competitive intelligence and business trend information, thereby increasing their decision-making abilities.

As the Internet and information literacy reduce job search costs, the revised employer-employee contract minimizes personal and professional job-switching costs. Ushered in by the downsizing of the 1980s, the new employment contract lets employees change jobs with relative ease and minimal sacrifice. No longer are employees limited to one corporation or career path as their sole route to promotion and increased rewards.

No longer an indicator of a problem employee, searching the external job market has become a sign of business acumen. In fact, the new norm is for workers to continually, electronically search the job market for better opportunities. Rather than being brand loyal, many workers use the employment intelligence they earn on the job to seek better offers. One survey found that 83 percent of workers are at least somewhat likely to look for a new job when the economy strengthens.[72] The Obama Era's increased health and retirement benefit portability is further serving this free agency..

During an economic downturn, management might take the shortsighted view that dissatisfied workers are "lucky to have a job." However, this stance can backfire as the economy recovers, making it a lose-lose approach. Through effective diversity and inclusion strategies, organizations can turn this "changed and charged" dynamic into a win-win.

Workforce Trend #5 – A Workforce with Multilayered Responsibilities

Without government and corporate guarantees, workers exert extra energy providing for their own stability, squeezing in errands during work hours and struggling to balance work and home. Many workers face added responsibilities as members of the "Sandwich Generation": adults who find themselves caring for aging parents and young children at the same time. Employers contribute to the stress: no longer are workers recipients of health care and retirement benefits so much as *consumers* of benefits, who must become educated buyers to ensure they are taking care of their family's needs. At the same time, employees find work increasingly intruding on their home lives via text messages in the evening and middle-of-the-night overseas conference calls.

As work interrupts personal life and personal life interrupts work, the work-life divide vanishes. Workers can best shuffle these multilayered demands if their jobs offer sufficient flexibility. "Employers need to enable their employees to tend to life from work, and work from life," says Cisco's Perry.

The Obama Era brings recognition that work-life boundaries have been erased. As the "First Couple," Barack and Michelle Obama juggle high-visibility roles, young children, and one still-living elder parent who moved in with them to the White House, while still tending to their relationship. The First Couple go to great lengths to negotiate the demands of home and office, from the President making time to eat with family to the couple exercising together. As they visibly demonstrate ways to deal with these kinds of multilayered responsibilities, the Obamas actually influence organizational culture. As they take time for date nights or join their kids on the neighborhood Halloween walk, they dismantle outdated expectations of how leaders and workers spend their time and juggle work-life responsibilities.

The Obama Era will be characterized by the ability to juggle various issues at once. Just as President Obama must tend to health care, the economy, education, wars, terrorism, the environment, immigration, infrastructure, and global relationships, and his family, workers must learn to manage their own multilayered responsibilities.

Taken together, the five workforce trends outlined above — smaller and less sufficiently skilled; global and highly virtual; vastly diverse; autonomous and empowered; and laboring under multilayered responsibilities — define a workforce radically different from even recent times. Employers will need to entirely rethink their approach to managing this talent. To do so requires diversity and inclusion approaches broader in scope, bolder in reach, and interdisciplinary in their solutions. It requires a different mind and skill set, to which we turn our attention in the next chapter. ☺

SUMMARY POINTS

- The world isn't flat; it's upside-down. Change is happening so rapidly in so many areas that no one — no organization, no geographic region, no society — can afford to avoid or ignore it.
- Five megatrends are roiling through work- places around the world:
  - Economic and political volatility
  - Multifaceted, unprecedented diversity
  - Fewer government and corporate guarantees
  - Rapidly evolving, game-changing technology
  - Globalization

- Correspondingly, five megatrends are shaping an emerging workforce:
  - Smaller and less skilled
  - Highly global and virtual
  - Vastly diverse
  - Multilayered job responsibilities
  - Autonomous and empowered

SHAPING YOUR STRATEGY

- How are these megatrends showing up in your organization? Are leaders and manag- ers making decisions that take them into account? If not, what can you do to influ- ence one key leader?

- What's the makeup of your organization's emerging workforce? In addition to their racial/gender/generational/sexual orien- tation makeup, how are their preferred workstyles enhancing and/or challenging the workplace?
- What can you do to surface a key need that's currently being overlooked?

An Upside-Down World

SUSTAINABLE DIVERSITY
RELEVANT, PROFITABLE,
AND GAME CHANGING'

SUSTAINABLE DIVERSITY
RELEVANT, PROFITABLE,
AND GAME CHANGING'

SUSTAINABLE DIVERSITY
RELEVANT, PROFITABLE,
AND GAME CHANGING'

SUSTAINABLE DIVERSITY
RELEVANT, PROFITABLE,
AND GAME CHANGING'

SUSTAINABLE DIVERSITY
RELEVANT, PROFITABLE,
AND GAME CHANGING'

SUSTAINABLE DIVERSITY
RELEVANT, PROFITABLE,
AND GAME CHANGING'

SUSTAINABLE DIVERSITY
RELEVANT, PROFITABLE,
AND GAME CHANGING'

SUSTAINABLE DIVERSITY
RELEVANT, PROFITABLE,
AND GAME CHANGING'

SUSTAINABLE DIVERSITY
RELEVANT, PROFITABLE,
AND GAME CHANGING'

2

Chapter 2

Sustainable Diversity: Relevant, Profitable, and Game Changing

It was a hospital built for White people.

Not that they had intended it that way. But that's what they got. In their rapid expansion into the fastest growing cities in the United States, the large hospital chain had failed to hard-wire inclusion into their growth plans. They had correctly identified expanding metros, but had not made note that the growth was due to the demographic tsunami of growing racial/ethnic representation. How could this affect their ambitious business plans?

During one strategic diversity and inclusion session, one astute real estate guy pulled out the template blueprint for their hospitals. Can you figure out why? Just what could a blueprint have to do with diversity and inclusion?

Considering the concepts behind the Inclusion Paradox, ask yourself this: What differences were not being called out in this hospital's services? For example, what happens in the waiting room when patients of different cultures get wheeled into surgery? If the patient is White, there will typically be one or two people in the waiting room. If it's an African-American patient, there could be six or seven people waiting. When it's a Latino, it could be more than a dozen! In looking at their designs, the business strategists realized they were about to build hospitals in rapidly growing racially diverse neighbor-

51

hoods — the very thing that was fueling their market growth opportunities — that inadvertently catered to white cultural preferences.

This was the turning point in their inclusion work. Once they pulled on the thread of cultural assumptions about the proper size of waiting rooms, they began to see that many other day-to-day hospital interactions — from the intake process to the layout of the emergency room to parking rules — were replete with cultural assumptions. Differences in beliefs and behaviors around modesty, faith, view of authority, illnesses, family support, and more had multiple implications for what would create a welcoming and comforting hospital environment. By discovering the mission-critical reason for diversity, this hospital chain has embarked on a diversity effort that, in large part, will be about offering crossculturally competent health care. Their focus on the diversity implications of their mission led right back to the need for a diverse staff at every level of the hospital and the need for all employees to be culturally competent to effectively do their jobs. This is what sustainable diversity and inclusion can look like.

Grounding diversity in a product and services perspective, rather than a human resources perspective, poses quite a challenge. As discussed in Chapter 1, a new financial and political order demands a new diversity and inclusion order. Creating pathways to sustainable diversity must be a characteristic of this new order. In the Obama Era, solutions must yield unequivocal, tangible benefits both to employees and to the bottom line.

Many diversity and inclusion professionals aren't aware just how vulnerable the work could be, were it to remain on its present course. That said, plenty of signposts point to a diversity and inclusion renaissance. In response to some of the megatrends shaping the emerging workforce, an explosion has taken place in the number of Chief Diversity Officer (CDO) appointments,[1] CEO statements championing diversity, and diversity and inclusion coverage in both the business and mainstream media. The rising tide of U.S. and global diversity is transforming the social and workforce landscape in ways that even the biggest skeptics can no longer ignore.

Still, the financial shakeout of 2008-2012 has resulted in a diversity initiative crash similar to that which happened to the dot.coms in the 1990s. While many things were riding on the World Wide Web wave, not all were equally financially sound or even good ideas to begin with. When the day of reckoning came, the non-sustainable ideas quickly imploded.

How do we ensure that the new diversity and inclusion order is relevant to the core of the business agenda? The answer to this question is critical.

During the dot.com implosion, winning ideas from Google, Amazon, Apple, and other organizations redefined the marketplace and positioned these companies for sustainable growth and evolution. The same will be true for diversity and inclusion. To survive the crash, we must make the shift from *programmatic* diversity to *sustainable* diversity by focusing on the approaches, ideas, processes, strategies, and tools that will lead to sustainability. The time for the deep reexamination and restructuring is now. Like there have been winning technology companies, there too are winning companies in diversity and inclusion who have been taking the steps that follow.

Making the Shift

Programmatic diversity has to do with affinity groups, diversity councils, diversity learning, and heritage month celebrations. It has to do with successful programs such as minority and women mentoring programs, diversity recruiting fairs, and Safe Space[2] for lesbian, gay, bisexual, and transgender (LGBT) employees.

These programs are — and will continue to be — important. But they're just the scaffolding for the structure that needs to be built. Eventually, as the building takes shape, the scaffolding will be dismantled. While it was once a necessity, it's no longer of use, having been replaced by the shiny new Otis elevator.

Consider the dot.com scaffolding — putting "e-" in front of everything, subscription-based access to "e-mail," and dial-up connections. All this was just scaffolding for the real structure being put into place: 24/7 online, customizable, self-service shopping, movies, music, and travel; the ability to find like-minded souls anywhere in the world through Facebook; open and free portals to anything; networking with tens of thousands through LinkedIn; ubiquitous broadband wireless connectivity.

In terms of our work, the equivalent sustainable edifice is a structure where diversity and inclusion is:

- Hard-wired into the organization's mission, growth, and profitability strategies and into the creation, design, marketing, and selling of the company's products and services.

- Embedded into every process and practice that touch employees, from their initial contact with the organization to the time they're brought in, oriented, trained, promoted, and made to feel part of the overall enterprise.

In the same way that the "e-"became assumed in every online interaction, sustainable diversity will be characterized by how much it has become part of how we do business and manage people. No longer will we have to put "diversity"in front of everything. "Diversity recruiting" will be replaced by "recruiting," with diversity sourcing and hiring fully integrated into how things get done. And "diversity management," will become just good management, where differences are taken into account proactively, with wisdom, and with savvy.

We can't get rid of the scaffolding yet, however, as we are still laying the foundation for sustainable diversity.

Laying the Foundation for Sustainable Diversity

Decisions regarding funding, staffing, and executive support must be grounded in the "business case." This is shorthand for: "How will the investment required to do what you're proposing bring greater value to the organization via higher revenue, cost savings, margin improvement, and/or enhanced corporate brand?"

In diversity and inclusion circles, there has been plenty of talk about the case for diversity for quite some time now. It sounds something like this: "Society is getting more diverse; therefore, the workforce is getting more diverse. In the midst of a growing skilled talent shortage, we must be able to hire the best talent from as many labor pools as we can find. Demographic growth is in the emerging workforce populations, but we have traditionally not known how to tap into the top talent we need." The more advanced version adds that "an organization's workforce should mirror the increasingly diverse marketplace the company is trying to sell to."

Compelling arguments, for sure. But they're incomplete.

As we've seen, the skilled talent shortage will be massive. Companies that cannot hire the talent they need will falter, fall behind, or even disappear. The case for inclusion is incomplete, however, because it's focused only on the talent dimension of the business case — what I call the "talent business case" — rather than a more holistic approach.

When it comes to the question, "What is the business case?," diversity work must have as compelling an answer as the competing requests for greater investment in new technology, a new advertising campaign, or a new product. When partnering with our client to shape a global diversity and inclusion strategy, the first task is to ensure a rock-solid grounding in the business case. The question we must answer before doing anything else is:

> *"Why is diversity important to you, specifically in the business that you are in, for the kind of company you are?"*

Before they can reply, I offer the following caveat, "There are three answers you cannot give: Right thing to do; War for talent; Compliance." Such answers are insufficient. They're generic, rote reasons that any company in any industry in any part of the world could give. It's crucial that each company find the differentiated reason for how diversity and inclusion will help them achieve their own specific business goals in the context of their particular products and services and how they run the business. I call these the *"marketplace* business case" and the *"operations* business case." Along with the talent business case, they give us the comprehensive framework to lay the foundation for sustainable diversity.

THE BUSINESS CASE FOR DIVERSITY & INCLUSION

How We Run the Business

Let's look at the structural elements of sustainable diversity in more detail.

The *Marketplace* Business Case: Hard-Wiring Diversity To Products And Services

Diversity as solely a human resources thing will wither on the vine.

Not only do people strategies need to support the business and mission, but organizations that fail to take the megatrends and their impact on the marketplace into account risk losing relevance. Like the hospital at the beginning of this chapter, they may find out that consumers with different cultural worldviews are looking for different features and value. Many Fortune 500 leaders are clear about the importance of diversity to their businesses. Valerie Crane Dorfman, former executive vice president of Bank of America, drives the point home: "Bank of America treats diversity as a business imperative." And it shows. During the first half of 2004, sales of checking and savings accounts to Hispanics increased 67 percent. And Hispanic customers had more than $15 billion in deposits with the bank.[3]

Former IBM chief diversity officer Ted Childs now runs his own consultancy, Ted Childs® LLC. He is widely recognized as the pioneer of hard-wiring diversity to the business. He has trademarked the following statement: "Workforce Diversity: The bridge between the Workplace and the Marketplace."® Childs' leadership and vision has served as a catalyst for many market penetration initiatives. Among them, a LGBT sales initiative targeting LGBT small business owners, which results in the sale of millions of dollars' worth of computer equipment and services. IBM was wise to take this step. In 2012, LGBT purchasing power was projected to be $790 billion.[4]

Marca Bristo, executive director of the disability advocacy group Access Living in Chicago, points out that people with disabilities are "a customer base with a bigger niche market than the coveted 'tween market." She could very well be right, as the market of people with disabilities is estimated to be $1 trillion.[5] Yet as Bristo explains, "Virtually no market research is ever done on people with disabilities, and they are missing out on a huge consumer base that is only going to grow as Baby Boomers age. They are already experiencing disability because of their parents and grandparents, and now they will be experiencing their own disability."

This kind of sustainable inclusion can only happen if differences are constructively called out using the principles of the Inclusion Paradox. It's not just at the moment of sale when signage may need to be produced in Chinese, Spanish, or Polish, but in the very creation of the product or the go-to-market approach. Here's a look at how a few companies are figuring this out:

- Japanese gaming company Koei Co. sought to expand its market share in Canada and the United States by developing product beyond its popular samurai games. However, executives knew up front the company wasn't good at making the kind of "gritty, realistic fare" preferred by Westerners. They worried the new games would miss the cultural mark. To overcome this challenge, they expanded their team in Toronto — which consisted primarily of a "handful of animators working on Japanese games" — hiring two dozen Canadians to design Western-market games. Granted, these Canadian designers are still entrenched in a Japanese working environment — complete with various daily rituals, including morning team exercises — but they are allowed a wide range of artistic control. They are trusted by executives to handle details, both large and small, that make games appealing to a Western market.[6]

- Around 1992-93, Allstate assembled a team to tap into the growing and untapped Latino market. Allstate approached this as a sound business strategy that would benefit this market and their company. The employees engaged to work on this effort were a team of current employees mirroring the diverse workforce whose "good hands" looked like this market whose insurance needs Allstate wanted to serve. They acted as subject matter experts, strategists, and advisors to the work. They revamped their marketing materials to reflect not only their language, but also their culture. A natural outgrowth of the strategy was the recruiting of strong Latino talent throughout the company. Today, due to these efforts, in certain metropolitan areas Allstate continues to have a strong presence among this market segment. This market keeps growing but it continues to be under-penetrated. When a senior professional at a rival insurance company heard this story at a conference, she sighed and whispered to me, "We live with that story every day."

- At Sodexo, senior vice president and global chief diversity officer Dr. Rohini Anand works closely with the business to add a competitive differentiator to the food services and facilities management it provides to universities, schools, hospitals, and corporations. "We assist our clients with their own diversity and inclusion strategy development," says Anand. "Our diversity and inclusion efforts, which include offering cultural competency training for our clients' employees who are working both with our and their own diverse employee base, have strengthened our relationships with them. This increases our chances of renewing contracts when they are due."

- Since Aon Hewitt is in the workforce business, Aon Hewitt has asked itself, "What implications do our clients' diverse workforces have on the design, development, and delivery of our human resources outsourcing and consulting products and services?" It quickly became clear that they have to help clients attract the best talent from as many diverse labor pools as possible. And as they help clients engage their talent, Aon Hewitt has to help them understand that different demographic groups may be motivated by different things. As Aon Hewitt designs 401(k) plans, for example, they have to ask whether there are differences in the use of retirement benefits based on demographics. When Aon Hewitt found out that there were, it begged the questions, 'Why does the gap exist?' and 'How do we close this gap?' For a closer look at where this journey took us when I was working there, see Chapter 13, "Why Not Acknowledging Differences Can Make Us Sicker and Poorer."

- In the past several years I have been working with companies such as Marriott, United Airlines, Home Depot, multiple health care and financial services organizations, and dozens of others where this strategic concept of marketplace diversity has seized the business leaders' imagination. In fact, several of these companies have declared that marketplace diversity is one of their key business growth strategies. Their special efforts are under non-disclosure wraps but most of these companies have been publically intentional of going after a multicultural market that is huge, growing rapidly, young, and underserved. A marketer's dream. In fact, the world's largest company, Wal-Mart, has gone as far as saying that since 100 percent of their growth will be multicultural, 100 percent of their marketing will be multicultural.[7] In other words, multicultural markets are shifting from being niche markets to going mainstream.

- For profits are not the only types of organizations that are going after the marketplace business case for diversity. Not-for-profits I have engaged with such as United Way Worldwide and their many local affiliates, arts organizations such as the 100-year-old Ravinia Music Festival in Highland Park, Illinois, sports organizations such as the United States Tennis Association (USTA), quasi governmental institutions such as Freddie Mae, and the Federal Reserve banks are looking at how integral diversity and inclusion is to them achieving their missions. The communities they serve are more diverse than ever and they must understand how their needs are different in some fundamental ways to the constituents they have served in the past. Several of these organizations also *must* diversify their volunteer and donor bases, and yes, their boards, lest they whither due to unsustainable support structures.

There cannot be true, sustainable inclusion until leaders, managers, and employees understand and believe that diversity is the key to their business and mission success. A mission-grounded rationale for diversity de-escalates many of the contentious issues surrounding the subject. Regardless of whether they're part of the majority or minority, employees see the relevance of diversity in their own day-to-day responsibilities. It also helps shift diversity from being about various constituencies to being about the whole enterprise.

The *Operations* Business Case: Hard Wiring Diversity to Processes And Structures (It's sexier than it sounds)

The hospital built for White people featured at the beginning of this chapter is a clear example of just how vital it is to take diversity and inclusion into account when determining how to provide services *and* run the business. Not only do doctors and nurses need to provide crossculturally competent care, but those designing the buildings and parking lots and laying down wireless connectivity need to consider that people from diverse backgrounds and experiences will respond differently to the surroundings.

One powerful influence in the movement to incorporate diversity into business management is Dr. R. Roosevelt Thomas Jr., author of the groundbreaking book, *Beyond Race and Gender: Unleashing the Power of Your Total Workforce by Managing Diversity* (AMACOM, 1992). Since his book's publication more than 15 years ago, Dr. Thomas has worked with innumerable corporations, spearheading conversations and serving as a catalyst for addressing diversity and inclusion issues inherent in operational strategies, such as vendor and supplier relationships, branding, and mergers and acquisitions. Despite his best efforts, Thomas says, "companies are still significantly overlooking how much addressing diversity issues in their operational areas can yield significant results."

Mergers and Acquisitions

One area that could definitely benefit from a closer examination of diversity issues is mergers and acquisitions. Seventy percent of all mergers do not achieve their promised financial value creation. Their failure is rarely due to a lack of financial or technological synergy, but because of cultural incompatibility. It turns out that the due diligence required to determine financial and marketplace compatibility rarely includes looking at the differing cultures of the merging companies — a diversity and inclusion issue if ever there was one.

There are too many tales to tell of painful, wrenching mergers, where bad blood lingered long after the ink had dried. Rather than referring to the new name of the merged company, people were still identified by whether they're "legacy company A" or "legacy company B."

"In a survey we conducted of corporate development and human resource professionals involved in a merger, they ranked cultural integration as the second top contributor to transaction failure, just behind failure to pay appropriate attention to workforce issues," says Elizabeth Fealy, EVP and global co-leader, Aon Hewitt M&A Solutions, that focuses on the human capital integration side of mergers. "Diversity and inclusion embedded into the M&A work can help mitigate these types of hiccups or convulsions. While culture can be viewed as amorphous, in our methodology we quantify cultural differences, identify the desired go-forward culture, and orchestrate an implementation process that fosters diversity and inclusion. It significantly increases the chances that the merger will succeed in achieving its financial objectives."

TOP FIVE REASONS WHY M&A TRANSACTION GOALS WERE NOT ACHIEVED

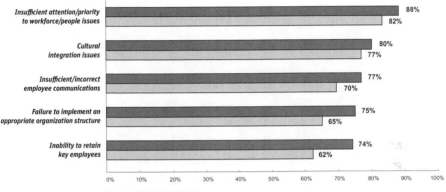

Source: Hewitt/The Deal's M&A Survey

Procurement

The name of the game in procurement is to get the greatest amount of services for the least amount of money. At the same time, corporations now are making a conscientious effort to use diverse suppliers directly or ask their middlemen to do so. The U.S. government is leading by example. In just the first few months of the Obama Era, we witnessed both increased government spending and a greater commitment to diversity, including in the area of procurement.

Diversity in the area of procurement is not just about using diverse suppliers, however. It's also about helping them learn the ropes of large-scale business. In the process, this creates win-win situations for the suppliers, buyers, and other groups. One person who is doing this with high-impact results is Douglas Freeman. He's a hard-core operations professional who through Virtcom Consulting, his strategy management consultancy, helps companies make and save millions of dollars on marketplace strategies and operational efficiencies by reexamining how they structure and run their processes.

His differentiator? Diversity. Here's an example of how he helped one client achieve $400M in new revenue through his application of the diversity operational business case.

A $400 Million Case Study of the Operations Business case

"Our core philosophy can be summed up as 'diversity focused,' where we seek to help our client generate profit through diversity," says Douglas Freeman, founder and CEO of Virtcom Consulting. Freeman uses the experiences he gained as a senior consultant at Deloitte Consulting, as an investment banker at JPMorgan Chase, and as the head of Business Development and Operations for Mondus, where he helped raise more than $170 million in private equity financing.

Freeman recognized that minority-owned businesses were inadvertently being shortsighted in their strategies for keeping their expenses down. As a result, they were losing out on a government mandate that 23 percent of federal agencies' procurement dollars must be spent with diversity vendors (spread across nine different categories).

The rub was that vendors qualifying as "minority-owned" businesses don't normally accept credit cards for two major reasons: 1) They want to avoid paying transaction fees that can amount to thousands of dollars, and 2) Most of them simply are uncomfortable accepting credit cards, due to a lack of experience with them. Instead, they typically take payment through direct deposit or checks, not procurement cards.

Here's where they were missing out. Because checks and direct deposits involve cumbersome processes to set up and use, government agencies were reluctant to do business with anyone who used the less streamlined check-writing process. They had the motivation to meet the mandate, but not the patience to work with outdated approaches.

Using hard data, Virtcom helped change the perception of diversity vendors in terms of the real costs of waiting 90 days for payment, the often-overlooked result of the check-paying process. By waiting three months, vendors were, in effect, paying interest charges on the unpaid invoice. When comparing the cost of the transaction fee on credit card charges (2 percent) to the cost of waiting for payment (2 to 5 percent), they were able to clearly show that accepting credit card payments resulted in cheaper transaction costs.

Virtcom then partnered with a major credit card company to develop a procurement card — a specialized credit card used by government agencies or large companies to purchase big ticket goods and services costing more the $5,000 — specifically for the African-American market. Virtcom initiated a supplier enrollment program that targeted and trained more than 2,000 diversity vendors. They also partnered with federal agencies to market the idea of procurement cards and trained bank sales force teams and processors.

Early in the process, Virtcom had to debunk the myth that diverse business to government suppliers (B2G) were a higher credit risk. Virtcom showed the banks, the processors, and the credit card company that the B2G market had a 0.0007 default rate. In other words, it was virtually risk-free. Based on their wrong-headed belief that diverse suppliers posed a higher credit risk, credit card companies had been charging a much higher transaction rate.

In the end, the card proved beneficial to suppliers and buyers, as well as the credit card company that issued it. Participating vendors now get their money in about two days, improving their cash flow and financial strategic management, while reducing the costs of not being able to pursue new business or make investments while waiting for payments to be made.

Boasting less expensive transaction costs (about $60 less expensive than a non-credit card transaction/payment), the procurement card saves the government billions of dollars, while significantly reducing red tape. Meanwhile, credit card companies have discovered a new revenue stream, since diversity vendors are now able to accept credit card payments for large purchases. The first year the diversity card was utilized, the credit card company gained $79 million in new revenues. Over the past four years, revenue has amounted to more than $400 million — all from what was just recently a totally untapped market and revenue stream.

According to Freeman, "We specialize in an area that we call 'blind spots' — missed business opportunity linked to diversity. In working with any large enterprise, we usually find six to ten of these. We propose quantitative value around those blind spots." And in this case study of the operations business case for diversity, $400 million worth of blind spots.

Regionalization

Think about the regionalization that's taking place in multinationals as they move away from country-specific structures to regional structures. Rather than have every function staffed in every country, they're spreading it out. The IT function for all of Latin America may be in Buenos Aires, while the HR function is in Mexico City, and the finance organization is in Santiago. They may all speak Spanish and most do the sign of the cross before praying. But listen to Argentineans, Mexicans, and Chileans speak about how they go about getting work done, and it's clear that any cost savings garnered by regionalizing will be undercut by cultural and diversity breakdowns.

Consider the management consultancy that's merging the real estate, HR, and technology functions of their Italian, Spanish, and Portuguese practices. The offices in each of these countries have to figure out how they're going to seamlessly serve all their constituencies across deep language, cultural, and regulatory differences. In order for it to be pulled off successfully, this is one operational strategy that desperately needs diversity and inclusion embedded into it.

We Can Bring Them In, But We Can't Keep Them: Hard-Wiring Diversity Into All People Strategies

Once grounded in the *marketplace* and *operations* business cases, diversity and inclusion can be more effectively brought to bear as part and parcel of a company's talent strategies. Even top leadership has become adept at recognizing the connection. DuPont president and CEO John Krol told a Conference Board audience several years ago,[8] "We have proof diversity improves our business performance." A leader from Quaker Oats told the same audience, "The talent and skills necessary to successfully drive our business are found in diverse people with different backgrounds." A vice president at Bell South added, "For us, inclusion is not only fundamental to our employee workforce, but also to our leadership structure, our supplier base, our charitable and corporate social outreach, and among the customers who make up our marketplace."[9]

So far, much of the diversity and inclusion work has been focused on getting those who are different in the door — hence, the focus on recruiting fairs, CEO proclamations on "the power of diversity," and tapping into affinity groups to help with the very act of recruiting itself. Many of these efforts have proven quite successful at attracting greater diversity — the mix.

But inclusion — making the mix work — continues to elude most employers because it's possible to have diversity without inclusion. If the members of a company's community do not feel they're full partners in the well-being of the corporation, if they feel their differences create both invisible and visible barriers to their ability to contribute to the fullness of their abilities and ambitions — then there is no inclusion. Conversely, we can have inclusion with no diversity when homogenous groups surround themselves with the comforts of their shared experiences.

The key to fostering inclusion is for the entire system to enable and nurture the mix. Even when attitudes are changed and majority members "get" the diversity business imperative, outdated systems and processes are still in place about how people join and grow within organizations. They are the legacy of the culturally bound wisdom and preferences of groups of people who were not too diverse at the time. In large part, HR processes themselves may be perpetuating old results, not because of their current intentions, but because of what they've inherited. Thus, diverse talent comes in, but it leaves at a higher rate.

Rest assured, I will not be revisiting the well-worn discussion on best practices for talent sourcing and recruiting. This is where diversity and inclusion has already made the most gains. Instead, I'll be taking a look at how legacy gremlins often get overlooked in the diversity and inclusion discussion and can sabotage even the most well-intentioned initiatives. When Don Wilson was Baxter's vice president of diversity, a few years ago he made it plain: "I see inclusion and diversity as being something that, quite frankly, if organizations don't become totally competent in embedding into their normal processes and procedures, in how they do business, that fundamentally, they will be out of business."

Let's take a look at a few HR processes where we must hard-wire diversity and inclusion.

The Skills For Constructively Calling Out Differences

The White, middle-class recruiter was convinced the candidate lacked confidence and in fact seemed like he was hiding something. When asked why, rather than give examples tied to the candidate's narration of his career history, she demurred to a gut feeling: "I don't know, I just didn't feel he was being straight with us. And he sure seemed nervous." When pressed further to identify what was informing her gut, she finally clicked into the specific behavior. "He totally avoided eye contact with all of us!" It turned out that the candidate came from an Asian culture in which direct eye contact with someone in an authority position — such as an interviewer — would be considered rude and disrespectful. The recruiter's gut — her intuition — that had served her so well in her career had failed her here.

In *Blink: The Power of Thinking Without Thinking*, Malcolm Gladwell lays out a treatise on how our intuition can serve us powerfully, yet lead us tragically astray. When we're observing and acting based upon our frames of reference — our *worldviews* — we can misinterpret what we're seeing because what means something in one culture can mean something quite different in another. The consequences can be serious.

The Inclusion Paradox demands that we know how to constructively call out our differences in order to create sustainable diversity. This requires *cross-cultural competence, the ability to discern and take into account one's own and others' worldviews, to be able to solve problems, make decisions, and resolve conflicts in ways that optimize cultural differences for better, longer-lasting, and more creative solutions.*

An overall organizational lack of crosscultural competence contributes to keeping the glass ceiling from shattering. To create inclusive environments, we must first address the traditional issue of power. That's because the work required to eradicate the *isms* of prejudice rests with the power realm. In fact, many best-known diversity strategies and programs — such as the call for CEO commitment plus the creation of affinity groups, inclusion councils, and mentoring programs — are aimed at reducing the barriers to greater access and connection to those in power.

Even when leadership has embraced the need to promote diversity and become personally involved, even the most well-intentioned efforts will quickly hit the limits of their ability to bring about change. Good intentions are simply not enough because diverse representation is still lacking in management and leadership.

The *isms* of the power realm are at play, but that doesn't explain the whole story. There are also white male cultural preferences for what strong leadership looks like. This is not an indictment, but rather an observation that every culturally bound group — Latinas from Miami, Ivy-league educated African-Americans, Japanese businessmen in Tokyo, White males in Omaha — have a preferred leadership style that they believe has contributed to their success. In a multicultural, global world, however, the diverse employees coming through our doors and moving up our ranks are going to exhibit great managerial and leadership qualities that are often not recognized as such because they look different from the cultural norm of the majority group currently in the leadership position.

Creating crossculturally competent individuals and organizations is essential for ushering in sustainable diversity. Only through crosscultural competence can employees and leaders gain a language, concepts, and tools for skillfully addressing cultural differences. It provides the tools with which to navigate the difference.

Performance Management: The Phenomenon of Overlooking Talent

To uncover the inadvertent assumptions keeping the mix from working, we must get into the very wiring of the performance assessment process.

As companies focus on their key or high-potential talent, they run the risk of perpetuating under-representation if this select group is not adequately diverse. The view that 20 percent of talent yields 80 percent of results has plenty of merit. It informs a strategy that an organization can get an even bigger payoff by focusing on this top talent even more. But if not managed in a way that diversifies who ends up in this talent pool, true inclusion will be elusive.

Inclusion Paradox principles clearly apply here. By design, the focus on key and high-potential individuals shrinks the pool of talent that receives special attention and developmental resources. How can we ensure these pools are diverse? Here, we still need some scaffolding to ensure sustainability. Along with the high-potential assessment, a multicultural talent review (MCTR) must be undertaken. The MCTR provides a macro view of the distribution of one's multicultural talent — for example, how many do you have, and in comparing different groups to one another, what is the bell curve of their performance levels, what are the turnover rates and their engagement scores?

Top performers who are people of color or people with disabilities already will have been identified during the high-potential assessment. Studies on the success of traditionally marginalized groups have shown that these individuals tend to be superstars who stand out dramatically. The potential blind spot is overlooking the strong — but not superstar — talent among these very same marginalized groups. Due to their different ways of thinking or acting, their strong performance is often not recognized as such.

As Russell Bennett, vice president of Latino Health Solutions at United Healthcare, says, "In corporate society it's easy to find leaders and managers who say they strongly support the concept of diversity. They want people who look different, but corporations still reward for conformity and are often uncomfortable with nonconformity."

We need to systemically ferret out this overlooked talent. But the question remains as to whether managers are able to tell the difference between a performance issue and a crosscultural misunderstanding? Think about the following performance assessment sound bites:

"trust"
"high performing"
"pay for results"
"proactive"
"executive presence"
"nice"
"assertive"

On the surface, these are all seemingly strong, positive traits. However, as we'll see later in the book, these sound bites are often tagged to individuals and can "label" them for the rest of their careers. Each is loaded with culturally biased assumptions that may inadvertently filter out positive assessments of diverse employees because the manner in which they express themselves may not fit an organizational view of what these traits look like when wielded effectively.

On the flip side, negative sound bites may sound like this:

"aggressive"
"not a team player"
"clients don't feel comfortable with her"
"shy"
"passive"

These, too, are terms that can mean different things depending upon the culture the individual comes from. For example, was the individual's behavior truly aggressive? Or was it actually a respectful and effective way of achieving business results had their behavior been observed within the context of their culture? Was the individual demonstrating passive participation in a meeting, or were they displaying effective, face-saving, influential leadership? By focusing specifically on diverse talent, an MCTR can create an opportunity to constructively call out differences. This enables a company to be better positioned to more accurately look at talent that could, ironically, be overlooked by the very nature of an individual's differences.

For a business to be truly successful — through the Obama Era and beyond — it needs to draw upon a diverse talent pool. Not only that, but it also needs to make sure this diversity of talent feels included in the culture of the organization. If this is the case, Baxter's former CDO, Don Wilson, said, "These diverse individuals will become talent magnets for you," creating a win-win scenario all around.

Benefit Programs Can Also Be Culturally Biased

Crosscultural competence also means that organizations can more clearly see the implications of diversity on programs that have not traditionally been thought of as culturally influenced. Inclusion is lacking, for example, when it comes to employees' optimal use of benefits. Although 401(k) and 403(b) retirement savings benefits and preventive care are available and communicated equally to all, African-Americans, Latinos, and women tend to under-save and exhibit behaviors that often sub-optimize their return on investment, according to research by Aon Hewitt and other organizations.[10] These studies have also shown that different demographic groups under- or over-utilize preventive care. Whether it's about health or wealth, these types of utilization disparities are evidence we do not have inclusion, even in benefits that are available and accessible to all employees.

While there are socioeconomic reasons for these gaps, cultural differences are also at play. How benefits are designed, communicated, marketed, and accessed inadvertently conform to — and are optimized by — the worldview of the traditional majority culture. Sustainable diversity demands that we be aware of why and how this is happening. As a result of this awareness, we can create solutions that make these essential well-being programs work equally well for all. We'll explore these phenomena and solutions in depth in Chapter 13, "Why Not Acknowledging Differences Can Make Us Sicker and Poorer."

There are other ways in which benefit programs can be tailored to meet diversifying needs. In addition to its standard benefits package, Xerox has given employees $10,000 for allocation to different programs.[11] This gives nontraditional families the flexibility to tailor benefits to their personal needs. Meanwhile, Merrill Lynch and Bank of America have instituted "extended family benefits." These flexible plans let employees add other household members to the plan, be it a domestic partner, an elder parent, or a grown child.[12]

This is not a trivial matter. As health care costs rise and a greater burden is placed on the emerging workforce to take responsibility for their retirement planning, the long-term well-being of employees needs to be a hallmark of sustainable diversity — even once they're no longer employed by the company providing these benefits.

Flexibility and Virtuality

Almost all diversity and inclusion issues point to the need for greater flexibility — not only in terms of benefits programs and the length of time they are extended, but also around the givens of career ladders, set retirement age, and fixed job descriptions. Calling out differences among a growing number of groups can quickly become complicated, particularly as we expand beyond the categories of race and gender. Two generations ago, the call for flexibility came from working moms. Now, it's coming from Millennials, Gen Xers, near retirees, and singles. This implies that it's less about tweaking systems and processes for greater flexibility and more about creating systems that are flexible by design. Meanwhile, nano and Web 2.0 technological breakthroughs challenge the paradigm that flexibility automatically means greater cost.

The 2008 financial meltdown accelerated the need to provide greater flexibility as organizations asked employees to do more with less. Work hours are increasing both out of need and fear, and flexibility can now be offered as a reward in a time when pay increases and benefits are reduced. (Check out Chapter 14, "Work-Life Flexibility: The Mother of All Battles," where I explore this further.)

Pulling It All Together

Make no mistake, the economic crisis has not just been a market thing. It's a "people thing" as well. There are the inevitable difficult decisions around job eliminations, treating laid-off workers with dignity, and maintaining a focused and engaged workforce for those who remain. It's a time when diversity and inclusion must be tended to — not in spite of the financial crisis, but because of it. There is desperate need for perspectives, skills, and worldviews that currently don't exist in organizations in order to interpret and prosper within the new upside-down world order.

As I've argued throughout this chapter, we must fundamentally tackle the work of diversity and inclusion in a different way in order for it to be sustainable. Those in diversity work need to build new capabilities and take on new experiences. "The chief diversity officer should have responsibilities that extend beyond traditional people issues," says 25-year veteran diversity consultant Mary-Frances Winters, CEO of the Winters Group. "The role should include international government relations, trade relations, manufacturing, design issues, selection of location, security, ethics, and global marketing."

This applies not only to CDOs, but to all HR leaders. Diversity is not something to be tended to on the side, but an integral part of managing all the dimensions of human capital. It must also be coupled with operations, with how the business is run, and with what an organization produces and sells.

"Unless we've got new, diverse people — new ways of thinking — we're never going to meet our new business goals," says Edie Fraser, a diversity pioneer and managing director of Diversified Search Odgers Berndtson. "Of the 86 companies that I've talked with about talent planning in the last 16 months, I'm a little shocked at the lack of talent planning and talent management that I've seen. Many business managers don't know who their vendors are across the board. They have not done a good job of including diverse and global vendors within their mix. Or they've not had their diversity officers or their diversity strategies at the table." This lack of a coordinated diversity effort — from the CEO down to individual vendors — ultimately results in inefficient business practices, a lack of innovation and strategic initiative, and ultimately, a lack of employee satisfaction and growth.

HR leaders are beginning to grasp the importance of diversity and inclusion. In the fall of 2008, the Society for Human Resource Management (SHRM), the leading global association of HR professionals with more than 100,000 members, convened a group of the top 100 diversity leaders and practitioners to give advice on how to best integrate diversity into their highly regarded HR certifications. This is a public acknowledgment that there had been an increasing number of HR professionals taking over the diversity agenda and seeing it as an inherent part of their responsibilities This has led to the development of three new HR diversity and inclusion organizational standards, which in 2013 will have been finalized by SHRM, in cooperation with the American National Standards Institute.[13]

This signals a fundamental shift in how HR professionals are viewing the need to get intimately and personally involved with diversity and inclusion. In April 2008, I was invited to lead a seminar for two dozen HR senior vice presidents who were "feeling stuck on diversity." What was telling about this invitation was that it was initiated by the SVPs of HR, not the CDOs. Clearly, HR leaders are feeling ownership for diversity and inclusion as never before. Why? In part, it's because they're not getting the results they expected from their long distance sponsorship and support for diversity and inclusion work. It's also because they're seeing diversity and inclusion issues spill over into every area of HR. They're seeing that to lead in HR means to lead on diversity.

"But the diversity field should not be expected to lead this debate," warns Ted Childs. "It's the business and government leadership who should lead it by seeing that diversity is one of the critical tools to success. The signals are mixed, however, of how this will play out. I'm seeing a climate change, where leaders are seeing things differently. But I feel that their motivation is less about recognizing the talent pool marketplace opportunities and more about following the political wind. There's a Black guy in the White House, so we got to be a little spiffy here. And with the crunch that's on right now, I'm fearful that I've seen this movie before. The things that we have come to know as important are the things they may view as expendable when they've got to reduce costs. They don't see this as a tool to achieve. They see this as baggage that has to be dealt with in the context of 'is it affordable?' — and as tough times get hard, it's less affordable."

The Obama Era offers a unique opportunity to bend the predictable story in a new way — through inspiration, but also through new legislation and policy. "The Labor Department is going to get revved up, so we're going to have audits again," says Childs. "The Commerce Department is going to get revved up with a vision of a global marketplace and opportunities for companies to do even more business around the world. So we need to take advantage of that. Whether the times are good or bad, it offers us the talent pool that's available, the diversity of the marketplace that's available. This opportunity is in front of us *right now.*"

This is part of the spirit of the cultural implication of a Renaissance in Values-Based Decision-Making demonstrated in the Obama Era. But embedding diversity — making it the cultural norm of how we do business and HR — is exceptionally hard work.

This is why many companies skirt the issue. They showcase diverse people in their marketing materials, offer minority scholarships, attend minority career fairs, subsidize minority internship programs, and fund minority community outreach programs. All of these are important and commendable efforts, but from a sustainability perspective, they don't engage the organizational machinery that defines the way things get done.

Programs come and go. In the process, they help raise issues, maintain interest, and mobilize people into action. Such programs must lead to systemic changes to existing processes or the creation of new ones to ensure that inclusion of the mix is taking place. Programmatic diversity is like riding a wave on a surfboard. It can be a spectacular, memorable thrill. But sustainable diversity requires harnessing the demographic wave to change the coastline. ♀

Wal-Mart Looks To Hispanic Market

By Jonathan Birchall
Published: March 12, 2009
Copyright The Financial Times Limited 2009

Wal-Mart plans to open its first Hispanic-focused supermarkets this summer in Arizona and Texas as the largest U.S. retailer continues its drive to expand its dominance of the U.S. grocery business.

The pilot stores, named Supermercado de Walmart, will open in Phoenix and Houston in remodeled 39,000 sq ft locations occupied previously by two of Wal-Mart's Neighborhood Market stores.

The retailer said that the stores were in "strongly Hispanic neighborhoods" and would feature a "new layout, signing, and product assortment designed to make them even more relevant to local Hispanic customers." The staff will also be bilingual. Wal-Mart's Sam's Club warehouse store also plans to open a 143,000 sq ft Hispanic-focused store called Más Club in Houston this year.

Several leading regional U.S. supermarket chains already operate Hispanic store brands, including Publix in Florida, which operates three Publix Sabor markets, and HEB in Texas, which opened a Mi Tienda store in Houston in 2006.

The markets include elements such as cafés serving Latino pastries and coffee, and full-service meat and fish counters.

Leading retailers are also pursuing Hispanic consumers online, with Best Buy and Home Depot having launched Spanish-language versions of their e-commerce sites in recent months.

Eduardo Castro-Wright, the head of Wal-Mart's U.S. stores since 2005, has also been an advocate of testing new smaller, more focused formats, and raised the idea of turning the Neighborhood Market into a Hispanic-style bodega concept several years ago.

He has also developed Wal-Mart's efforts to customize its larger Supercenter stores, which have been grouped according to differing community profiles, such as urban, suburban, Hispanic, and African-American, with customized merchandise.

A 195,000 sq ft Supercenter that opened in Texas last year included a tortilleria bakery, Hispanic foods, and a larger selection of Spanish-language music and DVDs. Mr. Castro-Wright was previously head of Wal-Mart's Mexican subsidiary, whose store network ranges from large U.S.-style Supercenters to small, local bodegas, an upscale supermarket chain, and two restaurant chains.

Last year, Wal-Mart also began testing four new 10,000 sq ft Marketside convenience grocery stores in the Phoenix area — its first new format in a decade. Tesco, the U.K. retailer, also has more than 25 of its small Fresh & Easy markets in the Phoenix area.

Reprinted with permission from The Financial Times Ltd.

SUMMARY POINTS

- Sustainable diversity is different from programmatic diversity, although the two are linked.
- Sustainable diversity is hard-wired into an organization's mission, growth, profitability, and operational strategies. It's embedded into every process and practice that touches people — recruitment, retention, training and development, promotion, and engagement.
- Leadership styles are culturally influenced.
- Crosscultural competence leads to sustainable diversity.
- While diversity missteps may be unintended, they're still very real. This can be evidenced in the gap between majority and nonmajority employees' use of company benefits.

SHAPING YOUR STRATEGY

- How much of your strategy relies on programmatic approaches, rather than the sustainable approach of hard-wiring diversity to your talent, business, and operational imperatives?
- How crossculturally competent are your leaders? If they're not, how much are they aware of the issue? What can you do to build a case for them to be crossculturally competent and then help them achieve that goal?
- As you look at the benefits that are available and how they're used, are they truly inclusive in addressing the needs, wants, and aspirations of the various different demographic groups in your organization? As you think about operational priorities and strategies, where do you think diversity inclusion can add something of value?

THIS THING IS GLOBAL! THIS THING IS GLOBAL! THIS THING IS GLOBAL! THIS THING IS GLOBAL!

3

Chapter 3

This Thing Is Global!

The Obama Era marks the globalization of most dimensions of our lives. Customer support for our cell phone can just as likely come from Gurgaon, Manila, or Albuquerque. The diagnosis of our chest X-rays can come from a radiologist in Bangalore or in Tacoma. Even our local city council news can come in the form of virtual reports from Filipinos watching council proceedings in Buena Vista, California. Americans are simultaneously managing virtual teams of workers in Buenos Aires, Brussels, Beijing, and Mumbai. Indian leaders, without having to repatriate, are directing American teams.

Diversity and inclusion must take into account these labor realities. While it's important to address diversity issues within a country, we must also address them across countries. Global teams may make sense in terms of overall compensation costs, 24/7 coverage, and local language support, but we mustn't forget they are complex organisms where inclusion/exclusion issues materialize in ways that affect both the quality of relationships and the work performed by these teams.

As U.S.-based multinationals begin planting the diversity flag in their operations outside the United States, they run the risk of inadvertently — and somewhat ironically — dismissing alternative national interpretations of diversity. While there's good reason to celebrate the global diversity push by American multinationals, many of which have strong diversity track records in the United States, there are pitfalls that could undermine the successful globalization of diversity and inclusion, if left unchecked.

During the past few years, I've given a number of presentations on diversity issues and trends to nearly hundreds of multinational client contacts in my native Latin America, Europe, and Asia. Speaking in Buenos Aires, Santiago, São Paolo, Mexico City, San Juan, London, Vienna, Shanghai, Beijing, and Delhi, I've heard these issues play out in a variety of ways. "This diversity thing is an American thing," is a common complaint outside the United States. "We don't see how the race issues in the United States are relevant to us — and yet we are being held accountable for targets for racial diversity that are not relevant for our workforce demographics."

A breakdown has occurred somewhere between the inspiring workforce and people strategies and the execution of diversity as a business imperative. As a result, we're beginning to see an increasingly resentful backlash against the American version of diversity abroad. In addition, there's an ironic blind spot that has emerged. While American companies are aggressively pushing diversity messages, many are failing to make the connection between the message of inclusion and long-standing complaints that HR policies, communication campaigns, and common business processes are culturally insensitive to Latin American or other non-U.S. realities.

Four Approaches to Global Diversity

In examining both the successful and unsuccessful approaches to global diversity, it's helpful to break them into four distinct archetypes: Isolationists, Idealists, Imperialists, and Globalists.

While members of all four archetypes are highly committed to the ideals of diversity, the differences lie in how they approach it.

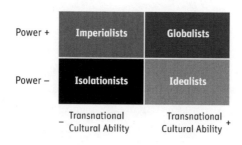

Isolationists and Idealists

Isolationists tend to have a limited view of the world and don't think very much about diversity outside the 50 states. To them, diversity is exclusively defined in the common U.S. terms of race/ethnicity, gender, sexual orientation, and physical ability, with a nod to secondary diversity issues such as thinking styles. These organizations may also take a more compliance-driven approach to diversity.

Idealists acknowledge that diversity issues must be addressed abroad but have a naïve understanding of how that could and should play out. Idealists tend to believe that programs that have proven successful in the United States will be equally effective when implemented abroad. Neither the Isolationists nor the Idealists have much power in the global diversity arena, though some may have power within the context of the United States. Whether they have true power or not, their limited exposure to life outside the United States undermines their ability to have a significant impact on diversity on a global level.

Imperialists and Globalists

Imperialists and Globalists are the most interesting and powerful of the diversity groups. Members of both groups are highly experienced and committed to global diversity, yet they differ in their diversity missions.

The Imperialists have earned their stripes through deeply committed work in forging cutting-edge diversity strategies built around thoughtful metrics, tough accountability, minority and women leadership, and succession planning. They have been so successful in the United States that they're now setting their sights abroad, where they seek to bring to bear all they've accomplished stateside.

Many members of this group are "inadvertent" Imperialists in that they would never describe themselves as such. While they may espouse values of inclusion, their actions belie a more Imperialist nature. For example, using Latin America as a case study, some demand that their company's offices in the region develop metrics of representation and plans for how they're going to bridge the diversity gaps in their offices. In doing so, they often describe the diversity requirements in terms of African-American, Latino, and Asian representation.

With the exception of Brazil, Latin America does not have the same degree of racial diversity as the United States, making these demands impossible to meet. In Latin regions, issues of diversity tend to be based more on class than race. During Colonial times, people of color could purchase certificates of whiteness. While this practice certainly acknowledged race as a factor, it placed greater emphasis on an individual's economic status in terms of privilege.

The pitfall in Imperialistic diversity lies not only in reactions to specific diversity messages, but also in corporate behaviors, including HR business and HR policies, procedures, and guidelines that Latin Americans may view as culturally insensitive. Ironically, many companies with an Imperialistic bent fail to see the contradiction between their emphasis on diversity and their cultural insensitivity in the deployment of other corporate initiatives.

Though both Imperialists and Idealists believe the U.S. approach to diversity is better, Idealists take a more social justice approach, rather than a pragmatic business approach. This results in less of an impact on the organization. In some ways, Globalists and Imperialists are cut from the same cloth. Both grasp the strategic importance of diversity to their businesses. They differ, however, in their level of focus on measurement and accountability and in their cultural sensitivities. Globalists do not assume what has worked in the United States will work elsewhere. Their first inclination is to deconstruct diversity — to unearth its true meaning in each country or region — rather than relying exclusively on the American definition.

With this approach, Globalists have been able to surface not only the cross-cultural issues between their non-U.S. offices and their American counterparts, but also the issues existing among the countries *within* the various other global regions themselves. For example, as U.S. multinationals regionalize corporate work in Latin America, cultural differences are surfacing between professionals in Argentina and Mexico. Latin American business and HR leaders have been caught off guard, having assumed the barrier would be low due to a common language, similar histories of being colonized by the Spanish, and cathedrals at the hearts of their cities.

"We were wrong," one Mexican business leader told me. "We are discovering in a painful way that there are very big differences between how business is conducted in Mexico and South America."

Despite trying to be sensitive to the spirit of diversity, companies often make unintentional missteps. A corporate video produced in the United States and intended for a Puerto Rican audience featured a moving interview with an employee who had gone through great sacrifice crossing the Rio Grande to seek a new life in America. He talked emotionally about his dream of one day becoming a U.S. citizen. For Puerto Ricans, who are already U.S. citizens and do not see themselves as having to resort to illegal immigration, this was a serious insult. Several people walked out of the screening. A Globalist approach would have avoided the assumption that what works for Latinos in the United States, where they are the minority, will also work for Latinos in Puerto Rico, where they are the majority.

The Way Forward

Diversity and inclusion offer a new platform for conversation and understanding among all involved. Diversity practitioners are strategically positioned to help broker new ways of talking about crosscultural issues that have long vexed multinationals conducting work outside the United States. However, those diversity professionals who have not had much exposure to life and work outside the United States are going to be at a significant disadvantage in stepping into this breach. Thus, chief diversity officers aspiring to lead diversity globally must make this developmental task a priority.

Setting a Globalist tone, rather than an inadvertently Imperialist one, can happen quickly in initial conversations on diversity. A variety of declarations have proven effective at disarming predisposed defensiveness against the perceived U.S. diversity Imperialist message. They include: "The key is for you to define what diversity means to you, your region, your country, your group," or "Our starting point will not be what diversity means in the United States," or "Diversity can open up new avenues for conversation on crosscultural conflicts between those in our region and U.S. Americans."

This does not negate the fact that every organization, regardless of its location, experiences some degree of resistance to change. There is a very real element of individuals and organizations digging in their heels and using the accusation of Imperialism as an excuse to avoid having the tough conversations and making the tough choices. Yet, no matter how uncomfortable, it's something we must do if organizations and workers are to thrive in the emerging environment and if we are to continue building on the gains made so far.

Globalist Views

While U.S.-based diversity practitioners wrestle with what it means to make their strategies global — versus exporting an "American thing" — non-American, non-European multinationals are confronting diversity challenges of their own. Much like the Americans and Europeans who preceded them during the first modern multinational expansion in the '60s, these new multinationals from emerging markets did not consider diversity issues as they mapped out ambitious global product launches and marketing strategies from their home countries. Yet here they are, running right smack into them.

It's not just cross-country, global diversity issues that are popping up either. As the demographic tsunami ripples throughout various countries around the world, hidden issues are beginning to surface. National inclusion realities are percolating at a local level in parts of the world where diversity talk had been dismissed.

In just four years' time — the time it takes to go to college and get a professional degree — a woman in India or China could find herself in a completely different place in terms of personal and economic power. As multinationals hire women in large numbers, a profound social change around gender roles is taking place. Income earned in her name and deposited in her bank account means greater individual power. This, in turn, lets her be more independent about the choices she makes, where she lives, and even whom she chooses to marry or when she chooses to marry, if at all.

The impact is not just societal. Glass-ceiling issues are increasingly sprouting up in these emerging economies as women succeed and expect to move up. In Latin America, for example, half of the workforce is comprised of women. Now that they've been in the workforce for one-and-a-half generations, Latino women are starting to bump up against the glass ceiling. Just 5 percent of listed board directorships are held by women, and only 22 percent of senior level corporate positions are held by women in Latin America. Latino women can't help but wonder why.[1]

As the world continues to shrink, a male bias in these traditionally male-dominated societies poses a real challenge for organizations. Without a change in their mindset, companies that fail to embrace women in the workforce — particularly in upper management positions — are going to fall behind those that do. "I see gender mismanagement as a global geographic liability. Women offer an extraordinary opportunity for access to talent," says Ted Childs, former chief diversity officer at IBM who now runs his own consultancy, Ted Childs® LLC. "And these male-dominated cultures or male-dominated companies, in both cases, are going to find that this attitude is a liability."

In Canada, a country rightfully proud of its tolerant and welcoming culture, the diversity conversation is catching Canadians off-guard as they begin to glimpse a fundamental gap between their inclusion ideals and their inclusion results. Here, the metaphor of the multicultural mosaic — where people retain their sense of group identity, yet together construct a beautiful social array — was intended to contrast with the American ideal of the proverbial melting pot in which immigrants were expected to shed their accents, dress, and customs and conform to Main Street ways. But Canadians are facing the stark reality that the mosaic is not displayed as expected in the managerial and more senior ranks. Roughly 17 percent of corporate officers are women, even though women represent nearly half of the Canadian workforce.[2] Meanwhile, only 3 percent of Canada's visible minorities hold senior management positions, despite representing more than 15 percent of the Canadian labor force.[3]

Sourcing Talent From Long-Excluded Groups in Canada

Canada's one-million-strong Aboriginal population comprises 4.1 percent of the population and 3.3 percent of the labor force. Yet, Aboriginals are underpaid compared to their White counterparts and face significantly higher levels of unemployment compared to the national average.[4] According to the Canadian Human Rights Commission, roughly 15 percent of Canadians with disabilities who are employed report being discriminated against because of their disability. At the same time, the number of Canadians with disabilities is expected to grow from around 4 million in 2009 to roughly 6 million by 2026.[5]

Headquartered in Regina, Conexus is an integrated financial services provider with more than 70 locations throughout Saskatchewan. After years of watching its workers lured away to work in the Alberta oil sands, Conexus decided to tap into a ready source of talent right in its own backyard: the Aboriginal population at a nearby community.[6] Gayle Johnson, executive vice president of human resources, marketing, and community development, admits the program required some trial and error before it ran smoothly. However, she attributes its ultimate success to these key initiatives:[7]

1. Before the recruitment process began, HR representatives from Conexus met with senior tribe members to explain the initiative. Only after garnering their endorsement did Conexus representatives begin meeting with community members.

2. Conexus introduced education and awareness training for its staff two years in advance of the effort, to help them understand and respect Aboriginal culture. More intensive training was provided to managers immediately before the arrival of the first group of Aboriginal employees.

3. To ensure companionship and support during the onboarding period, Aboriginal employees were hired in groups of ten.

4. Conexus brought in tribe elders to assist with communication during the ten-week training program it provides its Aboriginal employees. The program covered more than banking; it also provided social skills and personal financial training, like budgeting and how to use a checking account.

5. A First Nations liaison was hired to act as a "cultural intermediary" and advise on how to resolve issues. Since Aboriginal employees have a more relaxed attitude toward time, this made Conexus' standard 8 a.m. start time a challenge, for example. To avoid what was sure to be tardy showings for the group during their onboarding process, Conexus moved their starting time to 9 a.m.[8]

Thanks to the initiative, Aboriginals not only make up a significant portion of the Conexus workforce, they now hold financial services and administrative positions as well. Moreover, Conexus has a workforce that more closely mirrors the community — and a new customer base, to boot!

Even Europeans, who have been outspoken in questioning the relevance of diversity for them, feel the buffeting winds of an aging workforce, declining population, gender pay gap, and rising diversity through immigrants from North Africa, the Middle East, and Eastern Europe. The ideals of German meritocracy, British common sense, and French *liberté, égalité,* and *fraternité* face uncomfortable challenges to their credibility.

The Mix and Making it Work — Localizing Diversity and Inclusion

Talking about *global diversity* first requires shifting from a "United States-to-the-world" to a "world-to-the-world" perspective. In today's upside-down world, diversity is flowing every which way.

"Diversity" and "inclusion" mean different things to different people. Some reject the word itself as reflecting American corporate imperialism that has nothing to do with non-U.S. realities. In her extensive travels across the globe, Monica Francois Marcel, a deeply experienced interculturalist and co-founder of the consultancy Language and Culture Worldwide, sees signs that organizations are grappling with the varied aspects of inclusion. "Everyone is going to struggle with diversity within their own workforce," she explains. She goes on to say that while other countries, regions, and companies will have to face diversity and inclusion as they define those terms, "it would be ideal if they could glean from the United States' lessons learned without feeling as though the United States is pushing lessons on them — in other words, if they can take what they will from the experiences of the United States, they can improve upon them in their own regions and contexts."

Regardless of whether I'm speaking in Latin America, Europe, Canada, India, or the United States, I frequently ask audiences if they are willing to set aside their working definitions and see if they could agree to the definition of the two terms I introduced at the beginning of this book: Diversity is the mix, inclusion is making the mix work.™

With this approach, each location can define the mix and how it's working. Three concentric circles typically appear: things that pretty much everyone brings up, like gender; topics that outliers in the group may bring up, like race in Brazil and sexual orientation in Spain; and taboo issues that no one brings up, like race in Peru and sexual orientation in India. Here's a bit more of what I have encountered in a few of the countries where I have engaged in this conversation:

India — While race/ethnicity predominates when evaluating an individual's background in the United States, race rarely appears on that list in India. Rather, the top considerations are likely to be religion, caste, and geographic region. Each of India's 28 states has its unique predominant language and dialects (more than 300 in the whole country), as well as variations in cuisine, attire, and cultural focus. Understanding and dealing with such a broad spectrum of diversity presents a tremendous challenge in and of itself. The more expressive Punjabis, for example, are likely to dominate in the workplace, compared to the more taciturn folks from Uttar Pradesh. Managers from Northern Indian states have been known to say they will not hire anyone from a Southern state. Variances in corporate experience also cause discord. Those who grew up in outsourced, off-shored roles tend to clash with those who did not. The one-up dynamics of this issue are real and can be blatant.

"While inclusion presents an opportunity, as well as a tangible business case, to move past traditional barriers, it must be framed within the context and realities of the unique cultures of the country or location." says Sodexo's senior vice president and chief diversity officer, Dr. Rohini Anand. "For example, in India, where one of the defining issues is caste, some customers may be reluctant to eat food cooked by someone of a different caste, and this directly impacts us as a foodservice provider."

Brazil — Geographic region is also a top consideration in Brazil. The traditional rivalry between *Paulistas* from São Paolo and *Cariocas* from Rio — and the way both look down on *Mineiros* who come from the more agricultural and mining interior of Minas Gerais — plays out in unproductive ways in the workplace. In a roundtable discussion with a group of employees in Uberlândia in Minas Gerais, *Mineiros* talked with feeling about how their morale is affected by what they believe are superior attitudes on the part of coworkers and customers from the big cities. The put-downs are both subtle and explicit, creating a mix that is not working well. Productivity suffers as a result.

Japan — In the Land of the Rising Sun — where only 10 percent of managers are women[9] and 70 percent leave the workforce when they have children[10] — rigid workplace gender roles and the aging of the population are placing extraordinary pressures on Japanese society. With a negligible immigrant influx resulting in one of the most racially homogenous countries in the world, Japan's greatest source of diverse talent for managerial and senior roles will be women. But Japanese corporate culture is still a long way from creating pathways for women to rise into the leadership ranks. Fortunately, companies are beginning to recognize the problem. Recently, for example, Japanese electronics giant Sony appointed a head of diversity in Tokyo to address gender issues in its Japanese workforce.

Falling Into the Same Traps?
Multinationals From Emerging Nations

As multinationals from emerging markets continue to spread their global reach, they increasingly will face the kinds of diversity and crosscultural challenges American and European multinationals have been facing — and often not addressing — for decades. Remember Chevy's failed push to introduce the Nova in Latin

America? Who would want a car that, in Spanish, means "doesn't run?" Or Braniff's "Fly in Leather" campaign that invited Latin Americans to *Volar en Cuero* ("Fly Naked")!

Now the shoe is on the other foot. When Telefónica of Spain took over the state-run Brazilian telephone monopoly in 1998, it made the mistake of misspelling its own name on the logo plastered throughout the city, as well as on stationery and printed materials. They used the Spanish *Telefónica* instead of the Portuguese *Telefônica*. A public outcry forced them to get it right. Even Latin-American multinationals, *"multilatinas,"* are falling into the same traps as their American and European counterparts as they regionalize their corporate work in their own region. They, too, are running into below-the-waterline differences that go deeper than the Argentinean term *che* and the Peruvian equivalent *compadre*. Software development companies from India risk losing big accounts because their programmers are failing at crosscultural communications, with frequent misunderstandings about whether deadlines can truly be met.

So how can emerging-market companies strengthen their globalization by being diversity competent? These companies already are positioned to help broker new ways of discussing crosscultural issues that have long vexed multinationals. After all, they experienced firsthand what happened in their countries when the first multinationals came calling. And as Dr. Hammer says, "the ability to bridge across differences at the national, the ethnic, and other levels of difference is what is really going to determine our effectiveness in meeting global needs."

Emerging-market multinationals bring their cultural strengths and offer new ways of seeing things that could be mutually beneficial. For example, Brazilians exporting the country's spirit of *jogo de cintura* (a term from soccer-fevered Brazil describing soccer hip and waist feints used to get past an opponent) could offer just the right mind- and skill-set we all need to adapt to an unpredictable, global business world mutating at a dizzying rate.

Emerging-market multinationals must take crosscultural competency seriously. It is the bedrock that will improve interpersonal communications between workers, open new ways of thinking about product design, and sharpen sales pitches. Companies are beginning to awaken to this realization. The Indian company I referred to earlier, for example, now puts its teams and those of its U.S. clients through intensive crosscultural working sessions.

New Rules for the Changing Game

Everyone is spinning off-center in this new game. Emerging countries are facing global diversity, while Americans watch their long-cherished diversity assumptions and programs mutate and become owned by others. All players need to put their own house in order. Companies working to grow and prosper in this increasingly globally diverse world must deconstruct diversity and culture to unearth the true meaning in their own country or region rather than relying exclusively on each country's past definitions.

What new rules can we glean from this new space?

Listen to employees in your home country and global offices with regard to how they perceive each other. Is there a shared sense of working together in coordination or are colleagues convinced their peers in other countries simply can't get it right? Are workers blaming each other as the cause of low-quality work or slow response times, citing their "peculiar" way of getting things done? If so, your company may need to build crosscultural competence and instill some global diversity savvy.

Pay attention to your home country's diversity issues. Companies that have addressed diversity issues in a progressive way within their own countries tend to be better positioned for anticipating and addressing those issues on a global scale. If we define "diversity" as the mix and "inclusion" as making the mix work, what is the desired mix of your workforce and customer base given, say, Brazilian demographics? Do you have a workforce that reflects, as Brazil's national motto says, the land of *Ordem e Progresso (Order and Progress)*? Are women in managerial and leadership positions? Do they feel they're able to bring their full spectrum of talents to the business issues your company faces? With 50 percent of the population being Afro-Brazilian, are Blacks well represented in your pipeline? If you have the mix right, how well is it working?

In Brazil, private companies with more than 100 employees are obliged to hire people with disabilities. Quotas vary between 2 percent and 5 percent of the labor pool, depending on each employer's total number of employees.[11] Yet companies struggle to find enough skilled people from this group to employee for the jobs they have. Out of their own initiative, progressive companies are creating programs to equip this workforce even before hiring them.

Be a student of the major demographic shifts in the markets you want to serve. In Latin America, the major demographic shifts are age-related, as a large influx of young people has entered the workforce just as an older generation prepares to leave, creating generational clashes. The Chilean postal service, a 100-year-old state institution, realized that its patronage-style, family-based tradition of offering lifelong employment was not going to provide the workforce needed to modernize operations for the digital age. It needed college graduates with specific technical skills to help reengineer its way of doing business. The postal service was unprepared for the generational and culture clash that resulted between those who claimed the company as a family entitlement because "my grandfather worked here" versus those newcomers who came in with a different, more competitive mindset.

In the United States, progressive, diverse companies have recognized the emerging marketplace flourishing right in their midst. Financial institutions, for example, are seeing their greatest growth coming from the rising Latino population that is projected to comprise nearly one-third of the United States by July 1, 2050.[12] One officer at a major multinational bank told me that half of all new accounts in 2006 were opened by Latinos. This trend since then has been replicating at many other rival banks.

What new market needs are emerging in your country due to the demographic shifts?

Hard-wire it to HR. A growing number of Latin American employees are declaring that diversity, along with work-life balance, is a critical factor in what attracts them to an employer. According to Hewitt's 2005 and 2006 Best Employers in Latin America study, one of the top five characteristics of a Best Employer was its commitment to diversity and work-life balance. Some 87 percent of employees at Best Employers said their "organization is committed to creating a work environment that embraces diversity and differences" versus 67 percent at those who were not deemed Best Employers.[13] The path to inclusion lies in talent sourcing, recruiting, onboarding, compensation, and development processes that are fair, accessible, culturally appealing, and relevant to the various groups within your organization. Make it a priority to involve HR, as well as business leaders in your diversity efforts.

Bringing It Home

Diversity has become exponentially more complex as it has gone global. As Dr. Hammer explains, "The global leader today is somebody who is able to shift cultural perspective and adapt behavior appropriately to cultural context in order to accomplish goals that are important to the organization. Now that's a simple definition. But it's a very complex kind of capability." Along the way, some American diversity practitioners, while savvy and supportive about global diversity issues, have expressed a private fear that United States diversity issues will be lost because U.S.-based race and ethnicity issues present unique challenges. If one's diversity view is U.S.-to-the-world, that fear is legitimate: The United States will not be able to sustain its specific diversity issues on the top of the global agenda. But, in a world-to-the-world diversity view, where the United States is just one among many global regions that must address their own diversity issues, then the specific diversity issues found only in the United States remain on top of the agenda as a regional issue.

"Think global. Act local," says a popular slogan. But in an upside-down world, we must also follow all the permutations of this wisdom:

Think global. Act global.
Think local. Act global.
Think local. Act local.

These variations may not make for a nifty, pithy bumper sticker, but they make for far more effective global diversity strategies that truly will make the world more inclusive. ♀

SUMMARY POINTS

- In addition to addressing diversity issues within a country, we must deal with diversity and inclusion issues across national boundaries.
- Enterprises that are committed to diversity may assume one of four distinct archetypes: Isolationists, Idealists, Imperialists, and Globalists.
- Diversity and inclusion may take on different meanings to different people around the world. One definition that rings true across industries and societies is: *Diversity is the mix. Inclusion is making the mix work.*™ This definition enables every entity to define the mix and make the mix work for them.
- Multinational organizations from emerging markets may face diversity and crosscultural challenges similar to those which enterprises from developed markets have been addressing.

SHAPING YOUR STRATEGY

- As you think about how your company and your competitors have been approaching global diversity, which archetypes are they exhibiting?
- If your company is an Isolationist, Idealist, or Imperialist, what actions or steps must you take to shift your diversity and inclusion approach to a Globalist perspective?
- What is the mix in the various places where your company has a major presence? How does it compare and contrast to the mix in the United States? How well is it working? Wherever you identify places where the mix is not working well, what steps can you take to surface those issues and begin addressing them?

I NEED YOUR DIFFERENCES

need

mine

4

and

I NEED YOUR DIFFERENCES

need

mine

Chapter 4

I Need Your Differences ...
And You Need Mine

How could I have missed it? I really thought I had agreement from the group. After all, one of the team members had even said, "Andrés, I agree with you 100 percent." Yet when I started acting on the agreement I was sure we had, the e-mails and voicemails started flying in: "What are you doing? This is something we did not agree to!" Confused, I replied, "What part of 100 percent didn't I understand?"

As a Latino in corporate America, I once again had broken some unspoken rule, missed some commonly understood signal, and a foul was called. I was yellow carded. But unlike on the soccer field where I know why, on the corporate field I had no idea. Making things even more difficult: My colleagues weren't even aware I did not know what had gone amiss.

What had gone amiss — I was to learn through much trial, error, and observation of the Midwestern, European-American corporate culture — was that I was a middle-class Latin American guy with a direct style of communication inside an indirect-communication-style corporate environment. What I had missed were the body language and code words signaling disagreement that people with similar cultural backgrounds would intuitively interpret, but were lost on me. I had my own body language and code words that other Latin Americans would interpret correctly, but that my European-American colleagues had missed and misinterpreted on their end.

And so it went. They thought I was confrontational. I thought they were duplicitous. They thought I was disruptive. I thought they were inefficient.

Every minute, somewhere in the corporate world, someone who is different from the mainstream, someone whom the corporation wanted in their midst because diversity is a business imperative, is not feeling included. We're making missteps that lead to the raised eyebrows, the sidelong glances, the "tsk, tsk" of "doesn't she have a clue?"

We must not only acknowledge we're different from one another in vital ways, but we must be able to skillfully navigate these differences to succeed together. This is a must-have skill in the Obama Era. Whether in government, academia, nonprofits, or the corporate world, never before have we seen such an intersection of powerful, competent, and ambitious talent working together on behalf of common organizational missions — but with wildly differing ways of going about it. The requisite bundle of skills and behaviors is what's referred to as *crosscultural competence*, and it's something that must be exhibited by both individuals and organizations.

What exactly do I mean by "crosscultural competence?" As I shared earlier, it's "the ability to discern and take into account one's own and others' worldviews, to be able to solve problems, make decisions, and resolve conflicts in ways that optimize cultural differences for better, longer lasting, and more creative solutions."

How can companies bulk up talent and organizations in this competence? Not surprisingly, most initial answers will veer toward the need for training. In these transformational times, however, pinpoint solutions will not be enough. Building crosscultural competence is a developmental task similar to building great managers and leaders. One classroom or online learning experience won't do the trick. It requires a systemic approach that changes underlying assumptions about managing differences, how we assess and reward people, the kind of talent we hire, the structures and processes we put in place to get things done, and yes, the learning we provide employees. Even the learning must be staged out with the realism and respect this competence demands, however. In the same way that most of us would not be able to handle algebra without first learning basic arithmetic, so it is with learning how to navigate our differences in truly inclusive ways. The first thing we must tackle is our underlying belief about what we need to learn to do.

Since more than $8 billion has been spent on diversity learning in the past decade,[1] let's start by examining the ROI we've gotten for this investment.

The Faulty Paradigm of Tolerance and Sensitivity

Say "diversity training" and many people will immediately think about learning experiences based on a paradigm of tolerance and sensitivity. This approach made sense 25 years ago when more women and racial/ethnic minorities began to enter sectors of the U.S. workforce once dominated by White males. As they did, they encountered intolerance and insensitivity. Hence the birth of "sensitivity training." Born out of the civil rights era and the transformative feminist movement, sensitivity training taught how to be tolerant toward differences. It was appropriate for the first generation of diversity work. The guys *did* have to be made aware that the pin-up calendars had to come down, that their sexist and racist banter about women and Blacks had to stop, and that a female worker getting pregnant didn't mean she was not committed to her career. It was a disruptive time for old-timers and newcomers alike, as the workplace erupted in dislocations, antagonisms, fear, and explicit prejudice.

A generation later, tolerance and sensitivity work has established mechanisms for addressing the isms.

Tolerance is a good antidote to resistance and defensiveness on the part of majorities toward those who are different. It's a place of *truce* rather than *truth*. It's manifested in statements such as: "I won't resist you anymore." "I'll tolerate that you're here." "I'm okay, you're okay." "We'll agree to disagree." "Live and let live." It's the answer to, "Why can't we all just get along?"

Sensitivity takes it further. It finds its voice in statements such as: "I will work at understanding that you have unique needs and preferences." "When you say something bothers you and it doesn't make sense to me, I accept that it is important to you." "I won't question your views, and I won't resist them." In between the lines it says, "I'll let you have that gimme."

As a result of this approach, much *explicit* prejudice in the workplace has subsided or gone underground. Unfortunately, however, this paradigm has spent itself. It has been taken as far as it can, and it will not be enough to enable the transformation of global diversity.

Why has this paradigm run out of juice? A few reasons:

- **Paralysis.** Regardless of what opinions people may harbor, employees generally know what is and is not appropriate to say. Political correctness has paralyzed us from talking in constructive ways about the very real differences between us. Even those who have welcomed diversity often don't know how to move beyond the obligatory, "I'm glad you're here."
- **Impractical.** Tolerance and sensitivity aren't very helpful when facing a colleague whose mother taught him the exact opposite of what yours taught you to do. It's an attitude, not a skill, that's condescending at worst or superficial at best, as we sponsor international and ethnic food potlucks and teach each other our culture's dance steps.
- **U.S.-Centric.** Tolerance and sensitivity do not serve us well in developing a platform for global diversity. It's a construct that flows out of the civil rights movement that gets sniffed out as too American as soon as it crosses the border. Don't get me wrong. Americans are right to be proud of the movement. In global work, however, this approach is limited due to its historical context.
- **Finger-pointing.** Tolerance and sensitivity undermine inclusion because of its implied audience. Who is it that needs to be more tolerant and sensitive? The White heterosexual male, of course! So he's in the audience, thinking, "Okay, I get this. This is all about me, but I don't feel part of it." Right there in inclusion training, an important part of the community is being excluded.

It's time for more powerful concepts that go beyond, "You've got yours and I've got mine." We need to create a voice that asks, "What is ours — *together?* Out of our differences, what new progress can we create — *together?* How can I make how you view the world a part of how I see it, too?"

What could replace this limited, spent paradigm? Today's global world requires a shift toward the paradigm of crosscultural competence.

The benefits are many:

- **Competency-based.** Crosscultural competence is not about an attitude or stance, but discrete, observable, and trainable skills and behaviors.

- **Pragmatic.** It's applicable to resolving daily diversity issues. When facing that same colleague who learned something different on his mama's knee, it provides a means of resolving differing worldviews.
- **Globally relevant.** No matter where in the world I've presented or consulted, audiences readily acknowledge there are real differences in their midst — and they could use some skills to navigate them. Take Europe, for example. Europeans may have been quick to criticize diversity as an American thing, but crosscultural competence certainly resonates on a continent where cultural differences have led to wars, caricatures, and exasperation for a long time.
- **Versatile.** Given the expanding definition of diversity and the all-embracing nature of inclusion, it can be used in navigating all kinds of differences, not just traditional diversity issues. It's the same skill required to navigate differences in thinking styles, functional roles, organizational cultures coming together in a merger and acquisition, and so on.
- **HR system compatible.** Crosscultural competency can be embedded into an organization's performance, reward, recognition, and development system. Presented as just another set of expectations on which employees will be measured, the connection to work, expected outcomes, and pay rewards can be made clear.
- **Not accusatory.** No group, no matter how marginalized, has an inborn crosscultural gene. The implied audience in crosscultural competence is all of us. So the White male is in the audience, thinking, "Ah, okay, I need this but so does everyone else."

With crosscultural competence, individuals and organizations can begin to see that we all need each other's differences. It's not a matter of simply tolerating, accepting, or even appreciating those differences in some esoteric way, but rather understanding on a fundamental level that we need those differences for our very survival. This puts an entirely different spin on diversity and inclusion.

Crosscultural competence requires us to look at our cultural differences, call them out, ask deep questions about their underlying assumptions, and suspend our own cultural judgments. (We all have them.) We then need to tackle business or professional challenges based on what we've learned. It's an ongoing, ever evolving practice with no finish line. It's the hard work required to succeed in the Obama Era and beyond.

The payoff can be both personally and professionally profitable in these upside-down times. The crosscultural and intercultural fields have much to offer us in terms of tools and models to more competently navigate the cultural differences surrounding us.

Diversity Across National Cultures: Ay ay ay! Why Are the French so French, the Mexicans so Mexican, and the Americans so American?

Fons Trompenaars and Charles Hampden-Turner, European authors of *Riding the Waves of Culture: Understanding Diversity in Global Business,* were intrigued by how multinationals with strong corporate cultures, such as IBM, still struggled with national differences getting in the way of being able to work as effectively as they wanted. To better understand what was going on, they created an extensive survey with a series of "What would you do?" scenarios.

Here's one: You're riding in a car with a friend who you know is speeding. Suddenly, the flashing lights of a police car appear in the rear-view mirror. After pulling the car over, the officer asks you, "Was your friend speeding?" What would you answer? The answer depended on one's nationality. Ninety-seven percent of Swiss would say, "Yes, my friend was speeding," but only 32 percent of Venezuelans would give the same answer.[2] What's going on?

The authors came up with seven different cultural dimensions to explain the different ways people from different cultures would approach the same scenario. In the case of the speeding car, they developed a construct that identified what individual cultures determine is fair. Some cultures believe that rules apply to everyone equally. Trompenaars and Hampden-Turner referred to them as *Universalist.* Other cultures determine what is fair based on the context of the situations. These, they referred to as *Particularist* cultures.

In returning to the case of the speeding ticket, one can now imagine the judgments flying. The Universalist turns to the Particularist and says, "How dare you lie to a police officer!," while the Venezuelan turns to the Swiss and retorts, "How dare you betray a friend!"

Both want the same thing — fairness — but they have different ways of interpreting what fairness is. In their book, the authors explain how these kinds of worldview clashes happen daily in the workplace, as workers try to figure out whom to confer status to, how to get work done, and how to manage time, projects, and emotion.[3]

Here are the headlines from Trompenaars and Hampden-Turner's Seven Cultural Dimensions:

How do we define what's fair?
Universalism vs. Particularism
Focus on the rule vs. focus on the particular context.

How do we get things done?
Task vs. Relationship
Focus on the destination (outcomes) vs. focus on the journey/quality of the relationship.

How do we confer status?
Achievement vs. Ascription
Focus on the accomplishment vs. focus on the title.

Where do we get our sense of identity?
Individualism vs. Communitarianism
Identity comes from the self vs. identity comes from the group one is a part of.

How do we manage emotions?
Neutral vs. Affective
Focus on restraint in showing emotions vs. focus on showing them.

How do we define time?
Sequential Time vs. Synchronous Time
Time is linear; focus on one thing at a time vs. time is circular; focus on the big picture.

How do we manage our environment?
Internal Control vs. External Control
Focus on dominating the environment vs. focus on accepting whatever comes.

Before going any further, let me make a distinction between *archetypes* and *stereotypes*. An archetype is the tendency of a group of people to behave in a certain way. A stereotype is the belief that all members in a cultural group behave according to the archetype for that group. For example, people from Latin America are more likely to show emotions publicly than people from Japan. But this does not mean all people from Latin America show public emotion or all people from Japan do not.

As individuals and organizations use the Seven Cultural Dimensions framework to diagnose cultural clashes, they find language and concepts to interpret and analyze the situation, back off the judgment, and then be able to resolve their differences. When this occurs, amazing things can happen.

An example can be found at furniture maker Herman Miller, where designers had been trapped in the Universalist mindset that they designed one-size-fits-all chairs based on an assumption of five-foot nine-inch medium-framed males. Michelle Hunt, the company's senior vice president for people during the 1980s, recalls, "This, of course, left out a lot of people and limited sales." Once they started seeing the market through more Particularist eyes, they began designing chairs that adjusted to a multiplicity of body shapes. Their sales exploded.[4]

The tenets of the Seven Cultural Dimensions have also helped me to be more successful in the corporate world. For several years, my friendships were hindered by different interpretations of how to demonstrate respect through the management of time. Soon after arriving in the United States to attend college, I found myself bewildered by a new European-American friend looking at his watch in the middle of a heart-to-heart conversation about our life aspirations. "Omigosh, Andrés, it's 12 o'clock. I've got to go. Here's my half for lunch," he exclaimed, plunking down his money and taking off. I was hurt and offended. How dare he leave in the middle of an intimate conversation just because the clock said it was 12 o'clock? "Cold, rude, impersonal Americans!" was my judgment.

As I soon discovered, I was causing hurt and offense on the other end as well. Later that same day, I showed up at another European-American's apartment to hang out. He opened the door and was clearly upset: "Andrés, what's the matter with you? It's 7:30. We were supposed to meet at 6 p.m. You're an hour and a half late!" In all likelihood, his judgment was something along the lines of, "Irresponsible, disorganized, inconsiderate Latino!"

This went on for *two* years. In comparing notes with other Latin American students, I soon learned they were experiencing the same thing. We were having two different interpretations of time. European-Americans tend to be "clock-oriented" people, where time is defined by seconds, minutes, and hours. Conversely, Latin Americans are more "event-oriented." Things, such as a conversation, last as long as they need to and the rest of the day adjusts to that. Using Trompenaars' and Hampden-Turner's language, the first is a Sequential view of time, the latter a Synchronous view of time.

Armed with this insight, conversations with my European-American friends changed. Not only did we have a better understanding of how we viewed time — and, therefore, that we were not being intentionally disrespectful to one another — but we also now had language to navigate through the differences:

"Hey, let's get together this weekend!"

"Okay. Gringo time or Latino time?"

"Well, it depends. If it's dinner and a movie, let's make it gringo time because if we're late for dinner, we'll be late for the movie. And that's no fun for anybody."

"Okay. But if it's come to our place to hang out, let's make it Latino time, so we're not running around getting all stressed out, you getting your place ready, and me battling traffic to hurry up to start right at 7 o'clock so we can … relax!"

These seemingly minor mismatches and mutual judging of those who are different contribute to the underlying tensions between people. Its effect is to make inclusion more elusive. It's also part of what contributes to the common phenomenon of higher turnover among those who are culturally different from the majority. Employees who are different from the norm often are assessed as poor performers, at worst, or just not top-notch talent, at best. Depending on the dominant culture of the organization, they may be seen either as too abrasive or too passive, too controlling or too submissive, too standoffish or too friendly. And on and on, the judgments go.

Not only is this detrimental to diverse individuals, it also hurts the organizations that hire them. This leads to higher turnover among people of color across all industries in the United States and among women in male-dominated industries around the world.[5] Not only do employers have to deal with the costs of their replacement, but they also lose out on alternative ways of doing work. Baxter's Don Wilson explains, "If you're trying to solve your inclusion or diversity problems by just focusing on talent acquisitions, you're not going to solve it. The acquisition piece only impacts less than 15 percent of your workforce. If you have a turnover of only 15 percent, that's what you're going to be replacing every year. If the turnover is 20 percent, that's what you will be replacing. What about that 80 percent or whatever percentage of your workforce that exists today — how are you going to deal with that?"

In other words, employers can't think they're solving their diversity issues by merely bringing diverse talent into the workforce, only to have them leave in a year's time because they don't feel their different approaches are being understood or appreciated. This only contributes to a vicious cycle of replacing staff, which adds to the cost of replacement and frustrates existing employees — that 80 percent — who are continually having to adjust to a revolving door of new team members. Especially in a world where the rules are changing by the hour, we need innovative ways of looking at things. It requires seeing it through the very same perspectives many of us have been judging in negative ways.

Cultural dimensions can also explain different cultural groups' tendencies with regard to preventive health or with their long-term savings plans, a topic I turn to in a later chapter.

While much intercultural research has focused on exploring cultural differences between citizens of countries, frameworks like Trompenaars' and Hampden-Turner's can also be applied to differences of cultures within a country. Granted, very little has been done along these lines. However, Thomas Kochman, a White sociologist, has done some pioneering work in looking at the cultural differences between African-Americans and European-Americans.

In his book, *Black and White Styles in Conflict*, Kochman asserts that Black and White Americans use two different communication styles for establishing trust: truth over peace or peace over truth.[6] Though his book was written more than 20 years ago, Kochman's more recent research corroborates what he identified back then: that while both Blacks and Whites are looking to establish trust in communication, each group interprets and demonstrates the value of "trust" differently. Archetypically, African-Americans seek open and direct interactions, even to the point where vigorous disagreement occurs: truth over peace. The rationale is that, "I can trust a person who is this open — this honest — with me." However, White Americans generally seek to establish trust with a more indirect style focused on achieving peace. When approaching a point of conflict, they might simply agree to disagree. Peace is sought and valued. Their rationale is that, "I can trust a person who defers his or her position for the harmony of the relationship."

Given these differences, a White American with an indirect communication style might come away from an interaction with a Black American demonstrating a more direct style, thinking, "Why is this person being so aggressive?" On the flip side, the African-American might come away thinking, "What is this person trying to hide?"

This concept can be applied in exploring the interactions of any two cultures where direct and indirect styles of communication come into play: U.S. East Coast vs. U.S. Midwest. U.S. American vs. Indian. German vs. Japanese. The list goes on.

For the past several years, some colleagues and I have presented at the National Black MBA conferences. In discussing the cultural differences between African-Americans and European-Americans, we introduce these differing cultural dimensions. During the audience participation section, the group usually determines that in six out of the seven dimensions African-Americans and European-Americans are on opposite sides. The same pattern emerges when doing this exercise with Latino and Indian audiences. No wonder there's so much misunderstanding!

Everything Is Relative to Something Else

Along the way, I've realized that these dimensions serve as a relative scale between two cultures. As a Latino from an affective culture (one manages emotions by showing them), I've always viewed European-Americans as being from a neutral culture (one where emotions are not displayed). Compared to Latinos, they are. In working in Canadian and U.K. offices and meeting with local clients, however, I've learned that both Canadian Anglophones and the British see European-Americans (their racial kin) as "emotional" — or to use the crosscultural terminology, "affective." Compared to Anglos in Canada and England, they are.

These interpretations cannot be static. They must be dynamic. Compared to Northern Indian culture, are the French or Germans task- or relationship-based? Compared to Aboriginal Canadian culture, are Francophone Canadians sequential or synchronous? And how do Francophone Canadians compare on this same cultural dimension to Anglophone Canadians? The answers matter if one is to effectively navigate across various cultures. Not that one has to master every possible cultural permutation, but when work or personal circumstances bring us face-to-face with a new culture, success requires we possess this skill.

Why are affinity groups — among the most widely used diversity strategies — resisted so vehemently in France?

For the French, affinity groups are a strange concept. By contrast, Americans historically have had a mindset that makes them more naturally predisposed to affinity groups. In 1835 sociologist Alexis de Tocqueville (who was ironically French) wrote in *Democracy in America* how he marveled at how Americans got things done through the power of "free association." Americans accomplished things via what were basically *affinity groups* brought together by a common purpose.

Americans are naturally wired to organize themselves as groups to enact change. When discussing history, Americans frequently talk about affinity groups — Pilgrims, slaves, "Indians," Italian immigrants, Irish potato famine refugees, undocumented Latinos. This is particularly true in politics, as evidenced by CNN's digital voting map on election night. It offered an intense analysis of voting patterns by affinity group, answering questions such as, "What do low-income, White women from Appalachia want?"

By contrast, French history lacks a pattern of connection by affinity. Rather, family bonds were emphasized, so villages were organized and wars fought along bloodlines: the Hapsburgs vs. the Bourbons, for example. And election results are based more on right and left ideological votes than on voter demographics.

So why does an individualistic culture, such as that of America, paradoxically gravitate so easily toward communal affinity groups? To answer this question, let's compare American individualism to French individualism by contrasting heroes. American individualistic heroes stand for society. Loner John Wayne fights for his community, not himself. Batman defends Gotham City. Captain America defends the nation. Even the Most Valuable Player of a sporting contest is positioned in the spirit of a team win.

"In contrast, French individualism is significantly more shaped by the French philosophers, and by a sense of personal exploration which is the purpose of one's life," says Helene Baudet, a French national working as project leader for diversity and inclusiveness, in Ernst & Young's Global Diversity team. She explains that the "I think, therefore I am" worldview, where the self is at the center, leads away from communal heroes and toward French individualistic anti-heroes.

One such anti-hero is the comic book character Asterix, a non-muscular, disheveled iconoclast who fights for the village clan, rather than an affinity-based community. Baudet continues, "Other French heroes, like Le Petit Prince, Jean-Jacques Rousseau in 'Les Confessions,' Cyrano de Bergerac, Antoine Doinel (recurrent hero of Truffaut's films), have this in common: They are lonely products of a difficult childhood and no known parents. They are single men whose ambition is not to save the world, but to be the authors of their own lives. They spend a lot of time exploring their own emotions and speculating about the emotions of others, continuously debating the choices that will build their own identity and shape the relations they have with other individuals. Their goal in life seems to be to do things a la *premiere personne* — that is in the 'I' or 'me' sense. Truffaut himself says, 'I see life as a very tough thing. I think one should have a very simple, very basic ethic: Say yes, yes to all, and do only what one wants to do.'"

"Mon dieu!," the action-oriented John Wayne would say in his own way to these French iconic figures. While "The Duke" may never have *joined* an affinity group himself, his raison d'etre was to help affect a win for people from a similar background.

As they encounter each other in global organizations, could American and French perspectives influence each other and converge at some point in the future? If, after all, the spirit of diversity work is to bring about positive change, does it really matter whether it happens through affinity groups making their voices heard or through individuals fighting for an ideal that benefits others?

Bicultural Is More Powerful Than Bilingual (though, of course, it helps to be bilingual)

For generations, parents have encouraged their kids to learn other languages for the sake of opening up their horizons and creating opportunities to connect with people from other lands. While English has been the *lingua franca* of global business, there's an emerging power language that's commanding attention: Chinese. (You thought I was going to say Spanish, didn't you?) In an example of how emerging markets are bypassing the United States in their dealings with other markets, Chinese language academies are proliferating in Peru. "*El idioma del futuro es el chino*, the language of the future is Chinese," a student told the Peruvian news magazine, *Cuarto Poder* after mouthing his first-ever Chinese words.

Being bi- or multilingual does indeed open up new opportunities, but language should be seen as only the tip of the iceberg of the deeper knowledge of other people's worldviews within their cultures. While knowing more than one language is valuable in multiple ways, the benefit will be curtailed unless we also learn a country's worldview. "It's not enough to know the language, but also the culture," the student went on to tell *Cuarto Poder*, "to understand the Chinese way of thinking, which is so different to our Latin sensibilities."

Says Dr. Milton Bennett, "I call it feeling of appropriateness. And the assumption is that this is typically lodged in embodied ethnocentrism. How do we get to have the feeling of appropriateness in another culture? If we are going to go do business in China, for example, it's one thing to have the minimal and not very useful wallet card that says, 'When in China, do this/don't do that,' etc. It's a little bit better to have been through the program that says, 'Here's about U.S. culture, here's about Chinese culture, and here are the differences that you should be paying attention to.' But it's unclear that that really brings us to the point of being able to go to China and feel what the appropriate thing to do is there. And yet for us to operate competently and effectively in that context, that's what we need to be able to do. But how do we get there?"

Language actually contains the keys to these cultural insights. We may know how to say fluently, *"No gracias, estoy lleno"* ("No thank you, I'm full") when offered a third serving at a Latin American home, but fluency may create an easier way to be disrespectful. In a culture where "no's" are frowned upon, a "yes, please" in English would yield better results.

American vs. Indian Debate: Are Project Plans Necessary?

Accepting that differences exist and learning to call them out constructively sheds light on myriad daily interactions in increasingly multicultural teams, particularly when they involve teams from India. Much guidance about the differences between Indian and American cultures centers on tip-of-the-iceberg matters that, while important, are superficial. Numerous Web sites and travel guides offer advice such as, "Don't pick up food with your left hand," "Remove your shoes before entering private homes, places of worship, and even some shops and stores," and "The Western side-to-side head shake doesn't always mean 'no.'"

But these bits of advice don't explain the tension between Americans and Indians when it comes to project plans. Profound, below-the-waterline differences in worldviews come to a head among talented people on both sides with regard to how the work is going to get done. At Hewitt, I had the opportunity to work in-person on crosscultural tensions surfacing with both sides of an implementation team in Gurgaon, India and Lincolnshire, Illinois. All were highly committed to performance excellence, but misunderstandings and judgments were hindering progress.

"What is the thing that is most frustrating you about working with the Americans?" I asked the Indian team members.

"It's the project plans!"

"What about them?"

"They keep asking for them."

"And?"

"We haven't produced them yet."

"Why not?"

"We've got so many other more important things to be doing — the coding, the batch processes, the quality testing. We don't really have the time to create these detailed project plans they are asking for."

"Anything else?"

"It just feels like they don't trust us."

"Why do you say that?"

"We can't help but feel that by their repeated asking for it, they don't really believe that we can do the work. Rather than worrying about this document, about what we are going to do, we would rather just be doing it! We are all so committed to the project and we don't want to let anyone down, especially our American colleagues. We will work 'round the clock if we need to, including the weekend, to get it done. A project plan is just a piece of paper. We have told them we will get it done. Why don't they believe us?"

Back in the United States, I got in front of the other half of the team:

"What is the thing that is most frustrating you about working with the Indians?" I asked the American team members.

"It's the project plans!"

"What about them?"

"We keep asking for them."

"And?"

"They haven't produced them yet."

"Why not?"

"We just don't know! They keep telling us that we'll have them soon, but still nothing."

"And why do you think this is?"

It was in this moment that the assumption of similarity started to generate its uncomfortable side effects. If something so "simple" and "commonly understood" as project plans were not being produced, what explanations could there be for this except for … No one wanted to say. Someone changed the topic.

"The other thing that's frustrating is that when we go over there, there's a lot more socializing than we feel there's time for. We're only there for a few days, and we need to make the most of our time."

With both groups, I introduced various crosscultural concepts and models, including the Seven Cultural Dimensions. After talking them through these, I asked the Americans, "So, as a task-oriented group, how can you get comfortable spending a little more time socializing with your Indian colleagues so they feel respected?"

We went 'round and 'round until finally an astute American said, "I know! I'll make relationship building a task that goes into my project plan, maybe with a subtask of going out to dinner the first night we're there. And maybe with a note to self that says, 'Don't talk too much about business. Keep it personal.'" To which another American added, "Yeah, and when we get back to the hotel from dinner, we can pull out our project plan and check it off!" Amidst the laughter of self-recognition, there was relief.

In India, I asked the group there, "So, as a relationship-based group, how can you get comfortable creating that project plan for the Americans in order to reduce their anxiety?"

We went 'round and 'round until finally, an astute Indian said, "I know! For the sake of the relationship, we will create the project plan."

Not only does mutual adaptation improve team dynamics, it actually enhances each of the subteams' performance. Project planning invites consideration of time off due to holidays, vacations, and illness. At the same time, it triggers contingency planning to account for the upcoming monsoon season's weather-related power outages. Relationship building on the front end invites greater benefit of the doubt when time zone, language, and cultural differences create tears in the project's fabric. Personal connection reverses the emotional energy that, rather than ripping the fabric further, channels it toward mending the tear.

As a guy who moves through time in an event-oriented way, learning about clock-oriented time has enhanced my ability to execute my visionary ideas more efficiently and effectively. Conversely, the clock-oriented people in my life have found their experiences enriched by more consistently discovering the gestalt of the event itself.

In the end, it's not enough to tolerate differences or learn more about them. In the upside-down, 24/7 world of the Obama Era, to be successful means I need your differences. And you need mine. ♀

The Cappuccino Effect

In an in-depth interview for this book, Dr. Milton Bennett shared the following observation with me in his inimitable style:

One of my earlier experiences in Italy was to do what is commonly done here in the United States, which is to order a cappuccino after dinner. Following my normal proce-dure of always asking first, I was assured by my host that it was a perfectly fine thing, although strange, but certainly okay in this very international restaurant.

And so I said, "I'll have a cappuccino," to the waiter who looked at me rather ironi-cally and said, "Would you like a brioche with that?" A brioche is a *breakfast* bread and I realized that I had been skewered.

As I spend more time in Italy, an interesting thing has happened. I have developed an antipathy to ordering cappuccino after dinner. In fact, the very thought of a cappuc-cino that late in the day is now more or less *disgusting* to me. I'm thinking, why would *anybody* do that? Yet I remember that at the time, I felt perfectly fine about ordering that cappuccino. And I also felt surprised at being taken to task.

Since then, when trying to behave appropriately in an unfamiliar culture, I've start-ed paying attention to "How do I *feel* about that?" Although this is about a very small thing, it is a very big change. It's a change in how one makes an assessment about what the right thing to do is.

And this is the point: How is it that we know what is correct behavior? In our own society we're socialized into a whole constellation of correct behaviors, which mostly we don't have in our head. Mostly we just do them. You ask somebody, "Why do you do that?" and they say, "Because it's the right thing to do." And if you ask them even more deeply, "Well tell me how do you *know* that's the right thing to do." Usually they'll come to the point of saying, "Well, it just *feels* right." It just feels right, whether it's ordering cappuccino or approaching your boss for a promotion. It can be a very serious matter or it can be a very superficial matter, but it still just feels right or not.

I call it "the feeling of appropriateness." Or using intercultural terms, it's a case of embodied ethnocentrism. The feeling is in our body. The feeling of wanting that cappuccino is a physical feeling and the feeling of not wanting it is a physical feeling, too. The difficulty in moving out of one set of feelings and into another set of feelings is the essence of ethnocentrism.

We have our feelings that are centralized in one cultural context. So it seems to me that another cutting-edge issue is, how do we get the feeling of appropriateness in another culture? Say we are going to go do business in China, it's one thing to have the minimal and, by the way, not very useful thing of the wallet card that says when in China do this/don't do that — but it's unclear how to go to China and feel what the appropriate thing to do is there.

Yet for us to operate competently and effectively in that context, that's what we need to be able to do. But how do we get there? How do we *feel* what is right?

This is what I call the Cappuccino Effect.

SUMMARY POINTS

- Every minute in the corporate world, someone who is different from the mainstream is feeling excluded — even in companies that are committed to diversity.
- The Inclusion Paradox requires that we not only acknowledge the differences among us, but learn to navigate those differences as well.
- The current paradigm for diversity and inclusion training, which relies on sensitivity and tolerance, is inadequate for meeting the next phase of diversity and inclusion.
- Crosscultural competence is the ability to discern and take into account one's own and others' worldviews, to be able to solve problems, make decisions, and resolve conflicts in ways that optimize cultural differences for better, longer-lasting, and more creative solutions.

- Crosscultural competence is a learnable skill that everyone needs. Once acquired, it leads to the understanding that we all need each others' differences.
- Authors Fons Trompenaars and Charles Hampden-Turner explain Seven Cultural Dimensions that describe various cultural worldviews:
  - Universalism vs. Particularism
  - Task vs. Relationship
  - Achievement vs. Ascription
  - Individualism vs. Communitarianism
  - Neutral vs. Affective
  - Sequential Time vs. Synchronous Time
  - Internal Control vs. External Control
- *Archetype* and *stereotype* are not interchangeable terms. An archetype is the tendency of a group of people to behave in a certain way, while a stereotype is the belief that all members of a cultural group behave according to a specific archetype.

SHAPING YOUR STRATEGY

- How well do diversity champions in your organization understand that crosscultural competency is foundational in order to be able to move the work forward? How can you tap into those who do understand in order to deepen your organization's crosscultural competency? What things can you do to help those who don't make the paradigm shift from tolerance and sensitivity to crosscultural competence?

- How would you describe your organizational culture using the Seven Cultural Dimensions?
- Pick any minority cultural group in your organization. How does that group's archetype compare and contrast to the description of your company's preferred cultural dimensions?

PART 2:
CALLING OUT
DIFFERENCES IN
RELATIONSHIPS

Calling Out Differences in Relationships

What makes us uniquely human is our ability to put into language what we're thinking, feeling, and imagining. Strings of words are then woven into stories that capture what we fear, what we long for, what we can destroy, and what we can create. Since the beginning of civilization, stories have been used to pass history and values from generation to generation.

Our lives are resonant with stories. Bedtime stories ease children into slumber. News stories inform us. Reality TV stories seduce us. Business is also about stories. We are fueled by the narratives of how we and our competitors are doing in the marketplace. We celebrate the thrill of client wins. We feel the impact of narrow losses. Around the world, employees play both leading and secondary roles in their companies' stories of growth and decline, mergers and acquisitions, and stagnation and transformation.

Diversity and inclusion both compels and repels specifically because it is, at its essence, about the intimate topic of identity — of individuals, groups, nations, and organizations. In other words, diversity and inclusion is about how we and others seek to define what makes us who we are. Diversity ultimately is about biography — one's unique life path that shapes how each of us understands how the world works and how we choose to be actors in it.

In the Obama Era, biography, more than ideology, becomes essential in our ability to connect in a global world. Ideology has taken some big hits in recent history — from the fall of the Berlin Wall to the fall of Wall Street. In an upside-down world where the old rules are null and void, where we face challenges and issues never faced before, ideologies shaped when the world was right-side-up have little relevance. It is in one's personal story where we now seek answers.

To read Obama's autobiography, *Dreams from My Father: A Story of Race and Inheritance*, is to experience an intensely personal discovery of identity. The man who would be president wrestled profoundly with what it meant to be the biracial child of a White Christian woman from Kansas and a Black Muslim man from Kenya. How did his growing up in Hawaii and Indonesia shape how he viewed the world? What inheritance did he receive from the different influences in his formative years?

Obama is not just the first Black U.S. president, he's also the most global one. Obama's search for his roots did not take him to the deep American South. It took him to Kogelo, Kenya. In this narrative, we begin to see the contours of a life experience that shaped a leader who can successfully move across racial lines in the United States, walk just as comfortably through Ivy League halls as along inner city streets, and who can be seen as "one of us" by the 200,000 Berliners who came out to watch him deliver a speech at the city's Victory Column during the 2008 campaign.

It is in Obama's story that he came to understand his place in the world — and thus we can come to understand him. In the same way, the Inclusion Paradox demands we know our own biographies in ways that provide insight for ourselves and for others about our own places in the world. We need to be able to tell our own stories.

Inclusion is about both individual and collective stories. It is about our identities as men, women, parents, members of families, religious adherents, community members, citizens of nations and the world. It is also about our identities in the workplace as colleagues, coworkers, front-line managers, and leaders — from the shop floor to the executive suite. It is about exploring who we are in the midst of so many changes, celebrating that discovery, and valuing the journey.

The most powerful story is an individual's narrative of identity — of discovering and celebrating who they are. Regardless how different it may be from our own, each person's story contains something we can recognize. This is our quest to discover our life's meaning and where we stand in relation to the universe. In this discovery, we learn how to fit into the larger story of the society around us, helping us recognize those things in others' stories that we can relate to.

In diversity work, stories help us personalize controversial political or philosophical issues, so we don't forget we're talking about living human beings. They are our neighbors, siblings, friends, and coworkers — people just like us who are trying to survive and thrive during their finite time on earth.

Growing up in a bilingual/bicultural home with family in Peru and in the United States, I attended the American High School of Lima with the sons and daughters of multinational executives, diplomats, spies, and missionaries. Having Peruvian grandparents in Lima and American grandparents in Washington, I constantly crisscrossed physical and invisible boundaries between countries, organizations, and people. These relational and cultural junctions forged my understanding of worldview differences and how to navigate them successfully and profitably.

As I laid out in the Introduction, there's a three-step process to mastering the Inclusion Paradox:

1. **Learning it's all about me**
2. **Learning it's all about them**
3. **Learning it's all about us**

In Part 2, we focus specifically on the first step — learning it's all about me. We cannot even begin to make the interpersonal and group thing work with people different from us if we don't know *ourselves* as cultural beings. Many spiritual traditions and leadership books reveal that one secret to enlightenment, wisdom, power, and followership is self-awareness: Who am I? What has shaped me? What motivates me? How do I understand the world?

Only after we answer these questions can we begin to compare and contrast ourselves with those around us. In doing so, we learn to understand them better and help them better understand us. With this, we can address the implications of these differences among groups, which is the focus of Part 3, and among organizations, which we'll explore in Part 4.

The linchpin to inclusion exists in our ability to manage the differences between us and the person in front of us. Speaking at the Diversity Best Practices' Diversity Leadership Awards Gala on November 17, 2005, civil rights icon Dr. Dorothy Height summed up our journey, explaining that legislation was just the beginning: "We need to turn the laws into relationships — and the relationships into opportunities." ♀

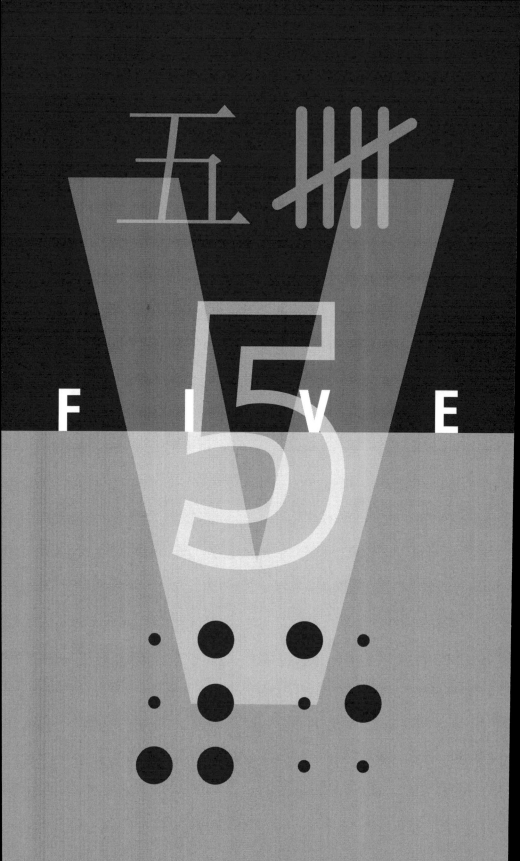

Chapter 5

Are You Evil, a Moron,
or Just Plain Incompetent?

Lori and I had been married only a short time when we decided to throw a party. In her German-American Midwestern way, Lori pulled out a note pad and said, "Okay, let's make an invite list." Quickly, we came up with about 25 friends and coworkers.

After we completed that task, Lori went on to deal with all the specific details for party planning — menu selection, music and entertainment, house preparation, and so on. Plans for the party were well under way. The following week, as I ran into friends and colleagues on the train, at work, or in the neighborhood, I would inevitably say, "Hey, Mark — we're having a party two weeks from Saturday. Here's my address. Be sure to come. And pass the word on!" When I mentioned to Lori that I'd invited Mark, Melinda, and Fareed, I got the look. "Are they on the invitation list?" she asked frostily. "Well, no. But hey, that was just to get us started." "Oh, *really?*" was her reply.

To Lori's way of thinking, the 25 names on the list represented the sum total of people who would attend our celebration. To *my* way of thinking, the invitation list was only the starting point for all the people who could possibly attend. *Todo el mundo* ("the whole world") is a phrase that frequently comes up in communal Latin America when discussing who's invited to a party or other social event. Rather than limiting an invitation list, as would be customary in the more individualistic United States, in Latin America, it's about expanding it. What Lori and I had was one invitation list, 25 names, and two culturally different ways of interpreting it. What started as a party for 25 turned into a whirlwind celebration of more than 100.

And so it has gone — navigating the deep waters of cultural differences, running aground in the shoals of cultural friction. As we found out quickly and painfully, cultural differences can seriously derail personal relationships, not only with one's spouse, but also with friends and coworkers.

Here's where it all begins to either fall apart or create something new. When someone does something different from what we've been trained to believe is the norm, we can only assume they are either incompetent or bad people. Why else would they do it that way? When we think about cultural misunderstandings with those close to us, don't we often end up being furious at their insensitivity? Steamed about their moronic behavior? Outraged at their selfishness?

Dianne Hofner-Saphiere, a crosscultural consultant with vast global experience, explains, "The most challenging thing is to get people to understand that their common sense isn't *common*. Common sense is really cultural sense. It's what you're expecting."

I Discovered My Latin Soul in Washington's Wheat Fields

My dad, Fernando Andrés Tapia Mendieta — the son of two school teachers from the fishing town of Pisco in Peru — earned his doctorate of medicine at San Marcos University in Lima. He came to the Cleveland Clinic to do his first residency as a cardiologist. My mom came from the small town of Harrington, Washington, 50 miles west of Spokane. She had always dreamt of getting out of small-town America, so she enrolled herself in an electrocardiogram technician certification program, also in Cleveland. So, between the heartbeats, the cardiologist and the EKG technician met, married, and moved to Chicago, where my father completed his second residency at Edgewater Hospital, where I was born.

When I was one year old, my parents got into their green Comet, drove to the port of San Francisco, hopped on a cargo ship, and sailed to the port of Callao off the coast of Lima, where I grew up.

Spanish was our first language at home, with English a close second. This bilingualism was interwoven with biculturalism. One night, we'd be having *arroz con pollo*, the next night meat loaf and potatoes. We celebrated Peruvian Inde-

pendence Day *and* American Thanksgiving, complete with turkey and stuffing —
though cranberry sauce was impossible to get since no one knew what my mom
was talking about when she asked for it at the store. She told us about Halloween,
so my siblings and I dressed up as goblins and cowboys and knocked on people's
doors and called out, *"Treekohtree!"* (our butchered version of "trick or treat").
People had no idea why there were goblins and cowboys at their doorstep, but
since we looked so cute, they gave us money. We quickly learned that the bigger
the house, the more money we got. We pulled in quite a haul — my first inkling
that becoming crossculturally adept could be profitable!

I first discovered differences when, as a third grader, I went to visit my American grandparents in my mom's hometown of Harrington over summer break.
Coming to the United States from Peru was already loaded with major culture
shock differences, which were compounded by the contrast between Lima, a city of
6 million at the time, and Harrington, population 500. Then there were the urban/
rural differences of pace, noise, animals, and occupations — just to name a few.

I stood out immediately. Though I'm not that dark-skinned, I was the darkest
person there. I spoke with a heavy Spanish accent, and when they threw a ball at me,
I would kick it. During this visit, I experienced both the underside and the upside
of being different. There were taunts and mean-spirited jests about my foreignness.
But there was also the genuine interest, on the part of the town folk, in this son of
a native daughter — Jackie Kay Graham, my mom. And so I was invited to ride
on the combine during wheat harvest season, to give a slide show on Peru at the
Methodist church potluck, and to play Little League baseball for the first time.

It was in Washington's Lincoln County wheat fields that I discovered my
Latinness. Until I was out of the culture I had grown up in and immersed in
another, I had little appreciation for the many ways in which my identity was outlined by the *absence* of the familiar cultural icons and customs of my upbringing.
Surrounded by people who didn't look or speak like I did made me aware of the
unique ways I looked and spoke. Here is where I realized I was a Latin American
from Peru and started to get an inkling of what that meant.

Returning to Lima, I continued my education in a parochial school run by
American nuns. I then prepared to go to college by getting a Peruvian and American high school diploma at the American High School of Lima. In Roosevelt's
classrooms I discovered the life-sustaining literature of Poe, Faulkner, and Mel-
ville along with that of Borges, Vargas Llosa, and Neruda. I learned about George

Washington's defiance of the British in his Christmas crossing of the Delaware in one class period, and about Tupac Amaru's rebellion in Cusco against the Spaniards in the next.

Every few years, I went back to Harrington, this time with my three younger sisters, to visit my grandparents, Brownie and Frieda. I played flag football, earned five bucks an hour pulling rye from a wheat field for a farmer who had mixed up his seeds, and watched the *Sha Na Na* show with my grandpa while munching on M&Ms. In turn, I taught my classmates where Peru was on a map, how to get by with a few choice Spanish phrases, and that when I threw a ball at them — to kick it. I told them stories of going to bullfights, professional soccer games, and political demonstrations.

By the time I arrived at Northwestern University to study journalism, I believed I was ready. I had even worked on my accent using my mom's voice as my internalized language tape. I would hear myself speak in an accented way and then repeat the same word ten times to match how she would say it.

But I was far from ready. So much of my preparation was tip-of-the-iceberg stuff — necessary, but only a beginning. I was soon to discover that most of my cultural differences were below the waterline. With icebergs, it's what's below the waterline that sinks *ships*. With culture, it's what's below the waterline that sinks *relationships*.

I've already shared my story of the differences between the Latin-American and European-American interpretation of time, but there were many other profound differences. As I relate these other stories, some of you may sheepishly recognize yourself in them because you've tripped the crosscultural wire in similar ways. Or you may end up scratching your head, asking, "Why would he do *that*?" And that is the point. We must come to appreciate the power of our differences and, as crazy (asinine, dumb, rude, weird may come to mind as well) as they may sound to us, understand that our ways can seem just as strange to others as theirs do to us. By sharing our stories, we can begin to forge new understandings where we can relate in more inclusive ways with one another.

Yeah, right

As a student at Northwestern, there was a problem paying my tuition every month. I had financial aid, but my dad still had to pay a portion. Now, keep in mind that my dad was in Peru. The country was undergoing hyperinflation and terrorism, and there were restrictions on transferring money out of the country.

To get around these multiple issues, Dad had to send cash with people he trusted who were flying from Peru to the States. I was depending on these flights to receive the money Dad sent for my tuition. But they weren't just flying to Chicago. They might be flying to Miami or Los Angeles. The money eventually came, but it could be two, four, even eight weeks late.

Tuition was due on the 15th of the month, with a $50 late fee applied on the 16th. So, on the 15th, I'd go to the Bursar's office, where students made tuition payments, and say, "My money isn't in yet." Every month, the clerk would say, "There's a $50 fine for being late." I would explain, "The money is on its way. It's coming from Peru. There's inflation, terrorism, restrictions on dollars. Can't you make an exception?" The university's response, from a Universalist point of view, was always the same: "If we make an exception for *you*, we'd have to make an exception for *everyone*." Exasperated, I would retort in true Particularistic fashion, "How many students do you have who come from a country 6,000 kilometers away where there is a 15,000 percent cumulative hyperinflation rate, a growing terrorist movement igniting car bombs in the Capitol, and restrictions for getting dollars out of the country?!"

So what was fair? One rule applied to everyone equally or taking into account that people's experiences could be very different? Every month, I fought with the administrator at the Bursar's office, and every month, I lost. The Universalist university system had no way to accommodate me. And so round and round we went as the Bursar and I drove each other crazy.

My parents sure had not prepared me for *this*.

Yours, Mine, and Ours

In the meantime, I was also driving my roommate, Leroy, crazy.

As someone coming from a communal culture, I had no problem borrowing people's things. My operating assumption was it was okay for me to borrow from others without asking, even if they weren't around.

I had come to school quite unprepared. Having not visited the campus beforehand due to cost and distance, I hadn't known what to bring. So I borrowed a slew of things like staplers, scissors, shampoo, and tennis rackets. Through various awkward moments, I eventually figured out I should not borrow without asking. It was important in American culture to ask permission. Ah! Okay, I got it. But there was a part two to the borrowing rule I was clueless about. Now I was asking, but I was doing it too often. It took me a while to figure out that one should only borrow sparingly and apologetically. "Why don't you have your own things? Get your own!" I started to hear in response as I applied part one of the borrowing lesson. I was so puzzled. "Why should I get my own if you're not using it? And this goes both ways. You can use anything I own — it actually would make me happy." But it didn't work that way. Coming from a developing country, I had a lot less that he would want to borrow — and he simply did not feel comfortable doing it.

When I became a homeowner many years later, I had to relearn the borrowing lessons. One neighbor had a lawnmower, another had an extension ladder, and a third had a snow blower. I had stuff, too, like an oil change drip pan, a shovel, and a rake. It took some time to figure out that even though I kept borrowing things from them, no one was borrowing from me. I just couldn't figure out why each household should have one of everything when these tools sat idle 95 percent of the time.

Since college, the crosscultural experiences have continued unabated, whether in the publishing and corporate worlds or on working trips to Kenya, India, Canada, the United Kingdom, and throughout Latin America. Each time, there are new and surprising things to discover about myself, my friends, and colleagues in our close encounters of a cultural kind. Each time, there is a lesson to be gleaned to smooth out crosscultural interpersonal clashes. Such encounters also sharpen our insights into how differences make a difference in relationships and organizations — from how we work together to how we design human resource programs to how we market and deliver products and services.

I'm not Okay. You're not Okay.

My first job was at a magazine called *U. Magazine*, a publication geared toward college students of the Intervarsity Christian Fellowship in Downers Grove, Illinois. I was one of only two minorities in an office of about 55 people.

They were a caring group. I learned a lot during that time and made some lifelong friends. But boy, did I feel the differences. I was a communal, particularistic, synchronous, expressive, externally-controlled Latino guy in the midst of an individualistic, universalist, sequential, emotionally-neutral, internally-controlled culture. To those who are familiar with Myers-Briggs personality tool, I was an ENFP in an ISTJ milieu.[1] To compound the differences, I had grown up in a non-air-conditioned world and loved the heat, so I often felt cold in U.S. office buildings. Every summer, I would close my office door, open my window, and create a tropical oasis in my workspace. No one could stand being in my office. Even my packed lunch with the previous night's leftovers was problematic with its strong aromatic smells wafting in the small lunchroom as I heated it in the microwave.

The very things that worked for the majority didn't work for me and vice versa. They got the benefit of richer reporting due to a greater diversity of sources and an alternative way of looking at things. I had to learn to create a detailed project plan. I perfected my English grammar syntax and adopted more of a storytelling approach. I changed to peanut butter and jelly sandwiches for the office lunchroom, and my colleagues came with me to ethnic restaurants.

Crosscultural interpersonal lesson: It's all about mutual adaptation. To trigger a good reciprocal and virtuous cycle, the one in the minority often needs to be the first mover — whether an American in Lima or a Peruvian in Downers Grove — not just through assimilation but also through adaptation. In response, those from the majority culture need to be welcoming of those who are different, show genuine interest in who they are and what they have to offer, and adapt in return.

Out of Africa

This mutual adaptation often comes about through a process of trial and error. As we get to know each other and our different cultural norms and practices, we begin to understand where the other person is coming from. Through this process, we tailor our respective approaches and eventually come together. I experienced this shortly after college during my first trip to Africa with my wife, Lori, who was doing field study in ethnomusicology. As if dealing with crosscultural issues in the United States weren't tough enough, they were exponentially harder in Kenya, yet I attribute this experience for contributing to the growth of my own crosscultural competence.

That summer, Lori and I spent time in Nairobi, Mombassa, and Malindi. But for most of our stay, we were with the Sabaot people in Mount Elgon on the Kenya-Uganda border, where people lived in mud huts insulated with cow dung and covered with thatch roofs.

As a passionate soccer fan and player, I always brought my soccer ball with me. Through my many travels, I had often been able to make connections by kicking the ball with people who spoke different languages and had different customs — whether with Cape Verdeans in Boston, Quechuas in the Peruvian Andes, or tots in kindergarten in Highland Park.

The day we caught the train to Mount Elgon from Nairobi, I forgot my soccer ball. Given how much emotional investment I had in my making-cultural-bridges-through-my-soccer-ball plan, I was devastated. I had counted on it being my lifeline to bridge cultural gaps. It was also my cultural prop. I only knew a smattering of words in Swahili, and those didn't go much further than *Asante* and even fewer in Sabaot. I had no family links in Kenya, and I'd never been this far from home. I felt very vulnerable.

The Land Rover picked us up at the train station and made steep climbs up the mountain around gigantic craters and through lush vegetation teeming with baboons, cows, donkeys, and elephants. I felt exhilaration and dread at the same time. Soon, Lori got invited to various ceremonies to record the music of such milestone events as birth, coming of age, marriage, and death.

Wherever we went, the Sabaot were hospitable and welcoming — not to mention complimentary of my gum boots and jeans, to which I always said "thank you," only to discover they were more communal than my Latin self. I was perceived as rude and materialistic because when people complimented something I had, I was supposed to give it to them. And here I thought they were just being nice! The community was poor, and even though we were only three years out of college, we were viewed as wealthy. But it was not just an income difference at play. Communally, I was expected to reciprocate their appreciation for my gum boots with a gift of that very footwear. I came to understand that, thanks to the help of one of my Sabaot friends, Christopher. When we left the mountain and were done slogging through the mud, I gave him my gum boots and jeans.

Another time, a large group of our newfound friends took us on a two-day hike to the top of a mountain, which was really a dormant volcano. On the way up, we stopped to meet one of our Sabaot friend's nearly 100-year-old grandmother. The greetings were formal, hierarchical, and full of symbolic meaning. The Sabaot subsisted on farming, and rain was both essential and capricious. When offering one's hand in greeting, the elder person spits on it as a blessing. One responds in kind. Since we were a large delegation of visitors, our friend's elderly grandmother worked her way through blessing each one of us. I was the last one. By the time she got to me, my salivary glands were so worked up and ready that, well, let's just say I *really* blessed her.

Halfway through our time there, Lori was recording a children's song with some girls next to where the just-harvested corn was being husked. Suddenly, a small, round object rolled by my feet. It was about eight-inches in diameter and made of balled-up plastic bags held together by twine. I looked in the direction of where it had come from. There, I saw a group of boys and men playing a game I knew very well. I picked up their soccer ball and drop-kicked it over to them. They waved me over to join them. *Yes!*

Interpersonal lesson: No matter how much you prepare ahead of time, there is no way to avoid mistakes. You will embarrass yourself, but your good intentions go a long way. It's all in the recovery, as you work it through the necessary, trusted cultural informant. To call out differences constructively, find points of commonality — though they will likely be on *their* terms, not yours.

India: My Polite Is Impolite

Prasheel and I had a great day together in the crosscultural train-the-trainer in Hewitt's offices in Gurgaon. Along with 25 of our colleagues, we had experienced exhilaration — of facing perplexing cultural dilemmas, discovering the break-through insights of what was going on, and having that understanding enable our ability to work together. To celebrate that successful first day, Prasheel took a group of us to an Indian restaurant for dinner. I worked my way through plates of this, that, and the other. We shared many laughs and learned much from each other that day and over dinner.

When it came time to say good night, Prasheel walked me to the outside of the restaurant so we could hail a taxi. As one was pulling up, I reached out my hand, and he took it. But when I said, "Thank you, Prasheel," I could see him visibly pull back. The smile on his face disappeared, and a grave formality descended between the two of us. I knew something had gone amiss, but I didn't know what.

"Anything the matter?" I asked him.

"Um..."

Sensing the awkwardness, I decided to lean into our crosscultural work of the day.

"No need to answer now if you don't know. But given how we talked today about calling out differences and how we need to do that as they come up, rather than assuming similarity, this may be one of those times."

By now, the cab had pulled up and the door was open, waiting for me to get in. I did, and a lively day came to a close in a less than ideal way. The next morning, Prasheel jovially came up to me as soon he saw me.

"Good morning, Andrés. I hope you had a good night's sleep. And by the way, I think I know what transpired last night."

"Yes?"

"It was the moment you said, 'thank you.'"

"'Thank you?' What's wrong with that?"

"Well, it can be seen as rude or inconsiderate."

"Yikes! Back in the United States, it would be rude and inconsiderate to not say it! Please explain."

"For us, 'thank you' implies that someone did something for you that they would not have wanted to do. It is said in response to someone doing things out of an obligation. When you said 'thank you,' to my Indian ears, it sounded like a dismissal of our newly evolving professional relationship and friendship. Taking you out to dinner was something I wanted to do for you in appreciation. You made me feel like it was done out of duty, a must-do."

"Ayayay!" I replied. After explaining the Spanish meaning of this expression — "Wow and my God" rolled into one — I said, "This is so helpful. Now I understand why Americans often think Indians are rude because they don't say 'please' and 'thank you.' But I still need more help. Because gratitude is clearly something you value here in India, as you have clearly stated that your taking me out to dinner was a way of showing that, how do I demonstrate my gratitude in return if I can't say 'thank you'?"

"When I'm up in Chicago next month, take me out to dinner."

Which, you can bet, I did!

Interpersonal lesson: We often have the same value, but a different interpretation. Gratitude was the shared value, but we clearly had different interpretations of how to show it. Our ways of showing gratitude were considered ungrateful, the very opposite in our respective cultures! If we had not established a protocol and assumption of the need to call out differences, that awkward exchange outside the restaurant would have remained unspoken for the rest of our relationship. This is just one example of awkward, unexplainable, can't-put-your-finger-on-it-but-it-didn't-feel-right kinds of comments that infest crosscultural relationships. By being able to respectfully call out the differences, we were able to discover where our relationship veered off the path of trust and get back on it.

In the Corporate World:
The Power of Teamwork Using Differences

As you become more crossculturally competent as an individual, the next challenge is to create and nurture a crossculturally competent team with healthy interpersonal relationships. This does not mean these relationships won't be without friction. In fact, the more diverse the team, the more *guaranteed* the friction.

As has been an underlying premise of the Inclusion Paradox, diversity is more complex to manage than homogeneity. That said, diversity is not only a demographic inevitability, but also a requirement for innovation. The innovative, creative combustion of a diverse team can either lead to destructive explosions or generative bursts. As in one-on-one interactions, team relationships across cultural divides require shared knowledge and understanding of crosscultural issues. Also needed are skills to manage these differences and a commitment to doing so. This intentionality channels the friction in ways that move the work forward.

Here's a panoramic snapshot of what happened on my diversity and inclusion team at Hewitt:

Tyronne Stoudemire, global D&I director, and Susan McCuistion, global D&I operational leader, are two very different people in more ways than just gender diversity. At the tip of the iceberg, Tyronne is an African-American from Detroit and Susan is a biracial White/Native American (Oneida tribe) from Las Vegas. Below the waterline, the differences only get magnified.

When Tyronne and Susan worked on my team, they were both responsible for operationalizing strategies, though in different spheres of responsibility. Susan was very task-oriented, while Tyronne was very relationship-oriented. Our project-related interactions sound something like this:

"Hey, Susan! I have an idea for a new strategic initiative. I want to get your thoughts on whether we can get it done by mid-June."

After I would explain it, Susan immediately would start sketching out the tasks, sub-tasks and sub-sub-tasks. She would figure out how many days each one would take, factoring in holidays, workloads, slippage, vacations, *and* the probability of sick days. Then, Susan would map out the timeline, along with project details, and say:

"Andrés, I know that you want it mid-June, but because of these other issues, I'll need an extra two weeks. So let's plan on the first week of July for a final completion date."

Contrast Susan's response with Tyronne's:

"Hey, Tyronne! I have an idea for a new strategic initiative. I want to get your thoughts on whether we can get it done by mid-June."

After I explained it, Tyronne immediately would start verbally brainstorming:

"I know so-and-so is going to be in town at a conference ... maybe I can bring him in. I don't know anybody in this other area, but I know someone who knows someone in that particular area. I know that you want to have this done by mid-June, but if we plan on doing it early in July, we can piggyback on another conference when one of the speakers will already be in town."

Same end date, but approached in an entirely different way.

Given these two disparate approaches, Tyronne and Susan sometimes drove each other a little crazy. Both were very effective, but their processes differed in nuanced ways. They operated on completely different systems. Susan's anxiety rose when she didn't see a written plan. Tyronne's anxiety rose when he didn't see a list of the right people who would be contacted and drawn into the process.

Tyronne's cell phone was his baton for directing his project orchestra. Susan's project plan was hers. Each made music in their own way. Check out the table below for the harmonic and discordant notes of their styles as they worked together:

	TYRONNE	SUSAN
Focus is getting the job done through	Relationships	Tasks
Mantra	Seize the day!	Plan ahead!
Highest priority	Front stage	Back stage
Leads work team's symphony with	His cell phone	Her project plan
Shortcuts	Know the right people	Cut back scope
Sounds the alarm	We don't know the right people!	We don't have enough time or resources!
Source of anxiety in working with the other	Her structure	His spontaneity
Source of learning in working with the other #1	Her structure	His spontaneity
Source of learning in working with the other #2	Leverage project tools to structure fluid working relationships	Leverage relationships to lubricate rigid tasks

The power of diversity is that every worldview offers something someone needs. When it comes to turning strategy into tangible projects and programs, I need diverse talents and perspectives on my team. Having both Tyronne's and Susan's widely divergent approaches broadened and deepened our group's reach and impact. And yes, I had them focus on doing things that played to their strengths. The diversity and crosscultural curriculum that so far has been rolled out to more than 15,000 associates and clients worldwide lends itself better to a task orientation. Creating a strategic networking alliance of high-powered corporate, not-for-profit, and government leaders who can have much impact in the global diversity field lends itself better to a relational approach.

As a Diversity and Inclusion "Center of Expertise," we'd better practice what we preach, right? Sure, piece of cake. No hay problema. Hakuna matata. *Right*.

You bet it's not easy. We have to work hard to make this work or our differences could undo us. So we're intentional in talking through the impact of our differences in our interpersonal and working relationships. We have to remind ourselves to assume positive intent on the part of the other, to be self-aware of how our worldview may lead to subjective interpretations, to listen intently to our colleague's side, and finally, to navigate toward resolution. The waters can be rough, but like white-water rafters, we need to expertly navigate the rapids through the myriad rocks and bends.

You bet it pays off. When worked right, it leads to richer relationships that pave the way for more innovative and memorable results.

Leaders Learning Through Relationships

The most transformative experience I've witnessed in developing interpersonal crosscultural competence at work came about through the development of a program by Mary-Frances Winters of the Winters Group and myself. Initially developed for Hewitt leaders, we now offer the program, dubbed Crosscultural Learning Partners, to our clients.

Here's how it works. Twenty-five senior Hewitt leaders were partnered with someone culturally different from themselves for a year. After an initial group kickoff — including a personalized and confidential IDI debrief (explained in book's Appendix A) — they received monthly assignments via email of an article or book chapter to read, or a movie to watch, that touched on a diversity/crosscultural issue. The senior leaders also received a set of reflection questions that touched on their individual worldviews — to help process with their partner what they read or watched — along with a set of application questions of how to apply what they learned to Hewitt's day-to-day realities. They shared each other's cultural identity stories and points of view in the context of these assignments and were often surprised by unexpected similarities and differences in how they interpreted the very same thing.

At the end of the experience, all participants retook the IDI. As a group, they had all progressed in their crosscultural competence. Their testimonials sounded like this:

A Human Resources leader speaking about the Gen X African-American trainer with whom he was partnered: "Charles [not his real name] helped me see around corners I would not have ever been able to see around. I especially realized this when he took me to the Chicago Theater for an evening debate among Tavis Smiley, host of *Tavis Smiley, Late Night* on PBS TV talk show, Cornel West, author and professor at Princeton University, and Michael Eric Dyson, radio host and University Professor of Sociology at Georgetown University. I must've been one of only two or three Whites there in an audience of hundreds. I heard a perspective from these three prominent African-American intellectuals in front of a Black audience on the current issues of our day that I had felt pretty well versed on, yet that I did not even know existed."

An African-American Boomer learning and development manager speaking about the White male business executive with whom she was partnered: "Until I had the chance to hear my learning partner's story, I had never had an in-depth conversation with a White male. I realized that as much as I was providing him with new understandings of the Black experience, I had my own deep misconceptions of the White male experience. I was surprised to find out that this well-respected leader had come from a tough family situation, had faced many challenges in his professional life, and even today, did not have it all figured out. I honestly did not know that White males could also struggle in life."

A White, lesbian Human Resources leader speaking about the overall learning experience: "I will never look at an HR issue the same ever again." Despite her many years of experience as a highly regarded HR professional known for her effectiveness and wisdom, her experience with her learning partner busted open new ways of looking at familiar dilemmas in addressing breakdowns between associates and their managers. Given her own personal experience as an outsider who did not come out to her coworkers until she had been at the company for ten years, her self-perception was that she really had an insider's view of diversity. "In many ways that was true, yet my African-American partner helped me see how I did not know about the Black experience intimately and how it shows up in the workplace."

Initially, we worked with U.S.-based groups who were dealing with American diversity and inclusion topics. Since then, we've launched programs partnering Indian and American employees who are working on the same project. Here, in addition to using the IDI to measure the program's impact, we also looked at a handful of the operational metrics that we were already using for measuring the team's efficiency and effectiveness. In comparing the pre- and post-experience results, they were markedly better at the end the program 90 percent of the time.

The Watch Phrase

Constructively calling out differences in relationships is pivotal. Once we can manage these, we can start to be more effective in calling them out among groups and developing savvy strategies around this ability, to which we will turn our attention in Part 3.

Before we do, I realize that some of you may be wondering what happened with our *todo el mundo* party. We ended up having a blast, but it was not without its interpersonal costs. The crosscultural interpersonal lesson? "Don't do that again!" That's not to say one *can't* have a party for 100, just negotiate it up-front. Rather than starting the list at 25 and allowing it to bloat to 100, simply start at 100 or even 200, as we did a few years ago for our daughter's *quinceañera*. Yup, that's big. But this synchronous, externally-controlled, relationship-based, communal guy has found a way to make it possible for my German-American, internally-controlled, sequential, task-oriented wife to go grand. It requires willing, mutual adaptation to work.

The watch phrase for those in crosscultural relationships? Challenge me, yes. Opportunities to grow, yes. Just no surprises, please.

Thank you. ♀

SUMMARY POINTS

- Cultural differences and worldviews can derail relationships among coworkers, friends, family, and neighbors.
- Most significant cultural differences exist below the waterline and resist the easy-to-describe differences of language, mannerisms, and other diversity descriptors.
- When encountering an unexplainable behavior that makes you feel the other party is evil, incompetent, or a moron, it's always helpful to assume positive intent.

With that as your starting point, begin to navigate what lies below the waterline between what you believe and what that other person believes.

- Good intentions go a long way, particularly when it comes to the inevitable inadvertent, cultural missteps.
- Across cultures (societies, people, and geography), similar values may be expressed differently and lead to different interpretations.

SHAPING YOUR STRATEGY

- Think about relationships, offices, and locations where you have particular challenges in being able to relate to and understand your coworkers.
- What is it that's below the waterline in terms of how you and members of that group may be interpreting conflict, ability

to seize opportunity, or approach to negotiation?

- What are some steps you can take to navigate the difference?
- Think of a personal relationship and apply the same principle.

PART 3:
CALLING OUT
DIFFERENCES
IN GROUPS

Calling Out Differences in Groups

"What color is the sky in your universe?"

I've been asked that question many times — through spoken words or silently, through raised eyebrows. Once I figured out the sarcastic meaning of the phrase, I began to wonder the same about others. But it's one thing to call out differences in personal relationships with your spouse, partner, children, family, friends, and associates. It's quite another to do so in groups. The dynamics quickly change when calling out differences at work or school, in religious communities or neighborhood associations, or as you perform civic or community service efforts.

Groups can be as small as two people or as large as an entire country. Even two people with similar backgrounds will share some cultural norms. Should a third individual enter the picture, they may not understand or be understood — even if they are speaking the same language and dressed in similar clothing — because they happen to come from a different upbringing. Our racial/ethnic background, gender, nationality, sexual orientation, disability, generation, faith practices, or other identity dimensions all come into play as we move through different environments — at work, at home, and in our community.

While self-awareness of what has shaped our own worldviews is an important first step in becoming crossculturally competent, we must move on to understand what has shaped the worldviews of others. What dynamics are inherent in the many ways in which we're different? What biases and misperceptions are shared by African-Americans, Latinos, and other ethnic groups when it comes to their European-American male coworkers? How do White males view diversity and inclusion and the part they play in these efforts? What unique experiences have affected female professionals? How did the Great Depression shape the Silent Generation? How did the '60s form the Boomers? How did the space shuttle Challenger's midair explosion mark the Xers? How has global terrorism influenced Millennials? Does life really look different from wheelchair height? How does the workplace experience differ for gays and lesbians who have to decide every day whether to be out or not? How can the performing arts help us further explore the differences among us?

To make the Inclusion Paradox come to life constructively, we must know how to call out these differences. It's the only way to find out where we share a common worldview and where we diverge from those who differ from what we're used to. What is their truth and what is yours? Only then can we move to the third and vital step of being crossculturally competent, navigating the differences to a mutually satisfying solution.

The color of the sky in our universes may indeed be different. We may even have different interpretations of a "blue sky." For me, a blue sky means a nice, warm day, but in the middle of a January deep freeze in Chicago, a blue sky day could appear on the coldest of days. A blue sky can represent a threat for a farmer hoping for rain to ease parched crops. Or it can bring elation to a tourist on a cruise to The Bahamas. A blue sky might be wishful thinking in a high-pollution city like Beijing or Mexico City. Such vastly different interpretations arise from our own personal experiences of our culture.

In Part 3, we examine in greater detail differing cultural dimensions and their impact on various diversity issues. At the G-20 Summit meeting early in his administration, President Obama said, "Each country has its own quirks."[1] Obama's assertion easily could be expanded. Whether defined by race/ethnicity, gender, sexual orientation, disability, generation, faith, or other, each *group* has its quirks. By understanding each other's quirks, we can more fully live out the paradox of inclusion.

In the following chapters, we'll apply the Inclusion Paradox to dimensions of identity and examine areas where conflict can and does occur — despite everyone's best intentions. We'll examine specific areas where calling out differences can encourage greater diversity and inclusion. Whether the sky in our universe is blue or not, we still can co-exist on the same planet. ↻

Chapter 6

I See White People

An American Story

Yup.

The White, heterosexual Boomer male is sick and tired of being the target of all those tolerance and sensitivity messages — fed up with feeling blamed for others' lack of progress, worried that diversity and inclusion advances will be made at his expense.

Many White males are also bewildered by the changing culture around them. And who wouldn't be, having grown up in a society where 90 percent of people looked like them, only to find just two generations later that only half did? By 2040, the United States will be well on its way to becoming a country where minorities are the majority, with non-Whites today making up 44 percent of those under the age of 10, according to the U.S. Census Bureau.[1] And in 2012, we officially reached the tipping point where babies of color (age one and under) reached the majority at 50.4 percent.[2] Not only has the White male become a minority in the 50 largest U.S. cities and a minority among all new entrants into the workforce, even the American president doesn't look like him anymore.[3]

To complicate matters further, the meteoric rise of emerging economies means growing numbers of White males are reporting to Indian, Chinese, and Middle Eastern bosses.

Let's make one thing perfectly clear: The White male must be part of the diversity story, not just for his own sake, but for the sake of true inclusion. If in inclusion work we exclude an important part of the community, we might as well hang it up.

That's not to say the White male doesn't have work to do. The Inclusion Paradox means none of us are off the hook. We may be on that hook for different reasons, leading to different outcomes, but we're all on the hook nonetheless. If we are to avoid diversity's mutually assured destruction — where White males feel that diversity is advancing at their expense — we must see in one another the keys to collective and individual success.

"Affirmative action has created a stigma in the workplace that has resulted in us having politically correct conversations about diversity rather than the ones we need to be having," says Candi Castleberry-Singleton, chief inclusion and diversity officer of UPMC. Political correctness, while it certainly has its place within the diversity/inclusion discussion, has led to a sense of burnout, particularly among the White male to whom many PC-related initiatives have been directed. Candi goes on to say, "There's burnout on both sides, from those who have been carrying the torch of diversity, to those that feel burned by that very same torch. On one hand, burnout comes from constantly redefining, readjusting, rebranding, and remarketing diversity to try to engage people. On the other hand, if you're trying to adjust to diversity's ever-changing landscape, you get tired." And when you're tired — as White males are — you tend to tune out of constructive dialogue.

So let's say the political correctness posse backs off a bit. What would it take to get White males engaged in a constructive dialogue resulting in new conversations and actions? The Obama Era does create new opportunities for changing how these unfold. While there still remains within American society deep racial issues that did not disappear on November 4, 2008, many have still raised the question of whether Barack Obama's election proves the United States has entered a post-racial era. The answer is yes ... and no.

But before tackling this debate, I want to set the stage for changing how we talk about racial differences. Much has been written about the power issue, and vigorous debates have surrounded matters such as equal representation, access, and opportunity. Fierce and touchy discussions still take place around "racism" and "white privilege." Even the question of whether we're now in a post-racial society gravitates around power dynamics. This conversation occurs within a zero-sum-game mindset, where one group's gain is the other's loss. And in politics and business — competitive realms by nature — it's particularly difficult to get beyond the scoreboard of winners and losers.

While we must still address dynamics of power, we must also add the dynamics of cultural difference to the mix. Adding the cultural difference dimension to the still relevant and vital dynamic of power opens a new avenue for getting past polarized debates. At the same time, it creates greater opportunities for what Dr. Michael Broom, author of *Power: The Infinite Game* (Sea Otter Press, 1999) refers to as the "infinite game."[4]

To shift the discussion from power toward cultural differences within relationships invites the following provocative question: What is white or European-American culture? There's actually an emerging field of study of white culture in schools such as Princeton, UCLA, the University of New Mexico, and 30 other colleges and universities. In some ways, they're comparable to that of African-American or Latino/Chicano studies. However, the thrust of several of these programs is to address the rise of racism and white privilege, rather than to celebrate and chronicle the emergence of white culture within the United States. That's indicative of the challenge we face.

Understanding the archetypes of white male culture is just as important as understanding those of other cultures. What are the historical, economic, political, and religious forces that shaped white culture? How do those who are from different cultures react and interpret the behavior of those with a European-American worldview? Without good answers, members of the majority culture will not be able to constructively call out their own differences or engage others in theirs.

The film *Undercover Brother* satirically explores the theme of white culture. In one scene, Undercover Brother, a secret agent played by comedian Eddie Griffin, plans to infiltrate a white-male-controlled corporation and save the world from domination by "The Man." To become a White-man-expert, Undercover Brother undergoes vigorous training, viewing a rapid montage of mainstream movie and TV clips, including Leave It to Beaver, Murder She Wrote, polka dancing, stock car racing, and Irish step dancing.[5] He begins screaming at the visual onslaught, whereby his colleague Smart Brother asks, "Are you alright?"

Undercover Brother responds in a whisper, "I … see … WHITE … people."

Whether White males recognize it or not, the pervasiveness of white culture in mainstream publishing and media is recognized by people of color. Yet it's not uncommon to hear White males respond, "But we don't have a culture." When white culture is the mainstream culture, it's hard to see it as being anything other than "just the way things are."

But people of color quickly recognize Seinfeld, Friends, The Daily Show, Led Zeppelin, Aerosmith, and Nirvana as examples of pop culture that cater more to white sensibilities and aesthetics than to their own. While these are tip-of-the-iceberg preferences (which don't represent all members of the group), discovering what's below the waterline is the prize.

White Males Have a Story, Too

Both Whites and people of color would be more successful at making the mix work if they understood European-American culture in the same way White males are increasingly expected to understand the cultures and histories of various other groups. True, European-American history is better known because it has been taught in schools as de facto American history — which then cloaks the history, heroes, and writers of other American ethnic groups. But we rarely explore the cultural preferences of the descendents of those who came through Plymouth Rock and Ellis Island.

Under the umbrella of "white," European-American culture has its own diversity, equivalent to that which encompasses African-Americans, Afro-Caribbeans, and Africans among Blacks. It's also equivalent to the diversity among Latinos, which encompasses first, second, and third generations, in addition to Guatemalan, Colombian, Mexican, Puerto Rican, and 24 other nationalities.

There are differences in worldviews shaped by the various historical and religious influences of White Americans of Italian, German, Irish, Greek, Polish, Slavic, and Anglo descent. When their ancestors emigrated to the United States, they found their way to ethnic enclaves — New York's Little Italy or Chicago's Greektown, for example. To this day, several generations removed from their arrival, these groups' cultural distinctiveness survives. It emerges particularly strongly at christenings, weddings, and funerals, as captured in movies such as My Big Fat Greek Wedding.

As monolithic as white culture seems today, each European ethnic group that came through Ellis Island faced discrimination from those who had preceded them. The colonizing Anglos found ways to discriminate against the immigrant Germans, Italians, Irish, Poles, and Slavs. And the Jews were discriminated against by every group, even when they shared the same country of origin.

The prejudice was deep and vile. Consider how the Irish were viewed in the second half of the 1800s when they fled the ravages of the Irish potato famine and arrived in the United States. In American Pharaoh, a biography of Chicago Mayor Richard J. Daley (son of Irish immigrants and father of the former 22-year tenured Chicago Mayor Richard M. Daley), authors Adam Cohen and Elizabeth Taylor write:

> *"Who does not know that the most depraved, debased, worthless, and irredeemable drunkards and sots which curse the community are Irish-Catholics?' the Chicago Tribune asked in 1855. The Irish were regarded as particularly disposed to crime. 'Scratch a convict or pauper,' the Chicago Post declared in 1898 and 'the chances are that you tickle the skin of an Irish-Catholic at the same time ... an Irish-Catholic made a criminal or a pauper by the priest and politicians who have deceived him and kept him in ignorance, in a word, a savage, as he was born.*
>
> *"America reserved some of the lowest rungs on the economic and social ladder for the new Irish immigrants. Signs proclaiming 'No Irish Need Apply' were common. Advertisements for housekeepers often specified 'Protestant girls' only, because young Irish-Catholic women, as one account had it, were 'the daughters of laborers, or needy tradesmen, or persecuted, rack-rented cotters, they're ignorant of the common duties of servants in respectable positions.' Irish men, for their part, were largely relegated to the jobs native-born whites would not take. They were the laborers who carved out the canals, laid the railroad tracks, and dug the ditches often at great personal cost."[6]*

We cannot have a fair and healthy conversation, unless we acknowledge the trials endured by European-Americans' ancestors. At the same time, we cannot merely expunge the legacy of racism in white culture and U.S. society in general. We must recognize the legacy of racism in a matter-of-fact, unflinching way so that we can move on to the deeper, more constructive work of crosscultural understanding and collaboration.

With the massacre and forced removal of Native Americans from their lands and the entrenchment of slavery in the emerging U.S. economy of the 1800s, race became a powerful societal construct. Eventually, White European groups found common causes and created boundary lines based on skin color rather than national heritage. After the Civil War, therefore, freed slaves migrating to Northern cities were viewed as a common threat by the European-Americans already living there.

The same groups that had themselves been persecuted turned their prejudice against people of color. Even in Richard J. Daley's own neighborhood of Bridgeport, where Irish immigrants had endured the ignominy and degradation of discrimination, Whites aimed their prejudices against Blacks. It was the era of Jim Crow laws and lynchings in the South — and segregation, white flight, and race riots in the North. The power of racism created common cause among White ethnic groups.

Over time, the construct of race and white superiority became so powerful that Whites piggy-backed on the issue of race, hopscotching over their own ethnic origin to gain acceptance and, with it, greater opportunity in society.

In the United States, race relations have been marred by points of progress and regress. Dr. King's march on Washington, President Lyndon Johnson's signing of the Civil Rights Act, and Barack Obama's election and re-election could all be deemed steps forward, while the Watts riots of 1968, the L.A. riots of 1992, and the O.J. Simpson trial mark steps backward. Together, they form an arc of lurching racial progress[7] — and demonstrate that there's still a long way to go.

There are still gaps in educational attainment, infant mortality, and the financial well-being of Blacks and Latinos compared to those of Whites. African-American infants experience mortality rates twice that of the national average. White households boast incomes two-thirds higher than Blacks and 40 percent higher than Hispanics. Seventy-five percent of Whites own their homes, compared to 46 percent of Blacks and 48 percent of Hispanics. And while 30 percent of Whites have a Bachelor's degree or greater, just 17 percent of Blacks and 12 percent of Hispanics do. In the 2012 U.S. Senate, there are two Latinos, one Asian American, and 97 European-Americans. In 2012, only 21 of all Fortune 500 CEOs were executives of color.[8]

One cannot tell the story of white culture through the lens of racial disparities alone. We must integrate cultural worldviews born not out of prejudice but out of religious, political, economic, and social experiences. It's not enough to simply equate whiteness with racism. While racism is and was a reality with many consequences, European-Americans are made up of communities, driven first to survive and then thrive. Along the way, they developed particular idiosyncratic interpretations of how to do just that.

This is why it's not enough merely to address power and law, but culture as well. Even as racism is legislated and socialized away, cultural preferences remain — not usually out of malice or intent — but in response to the primal need to seek similarity and equilibrium. These forces are at play in all cultures. Yet the group in power often institutionalizes their own preferences due to their numerical majority.

The institutionalizing of European-American preferences cannot be underestimated. To create true inclusion, we must first grasp how this deep enculturation may inadvertently create barriers for those who grew up with different cultural preferences, leading them to navigate the system with less savvy and effectiveness.

There's a key distinction between conscious barriers — which are designed to keep out people who are different (power issue) — and subconscious barriers that emerge out of a group's preference for how to survive and thrive (crosscultural issue). To identify and reduce or remove these barriers, we must first understand the conscious and subconscious choices being made. Since so much has already been said about conscious choices, I will focus on the impact of subconscious choices. This requires a more intimate understanding of the worldview of the culture in question.

European-American Male Worldview

"So what makes up this European-American — or white — worldview?" Whenever I pose this question, a discomfort descends on the crowd attending the seminar. Some eyes avoid mine; others lock in. Some heads shake no, while some begin to nod yes.

Usually it's the White and African-American women who make the first pass at the answer. They tend to focus on tip-of-the-iceberg descriptions verging on stereotyping, such as a passion for golf, sports on TV, and steaks. Several of the White men look up and nod their heads as if to say, "Well, yeah."

I then lead the class on an exercise where they capture their life values and how these values were interpreted in their families of origin. For White males, self-sufficiency, hard work, fairness, and honesty typically surface at the top of their lists.[9]

In the context of European-American history, these answers make sense. The opportunity to remake themselves in America propelled millions of Europeans to pull up roots and travel through vast churning oceans, scorching deserts, and suffocating wilderness. Out of this arose the mythology of the United States of America being the land of opportunity where anyone willing to work hard and create his or her own way could achieve their dreams. "Pull yourself up by your bootstraps." "From rags to riches." "God helps those who help themselves." These became the mantras of a people driven to succeed. Even happiness was to be pursued rather than realized from within.

As definable contours of European-American male culture begin to take shape, the men nod in recognition and then add more details. They own the description. "Yes, this is how we view the world. And it has served us well. It's how things work. It's what we learned from our fathers and what we are passing on to our children."

And so, not by design, but rather by their inherent norms and values, European-Americans collectively created a supra-white culture. Once they had immigrated to the United States, normalizing experiences of European-Americans blurred the deep cultural differences between them. The unifying value of democracy and its accompanying symbols of the Star-Spangled Banner and the Pledge of Allegiance took root. Acculturation forces of education, government policies, and mass media reinforced this self-image. And for European newcomers, an assimilationist invitation was made to become part of that great Melting Pot. Many European immigrants gave up their native language and traditional dress in order to fit in.

The white majority ran the institutions of power, commerce, and entertainment. As a result, the worldview preferences of European-Americans were systematically reinforced and standards set for what was acceptable and superlative behavior in the corridors of success and power. White culture became the norm. Thus, the archetypical behaviors from other cultures became deviations from that norm.

What values consistently emerge from other cultural groups? In that same seminar exercise I conduct almost all of the racial and ethnic groups also frequently list values such as Education and Respect. However, the greatest interest lies in looking at which values do not show up. Perhaps not surprisingly, the values most often cited by White men are not shared by others. On the African-American list of values, we see Giving Back and Justice. For Latinos, we see Commitment to Family.

So *now* we have something to compare and contrast between the intriguingly different worldviews of European-Americans and others. Why is it that some cultural groups don't place Fairness or Self-Sufficiency at the top of their lists? "Because this is not how it has played out for us," an African-American woman explained to her White male colleagues at a client session I facilitated. "I saw my father get good grades and was told he should only apply to a Black school to get his M.D. I heard about his repeatedly missing the IQ threshold by one point, which prevented him from getting on the officer track when he was in the military. Life is not fair. Hard work is not automatically rewarded."

So what's needed?

"Justice."

For many successful White men, the operating belief has been that hard work leads to success. For others, an outside intervention — justice — is required to achieve what is due.

No one list of values is more right than another. But they indeed are different. Even when the same value is shared, it can have different interpretations. Two Boomers — one Southern White male and one Northern African-American female — were paired to discuss their family's values in a course we designed titled, "The Power of Worldviews: Understanding Yourself and Others." Both agreed that they valued Respect. But listen for the differences in their interpretation:

White male: "For me, it was saying 'yes sir, no ma'am.'"

African-American female: "Oh noooo. For me, it was quite the opposite! To say 'yes sir, no ma'am' meant subservience. It was not the way to respect others or myself and my family."

At the tip of the iceberg, we may have shared values. But below the waterline, differing interpretations often materialize. It's at this juncture that workplace dynamics begin to go awry. White males who see themselves as open-minded and fair assume a level playing field where meritocracy rewards hard work and ambition. Self-sufficiency is a good thing. Meanwhile people of color, scrambling to keep from sliding off this tilted playing field, ask for support programs that can provide compensatory boosts to their efforts.

Over the years, we have conducted a workshop entitled "Why Don't They Get Me? Understanding Black and White Cultural Differences" at the National Black MBA Association annual conference. We present Trompenaars' and Hampden-Turner's seven cultural dimensions (defined specifically in Chapter 4; here I just want to point out the contrast), then ask the group to identify which ones seem more manifest in the European-American and African-American cultures. Their list looks like this:

White	African-American
Universalist	Particularist
Task	Relationship
Individualist	Communal
Sequential	Synchronous
Internal Control	External Control
Neutral	Affective

In six of the seven cultural dimensions, Black audiences have put Whites and Blacks on opposite interpretive sides! The only cultural dimension where the answer was not dichotomized between the two groups was Achievement vs. Ascription.* No wonder the gaps in the workplace continue to be deep and perplexing. It's not just about power dynamics — it's also about cultural differences.

When conducting this exercise with predominantly European-American audiences, they are reluctant to venture into what may be African-American archetypes. Instead, they make distinctions among different European-American ethnicities. The following dialogue with a group of leaders in Georgia is typical of my experience:

"As an Italian-American, I actually see myself and my family as more communal in that Family is one of our most important values. We're Affective in that we're much more expressive than Northern Europeans and we've got that Latin

---

* On the surface, the European-American celebration of accomplishment over title (admiring Bill Gates for his success despite not having graduated from college) and the high importance African-Americans give to titles ("I attend Second Baptist Church, Hycel B. Williams, Pastor"), makes clear the archetypical preferences of both groups — Whites seem to be more Achievement oriented, while Blacks seem to be more Ascription oriented. But dig a little deeper and you'll find that Blacks feel Whites put a lot of emphasis on titles, paying attention to who is VP, President, CEO, etc. For successful African-Americans from no-status families, status is conferred on the basis of overcoming all odds. Because of these complexities, a clear distinction between the worldviews of both groups was not evident.

Catholic fatalism External Control thing going on."

Fair enough. But remember that this model is best used when comparing one's own culture with another, however granular one defines it ("Calabrese Italian-American," for instance). And by saying "European-American," we're not saying "European" only. The "American" part is vital as well. Consider the case of Anglo-Saxon Whites who emigrated from England to escape an ascription society epitomized by the monarchy. For them, America became a place of reinvention of one's identity. Regardless of the family one was born into, if one worked hard enough, one could shape one's own destiny. Even today, England remains far more class-oriented than the United States. The term "rags to riches" is not part of the British cultural values vocabulary. But it definitely is in that of their American descendants.

European-American audiences initially put up their defenses when I ask if there's something that can be called European-American culture. Quickly, however, it becomes clear that their initial reaction is partly a means of deflecting what they assume will be negative characteristics, such as domineering, racist, sexist, etc. But as they start to describe the positive values instilled in them by the families they love and the heritage they're proud of, they begin to see that they have a distinct culture with certain values and interpretations that can consciously be described, compared, and contrasted with the increasing number of cultures they're interacting with at home and abroad.

White Men Have Feelings, Too

From this exploration of cultural worldview, let's return to the realm of power. Clearly, the White male dominates in positions of leadership, but this masks the struggles of many White males whom minorities may see as invulnerable. Much has been made of "white privilege." In fact, much of the work of diversity is about weakening and dismantling the dynamics that inadvertently strengthen white privilege. While a valid endeavor, focusing only on this concept only perpetuates the mythology of White male invulnerability.

In a training video used during "The Power of Worldviews" course, a White male engages in a frank conversation with a couple of African-Americans and an Asian-American. Upon hearing how he's perceived as invulnerable, he replies, "On the contrary. I feel quite vulnerable. I feel that when I reach out, I won't be able to touch anyone."

Diversity and inclusion work focuses a great deal of attention on those who have been traditionally marginalized. However, White men have their own workplace issues, too. Often, their issues are overlooked because they rarely feel their experiences fit into a specific culture worthy of attention, given diversity's traditional emphasis on their privileged position.

The Winters Group, a diversity consulting firm founded and led by Mary-Frances Winters, an African-American woman, has identified the following recurring themes as unresolved issues among White male employees in many corporate environments:

- Feeling undervalued and unrecognized for expertise
- Concern with lack of succession planning for their own aspirations
- Concern with work-life balance and flexibility
- Frustration with the addition of non-technical responsibilities, such as diversity training, inclusion programs, representations targets, etc.
- Believing that diversity equals quotas and that minorities are given privileges

Winters' research[10] also found that "both women and men have become more conscious of the personal tradeoffs they need to make to advance in their careers and that an increasing number are instead choosing to stay at the same levels, rather than continue moving up the career ladder." Work-life balance also has become increasingly important: "The hours and goals today are bigger than they were in the past. It takes more of a toll on my family time." "I'm on call 24/7." "I miss a lot of family events because I work so many days." "The time needed to complete daily paperwork comes off my family time."

Hearing the White male voice, both as a cultural group in a multicultural environment and as a group where individuals face their own share of challenges, can open up a new space where minorities see White males in a new light.

Without understanding, we have judgment. This is why one of the most powerful ways to develop crosscultural competency is to do so within the context of relationship. To facilitate this, Mary-Frances Winters and I developed the Crosscultural Learning Partners Program described in Chapter 5, where senior leaders and managers (many of whom are White males) are matched with someone culturally different for a year-long learning through personal dialogue.

Not only did we observe the expected ah-ha's among White males, but minorities themselves experienced their own awakening with regard to their biases toward White males. At the end of the year-long program, we sat in a circle sharing what everyone had learned. Referring to the White male colleague with whom she had been partnered, one African-American woman confessed, "I had no idea White men could feel vulnerable and not have all the answers. But my learning partner was so honest with me about his own challenges of growing up in a single-parent household and his learning disability, I had to face my own stereotyping of White men. It was eye-opening." A White male in the circle responded, "This process was liberating. For the first time, I could see the potential that really addressing diversity can have for our business without all the baggage of being the bad guy."

White Males as Partners in Diversity

What then are the possibilities when White men are more fully engaged in creating diverse and inclusive environments? Bill Proudman, founder of the White Men as Full Diversity Partners consulting firm, says that successful diversity and inclusion efforts must ensure we're addressing all employees, including White males. "It's vital that they become engaged partners," he says. "In fact, the real diversity goal for White males is to foster an environment where they feel part of the diversity and inclusion story and have options to get personally involved. Many White men have never examined the notion that they have a self-interest in diversity and inclusion efforts. To explore this is new terrain for them, as they mostly view diversity and inclusion efforts as about everyone else."

While White males are significantly more likely to say their company is actively working to support diversity, they're also significantly less likely to agree they're personally included in a company's diversity efforts, according to engagement survey data[11] from various companies. Their engagement scores are consistently lower than for other groups at the companies surveyed.

As long as White males feel left out of the discussion, inclusion — making the mix work — cannot be achieved. As Proudman explains, diversity initiatives that ignore the potential contributions of White males may only help foster the misconception that these efforts are nothing but a "chore" or a nuisance. "Most diversity work fails to fully engage White men," he says. "This leads people to view diversity as a win/lose proposition rather than a win/win. It's one reason why so many White men feel threatened or blamed by the topic." Because many White men don't view themselves as having a culture, they often think of themselves primarily as individuals, rather than members of a White male group. This mindset makes White men feel personally threatened and marginalized by their company's diversity efforts. They see it as only about changing representation (the mix), rather than including White men in the effort to make the mix work.

If White males are not engaged, they won't proactively move on progress. And since they make up the overwhelming majority of corporate America's middle managers (the very group essential for enacting cultural change), they can by sheer inertia choke off progress. Due to their size — plus their mandate to keep a company's essential services humming and product going out the door — middle managers are the most resistant to changing the status quo, regardless of the initiative. Usually, they are not required or rewarded for thinking and acting innovatively or strategically.

The converse is also true. "Ironically, while this group can squash change by inertia, it can, if motivated right, make things happen," Georgia Power's then vice president, diversity Frank McCloskey (a White male) told me at a diversity conference we both attended. "Action, not reflection, is their bias. And when the action is clear and compelling plus they're held accountable for results, big changes can happen. In order for this management and culture shift to occur, it must be seen as improving management effectiveness and employee performance. It can't be seen as 'adding to my pile of work.'"

What could this look like? Howard Ross, co-founder and chief learning officer of diversity consultancy at Cook Ross Inc., advises that White male employees become more actively involved in their organization's diverse culture, participating in a diversity-strategy group, mentoring and coaching, or being the person who directs the minority development programs and minority recruitment. Even more ideas are featured in Chuck Shelton's book, *Leadership 101 for White Men: How to Work Successfully with Black Colleagues and Customers.*[12]

We will see an even greater impact when White males see for themselves how diversity and inclusion can help them achieve the day-to-day business goals for which they're accountable — by finding and penetrating emerging markets both within the United States (over $1 trillion purchasing power by people of color and another $1 trillion plus by women business owners) and globally. When they start to see that what worked for them when dealing with people who looked and thought like them will not necessarily work when dealing with those from other cultures, the more these White males are going to want to have increasingly diverse teams and build the kind of crosscultural competence that will enable them to bridge the gaps and close the deal.

Post-racial? Yes and No

In the Obama Era, perhaps the hotly debated question is whether his historic election in 2008 and re-election in 2012 marks the beginning of a post-racial America. The answer is both yes and no. Speaking at the February 17, 2009 Chicago Dream Dinner honoring Dr. Martin Luther King, Jr.,[13] the Rev. Jesse Jackson, Sr. reached new rhetorical heights when dissecting how we see evidence of King's dream both achieved and deferred at this defining time in American history. Rev. Jackson said we cannot take lightly the fact that Obama's election is evidence of a dream achieved in a nation that outlawed slavery just over 100 years ago and gave Blacks the right to vote less than 50 years ago. At the same time, African-Americans are the largest demographic group in jail, in infant mortality, in poor academic performance, and in debt. In that sense, the dream is still deferred. Post-racial? Yes and no.

This color line doesn't just show up across the socioeconomic spectrum. It also runs right through racially diverse middle class groups.

Consider this scenario: It is 2008 and a group of about 40 people are holding 8 ½ x 11 sheets of paper, each containing a large handwritten number. They jostle to line up in numerical order, based on a self-scored questionnaire about their racial experiences. At the beginning of the line are those with the most negative experiences. At the end are the ones with the most positive. The visual is unambiguous: Those with the worst experiences are Black and the ones with the best are White. In between Latinos and Asians. How did this happen?

First, let's consider the make-up of the participants in the survey: a progressive group of Chicago area leaders from business, civic government, the legal profession, and non-profit organizations. They are White, African-American, Latino and Asian-American. All are college-educated, mid-career, successful leaders. They share a passion and commitment to community development. Age-wise, they are all post-civil rights era babies. They are an elite group selected through a rigorous process for a year-long program called Leadership Greater Chicago. Over the course of the program, they will build deep bonds with each other.

Despite the post-racial ethos of the group, a stark color line emerges. What defined the line? The answer may lie in Dr. Peggy McIntosh's[14] seminal work on "white privilege."[15] In it, she made 46 statements about her racial experiences in society that reflected "my own unearned advantages as a White person relative to African-American colleagues with whom I work."[16] As it turned out, her personal story resonated with many others who share her cultural and racial heritage — so much so that I felt it relevant to develop an exercise for the Chicago group based on Dr. McIntosh's list of "unearned advantages." Participants were asked to compare their experiences in housing, education, shopping, walking down the street, driving, and so on with those of Dr. McIntosh. Typical statements from her work included:

- I can go shopping alone most of the time, pretty well assured that I will not be followed or harassed.
- If I should need to move, I can be pretty sure of renting or purchasing housing in an area which I can afford and in which I would want to live.
- I can choose blemish cover or bandages in "flesh" color and have them more or less match my skin.
- Whether I use checks, credit cards, or cash, I can count on my skin color not to work against my appearance of financial reliability.
- I am never asked to speak for all the people of my racial group.
- If a traffic cop pulls me over or if the IRS audits my tax return, I can be sure I haven't been singled out because of my race.

An "Always" answer got a score of 5, a "Sometimes" 3, and "Never" 0. Participants added up their scores and then lined up from high to low across the room. That's how the stark color line materialized, with Whites scoring the highest with numbers above 100 (meaning, to their surprise, that their experience of having racial privilege was strong) and Blacks having the most negative scores — in the 20's and below. Asians and Latinos scored in between the first two groups, with their numbers ranging between the 20's and 60's. Regardless of when or where this exercise is conducted, the results are essentially the same.[17]

Let's return to my question from before: Are we now in a post-racial society? Unfortunately, the answer is no. And not for some time to come. Despite signs of racial progress there remain potent signs of racial distress with new dimensions.

Take, for instance, the arrest of Harvard tenured professor Henry Louis Gates in front of his own home when Boston police thought he was a burglar trying to break in.

Or take the 2012 Trayvon Martin shooting, where a 17-year-old African-American youth was shot and killed by George Zimmerman, who has been described as a multi-racial Latino male. Race shaped that public outburst around the case: from the presumption that racist motivations were behind Zimmerman's shooting of Martin, to accusations that race colored the police's initial decision to release Zimmerman instead of arresting and formally charging him to a legislative review of Florida's Stand Your Ground law.

These events are dramatic flash points that there continues to be a stark racial divide in how Blacks and Whites view the world. The 2012 Pew Charitable Trust's Economic Mobility Project[18] illustrated the many ways this is the case.

Blacks, Latinos, and Whites all believe in the existence of the American Dream. The differences show up in their expectations about it: whether they have already achieved the Dream or if reaching it will occur in their lifetimes. Forty percent of Whites believe that they have already achieved the American Dream, compared to 18 percent of Latinos and 16 percent of Blacks who felt the same.

Differences also crop up when you look at White, Black, and Latino expectations of reaching the American Dream in this lifetime. Fifty-seven percent of Latinos and 53 percent of African-Americans believe that they will achieve the American Dream in their lifetimes. However only 32 percent of Whites felt the same.

These racial differences continue to show up when it comes to the financial expectations for the future. Seventy-three percent of Blacks and nearly 70 percent of Latinos believe that their financial situation would be better in 10 years. Just slightly more than half (52 percent) of Whites believed the same. Just under a third (31 percent) of Whites believed that they would be worse off financially in 10 years, while only 22 percent of both Latinos and Blacks felt similarly. [19]

It's as if these two groups live in two different countries. And to some degree, they do.

Racial fault lines still show up across many sectors of society.

There's hope, however, in that we're having dialogues, making relationships, and finding new ways to collaborate across racial lines as never before. This is definitely true in the Obama Era. The election and re-election of President Obama pointed the way for a possible post-racial America and represented an opportunity to transform – not transcend or eliminate – our racial differences. As Obama said, his election is a chance "to continue the long march of those who came before us, a march for a more just, more equal, more free, more caring, and more prosperous America." [20]

The President recognizes the nation's complex racial reality and has always had to tread very carefully in discussing race. He is hyper-aware of the sensitivities, often to the chagrin of many of his supporters who had been hoping the nation's first Black president would more explicitly and often address race. While the debate will rage about how he best handles race he is clearly making deliberate choices about how he will negotiate this political and social third rail.

He explained, in the 2012 interview in *Rolling Stone Magazine*[21], "my view on race has always been that it's complicated. It's not just a matter of head – it's a matter of heart. It's about interactions. What happens in the workplace, in schools, on sports fields, and through music and culture shapes racial attitudes as much as any legislation that is passed. I do believe that we are making slow and steady progress."

Slow it has been. During this time we have seen some of the most uplifting evidence of racial progress as well as some of the ugliest expressions of racism we have seen in a very long time.

So President Obama mostly chooses not to address the issue head-on except on occasion when he had his Beer Summit with Professor Gates and Sergeant James Crowley, the police officer who arrested him, or in commenting in light of the Trayvon Martin case that "you know, if I had a son, he'd look like Trayvon."

But consider this: some of his most sweeping legislation have the potential of massive positive impact on people of color in the United States. Health care reform that will now insure nearly 32 million people, which disproportionately (about a third) are people of color. Education Reform in which the Obama administration has invested more than $100 billion[22], most of it is going to "failing schools" where 50 percent of Black and Latino kids are not graduating. The Consumer Protection Act benefits all Americans from potential abuses from credit card companies, but here again, disproportionately those falling prey to unsavory practices have been people of color.

Given his first-hand experience of being a person of color himself in the USA, President Obama has charted a highly nuanced approach to race. Some say it's not enough, others say it's best for him to remain low-key on it. Agree with his choices or not of what he should or should not put into words or not, his actions, while not framed under the banner of racial inequality, have been aimed in some large part to this very issue.

When it comes to race in America is the glass half-full or half-empty? Judge for yourself, but I'm going to say half-full. From tip-of-the-iceberg European-American cultural contributions, such as Rice Krispies®, Halloween, Rock 'n' Roll, hamburgers, hot dogs, baseball, and "Yahtzee" to the below-the-waterline world-view that believes in reinvention and can-do-ism, there's plenty to celebrate in white culture. American culture has also been heavily influenced by African-American culture when it comes to music, dance, and fashion, as well as below-the-waterline contributions of the higher value of expression, more direct communication, and a commitment to community. Then there are the Asian contributions — from the calming spirit of yoga to a more holistic view of health. Latino tip-of-the-iceberg contributions include salsa — both for chips and for dancing — and expressive architecture and interior design, in addition to below-the-waterline contributions of familia and community and work strategies that embed relationships at a deeper level.

Even as we redouble efforts to erase the racial legacies of socioeconomic inequality, do we really want to erase the unique and rich contributions that each culture, including that of the White male, contributes to the whole? "E Pluribus Unum," the saying on the Seal of the United States, translates to "Out of Many, One." The inverse may also be true — "Out of One, Many," as could be "Out of the Many, One" or "Out of the One, Many."

If post-racial means a place where we've erased legalized forms of inequality and a justification for lack of opportunity based on the color of people's skin, then we're surely post-racial. If post-racial means a land where our children are more likely than us to grow up with kids not looking like them as their classmates, as their best friends, and later as their lovers and intimate companions then we can call that post-racial. But if post-racial means erasing all those ways in which our uniqueness enriches one other, we may want to answer in the negative that we don't want to be post-racial. Or maybe it's time for a new term. "Maybe the desired state is *transracial*," wonders Mary-Frances Winters. "A national culture where race does not divide, but rather enriches."

We see White people. We see Blacks and Latinos and Asians and Native Americans. True to the American Way, we see Americans reinventing who they are every day, both as individuals and as a people. Americans are in the midst of an era of reinventing their racial relationships with one another — it's just too soon to declare what the "new" is. ℺

SUMMARY POINTS

- It's important for European-Americans to understand the American White male archetype in order to compare and contrast their cultural values and expressions with those of others.
- European-American culture has various nuances and its own intracultural diversity.

- White males need to feel included and involved in the diversity and inclusion effort. If they are left out of such initiatives, true inclusion will not be achieved.
- In the same way that there's African-American, Asian-American and Hispanic-American cultural history, there's also a European-American one.

SHAPING YOUR STRATEGY

- Are White males in your organizations engaged in supporting and moving forward diversity and inclusion work? Do they feel included? If not, why not? What actions can be implemented to include them? If they already feel included, how can you harness this sense of inclusion for greater and deeper impact?

- How knowledgeable and understanding are your non-white cultural groups about the White male experience?
- If there's a gap of understanding, how can you bridge the gap?

I See White People

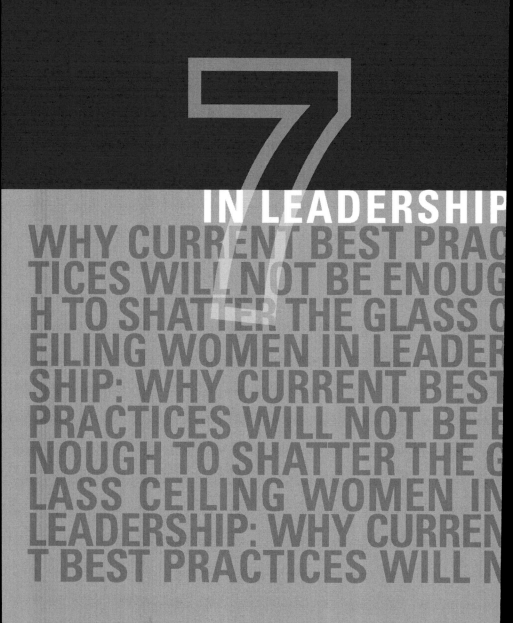
WOMEN

7 IN LEADERSHIP

WHY CURRENT BEST PRAC
TICES WILL NOT BE ENOUG
H TO SHATTER THE GLASS C
EILING WOMEN IN LEADER
SHIP: WHY CURRENT BEST
PRACTICES WILL NOT BE E
NOUGH TO SHATTER THE G
LASS CEILING WOMEN IN
LEADERSHIP: WHY CURREN
T BEST PRACTICES WILL N

Chapter 7

Women in Leadership:
Why Current Best Practices Will Not Be
Enough to Shatter the Glass Ceiling

It is one of the corporate world's greatest anticlimactic moments.

Throughout the world, women now represent half the labor force — in Latin America, Europe, the United States, Canada, Asia, Australia, and a host of other places.[1] In some of these geographic areas, it all started during World War II, when women headed to the factories as men headed off to war. As a result, we now have three to four generations of women who have been active in the workforce.

Yet the number and level of women at the executive leader ranks still have a long way to go. In 2012, women comprised 40 percent of the three billion people employed worldwide,[2] but held only 21 percent of senior management positions.[3]

Women have revolutionized the workplace, not only by their presence, but through their perspectives, skills, and demands. They've introduced new approaches to managing people and working in teams and led the way to new benefit concepts that support work-life balance, including alternative work programs and on-site childcare. Their true impact, however, is even more profound.

President Obama has often spoken emotively about the strong women in his life. During the 2008 Presidential campaign, he penned a white paper titled *Barack Obama's Plan to Support Working Women and Families*. In it, he cites the women in his own family as a testament to the contributions of women toward the advancement of female empowerment, not just in the home, but also in business. "My mother was a single mom who put herself through school, followed her passion for helping others, and raised my sister and me to believe that in America, there are no barriers to success if you're willing to work for it." He goes on to say, "My grandmother worked on a bomber assembly line during World War II — she was Rosie the Riveter. After the war, even though she never got more than a high school diploma, she worked her way up from her start as a secretary at a bank, and shouldered most of the financial responsibility for our entire family when I was growing up. My wife Michelle, the rock of the Obama family, has worked her way up from modest roots on the South Side of Chicago, and has juggled jobs and parenting with ... skill and grace ... My accomplishments are only possible because of these women."

It's not much of a stretch to think that Obama's personal experiences with a working mother and grandmother, and later a high-powered professional wife, were behind the reasons for his support of the Lilly Ledbetter Fair Pay Restoration Act, or to make it the very first piece of legislation he signed as president. In the spirit of equal pay for equal work, the act extends the time period that women can sue employers for paying women less than their male colleagues for the same job responsibilities. At the bill signing ceremony, Obama spoke of the impact the legislation will have on his daughters and the young women who follow. He said, "I sign this bill for my daughters, and all those who will come after us, because I want them to grow up in a nation that values their contributions, where there are no limits to their dreams and they have opportunities their mothers and grandmothers never could have imagined."[4]

While Obama attributes his personal success to the women in his life, women also have brought increased wealth to organizations and nations. According to a 2011 report by Catalyst, companies with the most women board directors had higher returns: Those with three or more directors outperformed those with none by 84 percent for return on sales and 46 percent for return on equity. Even in the financial sector, the presence of women makes a distinct difference. In the wild world of hedge fund management, between January 2000 and May 2009, women-managed hedge funds yielded a 9.5 percent return while men-managed funds returned 5.8 percent. And during the 2008 crisis, women-run funds lost just 9.6 percent compared to men's 19 percent loss. At a nation state level, the United

Nations published a report demonstrating a strong positive correlation between the education levels and income of women and the GNP of countries.[5]

The bottom line: The more educated and highly paid women are, the richer entire countries and companies are.[6]

Considering this degree of impact, women around the world are starting to say, *"Now just wait a minute!"* They are enriching the overall working environment and making companies wealthier, yet in Japan, women hold just 10 percent of all management jobs.[7] In Mexico, male employers outnumber female employers three to one.[8] In Europe, women represent only 31 percent of managers.[9] In the United States, among Fortune 500 companies, less than 8 percent of women are in the top five earners, 14 percent are corporate officers, 16 percent are corporate board members, and around 3.5 percent serve as CEOs.[10] The robust pipeline of women in various industries has not yielded the expected results at the most senior levels. At this rate of change, it will be 40 years before women enjoy parity with men at the corporate officer level.[11]

In light of the past ten to 15 years of heightened diversity work, women had hope that "the damned glass ceiling" would finally be shattered. Yet, the first five years of "patience, we've only just begun" evolved into the next five years of "patience, we're making some progress" to the past three to five years of "we're really stuck." It's true. Women are *really* stuck, despite having similar levels of ambition as men, and sometimes more education. In the United States, women now earn 57 percent of bachelor's degrees and 52 percent of doctorates.[12] By 2015 women will have accounted for two-thirds of undergraduates.[13] Increased education levels align with greater ambition, which can be considered a birthright of today's young women whose mothers struggled with these same issues.

According to recent research by Ellen Galinsky, president and co-founder of the Families and Work Institute, millennial women and men are equally likely to be ambitious and desire positions with greater responsibilities. This holds true whether these younger women are mothers or not. But the robust pipeline of women in various industries has not yet yielded the expected results at the most senior levels.

In certain countries, the dashing of rising expectations is making a growing number of women rethink the corporate deal. This could mean quite a loss for corporations. In the United States and Australia, for example, a growing number of senior women professionals have gained enough economic, personal, and professional power to abandon the corporate world entirely, opting to start their own businesses instead. In the United States, women and African-Americans are leading the way as the fastest-growing segments for start-up companies. Every 60 seconds, a woman — often a self-exile from the corporate ranks — starts her own business.[14]

The argument could be made that for women of color, the rise in business ownership is related to the lower rate of advancement up the management ranks. According to the 2012 Diversity Best Practices benchmarking study, participating companies promoted women of color into rising levels of management at much lower rates than White women or men of any race and ethnicity. In fact, women of color had the lowest promotion rate, implying there is an insidious double glass ceiling for women of color.

In this chapter, I explore what's required for breakthrough change in the advancement of women leaders. In the process, I examine some implications for corporations if women are to make the desired gains. It won't be enough to simply retool their diversity efforts. Corporate leadership will have to address the different perspectives and cultural behaviors women bring to the workplace and begin to discuss these differences openly and honestly, both with the women themselves and with their male colleagues, at all levels. This exploration will also touch on some of the gains women have made since the first printing of this book. The Obama Era aligns with the growing prominence of women and girls in the political, social, educational, and economic spheres all across the globe. The 21st Century is witnessing an emergence of female power. Despite the current stats pointing to stagnation in women's advancement into leadership, there are massive pressures against the glass ceiling that cannot be contained any longer. As Hillary Clinton mentioned at the end of the 2008 primary elections referring to the votes she had received, the 18 million cracks in the glass ceiling in politics and businesses have weakened the ceiling to the point that it's beginning to buckle against the pressure.

The impact of this female power is shaking the status quo in workplaces, homes, communities, schools and universities, legislative bodies, organizations, and informal and formal networks. Women are not only changing who is making decisions and doing work, but also how decisions are made, how work is accomplished, and the reasons underlying those changes.

In the past few years, the intervention most frequently requested in diversity today is for the advancement of women around the world. Current corporate best practices will have to adapt to this surge in female power and this growing acceptance that companies need to do more to enable women to rise to the fullness of their potential for their sakes and that of their organizations. Those that can't or won't adapt will be swept out to sea by this rising tide of women.

Best Practices

Yes, there are best practices to live by, and I will summarize what many have already deemed necessary for women to rise in corporate ranks. Diversity practitioners, think tanks, and women exec councils generally agree about what needs to be done, but existing approaches to the issue have their share of limitations. Shattering the glass ceiling requires more than mere diversity. Inclusion must be embedded into leadership development and succession plans, requiring that women be placed in the "ready now" and "ready in three years" boxes. Inclusive environments must be fostered where all manner of differences, including gender, are welcomed and embraced. Women must be mentored, and they must take part in open and honest discussions concerning their current skills and development needs. And yes, there must be pay equity.

These practices, *well executed,* will yield results. But only incrementally. Today's corporate structure and assumptions inherently prevent women from taking their rightful seats at the leaders' table. Thus, we must look beyond best practices to new paradigms.

Just what is it about being female that makes rising to the top so challenging? How can companies make room at the leaders' table for the archetypical female traits that now impede their advancement? Let's look at some new thinking on what needs to happen.

Beyond Best Practices

Corporations need to rethink their current paradigms to begin shattering the glass ceiling. It's time to:

- Rethink what strong leadership and management looks like
- Rethink the value of tenure
- Rethink compensation models
- Rethink whether competencies developed elsewhere are transferable to the workplace

- Rethink how unspoken rules around alternative work arrangements may be detrimental to women's advancement and their full inclusion into organizational life

Rethink what strong leadership and strong management looks like.
Quick! What attributes come to mind when you hear the words "leader" and "manager?" If you're like most respondents to various research studies, chances are you came up with characteristics like self-reliant, forceful, independent, analytical, assertive, willing to take risks, ambitious, makes decisions.[15]

Now consider this: When both sexes are asked to list attributes that come to mind when they hear the words "man" and "woman," there's a strong correlation between those cited for "leader," "manager," and "man" and a very weak overlap with those cited for "woman." In fact, the attributes most often associated with "woman" are loyal, compassionate, sensitive to the needs of others, and understanding — adjectives that are conspicuously absent from the leader and manager lists.

Women find themselves in a Catch-22. If they don't act like men, they don't get recognized as leadership material. If they do, other types of derogatory adjectives that rhyme with that of Halloween characters begin to surface. *This* is the debate raging at the glass ceiling fault line.[16]

"I simply got tired of having to act like a man," declare women who left their corporate jobs to start their own businesses. Others who choose to stay are pressing for the freedom to be more authentic. According to Kathy Flanagan, an executive coach on issues of women and leadership, 82 percent of female leaders say that remaining true to themselves in their leadership role without losing credibility is a top issue. "Books with titles such as *Games Your Mother Never Taught You, Hardball for Women,* and *Why Good Girls Don't Get Ahead but Gutsy Girls Do* are being challenged by new titles such as *Success on Our Own Terms, Swim with the Dolphins,* and *Pitch like a Girl,*" says Flanagan.

Ironically, it turns out that what corporations need more than ever is more archetypically female traits. New leadership requirements differ greatly from the traditional male military model of command and control. In today's upside-down world, the upper echelons of organizations (and really throughout enterprises) need leaders who are team building, multitasking, consensus building, stress resisting, and employee developing dynamos. In a March 2011 Harvard Business Review piece entitled "The New Path to the C-Suite," authors Boris Groysberg,

L. Kevin Kelly, and Bryan MacDonald wrote that "today, technical and functional expertise matters less at the top than business acumen and soft leadership skills."[17] In several performance management studies, female managers outperform their male counterparts on a variety of criteria.[18] In her article, "Women Leaders: Strategic Yet Invisible Assets," Kira Porter makes the case for what she refers to as the "post-heroic model" of leadership that includes communication, emotional intelligence, collaboration, negotiation, entrepreneurship, coaching, and mentoring.[19] All are traits that tend to show up more consistently among women.

The need for female influence is even more urgent, given the increased complexity and surging globalization of the marketplace. Rethinking leadership models would not only multiply opportunities for women, it would actually strengthen the effectiveness of multinationals. The punch-in-the-gut barrier is the immediate, intuitive, preprogrammed response that Malcolm Gladwell talks about in his book *Blink*. These knee-jerk assumptions and decisions made without thinking often sabotage our best inclusive intentions. *To shatter the glass ceiling, therefore, it is imperative that corporations develop crosscultural competence to acknowledge and act on gender issues.*

Throughout this book, I make the case for crosscultural competence. This can also be applied to traversing gender differences. Until males come to understand that their concept of what makes a strong leader or manager is culturally determined by their experience as *males*, they will never see they are inadvertently stifling the upward arc of ambitious and talented women. Until then, they'll continue to perpetuate an assessment of leadership and management that creates more and more *people like them*. Not only do they need to recognize the subjectivity of their leadership model preference, they must develop the capacity to value leadership styles different from their own — *even when they don't understand them.* The global economy creates a new opening for this type of approach, since the same "untethering" from familiar assumptions is required to excel globally.

Now comes the gutsy part: What might leaders begin to hear as they open themselves to new voices and approaches?

Rethink the value of tenure.

The correlation between tenure and assumptions creates a dilemma for women who choose to leave the workforce in the early years of child-raising. When they return, an employer will often welcome them back. Yet they fail to acknowledge the perils of being out of the workforce for a few years, causing them to fall behind their — male and female — peers. In one of the most comprehensive writings on this issue, *The Hidden Brain Drain: Off-Ramps and On-Ramps in Women's Careers*, the authors lay out what they refer to as the "penalties" for taking time out.[20] While off-ramping only lasts an average of two years, women lost an average of 18 percent of their earning power. (When they off-ramp for three or more years, the figure rises to 37 percent.) So here's the brain-drain impact: 93 percent of the women currently off-ramped want to get back to work. But only 74 percent succeed in obtaining jobs and *only 5 percent* of women who on-ramp want to return to the company they used to work for.

While the Talent War for specialized skills is still hot even in a downturned economy, experienced female professionals are waiting on the sidelines ready to get back in the game, but for a different team. Yet the Talent War is only part of the challenge. Calling out differences among various groups — in this case, women — enables all employees to feel valued enough to give their best efforts. Corporations have a prime opportunity to strengthen their talent pipeline by staying in touch with their female alumnae and enticing them back. Let's keep looking at some of the things that could do just that.

Rethink compensation models.

"Several studies have shown that women are not motivated by the same competitive compensation structures as those that have traditionally appealed to men," says Flanagan. "They prefer to measure themselves against their own Personal Best standard." The securities industry bemoaned for years that they could not recruit or retain female brokers because many women didn't like the competitive, transaction-based reward system, she explains. Yet the industry did not adapt to this difference until external customer pressures drove it toward fee-based (relationship-centered) compensation. Only then did the industry begin to see significant advances in the recruitment, retention, and advancement of female financial advisors. And the industry profited. The adoption of innovative strategies enabled the financial services industry to forge robust relationships with both new and current customers, enriching its financial standing in the overall economy. Navigating the gap among cultural worldviews — including gender-based perspectives — made this all possible.

Across industries, similar questioning must take the place of deep-seated assumptions about what types of rewards will resonate deeply with women professionals. In studies and focus groups, women have made a number of things clear:

- Pay is not the greatest motivator
- Competitive compensation models don't attract
- Meaningful work pulls
- A sense of belonging is prized
- Long hours disengage

Somewhere in these declarations lies the path to new ways of rewarding women. (Don't be surprised if a good number of men ride these coattails.) And beware the dangerous paradox that women are not as driven by high pay as men. This should not become the subconscious rationalization for not addressing the closing of the wage gap.

Rethink whether competencies developed elsewhere are transferable to the workplace.

What lies behind the whopping drop in earnings for women who off-ramped, but now want to get back on-track? An assumption that none of the experience garnered during their time off the corporate track is of value to the business. The corporate world is quick to make correlations between sports leadership accomplishments and business leadership. Why not do the same for family-raising accomplishments?

Consider the competencies required to raise a family. The ability to manage multiple responsibilities is a must, especially for the sandwich generation, which cares not only for small children but aging parents as well. In our complex modern life, each home is an economic profit-and-loss center. Everyone is burdened with multilayered responsibilities around carefully planning for one's own retirement or managing one's own health. At the same time, today's increasingly multiracial/international families require complex problem-solving, project-planning, and crosscultural skills.

It's a mistake to assume that a woman's skills will get rusty during her off-ramp time. Instead, we should imagine a development planning session that takes place right before she goes on maternity leave. The goal would be to itemize some of the experiences during her corporate time off that will result in new — and needed — skills. Can corporations assign an economic value to those skills that would then be factored into the woman's compensation once she ramps back on?

Maybe we should raise the ante by saying we need to measure not only *women's* advancement, but also *mothers'* advancement. In looking at women in top roles, how many of them are mothers? The answer to this question could go a long way toward supporting the notion — and convincing corporate leaders — that being a mother is no more of a disadvantage than being a father.

"In fact, being a mother can be a big advantage in growing professionally," says Linda Mateja, formerly a senior corporate human resources leader at Hewitt. "People who stay home with kids still develop competencies that are applicable in the workplace. Examples could be negotiation skills, time management, 'project' planning, even presentation skills if they are active in community or school activities."

Women who become mothers are confronted with a variety of issues and situations that require them to become experts at time management and prioritization, not to mention compassion. Don't these skills translate accordingly into a workplace environment? Don't managers need to be able to manage their time effectively, prioritize tasks and responsibilities, and show empathy, support, and understanding to their colleagues and partners both inside and outside of the organization? These maternal skills translate perfectly in a corporate environment. In fact, many men — if they're able to adjust their traditional male-oriented perspective — could stand to learn a lot from working mothers.

In 2012, Yahoo's board was able to overcome any discomfort with the hiring of its new CEO Marissa Mayer, who was brought on board while she was pregnant. A first. The public scrutiny of Yahoo's selection at this stage of the Mayer's life belies the often non-discussed notion that pregnant women are a hire risk. Despite blogsphere howls about Mayer's short maternity leave, her willingness to accept the post and return quickly to work speaks volumes about her confidence and ability to handle multiple responsibilities. Her example is more than 20 years in time and mindset from the 1992 speech by then Ceridian CEO Lawrence Perlman that asked, "A Pregnant CEO: In Whose Lifetime?"[21] Clearly in his.

Rethink how unspoken rules around alternative work arrangements may be detrimental to women's advancement.

Much has been written on alternative work patterns, such as reduced-hour jobs, flex hours, job shares, and so on. Companies that provide these benefits rightly pride themselves on their progressiveness. Yet we must ask: Is there a hidden "penalty" career- and income-wise for those who take this route? Sure, there's a logic that "time equals money." But plenty of studies demonstrate that the quality of the time and *commitment* of the employee may actually mean more money than merely looking at *total* time.

Study after study has shown flexibility is one of the most valued benefits for a workforce dealing with greater complexity and greater opportunities in the various facets of their lives. In the "Off-Ramps, On-Ramps" report, 64 percent of women cite flexible work arrangements as being extremely or very important to them. Just 43 percent say earning a lot of money is an important motivating force. Then there's the cultural stigma many experience when taking advantage of corporate-approved job flexibility programs. Often, managers are not supportive, and coworkers are judgmental. While the economic equation of the value of time away from the corporation may be difficult to calculate, it's clear that addressing the stigma can go a long way toward retaining female talent.

Unprecedented Opportunity

The outlook may sound gloomy, but the situation is far from bleak — particularly if corporations play to their strengths. *Multinationals are one of the most significant change agents for the advancement of women around the world.* After so much pummeling for their mediocre advancement of women leaders, let's take a moment to praise multinationals for their transformative impact on women's roles both inside and outside the corporation. While it's true that corporations have a long way to go in furthering the advancement of women, there's no denying that multinationals have been an accelerating force in the overall advancement of women.

Multinationals, particularly those rooted in American and European contexts, come from a worldview of meritocracy. Those who are the best performers tend to reap the greatest rewards. Of course, when we look at the dearth of minorities and women in top leadership, it's clear that these very corporations have fallen way short of living up to their value of meritocracy. Nevertheless, that value is there and it's the epicenter on which we base our diversity case. However imperfectly this value is lived, it still is at work.

As discussed in Chapter 3, women in India and China have seen their fortunes change tremendously in recent years. The opportunity to acquire a job with a multinational and earn her own keep has given her significantly greater power. She can choose where she lives and who she marries — if she chooses to marry at all. Of course, now we're seeing glass-ceiling issues sprouting up in these emerging powerhouse economies, as women are still in that first phase of entering professional workplaces. Nevertheless, women's standing in these traditional societies is changing, fueled by a multinational appetite for talent.

Corporations don't like to think of themselves as social change agents. But their impact is undeniable in the new capitalist economies of India and China. By finding new ways to attract and retain female talent, corporations contribute not only to the enterprise's bottom line, but to the greater health of society at large. Isobel Coleman, director of the Council on Foreign Relations' Women and Foreign Policy program, makes the case in an article in Foreign Affairs. Companies that adopt practices and policies that empower women can expect to see "their labor forces become more productive, the quality of their global supply chains improves, and their customer bases expand."[22] She predicts that this movement could be "the greatest cultural shift of the 21st Century."

But here's the rub: As national policies and practices attempt to harness this undeniable female energy, nations and societies face real challenges balancing their economic desires while remaining true to their particular societies' cultural traditions. Let's look at just a few.

Latin America

In Latin America, appreciating diversity and preventing workplace discrimination are nascent concepts that in the past five years have gathered quite a bit of force. Creating awareness of why diversity is important is critical. Although many countries have legislation about workplace discrimination, policies have not been commonly enforced. Worldwide, women make up about 40 percent of the managerial ranks, but only about 30 percent in Latin America. There are significant gender gaps in pay and leadership positions, with some statistics showing a 20 percent pay differential and a 1:17 female-to-male ratio in top leadership positions.[23] In Colombia and Venezuela, women make up 40 percent of the workforce or university student bodies, but earn roughly 40 percent less than men.[24] Women also deal with pressure to take on the traditional roles of wife, mother, and family caregiver. Many women see such endeavors as incompatible with a high-powered career. Pregnancy-based sex discrimination often is an issue for women in lower socioeconomic groups. For example, companies that operate in free zones in the Dominican Republic routinely screen women for pregnancy. The results are used in hiring and firing decisions. The fact that this practice is illegal — and prohibited by many international human rights treaties — has done very little to change actual practices.[25]

There can be ways around the work-life dilemmas faced by women in Latin America. Companies willing to hold difficult discussions and open executive minds can find ways to resolve those challenges. Consider a Fortune 500 global engineering firm with a growing Latin American presence that wants to promote its women employees. Here's the rub: Such promotions will require relocation of these employees, many of whom are married with children and many of them were resisting, even refusing, the promotion due to the need to relocate.

The initial assumption was that the barrier to the move was their husbands. But rather than going with that assumption they tested it. Turns out that what was holding these women back was not primarily their husbands, but their obligation to her and her husband's parents – a twist on the traditional relocation challenge for companies and families. So new question: what if relocation also included moving the parents? Companies could relook at the costs of relocation since now families throughout Latin America are decreasing in size from four to two children. Why not use that demographic reality to then also include elderly parents in the definition of the "family" to relocate? This win-win scenario would allow dutiful daughters to maintain their caregiving roles while enabling companies to retain and advance top female talent.

Asia

While women make up 16 percent of U.S. Fortune 500 board positions,[26] this number is only 9 percent in Hong Kong Hang Seng Index companies.[27] In 2012, about a third of all complaints to Hong Kong's Equal Opportunities Commission involved sexual discrimination, with about 80 percent being pregnancy-related.[28] This may have to do with stronger traditional values, including women's role in the family.

In Japan, a law was passed in 1986 to ensure equal opportunity for men and women, but it was not binding and faced fierce opposition from employers. The law was amended in 1999 to become binding, but many women still encounter strong discrimination because of Japan's rigid gender roles and the belief that women should retire upon marriage. Systems to enforce the law have not been put in place, and women find themselves relegated to clerical work or assisting their male counterparts. In 2012, Japanese women held only 10 percent of managerial positions compared to 43 percent in the United States.[29] In Japan, women also receive lower salaries and fewer perks. As a result, more Japanese women are choosing to work for foreign companies where there's less discrimination.

Despite these ongoing challenges, today's young women in Asia, and particularly in China, are pressing to break out of their traditionally defined gender roles. I witnessed this phenomenon at a November 2011 forum on the advancement of women held in Shanghai, China, which was hosted by *Working Mother* Magazine and Diversity Best Practices. Forum participants were women who are on the forefront of a social and economic revolution. These women are changing China's social and economic gender script. "It's our time to rise up to the fullness of our potential," a participant said. "It's what women have always wanted to do—our great grandmothers, our grandmothers, our mothers— but for the first time not only do we have the actual economic opportunity due to China's growth, but we also have the social opportunity due to China's opening up to the West."

These corporate and entrepreneurial women are sprinting to make up for lost time. They are devouring leadership development, women's conferences, mentorships, and sponsorships to find answers to questions their elders never faced. For them, work-life balance is one of their greatest pressing issues, and they apply the same tenacity to figuring that out as they do toward corporate politics and opportunities. In the process, their power in intimate relationships with men is also changing. Asian women are assertively transforming their nation's economies and social structure.

The Middle East

Perhaps the greatest culture clash between traditional gender roles and the rising tide of female ambitions occurs in the Middle East. The Arab Spring focus on toppling oppressive dictators can't help but be accompanied by the rise of a new modern order that redefines the place of Arab women. Young men and women are seeking opportunities for education, economic advancement, and freedom of expression. The logical offspring of that movement is a secular fatwa against the oppression of women.

Westerners can be confused by the images beamed from that part of the world. Veiled women demanding freedoms – not from wearing the veil, but to be licensed to drive, to attend school, and to be gainfully employed – creates a kind of cognitive dissonance for Western mindsets. Is this revolution political, economic, or social? It's all three. By willingly wearing their veils, these women may be embracing their cultural identity, while sloughing off other oppressions, and declaring their freedom of personhood and global citizenship.

In 2012, a fourteen-year-old girl from Afghanistan, Malala Yousufzai shook up the region when she was shot by the Taliban after she blogged in defiance to the group's prohibition to girls being educated, "Where in the Quran does it say that girls should not be educated? I have the right to play. I have the right to sing. I have the right to go to market. I have the right to speak up."[30]

And guess what? As the Taliban looks to the future of Afghanistan and their role in it as the United States winds down the war there, they have given indications that they may grudgingly support Malala's point. This reluctance shows both how much more work lies ahead on women's rights in the Middle East, as well as that today, beneath the veil are increasingly assertive women seeking to swell their voices in the Arab uprisings.

Women's Rights As Human Rights

As women make increasing demands for social freedoms, educational access, job opportunities, and control of their minds and bodies around the world, their calls represent nothing short of national and international security issues. While she was U.S. Secretary of State from 2009 to early 2013, Hillary Clinton said, "What we are learning around the word is that if women are healthy and educated, their families will flourish. ... If women have a chance to work and earn as full and equal partners in society, their families will flourish. And when families flourish, communities and nations will flourish."

Too many women and their communities and nations are not taking advantage of the female energy within their borders. Even in the female-friendly 21st Century, women around the globe still are denied full human rights. Secretary Clinton has made advocating a women's agenda one of her touchstones in every one of the dozens of countries she visited during her tenure. Whether she was in Burma, the Congo, Iraq, Afghanistan, China, India or Haiti, Clinton talked about economic trade, terrorism threats, missile deployments, and always, the advancement of women.

Secretary Clinton was bolstered in these discussions by cold enduring facts. The lack of full human rights for women has economic consequences. Though women perform 66 percent of the world's work and produce 50 percent of the food, they earn 10 percent of the income and own 1 percent of the property.[31] The best investment for the developing world is in educating its girls. Educating girls yields a higher rate of return than any other investment – social or economic. Socially, educating girls leads to a host of positive results, from delayed marriage and childbearing to healthier pregnancies, families, and lowered infant mortality rates. Economically, giving girls access to education increases their future earnings from 10 to 25 percent. Just as in the developed world, educated mothers tend to ensure that their daughters attend school, which boosts their life circumstances, and leads to these girls growing up to push their daughters into better life situations that start with schooling.

Secretary Clinton punctuates her messages to world leaders this way: "Human rights are women's rights, and women's rights are human rights." These rights, which men can take for granted, extend from the geopolitical realm to the shop floor, cubicle farm, and the executive suite.

A Woman's Place ...

... is in leadership and valuable jobs contributing valuable work. From the onset of women's migration into the workforce, they've been transforming it. The first wave could be called *accommodation*. It resulted in anti sexual harassment policies, childcare, family leave, and flex time. The next phase is about *empowerment*. The voices from focus groups, surveys, statistics, speeches, and writings are clear: "Either we're more empowered within the corporation's structures or we'll channel our empowerment into running our own businesses."

We must also consider the marketplace impact of women executives leading organizations whose products cater specifically to women. "What we have seen is the evolution of the value of woman," *Working Mother* magazine's Carol Evans observes. "In the past, companies like Avon or Procter & Gamble had men in most executive and management roles, even though more than 80 percent of their customers were women. Leaders like A.G. Lafley of P&G and Jim Preston of Avon changed that equation, bringing women into all levels of leadership. Companies with predominantly female customers have often been in the forefront of the advancement of career women. Today, Avon and Xerox have had two back-to-back female CEOs. At Avon Andrea Jung and Sheri McCoy and at Xerox Anne Mulcahy and Ursula Burns. Procter & Gamble has had a powerful cadre of women general managers and presidents. All three of these companies have been named to the NAFE list of Top Companies for Executive Women many times.

Still, companies still need to make transformational changes to attract, develop, and retain female talent to break the glass ceiling. Managing consulting firm Deloitte stands tall as one of the pioneers in moving beyond best practices that were only achieving gradual change. Through the leadership of Cathy Benko, vice chairman and chief talent officer, and Anne Weisberg, director of talent organization, the company changed many of its practices and ways. As a result, their representation of women partners climbed from 10 percent in 1997 to 17 percent in 2003. For more on this effort see the sidebar below, "Deloitte Case Study: If You Want Breakthrough, Challenge Long-Held Assumptions."

Deloitte LLP Case Study: If You Want Breakthrough, Challenge Long-held Assumptions

It was the early 1990s when professional services firm Deloitte LLP began examining high turnover among its female professionals. After years of investing in its workforce, Deloitte was losing its women just at the point where their contributions were going to be most valuable and needed. To their surprise, the study upended the prevailing assumption that women were leaving the workforce to stay home with young children. Rather, women were opting to pursue opportunities that were equally rewarding, provided better opportunities for advancement, and helped them achieve a more satisfying work-life balance.

Leaders' alarm at this brain drain, combined with the belief they could find ways to counter it, led them to sponsor a high-profile initiative called the Initiative for the Retention and Advancement of Women or WIN. It was the first formal program dedicated to retaining and advancing women instituted by a professional services firm. As part of the program, Deloitte examined its workplace practices to see how gender attitudes affected the work environment. The result was a multi-pronged response, including a program called "Men and Women as Colleagues," which addressed gender awareness building. Deloitte also instituted career development and leadership programs, networking and mentoring activities, and work-life initiatives. These programmatic responses,

coupled with accountability measures for leadership, helped Deloitte succeed in virtually eliminating the gender gap in attrition. Bottom line when it comes to shattering the
glass ceiling? The percentage of women partners, principals, and directors at Deloitte
increased from 7 percent to 22 percent from 1993 to 2009.

Still, flexibility was an issue for both women and men. Here's where Chief Talent
Officer Cathy Benko decided to move beyond best practices. She challenged the very
notion of a corporate career ladder whose fundamental assumption ties advancement to
40 uninterrupted years of work with ever-increasing responsibilities. "This was a structural issue," says Anne Weisberg, a Director in Deloitte's talent organization who partnered with Benko on the initiative. "The one-size-fits-all model for building careers was
fitting fewer and fewer."

So the corporate ladder at Deloitte became the corporate lattice™. As described
more fully in Benko's and Weisberg's book, *Mass Career Customization: Aligning the
Workplace with Today's Non-traditional Workforce,* the transition from ladder to lattice
is enabled by a framework called mass career customization (MCC)™. This framework
allows all employees — in partnership with their managers — to identify options and
discuss tradeoffs associated with choices made along the four core dimensions of a
career: Pace, Workload, Location/Schedule, and Role. In this way, employees customize
their careers based on their career objectives and current life circumstances within the
context of the needs of the business.

This approach has added a layer of rigorous management to flexibility and proactive career pathing in a firm that had already adopted a culture of informal flexibility.

Today, mass career customization has been rolled out to nearly all of Deloitte's
roughly 38,000 U.S.-based employees and is currently being piloted in the firm's India
offices. As Sharon Allen, Deloitte's chairman, says, "A culture of flexibility is a tremendous competitive advantage, so we pioneered MCC. For companies, MCC fosters greater
loyalty and employee retention, and for employees, more satisfaction by being able to
fit their life into their work and their work into their life."

It's not only women who stand to gain if corporations heed this call. So will communities, men, and children. If corporations can unleash women's power, they'll
unleash greater corporate profits. And we men need to acknowledge how we've
benefited from women taking a stand on work-life balance. Because women took
the heat, it's become more acceptable for men to take time off to watch their
daughter's soccer game or visit their son's classroom. Thanks to women campaign-

ing for family-friendly benefits, working men are spending a great deal more time with their children than their fathers did. So our children are benefiting as well. Whether seeing Mom work, seeing her home life more valued, or just seeing more of Dad, the result is a generation of children with stronger role models of holistic success.

Before corporate leaders can rethink current practices and assumptions, before they can take advantage of the unprecedented opportunity in front of them, before they can truly open up women's place in leadership, they will have to acknowledge the very real and sometimes uncomfortable differences women bring to the workplace — differences that go beyond biology, but that could form some of the basis for women's alternative perspective on goals, behaviors, and motivations. Corporate leaders may have to encourage some culture-altering discussions around defining and meeting organizational needs. In other words, they will have to learn how to call out those differences and act on them.

Linda Mateja while at Hewitt saw other advantages to creating greater inclusion for women managers and leaders. "In light of the economy and emerging labor retention strategies, this may be a labor force where the cost management strategies of reduced and flexible hours, sabbaticals, job shares, etc., may actually lead to win-win results for both employees and companies. This could have the outcome of retaining a broader pool of labor into the future who may be seeking more freedom to more flexibly manage their time plus be more open to trade-offs for flexibility (for example, modified pay for more flexible hours, working fewer hours to help balance the corporate budget and provide work-life balance, etc.). Taking these approaches now may be key in bringing many back to the same company as the economy turns up as a payoff for having done relationship-building with their female talent."

In the Obama Era, more opportunities for women have been opening up as women have started demanding more for themselves and greater recognition for their contributions — not just as working mothers and care providers at home, but also as leaders in the competitive world of business and in the political arena. The 2012 elections swept a groundbreaking historic number of women into national office, with 20 in the Senate and more than 75 elected to the House. New Hampshire with its all female delegation stands as a testament to the growing recognition of the issues women face, and their willingness to flex their growing political clout with their votes.[32]

The President has been vocal about the need for helping women break through that glass ceiling and celebrating their contributions. In his white paper on working women cited at the beginning of this chapter, Obama wrote, "We have a chance to move America in a fundamentally different direction, and that starts with empowering women and strengthening families." (More on what has happened since in Chapter 14, "Work-Life Flexibility: The Mother of All Battles.")

Corporate authenticity, connection, contribution, and flexibility. This is what many female leaders say they want in the workplace. Such components will be key to creating the conditions that will lead to the greater advancement of women. For too long, contribution has come at the expense of authenticity. But no more.

Women are asking pointed questions like, "Why are the traits that got me up to a certain point in my career now the very things that are keeping me from advancing?" And they're saying, loud and clear, through both words and deeds, "I refuse to compromise who I am for preconceived notions of what I should be. Accept me as I am or I'll walk out the door." ♀

SUMMARY POINTS

- Women have revolutionized the workplace by their presence and perspective, skills, and demands. Yet for the most part, their contributions have not resulted in representation at the highest levels of organizations.
- Even when well-executed, strategies for moving women into leadership roles have proven inadequate for the task. We must move beyond best practices by adopting new paradigms to shatter the glass ceiling.
- There are five ways to move beyond best practices:
  - Rethink what strong leadership and strong management look like.
  - Rethink the value of tenure.
  - Rethink compensation models.
  - Rethink whether competencies developed elsewhere are transferable to the workplace.
  - Rethink how unspoken rules around alternative work arrangements may be detrimental to women's advancement and their full inclusion into organizational life.
- Organizations need archetypal female characteristics and gender differences. Others — including men, communities, and societies — have benefited from women's efforts to make the workplace adapt to their needs.
- Multinational organizations are one of the most significant change agents on the planet.
- The Obama Era coincides with a female-friendly 21st Century.
- Women's rights are human rights, and human rights are women's rights.
- Workplace flexibility benefits companies. It enables women, men, and their families to meet their responsibilities at home and at work.

SHAPING YOUR STRATEGY

- What is the actual representation of women at the executive and senior management ranks in your organization? How will you assess the pipeline of female talent to feed those roles? How much resistance do you think you'll encounter in trying to go beyond best practices in addressing some of these structural barriers to the full advancement of women?
- What can women do to increase their visibility and chances of advancement?
- What can men do to increase their visibility and chances of advancement?

Chapter 8

The Millennials:
Why This Generation Will Challenge
the Workplace Like No Other

We are not ready for our children to go to work.

I don't mean this in a protective, letting-go sense. But rather in a "my-God-what-have-we-done" sense, as we hire and manage our children's generation. Are they, and our workplaces, on a collision course?

Unlike the Boomer flower children, the iPod kids are not about the counter-culture. In fact, they *are* the culture. It is our workplaces that are out of sync with the new 24/7, global, plugged-in, downloading, computer-interfacing rhythms of the digital society.

A few years ago, as I watched my 16-year-old do her homework, I realized the future was already here. Here's what my blog entry then captured: "She taps away on her wireless laptop, linking to assignments from the teacher's Web site. Researching on Google, she copies and pastes quotes and stats into Word. 'Yes,' I think approvingly, 'this is what the wise use of technology should look like.' But, of course, there's more. She's got six IM chats open. A couple, thankfully, are about the homework and an upcoming dance recital. But others are about week-end plans, a hot movie, a cute boy. It's all topped off by a flaming session among the girls. At the same time, she's updating her profile on Facebook, downloading music, burning CDs — *and* talking on the phone."

"Marisela, are you doing your work?" I ask with that father-knows-best tone.

"Yes, Papi, don't worry."

"But what is the *quality* of that work?" I continue with furrowed brow.

"Papi, don't worry. It'll be fine."

And sure enough, it is, as that quintessential scorecard, the report card, shows. I can just see her and her classmates at their first job. They're outside catching some rays. They're on high-definition wireless laptops they've slipped out of their purses. They're shaping a client report while planning their service vacation to Costa Rica, doing their holiday shopping, updating their résumé on Monster, and catching up on the latest outrage on YouTube — and always with ever-present, multi-instant communication with coworkers, family, and friends around the world to the beat of background music by their favorite artists.

Sure enough, the judgments about this generation are flying: "Not serious about hard work." "Distracted." "Self-centered." "Not interested in learning from how things were done in the past." "Don't want to pay their dues." "They spend too much time online." "They want to be CEO in just five years." And so on.

As a diversity leader, I know that a telltale sign of inclusion breakdown is when judgments pop up unchallenged and groupthink sets in about the newcomer. When behaviors by others are different from behaviors we believe are right, we assume they either are incompetent or just bad people. This is now happening in reaction to the Millennials. As in other forms of diversity, this kind of stance is not only exclusionary, it's not helpful in addressing the real issues.

Generational diversity has become just as much an issue as gender and racial diversity. We must seek to resolve this divide — not only to nurture inclusive environments that enhance corporate culture and optimize results, but also because the workforce will need to adapt to the Millennials' way of doing things. Just by nature of who they are, this generation will transform the workplace. Already they're transforming the U.S. political landscape: The 25-and-under generation voted in very large numbers, making them a key factor in Obama's 2008 election.[1] Not only did they vote in large numbers for Obama (giving him a 34 percentage point advantage in 2008 and 23 percentage points in 2012), but on nearly every social issue (women's equality, LGBT rights, immigration, the environment, role of government) they were overwhelmingly on the opposite side from the older Boomer generation.[2] More than just a one-hit wonder, both the 2008 and 2012 elections illustrated the stark contrast of the generational divide between this generation and older Boomers. But it wasn't just their values and idealism, but also their technological savvy that allowed them to build a digital grassroots movement advocating for their beliefs. The Obama Era will be significantly shaped by this group, as their impact will be felt not only in the United States, but around the globe.

If today's world is virtual, 24/7, global, diverse, networked, and digital, this same description could also be used to describe the Millennials. This generation and the Obama Era are one and the same. For them, the upside-down world is right-side-up because it's what they grew up with. As candidate and president, in both the 2008 and 2012 elections, Obama has fully tapped into Millennials' energy and worldview — through his strategies and polices, as well as his operational plan that fully leaned into Web 2.0 social networking. Obama even inserted Millennial slang into his political observations when he referred to one of his opponent's positions as "sketchy." Obama's social contract with Millennials helped mobilize the most effective and far-reaching presidential election grassroots effort, breaking records in terms of volunteers, donations, calls made, and doors knocked on.

Culturally, this was not just an election phenomenon. It is a way of life. What we saw in terms of bottom-up mobilization and the ability to influence a major outcome is indicative of the kind of transformation Millennials will have on the workplace and the workforce.

Who Are the Millennials?

Not only is there a lack of agreement on what they should be called (Millennials, Generation Y, Gen Xers, Nexters, and Un-Baby Boomers, to name but a few), but there are also discrepancies as to the actual size of the population and the birth years that categorize them.

Is it 1978–1995, 1981–1993, or 1980–2000? Depending on the date ranges, the cohort number ranges from 70 to 80 million. Either way, these are teens and 20-somethings — the quibbles will continue with regard to how far into the 20s and how low into the teens one goes. Regardless of the exact dates and ages, this is a very large group. In the United States, it is just as large as the Boomers and a third larger than Xers (85 million vs. 61 million).[3]

The life events that have shaped this generation include 9/11, Oklahoma City, Columbine, global warming, AIDS, Katrina, Enron, the Iraq War, globalization, the digital revolution, a wildly fluctuating stock market, the rise of India and China, and an overall decline in the United States' stature. In the workplace, the Millennials are coming of age in an era when layoffs, merit pay, and merit promotions are the norm.

These headlines of death, destruction, and increased competition make Millennials very present about today, intent on enjoying every moment to the max. They are a pragmatic bunch. They know their work arrangements are transactional and they must be prepared to move on when the deal no longer works for them — or their employer. At the same time, they are also more socially and environmentally conscious. Given the uncertainty both in the workplace and in the world, many Millennials place friends, family, and the community ahead of work.

A Special Relationship With Parents

Many Millennials grew up in hectic, dual-career households that tended to be more child-centric, with both mothers *and* fathers heavily involved with the kids. The relationship between Millennials and their parents is unprecedented. According to research compiled by Tamara Erickson of the Concourse Institute, 90 percent of Millennials report being very close to their parents. Compare that to 40 percent of Boomers who said back in the 1970s they would be better off *without* their parents! Millennials see their parents as role models. This translates into them trusting authority (parents 86 percent, teachers 86 percent, police 83 percent). With this closeness, many have become equal partners in family decisions, such as where to go on vacation or where to make major purchases like the new flat-screen TV, hybrid car, or dog.[4] Working Mother Media's CEO Carol Evans says, "We Boomers rebelled against our parents. Now as parents ourselves, we have vowed to not let social change become a barrier between us and our children."[5]

Millennial children are reciprocating by reaching out to their parents for help with their own major decisions. Parents get extremely involved in college applications and even in their child's job searches, earning the moniker of "helicopter parents" for their tendency to hover. Nevertheless, Millennials expect to stay close. To the chagrin of many parents, they're open to moving back home after college. Marrying later and being more deeply in debt earlier make living at home more appealing to Millennials, as they struggle to pay down both credit cards and tuition.

Diverse and Global

The Millennials are highly diverse. Among people 18 and under, nearly 40 percent report being racial or ethnic minorities, compared to 10 percent[6] of their parents' generation. For Millennial women, college is not only an option, it's an expectation. So, too, are they expected to compete equally with men for any job. And homosexuality is not a big deal for Millennials. Not only are teens more comfortable coming out, most find they're accepted by many of their peers. My daughter, in fact, assuaged my boy wariness by telling me about certain guys, "Don't worry, Papi, he's gay!"

Among my daughter's peers, global experience is common. Marisela spent six months in Lima, Peru, during her high school sophomore year, and her friend Rebecca spent a summer with her Argentinean relatives in Buenos Aires. Anna went on a multi-week service trip to Ecuador. Paulina traveled with her grandma to the Czech Republic and participated in a ceremony where she carried a Holocaust Torah back to its original synagogue home.

Our kids' global network extends through their digital network. Text messages fly between a café in Miraflores, Peru, and our car, as we drive along I-80 on our way to visit relatives in Kansas. Webcam chats not only allow for keeping in touch, but also for introducing friends to one another. Skype calls simultaneously connect family and friends in Guadalajara, Simi Valley, Miami, Chicago, San Diego, and Lima.

Millennials are emerging as the first truly global culture. Globalization supported by technology means a shared experience through world events like the rise of global terrorism, the acceleration of global warming, and the hyperlinking of the global economy. Meanwhile, technology, such as iTunes and smartphones, has also played a role in shaping Millennials' worldviews and how they think, play, and work.

How Millennials Are Challenging the Workplace

Who Millennials are affects what they're looking for in an employer. And they're looking continually. According to an Addecco Group study, in the two years from 2008 to 2010, the percentage of Millennials who looked for a new job more than doubled (14 percent to 30 percent) with more than half (51 percent) engaged in the interview phase of the job search.[7]

In the midst of the Talent War and as the economy recovers, this is worrisome. For organizations that traditionally attract and/or rely on a younger workforce, getting it right with Millennials is a matter of economic life and death.

This younger generation comes through the door more restless than ever. They want to be valued, put to work, rewarded, and affirmed from the get-go. Already, they are challenging the workplace in many ways:

They challenge the tenure paradigm. Experience and knowledge are no longer correlated with age, they argue, as they show up iPaded, smartphoned, globally traveled, socially networked, and multi-tasked. For the older generation, this is not just about being up to date with "what kids are up to nowadays" but about the very competencies and technical skills demanded by today's marketplace. Who is better equipped?

They challenge best practices mentality. Globalization and the technology that enabled it have been paradigm-busters that are not yet finished in changing the rules of the game. The power of Millennials rides on the speed at which knowledge doubles. It used to take centuries, now it takes months. The Boomer approach of "let me show you the best practices forged over time" is doomed to obsolescence simply because those practices worked *in the past*...and here the past is defined as early in the previous season of *Modern Family*. Millennials operate in a just-in-time mode where a "best practice" lasts only as long as the project.

They challenge traditional planning. Millennials live synchronous lives where inputs come from all over at all times and decisions are made accordingly. They coordinate, not plan. In a multitasking, hyper-connected, 24/7 world, "plans" don't hold up. I watched my daughter and friends coordinate where to meet on a Saturday night. When I was growing up it was, "Meet you at 7 p.m. in front of the bakery next to the movie theater. I'll wait for you for 15 minutes. If we don't meet up, then plan B is...." For her it's, "See you around 7 p.m. downtown." And then, at around 7 o'clock, "I'm downtown — where are you?" "Walking up the side street with the crazy mannequins." "Okay, I'll start walking there. Call me when you get to the fountain." Moments later, "Hey, we just ran into Ricardo before we got to the fountain. We are now by the ice cream place, meet us there...." This is how they're going to manage their projects in the workplace. Are you ready?

They challenge being told what to do. They want to be empowered: "Give us a problem to be solved and the right tools," they say, "and we'll figure it out." Paradoxically — and this may be due to their better relationships with parents — they want to be coached and mentored when needed. They want to be both autono-mous and connected at the same time. Command-and-control management is out. Coaching and collaborative management are in.

They challenge rigidity in time, space, job, and career. "Where and when we work should not matter, as long as the work gets done," they declare. "Connecting, even thousands of miles away, is as easy as connecting face-to-face. In fact, it's even better because we can all be in more places at once. Who I am, what I do, and the jobs and careers around me need to evolve iteratively and continuously, like soft-ware version releases." How will MyJob 1.0 evolve into MyJob 2.0? 5.3? 7.9?

How Corporations can Prepare and Change

Given these urgent challenges, current corporate philosophies, practices, and poli-cies will not suffice when it comes to attracting, engaging, and retaining this gen-eration. That's why I believe this generation will challenge the workforce like no other. Current people practices were designed during a very different era. So much of what is reality today did not exist when today's people practices were designed. Benefits, performance management systems, and corporate cultures were designed to solve a different set of needs and problems for a very different workforce.

Corporations need to start making some fundamental changes.

But in making these changes, corporations must never lose sight of the contribu-tions of the Boomers and Gen Xers. If the concerns of these older generations are not validated and addressed, corporations run the risk of alienating them. This leads to disharmony and a lack of willingness on their part to work constructively with the Millennials who are flooding the workplace. Millennials, in turn, must be open to the ideas of their predecessors and willing to work with them accordingly.

Boomers tend to approach their work like an assembly line approach, han-dling a specific task or project sequentially, perfecting each piece as it goes along and then only adding to it once each module is in tip-top form. To a Boomer, quality is a product of several sequential pieces that is not to be shared with any-one — let alone managers — until the very end. Given their familiarity with the World Wide Web, Millennials don't work sequentially, but rather synchronously. To a Millennial, quality is iterative. They demand feedback on each piece along the way, a little bit of encouragement so they know they're on the right path rather than waiting till the end to be told that more needs to be done.

If they're willing to listen, Boomers can greatly benefit from Millennials' technological prowess. But, in turn, Millennials can also learn from the experiences Boomers have acquired over the years.

While much has been written about the potential conflicts between Boomers and Millennials, little has been said about what Gen Xers can do to bridge this disparity or what all three generations can learn from each other. Given their closer proximity in age to the Millennials, Gen Xers are in a unique position to gain their ear and serve as mediators in this discussion. Gen Xers came of age during the rise of the post-modern world that has been the Millennials' only experience. Gen Xers exist at the crossroads between the traditional "this is the right way to go about doing things because this is how it's always been done" viewpoint of the Boomer and the more task-oriented, "give me feedback now," multitasking technologically savvy approach of the Millennial.

Millennials bring much energy and idealism to the corporate environment. However, they mustn't mistake their technical competence for experience. Indeed, their greatest weakness is their lack of experience. But what perhaps makes them even more vulnerable is their reliance on multitasking. They pride themselves on their ability to work on different projects simultaneously, but in doing so, they run the risk of not delving as deeply or completely into a project as may be required. Also a cumulative number of research studies are clearly showing that our brains really can't handle true simultaneous multitasking which is proven by the high number of accidents due to texting and driving. They also show that our productivity may actually go down.[8]

Each generation needs to listen to and respect the differing perspectives and experiences each brings to the table. If Boomers learn to appreciate that Millennials' contributions can benefit them and vice versa, then the overall effectiveness and output of an organization can increase tenfold: a win-win situation for everyone, regardless of age or work experience.

Let's take a look at some of these win-win benefits.

Create Designer Jobs, Careers, Benefits

Millennials don't get "standard." All their lives, they've been able to design everything — from travel experiences (extreme mountain biking in the Andes during the day, white tablecloth dinner at night) to tennis shoes (color, shapes, favorite saying stamped on the heel), to musical set lists (Shakira, Tony Bennett, Snoop

Dogg, all on one custom-burned CD).

This is fueled by three trends: technology, rapid change, and diversity. *Technology* enables a cost-effective way to customize products and services. *Rapid change* makes yesterday's standard antiquated. *Diversity* generates demand for multiple types of solutions — not only from the perspective of race/ethnicity, gender, and nationality, but also in terms of personality, thinking styles, and even hobbies. MySpace, MyYahoo, MyObama are only the beginning. Here come MyJob, MyCareer, MyBenefits. In this universe, time and place are not fixed. They bend, flex, blur into different dimensions that dislocate fixed structures.

Designer Benefits

Much like the Millennials busted up the paradigm that an artist or producer determines the music set list through a mass-produced CD, I believe they'll reject corporations that seek to determine their "set list" of benefits. What would be value-added for the programmer, financial analyst, or communicator who also happens to be a marathon runner, social services volunteer, or community thespian? To provide value to Millennials, benefits must address the needs of a culturally, racially/ethnically diverse generation that is virtual, autonomous, empowered, and continually digitally connected and has a multiplicity of worldviews around money, health, and success.[9]

Fixed benefits plans (even those with limited flexibility provided by cafeteria style design) will not be able to withstand these pressures and demands. Corporations must give up trying to figure out what's best for their employees within the fixed categories of health, wealth, and paid time off. Indeed, they would do well to emulate the new iTunes paradigm, which shattered the model of buying fixed set lists and reduced music purchasing to the basic unit of a song.

"Give us a budget and diverse options and we will decide what best enables our multifaceted lives," Millennials are saying. Think of the possibilities. Instead of a free physical, the 20-something may opt to take credits for solar-powering their homes or buying a hybrid car. Others may prefer to subscribe to short-term paid sabbaticals every six months. Still others may take a $500 credit at a camping retailer to fund their adventure travel or a paid community service day twice a month.

Corporations still have fiduciary responsibility, of course. Companies may want to require that at least 20 percent of employees' MyBenefits goes to catastrophic health insurance. Or they may employ automatic enrollment in their 401(k) plans and then empower employees to either continue in the plan or opt out.

Organizations must pay close attention to the interface necessary to enable these options. Content is important, but for Millennials, the interface is everything. If it doesn't sing, they will abandon it. The iTunes 99-cent one-song paradigm is brilliant, but it's the clean, attractive, easy-to-use interface that enabled the revolution. As people make more and more complex decisions, Millennials will value smart-decision support tools, particularly when they're offered in the spirit of coaching and mentoring. When I was at Hewitt we began at that time to move in this direction via a benefits delivery interface called People Like Me™. It provides decision support about what choices may work best for individual users by pulling up the stories of people in similar circumstances and with comparable backgrounds.

Designer Jobs and Careers

The job is dead! Long live the job! Jobs that look the same day after day, fixed in their definitions of roles and responsibilities, must go. For Millennials, the job experience must match the fast-moving, connected, iterative world in which they live. In fact, project-based work may better suit their restlessness. Millennials will be seek employers who have designed jobs to be broken into pieces or modules that can be easily manipulated into nonstandard work arrangements. What's more, they will expect to choose whom they work with across functions, geographies, and organizations.

Consider what kind of job Leah Campbell, a colleague's college-aged daughter, would have looked for. At Wesleyan University, she made up her own major, "Embodiment Studies." In order to better understand interpersonal and intercultural dynamics, she explored "how people move through the sociophysical environment, between individuals and among groups, in ways that distinguish, excite, blur, and uphold their conceptions of self-identity." Her course work included cultural studies, dance, architecture, psychology, philosophy, and anthropology.[10] Surely she, and many of her peers, have carried this drive for self-expression and meaningful relational thinking into their job expectations.

Organizations must create a process and interface for making individuals aware of available projects for which they can compete. Granted, job candidates will need to meet criteria for competencies and technical skills. But rather than living in a fixed job description, their competencies will be seen as portable from project-to-project. Clearly, some jobs are more conducive to this portability than others. But organizations must be careful not to get stuck in assumptions about what may or may not work.

These designer jobs should be shaped to offer meaning, as Millennials pursue a portfolio of diverse concerns: career, family, planet. In their commitment to a greener, safer, more progressive world, Millennials desire employers who share their philosophy of balancing hard work with having fun and giving back. This is not just about flexibility to take time off and pursue interests outside of work. It's about finding ways for the work itself to be more meaningful.

This can come in two different flavors: jobs that are advertised as contributing something tangible for the betterment of the world (developing medical devices for improving quality of life or green solutions that improve the environment) and jobs where the core skills and competencies can be devoted to improving humanity. Give engineers a percentage of time during which they can work on pro bono side projects, for example. How do you fund such programs? In focus groups I've conducted, Millennials have indicated they're willing to make trad-eoffs, such as a reduction in pay, in order to better live their values.

Designer jobs, of course, take us to designer careers for many of the same reasons. Wanting to save the planet, conquer Machu Picchu, or just do something different will take Millennials on what could seem like circuitous career paths. Corporations will not only have to offer greater flexibility for them to do this, but also not view these pursuits as detours but rather as opportunities for developing leadership skills and job competencies. And beware: Millennials are not the only people pushing this button. Already a growing number of working mothers and fathers want to off-ramp for a few months or years to raise their children, and then ramp back on without a sense that they're now forever in the corporate slow lane.

Can career maps be embedded with the developmental and experiential value of stepping out into a great new adventure — whether it be parenting, community development, or trekking in the Andes? In the midst of a Talent War, wouldn't companies want to find ways to nurture their growing alumni network as an already-developed talent pool that they can tap?

Create a Culture of Continuous Coaching, Support, and Collaboration

Provide Continuous Feedback

Accustomed to instant metrics on the Web (YouTube views, Amazon rankings, instant poll questions — "Who will win the election?" "Should paparazzi stop hounding Britney?"), Millennials expect to know at every moment how they're performing — but without too much analysis. Thumbs up/thumbs down will suffice, as they glance up from texting on their smartphones. And don't wait until the yearly review to tell them how they're doing!

A legacy of constant parental praise means Millennials expect attention. Mentors and managers who coach, rather than give directives, are welcome. Managers who give Millennials ownership of projects (whole or in part), along with the freedom to decide how to do their work, all the while staying constantly in touch (albeit unobtrusively) will motivate and get the best out of their young workers.

This is not an idealistic or cynical crowd. Above all, they are pragmatic. They are task-based rather than process-oriented. Instead of explaining best practices or spending too much time on upfront training, give them the opportunity to make important contributions from Day One. Get them started right away, with objectives to achieve and great technological tools to use. In their horizontal, flat world, they will find each other, share lines of code, URLs, e-mails, videos, photos, and Web sites to find solutions and accelerate goal achievement dramatically.

Employers will also do well by giving Millennials markers of achievement — frequently attainable goals and milestones, titles, new responsibilities, and small but frequent promotions. The days of pay broadbanding structures — that have workers slogging through vast expanses of time before a promotion is attained — are over.

Create Ultra-Collaborative Environments

In the Millennial social nerve center, all team members are connected to one another through texting, cell phones, e-mail, social networking pages, and mass media. Problem-solving is a group effort, particularly since today's technology makes instant collaboration possible. In helping a friend from Peru find colleges to attend in the United States, my daughter and her friend are connected via Skype and webcam. They surf the Web together and send each other links. They download media players and java scripts and watch campus orientation videos, while filling out forms and e-mailing them to each other. The thousands of miles between them are irrelevant. This kind of ultra-collaboration need not take place between just a few individuals or even many individuals within an organization. It's also possible with competitors, customers, and academics — even with avatars, virtual entities created by real people, but who have their own names and identities.

In *Wikinomics: How Mass Collaboration Changes Everything*, authors Don Tapscott and Anthony Williams show how masses of people are creating TV news stories, sequencing the human genome, remixing their favorite music, designing software, finding a cure for disease, editing school texts, inventing new cosmetics, and writing the global encyclopedia, Wikipedia.[11] The blogosphere is teeming with voices bouncing ideas, criticism, and opinions off each other in an ever-present, hyperkinetic fashion that accelerates the development of new ideas, products, and services which are then instantly disseminated globally.

Among its hundreds of case studies, *Wikinomics* shares the story of the Geek Squad, Best Buy's electronics and computer support service. One Geek Squad manager uses multiplayer games, such as Battlefield 2, for members to exchange best practices and solve problems. While inside the game, Geek Squad members intersperse fights with quick exchanges to solving clients' problems. They play, talk, and demo their solutions to each another, networking simultaneously — sometimes with as many as 384 members at a time. This mass collaboration has improved on-the-job performance by keeping members connected. In the process, it's helped deliver $280 million to the bottom line.[12]

At Hewitt, when he was CEO, Russ Fradin's blog allowed anyone across a global talent base of nearly 25,000 to reply with affirmations, challenges, and new ideas. This mass collaboration between the CEO and frontline employees led to changes in policies and programs.

Mass collaboration requires greater transparency and less spin. After all, things can't be hidden when thousands are connected. Hierarchy and control are no longer tenable in the same way as before. It may not be long before we see thousands of employees writing policies, co-creating with customers, and defining a company's best practices.

Develop Intergenerational Crosscultural Competence

In researching this chapter, I conducted separate focus groups with Millennials, Xers, and Boomers. As predicted, judgments fly when people are not crossculturally competent — in this case about differences in generational worldviews. One participant commented, "As an Xer myself, I find many of the Millennials I've encountered kind of repellent — rude, bossy, disrespectful, etc. — which I think a lot of people my age and older feel about the emergent generation." She went on to say that she needed tools to "help me better interact with these kids."

Among Boomers, there was clearly a deep divide between those who seemed to share this sentiment and those who were adapting their styles to get the most of their Millennials by engaging and learning from them.

A few of those learnings go beyond the well-worn "Well, they can teach us about technology."

Gimme feedback. "These Millennials want feedback all the time!" a Boomer manager complains. "We have a hard enough time doing it once a year, what with the 360-degree feedback requests, compiling the inputs, pulling it all into a well written assessment form." When I share this sentiment with the Millennial group, they respond, "Oh, they don't understand! We're asking for feedback in the lunch line!" Millennials are saying they can do with a 30-second, thumbs up or thumbs down, checklist-type assessment done on-the-fly while going through the salad bar or on the way to the elevator. Managers who master this type of feedback often get strong reviews from Millennials.

Smartphones: Privilege or basic tool? When it comes to company policies tying technological tools to pay grades or job titles, "it just doesn't make sense that you only get an iPhone when you reach a certain level in the organization," one 20-something said. "This is as much a daily business tool as the phone is — and we can be so much more productive if we had the right tools, the tools we grew up with. They're not parceling out landline phones just to managers, are they? Why should a smartphone be any different? I have an iPhone for my personal life. Why can't I have one for my professional life?"

You call that quality? Then there were the clashing worldviews around the interpretation of quality. Boomers were brought up with the technological paradigm of the assembly line — a sequential process where each step is an additive improvement and the product is not presented for evaluation until it comes out perfect at the other end of the line. "We learned to dot our i's and cross our t's," one Boomer remarked as she went on to describe the state of the output she received from the Millennials reporting to her: "It's incomplete. With typos. Half thought-out. I don't get why the work is so shoddy!"

In talking this through with the Millennials, it's clear their worldview is shaped by a different technological paradigm, the Internet — a nonsequential, synchronous process where multiple points lead to one point, and one point can lead to multiple points. The creation process is iterative and continuous. With three clicks on Facebook, one *publishes* a home page that invites friends to comment. The work is far from complete, but ready for interaction as the members of the network comment, send links to their favorite songs, pictures, or YouTube videos. "Our point of view is that in order to achieve quality, you have to show things as you're building them. Otherwise, you're going to spend a lot of time on a product that may turn out not to meet the need. Better to get the input early on throughout the process rather than after it's completed."

Reciprocal learning. Of course, Millennials have plenty to learn from Boomers and Xers. In our upside-down world, youth may actually mean more experience in certain things, but there is still the reality and power of actual life and work experience to distill wisdom, soften one's bravado. Millennials need that. As a Millennial male focus group member explained, "At some point, we need to face reality … no one is going to put me in charge on my first day, nor should they." There was acknowledgment that the newest approach to an issue is not always the best one. Group members understood there can be benefits to doing things in established ways.

"The thought of clocking in with face time at the office is my kryptonite," said one female Millennial focus group member. "But there has to be a balance between what we're looking for in autonomy and micromanagement. We don't want to be micromanaged, but at the same time we're looking for someone to provide coaching and advice and serve as a mentor." Another explained that Millennials want to make their own mistakes and learn from them.

Not content simply to throw stones at older generations, the majority sentiment in the Millennial focus groups was of wanting to work with them. They seemed to understand the diversity and inclusion imperative of needing each others' differences and the synergy that kind of collaboration offers. And Millennials remain optimistically pragmatic about the need for all generations to work together. "The company that can master that synergy could really use it as a competitive advantage in the marketplace," said one. The global medical technology firm Becton, Dickinson and Company is explicitly seeking to achieve this through an intergenerational affinity group called Network XYZ.

Melissa Giovagnoli, founder of Networlding and a thought leader in social networking marketing and community, throws out this suggestion: "Organizations should consider a high-profile contest for the best intergenerational collaboration initiative resulting in a new product, service, or process improvement."

Sidelined Xers? In this discussion, Xers felt somewhat on the sidelines. Some felt the Millennials were getting too much attention or that too much was being made of their differences. The challenge for Xers is twofold. Demographically they're a significantly smaller cohort — just a tad more than 60 million versus roughly 85 million Millennials and 81 million Boomers.[13] But they also are experiencing the very real dynamics of being the transitional generation. Xers were brought up by Boomer parents and became digital in their teens and 20s. Millennials, on the other hand, grew up in a digital, global, terrorism-threat environment that fully shaped their experiences, making their worldviews stand in stark contrast with their Boomer managers.

But rather than a detriment, Xers can lean into these realities to enhance their influence. Because they are indeed the generation in the middle, they, more than anyone else, understand what it's like to navigate through a major historical paradigm shift. They have straddled the transition from modernism to postmodernism. They can talk both Boomer and Millennial language. The challenge for them is whether they get stuck in resentment or move on to being influential brokers.

A Final Word

To create collaborative environments, organizations must focus attention on diversity and inclusion, equipping individuals and organizations to navigate differences. Building crosscultural competence across all workers is vital. In my crosscultural work, I advocate for reciprocal adaptation. The trick for Boomers, Xers, and Millennials is to stop judging each other and start valuing what each brings to the table. Creating a productive and winning enterprise means moving from "I tolerate your difference" to "I need your difference — and you need mine. Together let's solve the world's problems."

With every new wave — whether within the worlds of art, business, technology, or politics — there is resistance. Newcomers with new ideas invite skepticism and balking. This time it's the youth who are crashing the party. The Millennials are in the building.

RUUP4IT?[14] ♀

SUMMARY POINTS

- While some Millennial characteristics have to do with the common dynamics of youth, others are the result of unique, cultural, historic, political, and economic realities that have shaped their worldview.
- The younger generation comes through the door more restless than ever. They want to be valued, put to work, rewarded, and affirmed from the get-go.
- Jobs that look the same day after day — fixed in their definitions of roles and responsibilities — must go. Millennials desire job experiences that match the fast-moving, connected, iterative world in which they live. They will seek out employers who have designed jobs to be broken into pieces or modules that can be easily manipulated into nonstandard work arrangements.
- Millennials expect to know how they're performing at every moment, but without too much analysis.
- Rather than judging each other for their particular ways of doing things, Millennials, Xers, and Boomers should recognize each group has perspectives that each can benefit from.

SHAPING YOUR STRATEGY

- How are Millennials behaving in your work environment? How much acceptance or resistance are they finding on the part of the Boomers and Xers?
- Are your corporate policies and philosophies in alignment with or in opposition to the Millennial way of operating?
- If there are barriers, how can you begin to initiate to influence the change?
- What guidance and perspective can you offer Boomer managers about how to get the most out of their Millennial workforce?
- How is your Xer population feeling about intergenerational dynamics and how can you tap into their unique perspectives to generate greater intergenerational inclusion?

THE DIVERSITY ISSUE WE FEAR THE MOST

ability

Chapter 9

Disability: The Diversity
Issue We Fear the Most

It took only four seconds for John Vcelka's life to change forever. The five-foot-ten, athletic, rock-climbing, river-rafting, volleyball-playing 34-year-old skied into a tree going 40 miles per hour. His skull cracked, his left shoulder shattered, and his spine fractured. Airlifted by helicopter off Breckenridge Mountain and flown to Swedish Hospital in Englewood, Colorado, his battered body clung to life, breath by labored breath. By the time he was wheeled out of the operating room 12 hours later, John was alive, but with a bed-ridden, never-walk-or-talk-again prognosis. At the apex of his youthful vigor, John was disabled. Life as he knew it was over.

Or was it?

Stories like John's scare us. Like many, I thrive on intellectual challenges and work, but the pleasure of dancing with my wife, kicking a soccer ball with friends, or catching a wave on an emerald blue sea are how I experience living with vitality and joy. The fear of losing the ability to physically do the things we love is common. So are the myriad misconceptions that tag along with this fear.

Not only is this fear prevalent in society and workplaces, it's something even diversity practitioners struggle to address. Is it any coincidence that disability is the most neglected diversity issue in our organizations? Although we often include the concept in our one-word definition of diversity *(raceethnicitygen-*

dersexualorientationdisability), the issue of disability rarely shows up, even in a token way, when we design diversity and inclusion conferences, invite speakers, and develop enterprise-wide inclusion strategies.

As diversity professionals, we're good at converting dismay over a long-neglected issue into passionate advocacy and effective programs. But when it comes to disability, we've been passive. "If I'm in a diversity conference and some-one even mentions disability, it catches my ear because it so seldom happens," says Deb Dagit, recently retired vice president, diversity and work environment at Merck. This is our collective shame.

Dagit goes back to the early days of diversity efforts in the '70s and '80s, when it was extremely difficult to talk about race. "You couldn't be a good diversity leader if you had not crawled through the broken glass of all the programming you were subjected to, from the time you were a child, about people from different races. We've had to also face our fears in terms of gender, faith, and sexual orien-tation. To do so, we attended hundreds of workshops, read multiple books, and entered into one-on-one mentoring, courageous conversations, and just painful self-examinations. But we've yet to do this with disability." Dagit's disheartened by the many master diversity trainers who have told her how proud they were to be able to look at a person with a disability and not run away. "That's how bad it is … that they feel they've made great strides if they can just stay in the presence of someone with a disability."

Our inaction stems from our fear — fueled by the unknown, usually marked by misinformation about those who are different. As always, naming and facing the fear must be our starting point. Much of our work, then, is to confront this fear by deflating negative stereotypes and smashing common misconceptions about disability. Misguided views diminish us all.

Before going further, let's not assume we even have a common understand-ing of what we mean by "disability." What is disability? Is disability a handicap recognized by law? Is it something you are born with? The result of an illness or accident? Is it physical, mental, or both? Are aging or obesity disabilities? The answer is important because using all of these definitions, one in five Americans (57 million) has some form of disability, making this the largest minority group.[1] Globally the number is 1.1 billion.[2]

Various demographic issues will increase this number significantly, making it one of the most important emerging diversity issues in the workplace. For one, a majority of aging Baby Boomers (69 percent) plan to continue working past retirement, either because they simply want to keep busy or they can't afford to stop working.[3] That's significant because 30 percent of the U.S. population between the ages of 55 and 64 is disabled.[4] Then there are the veterans returning from the Iraq and Afghanistan wars. Nearly 45 percent of the 1.6 million veterans from those two wars are filing for disability benefits.[5] All told, 3.5 million of the 21.5 million U.S. veterans have a disability.[6]

Disability also intersects with other diversity issues. A cumulative effect of racism, sexism, and able-ism compounds the challenge. Around 20 percent of African-Americans have a disability, making them the group with the highest incidence.[7]

Some other statistics to consider: Fewer than half (41 percent) of people with a disability between the ages of 21 and 64 are employed. People with a non-severe disability are less likely to be employed than those with no disability — 75 percent to 83.5 percent, respectively. Not surprisingly, individuals reporting a severe disability are the least likely to be employed (28 percent).[8] Only 15.5 percent of those with a severe disability work full-time, compared to 63 percent of people with no disability and 48 percent of those with a non-severe disability. More than two-thirds (69.5 percent) of people with a severe disability are not employed at all, compared with 25 percent of people with a non-severe disability and 16.5 percent of people with no disability.[9] In the midst of a war for talent, we must keep in mind that 65 to 70 percent of people with disabilities of working age (16–64) are either unemployed or underemployed.[10]

In this chapter, I explore the roots of our underlying fear, address common misconceptions, answer questions many have been hesitant to ask, and share ways we can proactively address disability diversity.

Roots of the Fear

Why the fear? I believe it's because disability is the one diversity category that any of us, if not already in it, can join, either through an accident or by merely getting older — one is a possibility and the other is an eventuality few like to talk about.

"It's not like it's possible for me to one day wake up as a person of color," says Marca Bristo, president and CEO of Access Living, a disability civil rights and empowerment organization in Chicago. Bristo herself is in a wheelchair due to a diving accident. As happened to John Vcelka, just four seconds could separate any of us from becoming part of a group that previously seemed to have nothing to do with us.

Vcelka explains the discomfort expressed by able-bodied people he encounters: "I've found that there are three types of reactions to me being in a wheelchair. There are those who simply can't bear it and avoid acknowledging the disability, often by avoiding me. There are those who call out my condition, 'Oh, my gosh! How are you doing … is there anything you need?' And then there are the people who will say 'Hi' or whatever and interact with me as if they would with anyone else."

He explains that after the accident, most of his able-bodied friends, the ones that he spent time with regularly, drifted away. "It was not from a lack of attempts on their part, but as they visited me, they would say, 'I can't see you in a wheelchair.' What I came to realize was that it was true — it wasn't me they were seeing in the wheelchair. They were seeing themselves. They kept imagining that if they had gone through a similar injury, they wouldn't be able to cope with it." So, with excuses of being busy, the visits stopped and long-standing friendships withered.

Dagit, who is short-statured and uses a cane due to a genetic bone condition, brings up another dimension. "In my global diversity work, it's remarkable how consistently, across cultures, disability is viewed as some kind of punishment for an individual or a family due to past sins. Paradoxically, it's often also seen as evidence they're special, here to teach us special things around miracles, around the meaning of life. But in that specialness, they're set apart and not mainstreamed. Regardless of language, culture, or climate, it's amazing how consistent this belief is."

Corporate Barriers

Along with peoples' personal hang-ups around disability are corporate barriers, embedded in our systems and processes. These barriers reinforce our fears and ignorance and ultimately prevent successful sourcing, attraction, and retention of people with disabilities. Too few people with disabilities succeed in the workplace due to the spoken and unspoken beliefs that they can't do the job. Businesses worry, too, about the possibility of increased costs, safety, legal liability – and how employees and customers will react. These counterproductive attitudes create a 44 percent unemployment rate among people with disabilities, the highest of any demographic group.[11] To lower and dismantle these barriers, we must first explore how and where they show up in our organizations.

The Hidden Nature of Many Disabilities

Some people have visible disabilities, the most iconic of them being a wheelchair-using individual, the *de rigueur* picture when diversity wants to portray disability. Yet those with visible disabilities make up less than 29 percent of people with disabilities.[12] Many disabilities are essentially invisible by their very nature (that is, chronic pain, cognitive disorders, post-traumatic stress disorder, or malfunctioning internal organ). That is, you may not be able to tell simply by looking at the person that they are disabled.

Then there are those who seek to cover up their disability to fend off discrimination. Just as the first women and people of color broke through the glass ceiling by minimizing their difference (women who adapted by "behaving like men" and people of color who tried to "act" white through their speech and body language), disability pioneers did the same. U.S. President Franklin Delano Roosevelt went to extraordinary lengths to keep his wheelchair out of sight. Consequently, millions of Americans didn't even know he had polio.[13] An administrative assistant with an increasingly worsening hearing loss secretly recorded conversations and played them back at the end of the workday to get all the information she needed. A salesperson with diabetes worked as a diabetes technician, because that made it easier for him to check his blood glucose levels and administer his insulin medication without anyone detecting his condition.

Once women and people of color had entered the workforce in numbers beyond tokenism, they began changing workplace culture by their very presence. The same must now happen for people with disabilities. Companies try to excuse their dearth of women or minorities at certain levels by saying, "We can't find any." The same is true with disability — but employers won't be able to use that same old excuse much longer. A growing number of people with disabilities are aggressively pursuing education and training. Currently, 2.2 million college students in the United States (11 percent of the total student population) have disabilities,[14] with 25 percent of those majoring in computer science, engineering, and science,[15] key areas where the talent shortage is especially acute.

Assumptions About What People with Disabilities Can and Cannot Do

While everyone knows it's inappropriate and illegal to discriminate on the basis of disability, there is plenty of evidence it still happens. The Disability Funders

Network, a Midlothian, Va.-based membership and advocacy organization, reports the unemployment rate for people with disabilities is ten times higher than for the nation as a whole.

It is misunderstanding, calcified attitudes, and outright prejudice that are keeping so many people with disabilities un- or under-employed. The following story, told by a paraplegic we'll call David, is typical. Listen to the debilitating emotional thought process he goes through: "A lot of the jobs that I'm applying for are online, and they always have the EEO (Equal Employment Opportunity) thing on there. And on just about every one of them, they ask if you have a disability. I am so afraid to fill that part out. I know it says that they don't use any of the answers that you put on there for consideration for the job. I know that I have to answer truthfully if I answer it at all. Sometimes they give you an option of not answering, and I feel like if I don't answer they will think I'm trying to hide something."

This agony is compounded in the first face-to-face interaction. "I went on an interview the other day. When I showed up for the scheduled time, I asked for the hiring manager and when he came out, I said, 'Hi, I'm David. I'm here for my 5 p.m. interview.' He looked at me in my wheelchair, perplexed. 'We have a meeting at 5 o'clock? How can I help you? Uh … oh, yeah, right, okay!' But it was immediately clear I had no chance, despite my 24 years of retail experience."

Those with a visible disability must contend with pervasive assumptions about what people with disabilities can and can't do. "There is a societal belief that having a disability equals you can't work," says Bristo. She goes on to explain that this assumption is codified right into our Social Security system, shaping the beliefs of both the able-bodied and those with disabilities. The benefits provided assume the person will not be able to earn a wage. For children, the assumption is they will not have access to a competitive education, skills training, or equal access to academic preparation. "That whole system is based upon a model that people with disabilities have to be taken care of because they can't take care of themselves," Bristo says. "And while no one is going to argue that some people may need it, for many people it becomes a trap from which they can't get out. The system needs to be more flexible."

So if disability does not equal inability, we must rethink what's required for the job in terms of physical ability. Progressive companies are pretty good at answering the "what does the role require?" question when faced with a disabled employee and the need to respond to Americans with Disabilities Act (ADA) requirements. But this approach severely limits what opportunities are available for people with disabilities.

Able-bodied people's beliefs about what's necessary for performing a job are riddled with assumptions that must be questioned. One person who uses a wheelchair applied for a store manager's job at a video rental store, where the hiring manager's immediate reaction was, "You can't do this." The applicant responded by saying, "Give me a day-to-day listing of a store manager's responsibilities, and let's walk through them and see what a person in a wheelchair can't do." As they went through the list, the only thing that came up would be reaching the top shelf. The applicant said, "Okay, that's fair. But is that something I need to do, an absolute?" The manager answered, "No, it's not."

Myriad stories circulate of disabled people advancing against all odds. *DiversityInc* magazine captures the story of Melodi King, who has cerebral palsy, a neurological disorder that attacks the body's musculature. The condition mostly affects her right side, curling her hand into a fist.[16] In college, her keyboarding teacher told her she would have to quit the class because she couldn't type like the other students. She responded by teaching herself to type 60 words per minute with only her left hand. Cerebral palsy "has actually forced me to have stronger problem-solving skills and makes me prepared to deal with situations that other people can't handle well," this manufacturing development program analyst at Merck tells the magazine. "It forces you to be adaptable."[17]

Glass ceiling pioneers have had to "work twice as hard to get half as far." Many became super-achievers in ways that are not realistic for the bulk of the bell curve to exhibit. To truly be inclusive, "organizations need to meet us half way to give us a basic level playing field, hence the concept of reasonable accommodations," says Bristo.

Further complicating things are common misperceptions that one disability implies another. If someone can't hear, for example, people wonder if they can read. And if someone is in a wheelchair or has a speech impairment, people automatically assume they also have an intellectual disability. Some assume people with disabilities don't have a mind of their own. Says Vcelka, "I'll be at a restaurant with my girlfriend and the waitress will ask her what I'll have to eat." Some misguidedly jump to conclusions about what a person with a disability will need to be able to do their job — without even asking them. In one case, a manager insisted that a new hire, who is blind, have a guide dog, even though the employee had never used one and didn't need to.

Workplace Implications

If fear is the core barrier to creating true inclusion for people with disabilities, let's first work on dismantling it.

Disability advocates stress that we must recognize disability as a normal part of the human condition and acknowledge that it affects us all to some extent. When disability is present, we can accept it — not as an aberration or something gone terribly wrong, but rather as how life can be. As Bristo says, "When you're smack in the middle of dealing with a disability, most people find resources they didn't know they had. And what you thought you feared is not often what the experience ends up being." The simplest and most straightforward way to get comfortable with disability is to spend more time with people who have disabilities, she says. Once we do, "the mystique and mystery disappear, and then the person is seen for what they can do rather than what they can't."

Personal relationships are a powerful source in lowering barriers between able bodied and those with disabilities. But if we are going to keep dismantling the barriers, we must be ready to redefine ability. The embedded assumption that to be disabled means to be unable must be undone. This is the key to making the mix work.

Redefining Ability

John Vcelka sits in his wheelchair at a white board in front of a group of two dozen able-bodied students. "Which of these do you believe I've not been able to do since my accident?" he asks, pointing to the names of 36 different sports, including water skiing, rock climbing, and rugby. The students respond eagerly, calling out activity after activity. With the red marker in his hand, Vcelka circles one — canoeing. "This is the only one I've not done," he says as he taps the board, "and not because I've not been able to, but I just haven't gotten to it yet!"

People with disabilities are redefining what it means to be disabled and able-bodied. Check out Olympic-caliber athletes like South African open water swimmer Natalie du Toit and her compatriot, sprinter Oscar Pistorius, both of whom are amputees. In competing — not in the Paralympics, but rather for Du Toit in the mainstream 2008 Beijing Olympics and Pistorius in the 2012 London Olympics — they declared they didn't want their disability to put them in a different category. They wanted to compete with the best. Du Toit says, "In the water, I'm just like everybody else. [In competition, other swimmers] wouldn't hold back, saying, 'there's a disabled athlete, I'll go slower.'"[18] Pistorius had a tougher time as he sought to qualify for the team going to London. Was it his qualifying time or his Flex-Foot, a sharply-designed prosthetic, that track and field officials suspected might give him an unfair advantage?[19] In Pistorius' case, some even said having the disability meant great advantage!

Lais Kari is a blind proofreader. With the help of a digital replayer (with software that reads computer screen text aloud), Lais has become a top proofreader at Serasa Experian, a leading Brazilian global information services company. She sets the replayer to read back text at 10 times the normal speed and zips through documents, correcting grammatical errors as she goes. Her job allows her to work with one of her great passions—the Portuguese language—and she loves it. Disability isn't the problem, Lais explains. "What's a problem is convincing others that it's not a problem."

In the 2005 documentary film *Murderball*, quadriplegic men play quad-rugby. It is one of the more aggressively physical sports played by athletes who have, arguably, some of the most significant disabilities. They use "Stick-Ems" so the ball sticks to their hand, and they bang their wheelchairs into each other in hopes of knocking the ball out of the other person's hands or knocking the person over.

Vcelka climbs rocks by shifting rock-climbing's basic premise that it's mainly about leg use to making it mainly about arm use. The stories begin to mount: The paraplegic roofer; the visibly-impaired team manager of a joint United States-India technology team; the blind former governor of New York, David Paterson; and autistic mathematics genius, Daniel Tammet. His memoir, *Born on a Blue Day: Inside the Extraordinary Mind of an Autistic Savant* (Free Press, 2007), is the remarkable story of the author's experiences, beginning with being perceived as a useless drain on society and then describing how he went to school, got a degree and a job, sustained a long-distance relationship, learned how to speak Icelandic in a week, and even taught in Lithuania. Tammet's story is of particular interest to researchers because he is one of only 50 people today living with synesthesia (where the stimulation of one sense causes sensation in another — like when a sound produces a sensation of color) and autism. We all have a lot to learn from Tammet's life story, and from others whose disabilities may not be outwardly noticeable.

The growing number of "defying the odds" stories challenge the "unable" tag society has placed on those with disabilities. They are changing the way people with disabilities think about themselves. The Office of Disability Employment Policy (ODEP) at the U.S. Department of Labor has found that more young people with disabilities are graduating from high school and college. And according to the Job Accommodation Network (JAN), workers with disabilities have performance and retention ratings comparable to those without disabilities.[20]

This conversation often segues into wondering if people with disabilities actually have more powerful abilities than the able-bodied — moving from the extreme of "they can't do anything" to "they're superhuman." Dagit reflects on this phenomenon. "Yes, when you have a disability, it forces you to see the world in a different way and to not be afraid of things — to not be afraid of public speaking or be intimidated by an executive or to be able to negotiate through conflict that others see as impossible to solve because the muscles you have or the skills that you learn as a person who is differently abled — are things difficult to acquire for anyone if you're not forced to. And I don't mean if you're blind you can hear better. I mean if you're forced to rely on things other than the ableness of your body, you'll develop adaptive strategies that serve you well in a variety of circumstances. What you notice about people's tone and their body language, what you notice about human dynamics, it's just transformed."

There are parallels with historical diversity issues as well. "When African-Americans excelled at sports, society tried to make it like there was some innate biological difference. Couldn't it just be possible that they tried harder?" asks Dagit. "Or with women, society starts to go down this path: 'Women are better at multitasking because they're able to use more parts of their brain, but they're not as good at science and math.' We're trying to look for scientific proof, rather than see that there are adaptive behaviors where people apply more time, energy, and effort."

Wounded Warriors: Skills Intact

The face of disability today is partly, and movingly, defined by our country's wounded warriors, those soldiers who have come back from Iraq and are returning from the U.S.' longest war in Afghanistan. Thanks to the advanced technology of contemporary warfare and battlefield medicine that lead to a higher survivor rate many more vets, compared to wars before, are returning with prostheses rather than in body bags. Despite their injuries, for most, their skill sets are intact, and they're eager to work.

In Dan Senor and Saul Singer's book *Start-Up Nation: The Story of Israel's Economic Miracle*, the authors write about U.S. soldiers' ability to transition from the battlefield to the boardroom. They state, "Given all this battlefield entrepreneurial experience, the vets coming out of the Iraq and Afghanistan wars are better prepared than ever for the business world, whether building startups or helping lead larger companies through current turbulent periods...vets bring things to the table that their business peers could only dream about, including a sense of proportionality — what is truly a life-or-death situation and what is less than that; what it takes to motivate a workforce; how to achieve consensus under duress; and a solid ethical base that has been tested in the crucible of battle."

This has never been more apparent than when Obama's White House challenged private industry to hire or train more than 100,000 veterans by 2013. This, however, is requiring a culture change in these organizations. Culture changed from an able-bodied workforce to one that easily incorporates those with disabilities. And culture change for those old enough to remember that those who became disabled in previous wars did not have the technological and social support that exists today to help them demonstrate that they have valuable transferable skills and still can perform at the highest levels.

JPMorgan Chase is one of the companies taking up the Obama Era challenge. In a recent initiative, JPMorgan Chase employees partnered with the Wall Street Warfighters Foundation, an organization that helps service-disabled veterans transition from active duty to new careers. JPMorgan Chase provides ongoing support to veterans pursuing careers in the financial services industry. Wall Street Warfighters alumni have moved into financial services positions at Goldman Sachs, JPMorgan Chase, Citigroup, and Drexel Hamilton.[21]

Reassessing Ability

The other way to redefine ability is to see disability in new ways. Dagit describes a conference in Washington, D.C. attended by more than 700 people with a brittle-bones condition. It results in frequent bone fractures, which can be caused by something as seemingly harmless as going over a bump or even sneezing. They have heart valve and colon challenges, significant hearing loss, joint laxity that leads to chronic tendonitis, and severe spinal curvature. "And yet, this is not a group of unhappy sad sacks," she says. "These are people who are leaders in government, who are actors in the theater, who are holding all kinds of important and meaningful jobs, who have full lives that include family and community."

"But able-bodied people would walk into this conference and see something that is tragic, that needs to be cured, that we need to research. Ironically, those with a disability often look at the 'poor able-bodied people' who don't get to experience their unique perspective because they've not had to struggle with some dimension of disability." This is illustrated by a conversation Dagit recently had with her 13-year-old son, Van, who has the same brittle-bones condition. A homework assignment at the beginning of the school year asked seventh graders to answer questions about themselves, including the one thing they would most like to change about themselves. After giving the question some thought, Van asked, "Mom, what if there isn't anything I want to change?" "Just write that down if that is how you feel," she replied. As he was packing up his folders after finishing the assignment, Dagit asked, "Van, what about your bones breaking easily and you being smaller than the other kids … is that something you would like to change?" "No. I like me the way I am," he replied.

Let's Get Practical

The conversation starts deep, by looking at the people's fear and discomfort with people. Yet, moving into action on disability is about mundane, practical solutions.

Physical Space — It's More Than Just Parking Spaces and Restroom Stalls

While ramps and designated parking spaces are good to have, they're just a start. Moving within the building is equally as important as being able to get into it. To walk through Access Living's four-story building in downtown Chicago is to discover how much we've built the world for able-bodied people. Using a design principle called *Universal Design*, elevators open on both sides to eliminate elevator jostling, voice commands announce the floors, and light sensors automatically adjust lighting as the sun moves across the sky, keeping levels constant. All desks and chairs are easily adjustable, restroom entrances are set up without external doors so people in wheelchairs can easily enter and exit. Low-emitting carpet material (that doesn't require detergents to clean it) eliminates air contaminants that may be harmful to people with chemical sensitivities. And low-pile carpeted floors provide the right balance between traction and gliding for wheelchairs and walking aids.

Simply put, the building has been "designed for all." Advocates for Universal Design say it only makes sense, given how Baby Boomers will, as they age, be the beneficiaries of the principle.

disabilityworks Works

"What businesses don't know is what's keeping them from hiring people with disabilities," says Karen McCulloh, the former executive director of disabilityworks, a statewide initiative located at the Chicagoland Chamber of Commerce. "One of our objectives is to reach out to businesses that don't realize that the community of people with disabilities is an untapped resource of qualified workers."

disabilityworks partners with businesses through the Chicagoland Business Leadership Network (CBLN) and with service providers through the Chicagoland Provider Leadership Network to improve employment opportunities for people with disabilities. The initiative grew out of a task force focused on disability and employment started by former Chicago Mayor Richard M. Daley. The task force was in session for three years before disabilityworks was founded in 2005. "It's all about moving people with disabilities into the workforce," says McCulloh. In less than a year, nearly 200 people secured jobs from the leads distributed by disabilityworks via the Internet and email blasts to people with disabilities, service providers, and job placement specialists."

Adopting a business-oriented focus that balances labor supply and demand, disabilityworks seeks to make systemic changes in the attitudes and behaviors of the business community and the community of support for people with disabilities. Several times a year, disabilityworks CBLN holds special workshops on the American with Disabilities Act (ADA). These closed-door sessions, facilitated by an attorney well-versed in the topic, address the perceptions and issues that appear to hinder a company from hiring people with disabilities. Included is a discussion about employers' concerns regarding the cost of reasonable accommodations. Several studies have found these costs to be, on average, $500 or less. "No question is going to sound stupid, no question is going to sound discriminatory, because if you don't know, you don't know, and lack of information and education will keep businesses from hiring people with disabilities," says McCulloh.

disabilityworks' public-private partnership approach and its successes have been so distinctive that it has been awarded the Department of Labor's New Freedom Initiative Award. The initiative also has shared its message and methods with international delegations from Russia, the Ukraine, Great Britain, and Armenia, as well as various states across the country. As disabilityworks continues working on incorporating people with disabilities into all aspects of the workforce, McCulloh sums up the ongoing effort: "The employer outreach area is where the work needs to be done and, as lots of research shows, whatever helps people with disabilities helps customers as well."

At this point, you might be wondering how much it costs to implement services for the disabled. Are such accommodations just for a handful of people? If so, why should we spend thousands of dollars on programs and facilities that are only going to benefit a few? Well, first of all, there are more people with disabilities than you probably realize. And even if these services are only for a handful, there are compliance reasons for responding to their needs. From an ethics and philosophy perspective, it's all about inclusion for everyone — whether for thousands or for a few.

Dos and Don'ts

I usually avoid providing this kind of list given the reductive message that conveys all that inclusion requires is checking of boxes off a checklist. But of all the diversity issues we face, this is one where people are most often confused about what to say and do. Able-bodied people end up either not giving help when it's needed or offering it when it's not needed, creating an awkward and sometimes hurtful cycle we need to break. Here's some simple, yet often ignored, advice from the disabled people I spoke with for this book:

- Don't assume you, as an able-bodied person, know best what someone with a disability needs. Ask. This applies even when you see someone who may be struggling (pushing up an incline, for example). Ask first. They may indeed need the help and welcome it. But if they answer, "No, I'm fine," accept it.
- If someone who has a disability offers you a cup of coffee or a piece of pie and starts getting it for you, let them. The last thing you should do is say, "What are you doing that for? You don't need to do that, let me."
- Given how prevalent this problem is, I include this reminder: Don't use the stall for those with disabilities unless all other stalls are occupied.

Wheelchair Dynamics

You may have noticed that some people use wheelchairs that do not have push-handles on them. This didn't come about by chance. Those who use such wheelchairs chose this option on purpose. When able-bodied people see the push-handles, they have an instinctual response to grab them and push the person in the wheelchair. "It is one of the worst things you could do," says Vcelka. "It really makes one feel like less of a person when someone grabs a hold of your chair and starts pushing you even when I'm saying, 'Please don't push my chair, I'm fine. If I need help, I'll ask for it.'"

A female employee at a large Fortune 500 company uses an old, heavy manual wheelchair. She is constantly urged by her manager and coworkers to get a newer, sleeker version that's lighter and easier to push. Her response: "My wheelchair, the way that it is now, is also something that surrounds me, and if somebody bumps into me, they're not going to hurt me. I can sit on the armrest to reach things. I can climb down on the footrest to pick up something off the floor. If I get a different type of wheelchair, I forfeit all the other things that this chair does for me."

Like most diversity issues, we need to find the right stance between being pro-active and being paternalistic. Most importantly, we must respect the individual.

Cognitive Disability Dynamics

Admittedly, in this chapter, I've put my emphasis on physical disability rather than cognitive disability. But just as we need to rethink the realities of physical disability and what it does and does not mean, we need to rethink the dynamics of cognitive disability — such as, for example, Down syndrome, spina bifida, and autism. While we may have made some progress in addressing physical disabilities, society remains further behind in addressing its biases and misconceptions about people with cognitive disabilities.

Proving the ability in disability is especially difficult for people with cognitive disabilities. But increased research into autism spectrum disorders (ASD) is increasing our understanding of the unique abilities of this group. This is particularly true of those with Asperger's Syndrome, sometimes referred to as high-functioning autism. Although people with Asperger's Syndrome share with classically autistic people some of the same difficulties with social interaction, sensory processing, and repetitive behavior, they possess unique skills, such as synthesizing information in novel and complex ways. High-functioning people with an ASD pay precise attention to detail and routine processes; their minds are geared to order, complex systems, and mathematics. In other words, they have exactly the qualities valued in the sciences or computer lab. With 730,000 Americans under the age of 21 having an ASD, according to the Centers for Disease Control and Prevention, there is a pressing need to begin to channel their talents into appropriate jobs in areas such as science, technology, engineering, and mathematics.

Companies such as Danish software-testing firm Specialisterne are beginning to seek out this highly capable group. And there's growing recognition that in science and technology, some of the most brilliant people (Albert Einstein and Thomas Edison, for example) undoubtedly lived with learning disabilities or autism. Yet, their minds roamed the outer fields of thought and brought back ideas no one had yet considered. With so many critical 21st Century problems to be solved the world over, it's time people pay attention to these outliers.

Little By Little, More Acceptance

Bristo talks about freeing people with disabilities from the imprisonment of their homes and opening up more workplace opportunities for them. Legislative changes, the push for diversity and inclusion, and technological advantages are lowering the barriers, albeit slowly.

Unlike building designers, who have been slow to get onboard, techies love the challenge of programming their software to meet the needs of people with different levels of ability. Virtual and remote work creates more opportunities for workers needing flexibility, as well as for those who have difficulty getting around.

We've not yet hit the tipping point in terms of society's attitudes toward those with disabilities, but things are inching that way. "It used to be that if I saw another person in a wheelchair at O'Hare Airport coming toward me in a terminal, by the time we got up to each other, I knew them. There were that few of us really flying," says Bristo. "Now the airlines can't keep up with us because there are so many people with disabilities flying."

Approaches to cognitive disability lag further behind, but here, too, we see signs of progress. In many public schools, kids with Down syndrome, spina bifida, and autism have been integrated into mainstream classes.[22] Both research and practical experience show that those with cognitive disabilities are more able in thought and skills than previously believed. This leads to better post-school preparation, whether going into college, a vocational trade, or a service job. When the first edition was completed, my goddaughter, Jennifer, who has Down syndrome, was a senior in high school. She's had an active social life filled with friends, dancing, and movies that she balanced between school and her public library job, where she sorted and reshelved books. Since then, she's worked at the local chapter of the American Cancer Society, and currently volunteers several days a week at Misericordia, a residential community for people with developmental disabilities.

As we address the inclusiveness requests of those who have been on the margins, benefit flows to the full community. I don't mean this in a "feel good" way, but in a practical, helpful way. The working mother's battle cry for work-life balance ended up also benefiting working fathers, near-retirees, and Millennials. The clamor by people of color for mentors has also benefited up-and-coming majority talent. And now, disabled individuals' urging for user-friendly workplaces will bring benefits for all. Curb cuts and wider aisles help parents with strollers and carts and people with luggage, for example. Accessible doorknobs make it easier for people with packages to open doors. And voice recognition technology originally created to allow people with disabilities to write text on a computer without typing, is also now the basis for the technology many of us are using when navigating smartphone calls.

Beyond the medical and social models for looking at people with disabilities in society is the emerging market model. This model sees people with disabilities as a large and growing group of employees and consumers. In other words: huge marketplace opportunities.

If the workplace potential of people with disabilities is just beginning to be recognized, their massive purchasing power has yet to be capitalized. The global disability market has mushroomed to the size of China. Its 1.1 billion people control $4 trillion dollars in spending power. If you include family and friends who have a direct and emotional connection with people with disabilities, the numbers nearly double to a staggering 2 billion people controlling $8.1 trillion dollars.[23]

Take the ubiquitous Baby Boomers. The first legion of their huge demographic has already turned 65, and they are redefining what it means to grow older. Despite statistics that will render them increasingly disabled, they want to stay involved in their lives and in society. New products and services that help both able-bodied and disabled Baby Boomers stay independent are beginning to appear in the economic landscape, from walk-in therapeutic baths to retirement communities that reinterpret the communes of the 1960s as a mutually support-ive way for seniors to share housing.

In recognizing a customer service need, airlines are offering gate-to-gate trans-portation for people with less visible constraints, like respiratory ailments, though it first started the practice to help those in wheelchairs. Universal Design dovetails nicely into green design and the potential economic benefits that can accrue. Mak-ing necessary ergonomic adjustments for those with disabilities will make ergonomic furniture even more ubiquitous, meeting everyone's needs for healthy keyboard work in an era with a sharp climb in repetitive stress and carpal tunnel injuries.

We have been looking at how people with disabilities are beginning to strengthen the workplace and invigorate the marketplace. These advances alone, however, are not enough to bring about a fundamental shift in attitudes toward and opportunities for people with disabilities. We must develop cultural change strategies to undermine hard-held beliefs and attitudes that continue to create barriers to disability inclusion.

The ambivalence of many in the diversity field toward, and even the neglect of, disability is a reflection of larger societal attitudes. After the globally historic passage of the ADA in 1990, which put the United States in world leadership of disability issues by the early 2000s, the United States had lost its leadership in dealing with disability issues. However, in the Obama Era, we've been see-ing a renewed emphasis on bridging the gap between the able-bodied and those with disabilities. Though, as with many vote related legislation in the Obama Era, the emphasis has not been without controversy. President Obama announced, within months of taking office, that the United States would join the more than 150 other nations in becoming a signatory to the unprecedented United Nations Convention on the Rights of Persons with Disabilities. The President acknowl-edged this was merely a starting point. "And even as we extend our commitment to persons with disabilities around the world, we're working to deepen that com-mitment here at home," he said in remarks marking the 19th anniversary of the Americans with Disabilities Act (ADA) and the signing of the treaty. "We must consider what can be done to eliminate anti-disabled prejudices that exist – both consciously and subconsciously – within our society."[24] But as a reflection of the ambivalence toward addressing disability, along with the polarized politics of our times, this Obama Era intent has met resistance and in a vote taken late in 2012, the U.S. Senate rejected confirmation of the treaty.

Similarly in the Obama Era the Department of Labor has issued a directive that many see as too onerous: that anyone doing contracting with the Federal government employ at least 7 percent of their workforce with people with disabilities.[25] This is a heated debate but there's no question that it's Obama Era inclusive policies triggering the debate.

The resistance by politicians and business as well as the still indifference by diversity practitioners as a whole, means we still have a long way to go.

To address this seriously lagging diversity issue, we need to take a stand. Says Dagit, "Until we come to the realization that every single one of us is temporarily able-bodied, we're not going to make significant progress on this. It is enlightened self-interest that will drive us to a solution. If we create a world where people with disabilities can fully participate, then we'll have created an insurance policy for ourselves and anyone we care about. It's not an 'other' issue. It's a self issue." ℘

SUMMARY POINTS

- Misconceptions about disability are based on fear, which is prevalent both in society and in our workplaces. Some diversity practitioners even struggle with this issue.
- Disability is a normal part of the human condition and affects all of us to a greater or lesser extent. Sooner or later, we all will face our own disabilities, making it an issue of self-interest.

- Accessibility issues are about more than parking spaces and restroom stalls. When accessibility is based on the concept of Universal Design, buildings and environments will become accessible and welcoming to all — disabled and able-bodied people alike.
- Returning veterans with disabilities with all the skills learned on the battlefield possess multiple competencies that can benefit businesses.

SHAPING YOUR STRATEGY

- How proactive is your organization in addressing disability issues?
- What are the biggest barriers among individuals and within your organization

to assertively attract, hire, engage, and develop people with disabilities?
- Where would you assess your own comfort with disability in others? In yourself?

GAY 10

GAY

HOW MY GAY FRIENDS UPENDED MY UNDERSTANDING ABOUT MOST EVERYTHING

Chapter 10

How My Gay Friends
Upended My Understanding
About Most Everything

While working as a senior leader at Hewitt, Jocelyn Purcell also served as the business leader sponsor of the Lesbian, Gay, Bisexual, and Transgender (LGBT) affinity group. In that capacity, she was asked to speak at a Pride celebration. To prepare for the event, she decided to see what it would be like to not be able to talk about the people you love in everyday workplace conversation. Here's how she described the experience:

"It was not uncommon for LGBT colleagues to tell me how difficult it was to not be out. One person called it putting on the 'cloak.' She explained the constant decision about whether to put on the cloak or feel safe keeping it off. Many coworkers still wear that cloak because they don't trust they can take it off. Imagine how much more the work world could gain if the energy spent putting on the cloak was spent instead on the team and the client.

"So the idea was to try to put myself in the shoes of someone who was not out in the workplace and how that would feel. I have had the privilege of being able to be 100 percent who I am — in all aspects of my life — at work. And those of you who know me well, know that I like to talk about my family, my activities outside of work, and like to talk with others and find out about their families and their activities.

"So, I decided that for one week, I would not talk about anything outside of work. I would pretend that I was afraid to because it could lead to questions I did not want to answer. And because I couldn't talk about it, I would not ask others about it — because that would inevitably lead back to questions about me. As I thought about other implications, I realized I would need to take down all my pictures in my office of my family — because I wouldn't be able to have to answer questions like 'Who is this in the picture?'

"Every time I thought about entering into a week of shutting down part of myself, the energy that would take was overwhelming to me. The tremendous amount of restraint to be someone other than who I am would affect the focus and attention on my work I usually have. And the thought that in the middle of a stressful day, I couldn't look at pictures of my family and take some strength from their smiling faces and remind myself about what is important — the way I do every day — was too much.

"So, I didn't do it. I couldn't do it. And the truth is, I didn't have to do it. I have that choice. But many of our associates who are gay — but are not out — do not have that same choice."

Jocelyn's story comes from the perspective of someone who is an ally of those who are LGBT. We also had the opportunity to hear from coworkers who, on a daily basis, do not have the choice Jocelyn has long taken for granted. Let me share how this happened during a Gay Pride Month not too long ago.

My name is Diana.
I am 39 years old. I love the work I do...
and I consistently perform above expectations.
I am a lesbian.
I am the same person I was before you read the previous sentence.
– Affirmations Exhibit during Gay Pride Month

Forty LGBT associates — and their allies — joined Diana in telling their stories through a 130-foot photographic Affirmations Exhibit, nestled in the main reception areas of Hewitt's largest four U.S. offices. A virtual version of the exhibit was posted on the company's intranet.

Some gay associates took the opportunity to come out through the stories they shared in the exhibit. Others told of the anguish of having to watch their pronouns when talking about their weekend on a Monday morning. The impact was earth-shattering. After viewing the exhibit, a 20-something daughter chose to come out to her mom. And parents of LGBT children opened up about how the affirmation of gay employees as members of the Hewitt community felt like an affirmation of themselves as parents. This, in turn, freed them to be more open with coworkers about their own families.

The more people felt free to engage in conversation, the more it encouraged others. Given how divisive LGBT issues can be in society, in politics, and in corporations, the mood shift from polarized polemic to constructive dialogue made the event the most influential I have ever witnessed in shifting the discourse on LGBT issues within a community of people.

The Obama Era creates an opportunity to create an alternative to either/or polarization. Obama's 2009 Inauguration Day was marred with controversy when it was announced that two guests with diametrically opposed views on LGBT issues were asked to offer invocations at Inaugural events. This created great discomfort, even outrage, on all sides of the issue.[1] But it was clearly a deliberate attempt to include diverse, even opposing voices, and in that attempt, create a both/and opportunity to engage in a different kind of conversation. This is a manifestation of the Inclusion Paradox. In order to have inclusion, we must be able to constructively call out the differences among us.

It's not just about forging a better understanding of something that previously seemed foreign or elusive. Within the dialogue itself, insights emerge and shed new light on common conundrums. Hearing the stories of my LGBT friends and colleagues not only helped me understand them and their contributions better, it helped me discover new pathways to gender issues in general.

Before we delve into further insights, let's go back to the impact of the exhibit itself. We learned that charged conversations on LGBT issues had lost some of their edge. The impact could be measured through the engagement scores of LGBT associates, which we tracked by allowing participants to self-identify themselves. As one of the premier experts on employee engagement — how likely workers are to stay, say good things about the organization, and give their best — Hewitt has incontrovertible data which proves that lifting the engagement of groups of employees results in greater productivity and, ultimately, greater profitability.[2]

"Raising and maintaining engagement even a few percentage points can have a substantial impact on results for most organizations, so lifting engagement for what could be 5 percent to 10 percent of the population would surely provide significant returns," says Ray Baumruk, Aon Hewitt's Partner, Communication — Employee Research and Insights.

The Stories

From the Affirmations Exhibit:

My Question

Every morning I praise I thank You for blessing me with another day.
Throughout the day, I thank You for your grace and mercy.
And every night before I close my eyes,
I thank God for bringing me through another day.
Every day I live, I strive to be more like You.
More loving. More understanding. More forgiving. More patient.
As I am praising Your name, others condemn me.
They judge me.
They label me.
They outcast me and those I associate with.
My question:
Lord, why can't they see me as Your child and love me as You love me?
– Fatima

When we initially approached members of the LGBT affinity group with this idea, we were met with uncertainty. Steve Wasik, one of the leaders of the affinity group, told me, "I've had to deal with coming out to parents whose love, I learned, was conditional. I've spent years trying to find acceptance during a time when AIDS and gay hate crimes were in full bloom. Am I ready to share this pain, this very deep part of me, here at work? Why did I have to come out over and over again, each time bracing for whatever the reaction might be?"

But the more they thought about it, the more a growing number of members embraced the idea. As Steve explained, "I've been searching for a way I could help make my workplace more LGBT friendly without damaging the fragile existence I thought I had created. I didn't want to expend any more energy wondering if people knew, or should they find out, what the response would be if they did." He said yes, and others followed. We received more stories than we could use. The exhibit went up with 40 stories and accompanying photographs. As associates weaved their way through the exhibit, here's some of what they read:

"I am proud that I am Chinese and I am proud that I am gay. I have fought back and I will continue to fight back. How I am on the outside will be who I am on the inside ... once again" – Jimmy

"ADJECTIVES: Methodist. Politically Conservative. Gay. HIV positive. Employed. VERBS: Prays. Thinks. Loves. Hurts. Works. I've found that actions really do speak louder than words. Have you?" – Doug

"Did I just slip and say 'she' when I was talking with my coworker about what I did this weekend? For a year-and-a-half of working at Hewitt and not being out, I struggled almost daily with racing thoughts as I worried about my pronouns, or hoped that a coworker hadn't realized that I was with my girlfriend when I saw him at the restaurant the night before." – Andrea

"The hardest thing is explaining to my 8-year-old why some people might give him a hard time because he has two moms. He doesn't understand why some people would think there was anything wrong with that. He also doesn't understand why having a different color skin, or being a different shape or size, or speaking a different language, or having a disability causes some people discomfort. He keeps asking, 'But why, Mom? It just doesn't make sense to me!'" – Kaleen

*"Hewitt is the only place where I have ever worked that allows me to be myself and for the first time I can have pictures of **MY FAMILY** on my desk and my coworkers will come by and look at **MY PICTURES** of **MY LIFE**. I don't have to hide who I am for fear of being ridiculed or being fired for who I am." – Cynthia*

"Hewitt is a place where for the first time in my entire life I have been able to completely honest, feel acceptance, live my faith in my work, and openly love my nontraditional family." – Bill

"When my clients glance at the ring on my ring finger and ask, "What does your husband do?," I am faced with that inevitable moment of decision — do I gray the lines and boundaries of the truth or am I honest in my response and risk alienating my customer? The firm I work for requires honesty and integrity, but my truth at times risks alienating me from critical connections — my

clients and my team. Do I dance around with the words that hide her identity by saying 'us,' 'we,' or 'they'? This 'pronoun game' distracts when trying to build trusted partnerships." – Cara

Straight allies spoke of their coming out as well. "My friend Steve is gay. I knew this before I received a note from him inviting me to attend a GALAA [Gay and Lesbian and Allied Associates] meeting, but I wasn't sure how, or even if, I should talk to him about his being gay. I was nervous because I didn't know how open he was or if he was even out. I knew that sending that meeting invite took courage. He put his life out there for me to either accept or reject, just as my sister had 14 years ago with my mom. I'm so glad that Steve opened this new door to our friendship, because I was too afraid to do it."

Then there's Steve's response. "My friend Allison is straight. When I came out to her shortly after joining Hewitt, I was afraid I would lose our newly forming friendship, and I wasn't sure I could handle that. I had come out to my parents when I was 18. I couldn't understand why my mother was down on her knees, sobbing in front of the shelves that held all my high school pictures, after I told her I was gay. Tearing down the walls is what I thought of as I e-mailed Allison about becoming a GALAA ally. I loved her and myself enough to take the chance. My whole life, personal and work, is better because of Allison."

The outpouring of emotion was a cultural balm that brought LGBT and straight employees together. At the exhibit, associates wrote notes and placed them in a Comments box. To be sure, not all embraced the spirit of the exhibit. Overwhelmingly, however, those who took the time to write a comment were moved. "I was on the verge of tears after reading the stories. They really brought to light what those in my family who are gay go through everyday." "Awesome! The strength, openness, and honesty in each and every affirmation made me proud to be a fellow associate."

"It's time for me to get involved as an ally in GALAA. No one should ever have to live his or her life in hiding." "Thank you, Affirmations participants: I found myself on an emotional roller coaster as I read the stories. Everything from sadness for the obstacles many of you have dealt with, happiness for the weight I hope that has been lifted from your shoulders, anger with myself for times when I didn't have an open mind, and privileged to work with truly amazing people."

We went a step further the following year and created "Family Affirmations" for LGBT associates to share about their partners, children, and even pets with their peers. Even for those who have different beliefs about LGBT issues, the stories were humanizing.

"For me and the rest of us at Hewitt, it has been a great turning point," says Steve. "For those who participated, it was a courageous step into the unknown, yet we knew we weren't out there alone. We had the support of our CEO and CDO, business leaders, and allies. We had our own personal strength, which had brought us to this point in our lives. And, we had the strength of our stories, banded together, saying with one voice, "We survived. And today, we work hard for the company and search for joy, happiness, and love — just like you."

Why Did It Work?

Debates grounded in religious and political beliefs are inherently contentious when different belief systems are at play. Conversations grounded in relationships can foster a dramatically different dynamic. The inclusion goal in LGBT issues should not be about reaching agreement, but rather creating a workplace environment where anyone who wanted to be out could do so without worrying about real or imagined repercussions. Once we reached that realization, we came upon the idea of sharing stories.

This was influenced by my own journey. It was my best friend's story that obliterated my machista-influenced understandings of gays and lesbians. Married, with two children, a man of impeccable integrity and commitment, he told me one day over coffee that he was gay. It had taken him more than 35 years to say those words and to accept his own story — a story he had fought against since he was 8 years old; a story he tried denying in countless ways, including choosing to live a heterosexual lifestyle, when his orientation was homosexual. He had arrived at a point where the years of denial were increasingly asphyxiating him. Letting his story of his true self come out was his liberation.

It was mine too. From a story-less understanding of gays, lesbians, bisexuals, and transgendered people to one grounded in who they really are, my assumptions about LGBT people, based on religious, political and psychological beliefs withered in the crucible of my friend's story. It had been easy to hold certain beliefs with conviction while the issue was abstract. But once it was about my best friend of ten years, I came to realize my beliefs about gays at the time did not fit any dimension of who he was. He told me his story. I listened. And it changed me.

Authentic, engaging stories spur us to action. One person who saw the Affirmations Exhibit wrote, "How do I respond, live, behave at work to better support colleagues in similar situations? Where can I learn more and ask questions?" Yes! This was exactly the kind of dialogue we intended to elicit. In his introduction to the exhibit, Hewitt's CEO at the time, Dale Gifford, wrote, "These stories are also about courage, often in the face of rejection, fear, and distrust in overall society. Yet, each of them found the strength to overcome the barriers that stood in the way of being the best they could be. When we have an environment where this is possible, we can focus our energy on our talents and our work."

A New Era for LGBT

The Obama Era is leaving a lasting legacy on LGBT issues. Whether it's President Barack Obama's declaration that he supports gay marriage making him the first U.S. president to do so, the appointment to the Commerce Department of Amanda Simpson making her the first ever presidential transgender appointee, or the repeal of the U.S. military's Don't Ask, Don't Tell policy, we have entered a new era in how mainstream culture views lesbian, gay, bisexual, and transgender issues.

The repeal of Don't Ask, Don't Tell (DADT) was a watershed moment in U.S. and LGBT history. The U.S. Department of Defense — one of the most conservative institutions in the United States government and one of the largest employers in the world — changed a long-standing policy regarding gays and lesbians when it declared gays and lesbians could serve openly as military personnel.

DADT had been an awkward, convoluted, and ultimately dehumanizing compromise enacted in 1993. As is true with most culture change, organizations and societies often have to take an interim, contrived step to move the real change. DADT was particularly "sin querer, queriendo" (without wanting, wanting) in terms of accepting the reality of same-sex orientation. It had required military personnel refrain from requesting information about someone's sexual orientation, yet officials who admitted to homosexuality or bisexuality in identity or behavior were to be discharged from the military. Gay and lesbian servicemen and women were forced to choose between never discussing an essential aspect of their identity or leaving military service, while the sharp edge of suspicion remained hanging over their military careers.[3]

It also lingered in all its contradictions for way too long. But in December of 2010 in the midst of much political wrangling about a whole bunch of things from the economy to nuclear treaties with the Russians, DADT was repealed by Congress and signed into law by the president soon thereafter. In June 2012, the Department of Defense celebrated its first ever Gay Pride Month with Secretary of Defense Leon Panetta kicking off the day with a live video conference message to the entire DOD.

The bottom line message: one can be brave, loyal, strong, willing to die for one's country, and gay.

This indeed is culture change. To prove it, since the repeal of DADT, nine states, plus the District of Columbia, have approved same sex marriage – Connecticut, Iowa, Maine, Maryland, Massachusetts, New Hampshire, New York, Vermont and Washington State. In three of these states it happened by popular vote, the first time in 30 previous attempts across the U.S. to do so.[4]

Highlights of Key LGBT Events during Obama Era

• In 2012 – 252 companies participating in the Human Rights Campaign's (HRC) Corporate Equality Index received a score of 100 percent. This was a drop from 337 companies in 2011. The decrease was due to the HRC raising the criteria for reaching 100 percent and recognized the growing number of businesses adopting basic workplace equality practices for LGBT employees.[5]

• President Barack Obama is the first U.S. president to declare support for marriage equality.

• December 2011 – LGBT rights is used as a criteria for whether a country will receive U.S. foreign aid.[6]

• The high court in New Delhi, India rules that the law making same-sex sexual activity illegal is unconstitutional and discriminates against gays and lesbians.[7]

• Nine states, plus the District of Columbia, have approved same sex marriage – Connecticut, Iowa, Maine, Maryland, Massachusetts, New Hampshire, New York, Vermont, and Washington State.

• In 2007, 20 percent of same-sex couples had minor-aged children in their homes.[8]

• About 4 percent of adoptive parents are same-sex couples.[9]

• 65, 000 adopted children and 14,000 foster children live in households headed by gays or lesbians.[10]

LGBT in the Workplace and Marketplace

As we are witnessing changes taking place in the Department of Defense, the more included LGBT employees feel in their working environment, the more organizations learn about this often invisible and misunderstood group. According to the San Francisco-based LGBT workplace advocacy group, Out & Equal, there is no precise count of the total number of workers in corporate America who identify as LGBT. However, 324 out of 2,932 survey respondents identified themselves as LGBT, and seven out of ten heterosexual respondents say they know someone who is gay.[11]

Despite progress, there are myriad workplaces in which talented employees are leaving behind a part of who they are in order to get ahead. It's no surprise given that it's still legal in 29 states to fire employees because they identify as lesbian, gay, or bisexual. In 34 states, it's legal to fire someone for being transgender.[12]

Many of these workers are forced to stay closeted at work in order to keep their jobs or avoid harassment. In 2011, crimes against LGBT individuals ranked second among all hate crimes, accounting for more than 20 percent.[13]

LGBT people face other challenges, too. Most are not able to benefit from inheritance laws, have a guarantee that their health care proxy wishes will be honored, marry their partners, buy life insurance for them, or put them in their wills. They must anxiously wonder whether long-term care facilities will accept them when they can no longer take care of themselves. Choosing doctors is fraught with difficulty since they don't know which physicians will be both accepting of them and knowledgeable about particular LGBT health issues.

Other dilemmas remain unresolved. While many companies now provide domestic partner benefits, LGBT employees typically get taxed for the portion of insurance premiums that cover their partner, incurring a financial burden that does not apply to married heterosexual couples.

An increasing number of companies are rethinking common assumptions about who LGBT employees are, the issues they face, and what they're looking for in the workplace. Nearly 1,400 people, representing 22 countries and 118 corporate and organization sponsors attended the Out & Equal Workplace Summit*,

---

* Initially, 2,500 participants were expected to attend the 2012 Out & Equal Summit. However, attendance was affected by Hurricane Sandy, which caused massive East Coast disruptions.

a conference for the LGBT community held in Baltimore, Maryland, in October/ November 2012.[14] This growing awareness has led to more inclusive policies. In 1992, only three Fortune 500 companies offered domestic partner health benefits. Within five years, that number jumped to 46. By 2006, it was 249.[15] A 2010 Mercer study found that 72 percent of companies with at least 20,000 employees offered same-sex benefits, up from 62 percent in 2006.[16]

The Human Rights Campaign (HRC) rates large U.S. businesses on how they treat LGBT stakeholders. Conducted annually, the Corporate Equality Index ranks companies on a scale of 0 to 100 percent, based on a checklist of about a dozen LGBT-inclusive practices. The first report, issued in 2002, found 13 out of 319 companies achieving a 100 percent score.[17] In 2009, an astounding 260 major U.S. businesses received a 100 percent score, an increase of one-third over just the year before. Increases in the number of companies reaching this rating continued in 2010 with 306 until 2011 with 337 companies achieving a score of 100 percent.[18] (See sidebar for more information.)

Seeing this high water mark in 2011, the HRC, as part of their methodology, raised the bar of what it took to reach 100 percent by inserting harder to achieve standards now that certain things such as domestic partner benefits so revolutionary a few years ago had become standard in so many Fortune 500 companies. Predictably, the number of companies achieving 100 percent dropped in 2012 to 252. But the gambit is working in that it is spurring those who had previously achieved 100 percent, but who had slipped due to the new standards, to enact the polices that will get them back to the coveted designation of 100 percent once again.[19]

Companies are also starting to see the marketplace through LGBT eyes. And with good reason. The purchasing power of the LGBT population reached $690 billion in 2007,[20] and is estimated to be $790 billion in 2012.[21] This surpasses U.S. Asian 2012 buying power by nearly $75 billion[22], and is a $100 billion increase from 2007. In addition, the average household income for married or partnered gay men is $116,000 compared with $94,500 for married heterosexual men; for married or partnered lesbians the average household income is $99,700, compared to $92,500 for married heterosexual women, according to the 2012 LGBT Demographic Report by Experian Simmons.[23]

In light of those figures, advertisers are beginning to wise up the enormity of the LGBT market, which is, by far, one of the fastest growing and largest in the world.

Adding to the vast purchasing power of the LGBT population is strong brand loyalty and willingness to support brands that back LGBT issues. Eighty-seven percent of LGBT adults say they would choose a brand that offers equal benefits for their LGBT employees over ones that don't. Interestingly, 75 percent of heterosexuals are also likely to consider if a company provides equal workplace benefits when making buying decisions.[24]

Who knew?

IBM, for one. In 1994, they launched a small business initiative aimed at LGBT business owners.[25] Responding to management's challenge that they offer ideas to help strengthen IBM's business, the LGBT Diversity Committee mapped out a market analysis that demonstrated a significant untapped market of LGBT business owners who needed computers and networks. This led to a deliberate strategy on Big Blue's part to go after the LGBT market, which they eventually grew into a multimillion-dollar business.

Checklist For An LGBT Inclusive Workplace Environment

The HRC's Corporate Equality Index rates Fortune 500 and other large U.S. businesses on how they treat LGBT stakeholders. Conducted annually, the Corporate Equality Index rates companies on a scale of 0 to 100 percent based on whether they:

- Include "Sexual Orientation" in primary written nondiscrimination policy.
- Offer same-sex domestic partner benefits that are equivalent to those offered to employees with opposite sex spouses.
- Offer equal health insurance coverage for transgender individuals without exclusions for medically necessary care.
- Recognize and support an LGBT Employee Resource Group or Diversity Council.
- Offer diversity training that includes sexual orientation and/or gender identity and expression in the workplace.
- Include LGBT data in employee engagement or demographic research by asking optional and confidential LGBT identification questions.
- Engage in respectful and appropriate marketing to the LGBT community, outreach to certified LGBT suppliers, and/or provide support through corporate sponsorship or philanthropy.

> - Do not engage in any actions that would undermine the goal of equal rights for LGBT people.
> - Include "Gender Identity or Expression" in primary written nondiscrimination policy. This is intended to cover those who are transgender. This item has kept many companies from achieving 100 percent, despite other inclusionary policies for their LGBT employees.

When Wendell Became Breanna

Through each L, G, and B story, my assumptions about identity, sexuality, gender, and the workplace implications of what it meant to *not* be out have frayed, ripped, and torn. But it was the T that ultimately dissolved so many things I thought to be true.

The first time I met Wendell Speed, I was having lunch with about 25 members of Hewitt's LGBT affinity group. Out of the corner of my eye, I saw someone pass by the meeting room's open door once, twice, and finally a third time before he walked in and took a seat at the far end of the room. In between bites of pizza and salad, associates introduced themselves with their coming-out stories. And then it was Wendell's turn.

He looked around the room, uncertain for a beat, and then gathering his courage, he shared. "I work in information services, and when my manager assigned me a pager it precipitated a crisis for me. 'If I come in right away, you won't recognize me,' I told him. 'What do you mean?' my manager asked. I explained that even though he knew me as a man, I dressed as a woman when not at work. And in responding to an urgent page, I would not have time to change back."

Wendell was a charismatic and respected IT database administrator for Oracle/SQL servers. He also happened to be African-American, plus a gifted musician who eventually ended up directing Hewitt's diversity chorus, a multiethnic singing group. This was the first time he had told a group of coworkers he was transgender.

Transgenderism is a little understood dimension of sexuality and identity, not just among the straight population but also in the L, G, and B communities. Transgender is an umbrella term used to refer to individuals whose biological sex is not entirely congruent with their gender identity. This encompasses a full range — from the occasional, recreational crossdresser to the transsexual.

Crossdressers sometimes dress in clothing traditionally associated with the opposite sex. They change back and forth between presenting themselves as a man and woman. Transsexuals are people who desire to permanently live as the opposite of their birth sex. Some choose to have sex reassignment surgery. This is what Wendell intended to do.

Over the next 18 months, we supported Wendell, his manager, and peers as he became Breanna. While Breanna was relieved that she experienced more acceptance than she had anticipated, some of her peers were relieved for an altogether different reason. "I finally had an answer to the great mystery: Why were Wendell's nails so perfect?!" exclaimed a fellow colleague.

While all of us — Breanna included — found joy, relief, and even humor in the situation, these were tricky waters to navigate. Hewitt's nondiscrimination policy at the time covered sexual orientation, but this was different than transgenderism. In consultation with the HRC, we recommended that Hewitt revise its policy to state that the company did not discriminate on the basis of "gender identity and expression." The CEO endorsed our recommendation and policy was set.

As usual, principle is one thing, implementation another. How and when do we introduce Breanna to Wendell's coworkers? What's the process for legally changing a person's gender and what implications does it have for benefits coverage? How do we deal with the very practical, yet sensitive issue of restroom use? The very real story in front of us jarred our ingrained presuppositions about what is proper.

But navigate we did. Wendell started to show up at certain after-hours events as Breanna. He began taking hormones and his body began to change. Eventually, Wendell transitioned to showing up as Breanna all day at work. We had a carefully choreographed change management process that included e-mails and face-to-face meetings with managers and peers. *New York Times* writer Lisa Belkin interviewed Breanna and wrote, "The workplace piece of her transgender puzzle, the part she had worried about most, 'turned out to be the simplest,' she said. 'That was a surprise.'"[26]

Along the way, we not only got educated on transgender issues, but — as often happens when we learn to constructively call out differences — we suddenly gained new insights into other issues, such as gender. What does it mean, when you really think about it, to be male or female? Is gender a binary either/or identity or is it more of a continuum? What does masculinity and femininity mean after all? Right now, picture in your mind what masculine and feminine look like to you. Now think about all the men and women you know. How much do they overlap in their gender expression in terms of what it means to be a man or a woman?

The transgender issue got me thinking about male/female workplace team interaction in ways that go beyond the Venus/Mars dichotomies or even some of the excellent social linguistic work by the renowned Dr. Deborah Tannen, who has written extensively on male and female differences in the workplace and elsewhere.

Today, 57 percent the Fortune 500 include "gender identity" in their non-discrimination policies, compared with only 3 percent in 2002, according to the HRC.[27]

The day after Breanna was introduced to her colleagues, she sent me an e-mail: "Today I could finally be me."

In the cacophony of contentious debates, what can we learn from LGBT in our midst?

Shhhh. Listen. ♀

SUMMARY POINTS

- Many LGBT employees are forced to remain in the closet at work in order to keep their jobs.
- A growing number of companies offer benefits and have adopted inclusive practices directed toward LGBT employees and consumers.
- Companies are starting to see the marketplace through LGBT eyes. Consumers from emerging markets, particularly LGBT, are actively considering an organization's internal diversity policies when selecting a company for business plans or when making purchasing decisions.

- Conversations grounded in relationships can foster dramatically different dynamics than those grounded in religion, politics, or other belief systems. Knowing someone on a personal level matters.
- In addressing many diversity issues, particularly those that deal with transgender employees, principles, practices, and policies may by easier to manage than actual implementation. Calling out differences and navigating the gap between assumptions and reality can make the constructive difference.

SHAPING YOUR STRATEGY

- On a scale of one to 10, where 10 is full acceptance, openness, and supportive policies of LGBT, and one is a place where LGBT employees are afraid to be out, where would you rate your company in terms of LGBT diversity?
- How would your LGBT employees answer the previous question? How would the rest of your work population answer it?

- Do you know your company's HRC Corporate Equality score? Do you know what you need to do to improve that score? If you have not participated, would you consider doing so? To find out more, please visit www.hrc.org/issues/workplace/cei_criteria.htm.
- Is there a way to use the strategy of focusing on relationship versus debate to create a more participatory and inclusive conversation around LGBT?

ABBREVIATED LGBT GLOSSARY

Bisexual
A person who is emotionally, romantically, sexually, and relationally attracted to both men and women, though not necessarily simultaneously. A bisexual person may not be equally attracted to both sexes, and the degree of attraction may vary as sexual identity develops over time.

Coming Out
The process in which a person first acknowledges, accepts, and appreciates his or her sexual orientation or gender identity and begins to share that with others.

Crossdresser
A person who sometimes dresses in clothing and/or accoutrements (such as makeup and accessories) traditionally associated with the opposite sex.

Gay
A man or woman who is emotionally, romantically, sexually, and relationally attracted to members of the same sex.

Gender

An internal sense of self and the role a person takes in social interactions, as in "man" or "woman," "masculine" or "feminine," "he" or "she." Gender involves a person's internal feelings of "gender identity," as well as external "gender role" or "gender expression." Gender is not a synonym for "sex," although the sex and gender of most people are congruent.

Gender Identity Disorder

Gender Identity Disorder is a psychological diagnosis recognized by the American Psychiatric Association. This disorder is marked by severe distress and discomfort caused by the conflict between one's gender identity and one's designated sex at birth. Not all transgender people experience gender dysphoria or are diagnosed with Gender Identity Disorder.

Gender Expression

All of the external characteristics and behaviors that are socially defined as either masculine or feminine, such as dress, grooming, mannerisms, speech patterns, and social interactions. Social or cultural norms vary widely and some characteristics that may be accepted as masculine, feminine, or neutral in one culture may not be assessed similarly in another culture.

Gender Identity

A person's innate, deeply felt psychological identification as masculine or feminine, which may or may not correspond to the person's body or what sex was originally listed on their birth certificate.

Gender Roles

Societal expectations of how we are supposed to appear and behave depending on one's being male or female. Among the most explicit social rules is that one is expected to present oneself in public in a manner consistent with one's sex, and that presentation is to be unambiguous.

Gender Transition

The term "transitioning" refers to the process through which a person modifies his or her physical characteristics and/or manner of gender expression to be consistent with his or her gender identity. This transition may include hormone therapy, sex-reassignment surgery and/or other components and is generally conducted under medical supervision based on a set of standards developed by medical professionals. The transition process typically includes a one-year "real-life experience" in which the individual lives and presents consistently with their gender identity under medical supervision.

Gender Variance

The degree to which a person's gender identity or gender expression is different from cultural expectations. A gender variant person is one whose gender variance is high enough for them to be harassed or discriminated against.

Homophobia

The fear and hatred of — or discomfort with — people who love and are sexually attracted to members of the same sex.

LGBT

An acronym for "Lesbian, Gay, Bisexual, and Transgender" (also written as GLBT).

Lesbian

A woman who is emotionally, romantically, sexually, and relationally attracted to other women.

Living Openly

A state in which LGBT people are open with others about being LGBT.

Outing

Exposing someone's sexual orientation as gay, lesbian, bisexual or transgender to others, usually without their permission – in essence "outing" them from the closet.

Queer

A term that is inclusive of people who are not heterosexual. For many LGBT people, the word has a negative connotation. However, younger LGBT people are often comfortable using it.

Sexual Orientation

An individual's physical and/or emotional attraction to the same and/or opposite gender.

Sexual Preference

What a person likes or prefers to do sexually – a conscious recognition or choice, not to be confused with sexual orientation.

Straight Supporter/Ally

A person who supports and honors sexual diversity, acts accordingly to challenge homo-phobic remarks and behaviors, and explores and understands these forms of bias within him- or herself.

Sex

Categorization as female or male based on anatomic features or other biological mark-ers such as chromosomes or hormones.

Sex Reassignment Surgery (SRS)

Surgical transformation of the genital area from the appearance characteristic of one sex to that of the other sex; may also include breast reduction in transsexual men.

Target Sex

The sex toward which an individual is transitioning.

Transgender

A term describing a broad range of people who experience and/or express their gender differently from what most people expect. It is an umbrella term that includes people who are transsexual, crossdressers or otherwise gender non-conforming.

Transsexual

A medical term describing people whose gender and sex do not match, and who often seek medical treatment to bring their body and gender identity into alignment.

Definitions by the Human Rights Campaign (HRC) and Hewitt Associates.

Chapter 11

The Power of Diversity
Through the Arts

As I've stated repeatedly throughout this book, diversity is the mix and inclusion is making the mix work™. I want to conclude this section on Calling Out Different Groups by turning our attention to the world of the arts, where making the mix work is an everyday part of the artistic experience. The stories in this chapter — about the Luna Negra Dance Theater, the Chicago Sinfonietta, the Ravinia Summer Music Festival, and the Sushi Samba Rio restaurant — demonstrate how art is diverse and inclusive. The mix is an end in itself as well as a means to an end. It is literal, and it is a metaphor. The mix is there, and it works!

The ability to experience Luna Negra's *Mi Corazon Negro* (My Black Heart) set to Afro-Peruvian songs performed live by South American singer Susana Baca or taste Sushi Samba Rio's yellowtail sashimi tiradito is a powerful, inclusive experience for someone who deeply misses home. As a Latino who grew up in Peru with a Peruvian dad and American mom, and is now living in the United States, these diverse artistic experiences let me see my work, my family, my cultures, my friends, my communities, my countries on stage or on a plate. It is seeing, feeling, and tasting my life.

The first time I saw Luna Negra Dance Theater perform, my heart skipped a beat, then raced. By the end, it soared. Its artistic fusion of Latin, modern, and classical dance forms created something new, beautiful, and inspiring. Watching Luna Negra's dancers spin, twirl, jump, turn, twist, spiral, bend, and float moved me to imagine new possibilities — not just personally, but also for the work of diversity.

Here in Chicago at the Harris Theater for Music and Dance at Millennium Park, the stage bursts with exuberant and inclusive diversity. Luna Negra's choreography fuses Afro-Latin three-two beat syncopation with modern dance's boundary-breaking moves, all grounded in classical ballet rigor. The challenges, contradictions, and never-before-seen possibilities of these divergent influences blend to build a creative tension with an exhilarating payoff for audiences and dancers alike.

Fusion involves recognizing something familiar at a visceral level, yet feeling surprise and delight at some facet that's never been seen or felt before. Luna Negra's dance fusion plays to an audience that's truly representative of Chicago's racial, ethnic, age, and income diversity. Walking through the marvelously diverse crowd during intermission, I wondered if a few shows appealing to different demographics had let out all at once. Suddenly, I realized that this beautiful, fascinating collection of people was connected by a common desire to celebrate differences, to see new creation in movement and expression.

Down the street at Orchestra Hall, the Chicago Sinfonietta — which bills itself as "the nation's most diverse orchestra" — is doing some musical fusion of its own, marrying classical music and alternative rock. During *Carmen Remixed*, multiple interpretations of George Bizet's classic romantic opera are played by-the-book, reverently, and then reinterpreted, at times irreverently, through the arms, hands, and mouths of the multiracial, multiethnic Sinfonietta, performing alongside the Chicago-based alternative rock band Poi Dog Pondering.

By combining the ancient and genteel sounds of winds and strings with the rebellious rhythms of rock 'n' roll, the Chicago Sinfonietta creates an exquisitely stirring, insightful, and redemptive musical experience that brings down the house. By the final crash of cymbals, old and new, traditional and alternative, control and exuberance are on full display as point and complementary counterpoint. For the Sinfonietta — like Luna Negra — diversity is not just something different to appreciate, but the vital ingredient in a never-before-experienced event.

Near Chicago's Magnificent Mile, Sushi Samba Rio artistically fuses the cuisine and spices of Brazil, Japan, and Peru. Executive Chef Abel Cortes brings forth mesmerizing and passionate creations, combining Peruvian Andean corn and purple potatoes with Japanese sushi and Brazilian spices like *malagueta*. In this creative culinary expression, unconventional ingredient combinations bring forth new bursts of flavor that excite diners day and night.

The underlying premise and promise of diversity is that, in the *paella* of differences, new solutions, new products, and new ideas are possible — ideas that could not be envisioned in a monochromatic *caldo*, or broth, of uniform environments where everyone is the same.

Powerfully and poignantly, art captures this vision. Whether through dance, music, or food, we experience more sensory dimensions of diversity. This, in turn, inspires us to tap into new vehicles for deepening and widening the reach and impact of our work.

With the arts enjoying a renaissance in various U.S. cities (including Chicago),[1] we have the perfect opportunity to bring the arts into diversity work. Art infused with diversity can bring to life game-changing inclusion principles. Consider creating inclusion by:

* Bringing down barriers
* Accepting new ways of excelling
* Diversifying offerings
* Challenging all to see themselves and others in new ways
* Equipping newcomers to navigate the legacy culture
* Surfacing difficult truths

Create Inclusion by Bringing Down Barriers

From its beginnings in 1987, the Sinfonietta was about getting the mix — *diversity* — into one of the most segregated forums in the Western World, the symphony orchestra. And while the story of how they did it demonstrates how difficult this can be, they also found how much more powerful inclusion — making the mix work — can be. The Sinfonietta's founder and conductor (until 2011) and its Board figured out that it needed to embrace the Inclusion Paradox — that is, it needed to call out differences among its members and among different musical styles — to create truly inclusive environments.

But first, the mix. Since childhood, Maestro Paul Freeman pursued classical music passionately through the clarinet and the cello. In public, however, he had to listen to the Richmond Symphony Orchestra from the segregated black balcony. He vowed then to someday be part of breaking through this color barrier.

Freeman earned a doctorate from the prestigious Eastman School of Music, yet still encountered difficulties securing a job as a conductor. There were almost no African-Americans conducting symphony orchestras at that time, and it looked like no one was inclined to give Freeman the opportunity he had worked so hard to earn. Three weeks before Dr. Martin Luther King, Jr.'s life was cut short by a sniper's bullet, Maestro Freeman ran into the Civil Rights icon late one night at the Atlanta Airport. He told King *his* dream to create and lead a diverse orchestra. On hearing about his vision for an integrated orchestra, Dr. King replied, "The symphony orchestra. The last bastion of elitism. Hallelujah."

Nineteen years later, Maestro Freeman founded the Sinfonietta. Today, 35 to 40 percent of the Sinfonietta's musicians are people of color and half are female. Minorities hold the lead chairs in viola, timpani, and clarinet. This mix of musicians consistently garners acclaim. By comparison, the Chicago Symphony Orchestra counts just one African-American and no Latinos among its 110 musicians.[2]

The Sinfonietta's diversity story demonstrates that breaking down barriers requires commitment and intentionality. It does not happen organically or through good intentions — not in the arts nor in corporations. And it definitely does not happen by lowering standards. Though musicians of color are underrepresented in classical music, plenty of female and minority musicians with world-class skills are available. This is also true for engineers, accountants, lawyers, and technologists.

Create Inclusion by Accepting New Ways of Excelling

Watching Luna Negra's principal dancer, Vanessa Valecillos, manipulate a classical arabesque into a poem of culturally-specific memory is like drinking a *mojito* during *Swan Lake*.

Founder and artistic director in its first ten years, Eduardo Vilaro has always dealt with imposed identity. "Everyone, from audience members to theater representatives, sees our name and immediately expects a representation of a mainstream idea of Latino," he says. "Some people want us to be salsa dancers, others want us to be a trendy contemporary company. We are championing fusion."

Over the years, we've gotten better at bringing the mix into corporations as we've gotten relatively comfortable with people who *look* different. But we've been surprised when people *behave* differently. That's when the corporate organism begins to release "we don't do it that way here" antibodies that exclude newcomers. In the talent acquisition arena, the onboarding process is often referred to as "assimilation." In assimilation, the idea is that all melts down into indistinctness. No wonder we still witness exclusion and higher turnover for diverse talent.

Not only should we *accept* new ways of doing business, we should recognize that we *need* these different approaches to prosper. Through art, we see and feel how diverse elements can be brought together to create something powerful and unimaginable. In a global, 24/7, upside-down world, where European-American wisdom and power face brazen challenges, new influences fused with legacy experience are a must. In fusion, the different elements retain their essence even as they morph. Luna Negra's eclectic repertoire unveils dualities that help us discover new insights into our personal and corporate quests for inclusion.

Create Inclusion by Diversifying Offerings

As the arts extend their diversity exploration and outreach, they pull in new audiences that never before would have even thought about entering the carpeted steps of Orchestra Hall or going online to buy tickets to a ballet.

Welz Kauffman, CEO of the Ravinia Musical Festival, is fully aware of the need to reach these new audiences. The 100-year-old, one-of-a-kind outdoor musical festival serves as the summer home to the Chicago Symphony Orchestra. Yo-Yo Ma, Luciano Pavarotti, Christopher Parkening, and Itzhak Perlman have graced its stage as thousands of classical music lovers relax on the lawn, sipping wine and savoring Brie cheese on sesame seed crackers. Ravinia's classical music tradition endures, sustained by the presence and donations of predominantly older White audiences, the primary cultural demographic for symphony music.

Yet Ravinia has long pulled in other musical traditions, too, such as jazz from Ramsey Lewis, and Boomer and folk music from Peter, Paul, and Mary. But even these musical acts catered to predominantly White audiences. "While retaining our core traditional audiences," says Welz, "we must attract new audiences." Welz understands the major demographic tsunami swelling in the United States. In 1950, when Ravinia was just 42 years old, 90 percent of the United States was White. But, as the Census Bureau recently reported, only half of the United States will be White by the time the festival celebrates its 134th birthday in 2042.[3] This dizzying rate of demographic shifts calls for radically different musical acts to enhance the Ravinia musical smorgasbord.

So Luna Negra and Tiempo Libre — a Miami-based salsa band — made opening night performances for Ravinia's 2008 season. In the middle of Ravinia's fabled lawn, a Latin dance contest was held under a tent. Los Tigres del Norte, a south-of-the-border *ranchera* band, pulls in Mexican families from a 50-mile radius, while Led Zeppelin frontman Robert Plant pulls in rock 'n' roll Boomers and hard rock fans; Feist draws the Millennials, while the Temptations and the Four Tops attract African-Americans.

Ravinia's 2009 line-up was even more diverse, boasting current hitmakers like John Legend (an African-American R&B singer/songwriter) and Carrie Underwood (a country songstress). Also on the docket were long-time favorites like Jackson Browne, Elvis Costello, Tom Jones, and Emmylou Harris, along with legendary crooner Tony Bennett and top classical artists Jessye Norman and Thomas Hampson.

Tapping into new audiences means growth. Since aggressively mixing its lineup, Ravinia's attendance and revenue have increased by nearly 10 percent, according to Welz. Similarly, as Luna Negra continues to draw these same emerging audiences, the company has seen its income triple in just three years.

The Sinfonietta's diverse musicians and repertoire have brought new audiences into Orchestra Hall. While Chicago Symphony Orchestra audiences and those of other big city symphonies are around 1 to 2 percent diverse,[4] the Sinfonietta's is 35 percent. Says Maestro Freeman, "It's about diversity, top to bottom. Our primary social mission has always been to provide music for everyone — all races, all creeds." When asked his favorite color, he replies, "All of them."

New audiences bring new behaviors. At Luna Negra performances, when the curtain rises, the audience cheers before the dance has even started — something unheard of in concert dance circles. New Broadway audiences also are bringing a new vibe, as *New York Times* reporter Josh Getlin describes in writing about the 2008 Tony Award-winning musical, *In the Heights*, which focuses on a Hispanic New York City neighborhood facing gentrification:

"There are telltale moments when Lin-Manuel Miranda, the star and creator of *In the Heights*, ... whenever he mentions the Dominican Republic or Puerto Rico in a rap song, or watches cast members unfurl the Mexican flag, ecstatic cheers ring out. Similar moments occur for Stew, who wrote and performs in *Passing Strange*, the new musical about a Black kid from Los Angeles ... At key points, large blocks of the audience — often Blacks and young people — rise to their feet singing, as though they are in church or at a rock concert. 'I wanted to put on a show that looked like the world I grew up in,' says Miranda. Meanwhile, *Passing Strange*, Stew says, draws new patrons 'because we encourage people to participate. It's like we've given them their own voice in the theater.'"[5]

As corporations seek to attract diverse talent — and keep diverse workers excited about staying and giving their best — they can learn some lessons from the arts. Practices that have succeeded for years in attracting talent — the corporate equivalent of attracting performers — are now losing their magnetic power when it comes to talent with different experiences, backgrounds, and expectations. Companies need to continue pressing themselves to better understand these new and talented workers by tapping into the diversity they already have. Leaders and managers must also be ready for new behaviors in their hallways and conference rooms. While such endeavors can be challenging, when successful, they lead to this talent's deep connection with the organization.

THE ARTS AND DIVERSITY WORK

The Arts and Diversity
How closely related are the arts and diversity?
Consider the following characteristics about art:

Art exists in all cultures.
Art challenges us to see others and ourselves in new ways.
Art helps us face difficult truths.
Art provokes.
Art inspires.
Art reveals what is hidden.
Art teaches.
Art creates something new.
Art brings down barriers.

Now read the list again and substitute "art" with "diversity."

Create Inclusion by Challenging All to See Others and Themselves in New Ways

Quinceañera is one of Luna Negra's signature pieces about the quintessential Latin American rite of passage when a young girl becomes a young woman. During this piece, Vilaro's choreography takes deep tradition symbolized in rituals, such as the girl receiving her last doll and her first pair of high-heeled shoes, and creates something simultaneously familiar and new to both Latino and non-Latino audiences.

The quinceañera rituals may feel unfamiliar to non-Latino audiences, but the classical dance movements offer a culturally resonating experience coupled with a universal coming-of-age narrative. For Latinos, there will be the knowing nods of "I've lived that" and yet unfamiliar movements from different dance traditions that shed deeper insight into their own Latin culture. In this fusion, Vilaro brings different audiences together in one shared experience, despite different starting points.

"We take Latino traditions and deconstruct work that reveals who we are as Latinos today, to then reconstruct it in a new way of looking at culture, dance, movement," says Vilaro. "It's very difficult to capture what is Latino now when there are such icons of what Latino has been through the ages. People usually refer to the regular stuff such as the red dresses, the castanets, the tropical island. That's not all that we are today. We are all that and this more contemporary being."

Successful corporate diversity efforts also challenge us to rethink common assumptions about our identities and how they show up in the workplace. They require a combination of affirming our roots, while at the same time examining how we're changing based on diverse interactions in society and the workplace. Culture is never static. We need to deconstruct where we came from, consider its effect on how we approach our work and coworkers, then reconstruct what it means to be a worker in the new global economy.

Create Inclusion by Equipping Newcomers to Navigate the Legacy Culture

During a 20-year period at the helm, Maestro Freeman had set a foundation that would continually create opportunities for talented musicians of all cultures. Maestro Freeman's legacy is not only doing this with musicians of color just starting their careers, but also with those who are experienced but looking to break through into a bigger arena. The epitome of this was when he handed his baton to his successor, a female, Taiwanese conductor Mei-Ann Chen. Since then Chen has rocked the orchestral world, and in 2012, just one year after her tenure as conductor and artistic director began, the League of American Orchestras awarded the Sinfonietta with an ASCAP Award for Adventurous Programming and Chen the Helen M. Thompson Award, which honors one conductor every other year that they believe has the potential for an important national and/or international career. Receiving both awards in the same year is an extremely unusual occurrence.

From its inception, the Sinfonietta's personnel manager and Maestro Freeman actively sought talented minority musicians to occupy the seats. Candidates had to go through a rigorous audition process, and once selected, they were expected to display the highest levels of professionalism and musical ability. The orchestra's diverse representation and consistently high levels of performances have proven the veracity of this approach. Continuing this effort, the Sinfonietta launched Project Inclusion, which focuses on building a pipeline of talent by identifying and mentoring college-age musicians of color.

Studies have shown that the gender and race of auditioning musicians influence selection juries composed of mostly White males. Recognizing that this perpetuates the lack of diversity, some orchestras have begun instituting color-blind auditions where a curtain separates candidates from selectors. Assessed only on musicianship, audition winners tend to be more diverse.

Despite its Latin roots, Luna Negra is a diverse company, boasting dancers from all ethnic groups. Still, it deliberately maintains a pipeline of Latino and women choreographers. While women dominate the dancer ranks, they are almost nonexistent among choreographers. Luna Negra accomplishes this seemingly impossible task by commissioning works from Latinas and having all-female choreographed performances.

While corporations don't hand out bows and music stands, they face the same challenges around lack of representation in different types of roles. In many organizations, certain jobs and certain levels remain remarkably homogenous, so much so that it's hard to imagine things being any different. A diverse symphony orchestra? A diverse executive team? To find and assess diverse talent, we must defy convention. Like Luna Negra, companies must do their part to pave the way for minorities and women to enter fields they've avoided in the past. This can be accomplished by investing in apprenticeships, scholarships, and internship programs. Neither orchestra nor corporation can depend on someone else to build a pipeline of diverse talent for them.

Create Inclusion by Surfacing Difficult Truths

Hunched, hooded figures walk single file across the stage. Moments later, shadows run in the opposite direction. Gathering in the middle, they pirouette a protest. They stag leap away from the authoritarian response, arms raised, index finger pointing, thumb pointing upward, and then up against their temples. The percussion beats louder, the sharp clap, the figures swivel convulsively down to the floor, as the Luna Negra dancers resurrect the ghosts of the 1968 student massacre in Mexico City. The performance is a fusion of contemporary dance, West African movement, and indigenous Mexican patterning. The music is Café Tacuba, heavily influenced by Mexico's indigenous population and folk music traditions, but also by punk and electronic music. The rich, multigenerational mix of influences makes history immediate, as shameful pasts find echoes in current world events. Art confronts denial.

It's the Sinfonietta's annual Dr. Martin Luther King, Jr. tribute. It's quite an event, complete with historian Lerone Bennett, an African-American teen piano virtuoso, a storyteller, and spiritual music backed by a 200-person gospel choir. In this mix, where differences are called out, the audience connects not only with the artists in the orchestra, but with each other. In the tribute's final crescendo, the audience is on its feet holding hands ... swaying ... swinging ... singing *We Shall Overcome*. The drums swell, horns blare, and strings soar, as the gospel choir belts out the classic civil rights anthem. The mix is in the house and it's working, leaving all connected, uplifted, and hopeful about tomorrow. Remembering to keep hope alive. Art confronts despair.

The arts serve well as a metaphor for diversity, but I believe they can do more to help us further the work. Corporate diversity events resonate with inspiring speeches, testimonials, and exhortations. CEOs and other execs express their support. But tapping the drama of the arts, we can go further and deeper to puncture retro beliefs that have been hardened into words. The arts can be harnessed to confront the denial and despair around diversity that often shows up in the corporate world.

Sparking Innovation

In reflecting on Maestro Freeman and his effort to build the Sinfonietta, getting the mix was not enough. Freeman believed diversity was not just about equal opportunity and building an orchestra that looked like society, but that it could actually stimulate greater creativity and innovation. He recognized that calling out differences, rather than minimizing them, would enable him to exploit the power of the diverse symphony he had created. The results have been mind-bending and exhilarating. Said Freeman, "It was not only about bringing down barriers, obliterating presuppositions, knocking down stereotypes, but the question we sought to answer was, what will be different now that we are more diverse. So what?"

That *so what led to what if*. What if instead of cell phones being the enemy in the concert hall, they were part of the experience? This led to the penning of the *Concertino for Cell Phones and Orchestra* by African-American composer David Baker — a work where, rather than being asked to turn off their cell phones, audience members were asked to make them ring — and then to listen to their pitch and tone. In this way, the audience was given their own part to play. Maestro Freeman led both his classical orchestra on the stage and his cell phone instrumentalists on the floor. And so it goes. The Sinfonietta gives us *Tango Beethoven*. Luna Negra does *Nuevo Folk*. They make the mix work by offering paradox, duality, and unexpected syncretism.

In the process, the past is honored, as Bach, Beethoven, and Strauss are played to perfection according to traditional interpretation. Then they go into an innovative space where tradition and legacy, technique and innovation blend and create something new and powerful and beautiful. Fusion also means a mastering of the core essence of the cultures one is fusing. Luna Negra's choreography works because its core, ballet, is mastered by choreographers and dozens of dancers who all have classical dance training and performance experience. By mastering the rules of the classical, they now have the authority to break the rules as they bring in other influences to create something new. "Artists can only take risks when they have a strong foundation," says Vilaro.

As Frans Johansson writes in *The Medici Effect*, the greatest innovations happen when unrelated things, such as spiders' silk and goats' milk, are combined, resulting in a material that's stronger than steel. Or when the rigid classical lines of ballet are combined with the undulating movements of Latino folk dances like salsa or mambo.

One can taste the Peruvian spice within the Japanese raw fish preparation and celebrate a combination never tasted before. One can recognize the "pa-papa-pam" of Beethoven's Fifth, the classical pirouette en pointe that then leads into a salsa sashay that ends in a Paso Doble. After mastering legacy, exhilaration can follow when rules are bent or broken. We earn the right to create new by mastering tradition.

In the workplace, we need to understand the legacy culture — the traditional rules required to succeed. We must master those techniques so there is no question to our own competence. And when we do, we are best positioned to break the rules, introduce the unfamiliar, and invent the new.

Invading Spaces

In the same way that traditional art forms must seek new audiences, so must the work of diversity and inclusion. The challenge lies in figuring out how to reach those audiences within organizations that have long dismissed diversity events as something not intended for them.

We've begun invading the corporate public space by using the arts. Rather than asking people to come to an auditorium to experience a diversity event, we are taking diversity to public spaces to reach people who have not been reached before. Mariachis in the cafeteria cast a spell over workers eating their sandwiches. Luna Negra performs in the workplace, their costumes and soaring bodies catching the uninitiated in an emotional moment that conveys a truth about inclusion without any words being spoken.

The great diversity in the arts world has also invaded the White House during the Obama Era with public events that hosted a hip-hop performance by the artist Common, Latin musicians such as Gloria Estefan, Jose Feliciano, and Los Lobos, diverse dancers from the New York City Ballet and the African-American modern dance company Alvin Ailey American Dance Theater, and comic performances by George Lopez and Jaime Foxx as well as traditional classical and jazz artists. The extensive range of music and artistic diversity invited to perform mirror the diversity of the country. During the Fiesta Latino performance at the White House, which included musical offerings of reggaeton, Tejano, and salsa, President Obama quoted singer Gloria Estefan saying, "The most beautiful things in this country have the flavor of other places."

President Obama sees how the arts can help us see the common experiences that unite us and, at the same time, bridge our differences. He said, "One of the most extraordinary features of America's cultural inheritance is its dynamism and its diversity. It's a culture that produced Mark Twain and Toni Morrison, John Philip Sousa and Louis Armstrong, Marian Anderson and Alvin Ailey. It's a culture in which all of us can find a place, in which all of us can take great pride. ... No matter what community we call our own, all of us can be moved by a symphony, or an aria; all of us can be moved by a soprano's voice; all of us can be moved by a film's score. The arts, the humanities, they appeal to a certain yearning that's shared by all of us — a yearning for truth and for beauty, for connection and the simple pleasure of a good story."

Through diversity and inclusion, each group has cultural gifts to offer others. It's not by simply learning about each other, but by sharing who we are that we unlock new ways to see ourselves.

"In Luna Negra's fusion, the diversity we find enables each of us, regardless of whether we are Latino or not, to find ourselves in the many cultural stories," Vilaro says. He goes on to share the story of an Eastern European woman who approached him after the performance of *Vuelo del Alma* (Flight of the Soul), a dance about immigration and what we end up leaving behind. Though the symbology in the piece had Latino influences, "she told me excitedly, 'You made my story!'"

The arts help us see in new and insightful ways the lives and aspirations of others — and new possibilities for us all. ○

SUMMARY POINTS

- The arts enable society to powerfully and poignantly capture the vision and reality of diversity and inclusion. Whether through dance, music, or food, we experience more sensory dimensions of diversity while tapping into new vehicles for deepening and widening the reach and impact of our work.
- Art infused with diversity brings game-changing inclusion principles to life.
- Corporations can borrow from the diversity of the arts to infuse their own efforts. Successful corporate diversity efforts mirror diversity in the arts by calling for approaches that challenge us to rethink common assumptions and reaffirm our roots, while at the same time examining how we're changing based on the diverse interactions we have in society and in the workplace.
- Diversity and inclusion, like culture, is never static.
- We need to deconstruct where we came from, consider its effect on how we approach our work and coworkers, then reconstruct what it means to be a worker in the new global economy.
- The arts serve well as a metaphor for diversity, but they can do more to help us further our work. As with all aspects of the human existence, the arts can be harnessed to confront the denial and despair, as well as the hope and opportunities surrounding diversity in the corporate world.

SHAPING YOUR STRATEGY

- How can your corporation borrow from the arts to infuse its own diversity efforts?
- What are some common assumptions you and your coworkers share about diversity, both in the workplace and within society as a whole? How can you examine these assumptions and, using art as a metaphor for diversity, change them to benefit your workplace?

PART 4: CALLING OUT DIFFERENCES IN ORGANIZATIONS

Calling Out Differences in Organizations

Organizations are living organisms. In many ways, they act like people. They're equally as culturally complex as the humans who comprise them. So while we are bulking up our own crosscultural strengths, we must remember to develop this competency within our organizations as well.

Beyond essential strategies and techniques for creating organizational change — such as rewards, training, leadership, and engagement — this section of the book focuses on the actual cultural dynamics that take place in increasingly diverse organizations. These are, in essence, the worldviews that shape organizational culture and, in turn, suggest approaches for defining good work, fair policies, and engaging environments.

As with people and groups, what seems "right and true" in an organization may simply be, as Dr. R. Roosevelt Thomas Jr. says, "a preference, tradition, or convenience," but not necessarily a "requirement" for getting the job done.[1] To create true inclusion, where the mix is working creatively and efficiently, we must call out our differences within the organization. For example, do the needs of Millennials, Xers, women, and racial minorities within an organization vary significantly from the needs of the mainstream workforce? Are leaders adequately equipped to lead diverse and multicultural teams in the global marketplace? And how do organizations adequately prepare for the Talent War, especially one that's already being lost in junior highs and high schools, where students of color are graduating in decreasing numbers and without relevant skills?

We must consider the unexpected places in organizations where exclusion may inadvertently occur — within benefits offerings, for example. You may be surprised to learn the different perspectives African-Americans, Latinos, women, and White men bring to retirement investing or maximizing their healthcare benefits. What works for one does not automatically work for another. Organizations must take special care to develop benefit plans and marketing tools tailored to each community's specific worldview.

It's hard enough to manage individual change, but in the end, will, strength, skill, and motivation can be enough. When it comes to organizations, change is even more difficult to achieve, and these four dimensions are simply not enough. The inertia of "how things have always been," the Herculean task of changing people's minds, and the ability to create a new path where one previously did not exist create barriers to delivering organizational change. This is why many companies often fail to round the bend when dangerous curves lie ahead, instead plunging off the precipice because they cannot control their momentum.

In spite of these obstacles, a number of organizations have managed to round the curve of change successfully. Their leaders sounded the clarion call for change just in time to make the hairpin turn, allowing them to make the necessary adjustments and investments. These organizations grasped the depth of the challenges posed to systems and structures created for another era and were courageous enough to engage in what Joseph Schumpeter referred to as "creative destruction."[2]

In the Obama Era, entire nations are facing this type of transformational challenge. If ever there was a time to begin an honest evaluation of our programs, policies, and processes — the very ones that contributed to past successes — that time is now. ♀

MENTORING

COMMUNITY

RECOGNITION

ADVANCEMENT

Chapter 12

The Four Pillars of
What Makes People of Color
Stay and Thrive

Her dismay was palpable. As chief diversity officer of a Fortune 500 company, she rightfully felt proud of the ten MBA hires they snagged at the National Black MBA Association annual conference. But within a year, they were all gone.

She reviewed the massive effort it had taken to recruit them, beginning with obtaining the commitment from the CEO and senior VP of HR for the budget and resources to stage a convincing presence at the conference. Those costs were substantial — $50,000 to sponsor the event; $35,000 to transport and set up their booth; and the travel costs of more than 30 recruiters, hiring managers, and diversity practitioners, along with the costs of setting up follow-up interviews, flying candidates to corporate offices, onboarding, and then training in the company's methodologies. And now once again, they had ten open positions to fill and all the extra time and money it would require, not to mention the economic loss in productivity. This "revolving door syndrome" is one particularly painful aspect of our ongoing two-steps-forward-one-step-back work.

Many of our companies have gotten quite good at multicultural recruiting. We show up at the marquee diversity events, such as The National Society of Hispanic MBAs (NSHMBA), Black Data Processing Associates (BDPA), State Health Insurance Assistance Program (SHIP), and the National Association of

Asian American Professionals (NAAAP). We hound recruiters to maximize local diversity job fairs. We spend big bucks on four-color ads in *DiversityInc, Black Enterprise, The Advocate, and Hispanic Magazine*, among a few dozen others. We've got our story down to a compelling, inspiring "we-want-you-because-we-believe-in-diversity" message. And the recruits buy it ...

... until they hit the hidden barriers of exclusion ... until they experience the raised eyebrows of disapproval when they apparently said something out of turn ... until they see someone from the majority who started at the same time get the plum project that's often followed by the even "plummer" promotion ... until the great effort with the high-impact result passes without comment or is minimized with a "that's the least we expect from you" shrug ... until they get that first per-formance review with the message of "you seem to be doing fine, *but* ... " And so the engagement strands that connect the employee to the organization begin to snap, one by one. This weakened connection gives way then to the third or fourth call from the headhunter that this time gets returned and soon the employee is gone. The gain for the company is then erased.

According to a Hewitt client survey a few years ago, two-thirds of companies focus on recruitment, but only one-third focus on retention.[1] In response to this gap, chief diversity officers are increasingly shifting their focus from merely finding employees to keeping them. Good work is indeed happening in the areas of men-toring, development, promotion, rotational roles, and other creative approaches — yet we still have a way to go in mastering their implementation. What is often overlooked is the elusive element of creating a culture of inclusion. Companies must ask themselves, what must be put in place so people who have traditionally been outside the mainstream feel they're truly part of the community, rather than intruders at worst and guests at best?

At this point, using the principle that cultures are different, I'd like to present what I consider the four pillars for engagement and retention:

• Community
• Recognition
• Mentoring
• Advancement

While more than a dozen best practice engagement factors are important to all majority and minority employees, this quartet of factors resonates especially deeply with multicultural employees. Together, these four pillars will create a solid foundation for the engagement and retention of multicultural talent.

Community

Let's return to the cultural studies discussed in Chapter 4. As you will recall, Trompenaars and Hampden-Turner identified seven cultural dimensions that manifest themselves differently in different cultures. Some cultures believe identity comes from the group they belong to. Others believe it comes through the individual. They refer to this as Communitarianism vs. Individualism. All four major racial/ethnic minority groups in the United States (Black, Latino, Asian, and Native American) are communal cultures where the sense of group identity — as expressed by *la familia*, the clan, the church, the affinity group — is deeply ingrained. This is in contrast to the majority culture of European-Americans, which is more individualistic. It's no coincidence that the first-person pronoun in English ("I") is the only pronoun that is capitalized in any language.

This is why affinity groups are of particular importance to multicultural employees. A minority needs a place of refuge in a majority sea. There's a primal desire to be connected to others "like me." This centering, connecting practice — which nurtures a full sense of identity — explains the allure of affinity groups. But there's another community connection that's often overlooked. Members of communitarian cultures long for a sense of connection to the larger community, which is the enterprise. If their only connection is to the demographic affinity group and not to the full corporate community, their sense of identity within the corporate walls will be incomplete, leading to disengagement and eventually turnover.

This is why it's critical to identify those elements required to have an inclusive culture. No one likes being excluded. To be excluded from the community is to have part of one's identity truncated. For multicultural employees, exclusion has not only been painfully real, its negative impact goes deeper, given their longing to be part of something larger than themselves. Corporate cultures, so dominated by the European-American individualistic culture, often overlook the higher-octane energy that could be infused into their corporations by more effectively nurturing enterprise-wide community building. They ignore the reaction of multicultural employees who never fail to notice when CEOs and other executive leaders — even middle managers — show up at heritage month events.

Nor does their absence go unnoticed. Individualistic cultures may minimize the potential impact of their presence since all they did was show up. But for the communal cultures, showing up does something vitally important: It affirms the multicultural group as part of the larger community. More importantly, it's a declaration that the leader also wants to be part of the multicultural community. Those with individualistic worldviews must evaluate the benefit of the event not in terms of how it will benefit them personally, but how their presence will benefit the community.

Another example can be found in the "default settings" — the themes, food, and entertainment that get selected for community events sponsored by the enterprise. Is there a cultural bias toward rock 'n' roll, golf, and pizza? How about some soul food, salsa dancing, and soccer? Or the inclusion of *arroz con pollo*, greens, and Filipino *pancit*?

Corporations must take these same factors into consideration when contemplating their benefits administration. Are they relying too much on an individualistic approach to preventive care ("take care of yourself, go for your physical")? Would they be better served by fostering communal on-site health care clinics where employees can bring their families as part of a communal event complete with free checkups, immunizations, and health risk assessments?

The idea here is not to be prescriptive, but to acknowledge that the active nurturing and building of community goes a long way toward engaging and retaining multicultural employees.

Recognition

For multicultural groups that have traditionally been oppressed and marginalized, public recognition is like water in the desert. Oppression and marginalization are acts of dehumanization. They are declarations through words and deeds that certain groups are not fully human since there are restrictions on their universal human rights. When a person of color is recognized publicly for his or her achievement, it's more than an affirming statement. It is a frontal assault on centuries of messages implying that people of color do not matter, that they cannot achieve, that they cannot excel. It is an act that bestows dignity by declaring, *You exist. You are valuable. You matter!*

Given the communal nature of multicultural groups, recognition of the one is recognition of the many. The community as a whole takes pride in the achievement of one of its own. Postings of recognition are often widely circulated by leaders of affinity groups to their membership lists. Of course, recognition can come in many forms. But for people of color, the public nature of recognition is vital. That's why corporate cultures with understated approaches to recognition may inadvertently undermine the desired payoff when recognition is done quietly rather than shouted from the rooftops. For people of color, recognition reverberates even more powerfully when it's done outside the corporate walls. This is why talented professionals of color are often the recipients of numerous awards and recognitions granted by community, not-for-profit, and volunteer organizations with an array of honorifics — such as Outstanding African-American of the Year, Community Role Model Professional, Latin Pride — awarded at elegant banquets and trumpeted through press releases.

Too often, these third-party recognitions are overlooked by the corporations where these individuals work. If colleagues and leaders from the enterprise would show up more regularly at these events, the third-party recognition would be magnified exponentially. Why? Because showing up on their turf further reinforces the message that these associates matter. It declares that where they live and the communities they're a part of have value and legitimacy. They're as real and genuine as the places frequented by the enterprise leaders. Companies can also do a better job of making the community and the press aware of recognitions and promotions awarded to their multicultural talent. When these types of approaches are used, we start getting into the synergistic power of the pillars of multicultural engagement and retention. Recognition to the individual speaks. Recognition among the internal community sings. Recognition among the external community proclaims.

Mentoring

Much has been researched, quantified, qualified, and written about the role mentoring plays in the advancement of multicultural talent. Every day, conversations with multicultural talent reinforce how mentoring from senior leadership increases their possibilities for *advancement* and adds to their sense of connection to the *community*. Mentoring is also a form of *recognition* that leads to multicultural talent being more public about this pivotal relationship with members of the majority group. Mentoring, then, is a pillar with deep structural connections to the other three pillars.

That's not to suggest that mentoring is entirely without flaws. There is a problematic, potentially undermining assumption behind traditional mentoring — that it's still a one-up, one-down relationship. More often than not, it's the White male who remains in the position of authority. And it's the multicultural employee who is left to glean secrets on how to enter the inner circle.

Even here, there's still value because in all communities — whether executive-floor corporate swamis or Amazon-like tribal executives — the ushering in of the new by those who have come before is as human and ancient as the creation of hierarchy. However, we must recognize this for what it is. Receiving tips about what will or will not get you acceptance or the types of behavior that will elicit the sidelong glance of disapproval and silent gonging is priceless. But at what cost?

Traditional mentoring has the inherent contradiction of creating a vehicle for inclusion — not necessarily by dismantling the barriers of exclusion, but by revealing the paths around them. "It may indeed be an old boys' network, but let us teach you the ropes" is the name of this game. While unspoken, it is still understood: "Yes, deals do take place on the golf course, so we'll foster this mentoring relationship on the back nine as I help you get to know some of the company's movers and shakers."

We can't be naive and say this is not helpful. For those on the receiving end of the mentoring, it's incredibly advantageous in terms of getting connected to leaders who can open some doors. But this is not the way to sustainable, transformative change that would positively benefit professionals of color beyond a mere handful. It perpetuates the exclusiveness of a process that continually puts those who are different at a disadvantage. It also perpetuates an asymmetrical view of mentoring.

We need to rethink this concept.

Does mentoring have to be hierarchical? What about reciprocal mentoring, where the assumption is that executives not only have something to impart, but also something to learn from the multicultural employee they're partnered with? We saw the impact of this in Chapter 5, where I described the Crosscultural Learning Partners Program.

Traditional mentoring is intended to overcome a risk aversion on the part of the power elites about whom they let into the cockpit. That anxiety is assuaged in large part through relationships. "I know who he or she is when no one is looking," is the sought-after testimonial. "She's good people." This relational dynamic can lead to the inadvertent exclusion of multicultural talent from job-advancement opportunities because they simply are not known. This then causes a greater risk aversion on the part of the majority leaders when it comes to their advancement. The bigger barrier in these cases may not necessarily be race/ethnicity or gender, but rather that majority leaders simply don't *know* their multicultural talent. Yet it's that very diverse background that has inadvertently created social barriers for getting to know them.

Reciprocal mentoring addresses this need for leaders to get to know these individuals up close and personal, without falling into the hierarchical form of mentoring. At the same time, it provides a learning environment for the corporate executive to personally and professionally benefit from one of the basic premises behind diversity — diverse talent brings new and fresh perspectives to age-old as well as cutting-edge business issues.

Mentoring programs that are not reciprocal — where the burden of guiding the other is carried by the senior leader — are well-intentioned, but have inherent limitations. They assume the minority or woman being mentored has little to offer the senior leader in return. Reciprocal mentoring programs, on the other hand, help break through cultural assumptions about what is good and strong leadership.

Advancement

This pillar cannot be realized without the other three, but the first three do not guarantee this final one. No advancement means there has been no progress.

In 2012, 70 percent of the U.S. workforce became women and minorities.[2] Yet, the lack of meaningful representation of these key populations in leadership is one of the greatest challenges for today's corporations. The presence of role models for diverse talent across the organization is vital. And considering the accelerated globalization of the marketplace, it's clear that diverse leadership is essential to addressing the unique and complex challenges of global markets, customers, and employees.

In corporations where labor relations are healthy, where no systemic issues of discrimination exist, and where diversity is celebrated, leaders are perplexed by the slow progress of diverse representation at the executive level. For multicultural talent, there is downright frustration and even outrage. This is one of the most significant indications that it's time for the next generation of diversity and inclusion work.

Various studies, in addition to our own analysis at Diversity Best Practices on the talent-management issues of minorities and women, reveal some of the unique leadership development challenges they face. Typically, they revolve around issues of risk aversion and leadership culture.

Risk Aversion

In terms of risk, a complex dance transpires between majority-dominated management and high-potential female and multicultural talent. On all sides, the different players tend to shift away from their default risk tolerance levels when it comes to the corporate ascent of diverse talent.

According to a number of studies, minorities tend to either make the lowest risk moves or the highest risk moves, while midlevel women opt for the lower risk options. By contrast, White males consistently take more calculated risks. Since leadership advancement is helped by the demonstrated ability to take calculated risks, an individual's or a group's comfort with risk can be a predictor of advancement. Various studies show that when it comes to risk taking there are distinct differences between those in the majority and those in the minority — differences that put those in the minority at a disadvantage.

One observer of these differences is Harvard-trained social psychologist Dr. Jeff Howard. Through his consulting practice as well as through his innovative "Efficacy" training he saw patterns of clear differences emerge.

Howard's Efficacy training stands apart as one of the most effective professional development programs for people of color, and training in moderate risk taking is a critical component. In a conversation, Dr. Howard shared the remarkable results of a variation of the classic ring toss game that is part of his program's design. In this exercise, participants are given four plastic or rope rings to try to land on a small post. Using a tape running 16-feet away from the peg, and measured off in one-foot increments, the participants decide how close or how far they stand from the post. The closer to the post they stand, the lower the risk; the farther from the post the higher the risk of missing the post. Of course, with four rings, participants have four chances at "ringers," with more points gained the farther one is able to successfully nail it.

Simple enough. Except that while initially the exercise was designed to gauge risk tolerance levels of *individuals*, throughout thousands of training sessions clear different patterns emerged in the behaviors of different *groups*. Participants of color, European-Americans, and women within both groups showed different behaviors. The women seemed more inclined to stand within 1 to 3 feet of the post and went for the safe, almost sure bet. Many of the Black and Latino men either went for this same safe bet or for the low probability Hail-Mary toss of 9 to 16 feet. The White men, in contrast, however, seemed more inclined to stand about 4 to 8 feet or at a medium distance from the post. *The calculated risk.* There were clear differences within each group, of course; some women took a wild risk, some people of color went for the moderate risk, some White men went straight for the one-foot marker. But the overall group patterns were clear; people from different groups seemed inclined toward different levels of risk.

How does the ring toss game show up in real life? In his corporate consulting practice, Dr. Howard observed that "White males were more likely to use a moderate risk strategy to learn how to succeed. They seemed more willing to volunteer for assignments that represented a calculated risk — the kind of risk that is a stretch, yet where the chances of success are realistically within reach. This type of moderate risk taking can result in rapid development of new knowledge and skills, and is something successful organizations look for in their next generation of leaders."

And for many minorities the story is different. Given various and multiple social psychology dynamics that include the internalization of negative assessments made by society and people in their lives toward people of one's racial/ethnic minority group, many people of color tend to avoid moderate risks, playing it safe, and therefore guaranteeing slower skill development, and that they will not be noticed as emerging leadership talent. Or conversely, really having little hope for any advancement due to believing the system is stacked up against them, they will take a "what-the-hell-attitude" and swing for the fences hoping against all hope that they just may get lucky because of a belief that merit and effort really seems to have little to do with whether they advance or not.[3]

Management also shifts its own risk tolerance. It may be more inclined to subconsciously say, "Go for it!" in giving a chance to an up-and-coming White male leader, the belief being "we should give him a shot." Yet management is less inclined to give similar opportunities to women and minorities. Instead, risk averse comments begin to emerge such as "she is still two jobs away," or "since it would be a very visible position, we can't afford for him to fail," and so on. Failing to address these risk-aversion actions inhibits the advancement of women and multicultural talent.

Leadership Culture

The leaders of successful companies understand that they stand on the shoulders of those who came before them. They are also the beneficiaries of a culture that spotted their talent and gave them opportunities to prove themselves. While they may be sincere in their desire to diversify their representation, homogenous leadership teams often don't realize that their assessment filters can be culturally biased. Strong leadership can look very different in different cultures or among women. But a majority-dominated leadership team tends to overlook these qualities because they differ from what is considered strong leadership in their culture.

To develop more female and multicultural leaders, management teams must cultivate additional crosscultural competence for spotting alternate leadership qualities they themselves have not demonstrated. In an increasingly diverse and global environment, such qualities are vital. There are already some best practices that have yielded good results in achieving greater advancement of multicultural and female talent. Many companies make it a requirement, for example, that multicultural talent and women be included in all succession plan boxes. But we need to go beyond this practice and find new ways to address the unintended barriers created by risk aversion and leadership culture.

Lifted up together, these four pillars will strengthen the foundation for the engagement and retention of multicultural talent. Under the tent that can be supported by the four pillars, we must continue to find alternate ways to address the challenges of the revolving door syndrome for multicultural talent.

The challenges of multicultural engagement and retention are multiple and vexing. Yet we have hope, because many great ideas have led to significant progress over the past couple of decades. In one chapter of the Judeo-Christian scriptures, there's a verse that reads, "We are perplexed but not in despair."[4] This certainly applies to the inclusion work of diversity practitioners and business leaders today. This half-full reality is what propels us to continue to find new ways to address the half-empty reality.

CHAPTER SUMMARY

- All four major racial/ethnic minority groups in the United States (Black, Latino, Asian, and Native American) are communal cultures where the sense of group identity — as expressed by *la familia*, the clan, the church, the affinity group — is deeply ingrained. This is in contrast to the majority culture of European-Americans, which is more individualistic. It's no coincidence that the first-person pronoun "I" in English is the only pronoun that is capitalized in any language.

- Corporate cultures, so dominated by European-American individualistic culture, often overlook the higher-octane energy that could be infused into their corporations by more effectively nurturing enterprise-wide community building.

- For multicultural groups that have traditionally been oppressed and marginalized, public recognition is like water in the desert.

- Corporations need to go beyond putting women's or multiculturals' names into their succession planning boxes and find new ways to address the unintended barriers created by risk aversion and leadership culture.

- Employers should consider reciprocal mentoring, where the assumption is that the executives not only have something to impart, but also something to learn from the multicultural employee they're partnered with.

- The advancement pillar cannot be realized without the other three pillars (community, recognition, and mentoring). However, the first three do not guarantee this final one. And no advancement means there has been no progress.

SHAPING YOUR STRATEGY

- What are the racial/ethnic minority groups that exist in your corporate environment? How do they interact within their own group, with other minorities, and with the majority culture? Are members of the majority culture aware that the way they interact with people from their own culture may differ from how they interact with those from other cultures?

- How well does your organization recognize the contributions of its minority employees? How can your company better publicly acknowledge their efforts and contributions?

- How risk-averse are your leaders? What barriers does this risk aversion create, and how can you overcome these barriers?

- Does your organization have a reciprocal mentoring program? If so, what have been the results? If not, what steps can you take to implement such a program?

WHY NOT ACKNOWLEDG
ING DIFFERENCE$ CAN
MAKE U$ $ICKER AND
POORER WHY NOT AC
KNOW EDGING DIFFER
EN E$ CAN MAK U$ $ICK R
AND P OR R W Y NOT
A KNOWL DGING DIF
FER N E$ MAKE U$ $I K
R A ND P O ER W Y
N T AC NOW EDGING
D FFE E E$ MA E U$
ICK R A ND P O ER
ING I FE EN E$ MA E
$ IC E A D OO E
W Y OT A K L D
N IF RE E A E
U IC A D O
H O WE
I F N
Y O D

Chapter 13

Why Not Acknowledging Differences Can Make Us Sicker and Poorer

I

A blur of cars, multicolored microbuses, and motorcycles zoomed past us. We broke into a sweat running up the street, frantically jumping to hail a cab — all of which passed us by. It was 20 minutes before the start of the citywide state-of-emergency curfew, and we were 30 minutes from home. Yet no one was stopping for us. We had already begun making plans for our walk down the middle of the avenue waving our underwear, the only white thing we had on us, as required by martial law if you happened to be out after curfew, when we succeeded at making a VW Bug screech to a halt as we threw ourselves in its path. "Monterrico!" we cried out. "Ok, yes, that's on my way," the driver said. "Hop in!"

Growing up in a Latin American military dictatorship shaped how I view the world. I was just 17 when I jumped into that VW Bug to avoid getting arrested, but the volatility of that era — 12 years of a military dictatorship, and the economic and political aftershocks when the *generales* gave back power — permanently shaped my stance toward so much of life. How I view time, money, health, and risk were subconsciously shaped by the forces of growing up in an underdeveloped Latin American country that alternated between populist and right wing democracies and military dictatorships.

The uncertainty of the government, the savings-devouring wildfire of hyperinflation, and the sense that so much was out of our control led to the need for creative
improvisation. Whether dealing with military checkpoints on our way home from
the movies or figuring out how to secure a kilo of rice and sugar in the midst of
shortages, those effects linger long after the headlines have become history.

Through this upbringing, I developed insights into effective multicultural
marketing. As an employee, the subconscious ghosts of that time haunt my decisions when I do something seemingly mundane, such as signing up for employee
benefits. After the economic and political roller coaster of growing up in Peru
where we did not know what the government was going to be in the next four
years, projecting my nest egg for the next 40 years was quite an abstraction. After
a five-year cumulative inflation rate of 15,000 percent, who wants to save their
money? Inflation was so rampant that restaurants wrote their prices on a black-
board because by the time you ordered your food, ate it, and got the bill, the prices
would have changed!

Even long after circumstances have changed — and they have changed dramatically as Peru now has a prospering economy and a stable democracy — our
worldviews are wired in the past. After managing food shortages due to a bureau-
cratized economy and constant blackouts caused by terrorist bombs, how much
of a priority is getting an annual physical? Present circumstances often have little
impact on cultural perspective — unless there is an effective intervention.

As chief diversity officer at Hewitt and now as president of Diversity Best
Practices, I have wrestled with what these interventions could be. In my role, I am
responsible for identifying the various ways in which exclusion may inadvertently
be taking place. There are the classic issues of representation and advancement
of women and minorities, but there are other areas that get overlooked. For example, are non-majority groups equally taking advantage of the benefits available to
all employees?

It turns out that in many circumstances, they are not.

For instance, African-Americans and Latinos both under-save in their 401(k)
plans compared to Whites and Asians — even when they earn the same amount
of money. Women sub-optimize their returns by investing more conservatively
than men. And minorities under-participate in preventive health care, even when
it's available to them at little or no cost.

Why is this happening? How can we bridge these gaps? The search for these answers has led to a treasure trove of information and insight. It has also led the way to some new types of solutions, including the need to communicate — or *market* — these benefits in ways that are inclusive of the worldviews of different diverse groups. In our research, we found solutions that tapped into cultural behavioral drivers — often quite divergent from mainstream assumptions — that motivated individuals into actions that were good for them and their families. The Inclusion Paradox requires that we call out differences in doing this.

Rather than comprehensively addressing the many ways in which differences show up, I will delve deep into a case study of racial/ethnic differences. This exploration serves as a template for how we can do the same with other types of differences to surface the most effective ways to motivate employees to better manage their health and finances.

Multicultural Marketing of Employee Benefits

Think of the last time you turned on your favorite TV show and one of the ads moved you — not only emotionally, but to action — to buy a product, go on a trip, or support a cause.

Marketers spend much time and money figuring out how to reach you, whether you're a 20-something or a senior citizen, an Xer or a Baby Boomer, a man or a woman, a Latin American immigrant or a Texas cowboy. Not only have they figured out how to reach you, but how to move you as well.

Their approach is based on sophisticated market research data that reveals patterns in the way different demographic groups tend to move, act, and believe. Marketers understand, of course, that not all members within these demographic groups move according to the group norm, but there's enough of a pattern for them to shape messages and find channels that hit the broad mark time after time.

Quick! What audiences come to mind when you do the following virtual channel surfing: Sunday afternoon NFL game, *Sabado Gigante* on Univision, *The Jamie Foxx Show* on BET, any movie on Lifetime TV, *Blue's Clues* on Nickelodeon, *Modern Family* on ABC, *Friends* in syndication?

How much of this same market research knowledge applies to human resources products and services? Quite a bit, actually. Cultural studies show that different demographic groups approach issues of health, wealth, and career in distinctly different ways.

Let's consider these differences with regard to health care. Mary Lynch is senior vice president for Human Resource Services for CHRISTUS Health, a Catholic healthcare organization in the southern and southwestern United States and Mexico. She speaks of the challenge to be inclusive and provide care and services to those with differing worldviews especially when they are from a different religion: "When we talk about inclusion, growing up in the western world and having things done a certain way challenges us today to really broaden our horizons and look at other perspectives, such as Eastern medicine and beliefs of people because many come to the healthcare environment with very different beliefs. For example, different people believe that different kinds of foods are healing foods. One of the hospital's lessons was that not everyone considers eggs or oatmeal to be a suitable breakfast. Hospital staff learned that Vietnamese patients might actually prefer chicken soup for breakfast."

If *oatmeal* could be wrong, then what else could we be missing when designing benefits that touch the critical needs of physical, emotional, and financial health? The search for answers must start with determining where differences exist, getting a handle on *why*, and then finally, identifying crossculturally savvy ways to bridge unhealthy gaps.

Employees as Consumers

Employers must start to view employees not as passive recipients of benefit packages, but as consumers — consumers of jobs, of career opportunities, of benefits. This is not only from the perspective of attracting the best talent, it's also a smart way to achieve optimal results from benefits plans that are less generous than before.

Making it all more difficult: Companies are finding that the one-size-fits-all approach — meant as a way to better manage costs — is increasingly ineffective. Already, employers are forcing employees to make tough choices on their healthcare packages as they weigh the tradeoffs between high deductibles and lower premiums. And how about the alphabet soup choices between PPO, HMO, POS, HRA, HSA? Late at night, on the eve of the deadline for the annual benefits enrollment, with forehead in hands, employees are truly benefits *shopping*.

These are *consumer choices*, and they must be packaged and marketed as such to help employees make smart choices on behalf of themselves and their families — in ways that also help employers better manage their costs.

Choices now are more dependent than ever on the employee than on the employer. And in a multicultural, multigenerational workplace, communications that worked when audiences were more homogenous will not work today.

Today's HR programs are legacies from the philosophies and structures of more than 50 years ago — when most of the workforce was White and male. So while the workforce has changed dramatically, why is it that benefits have not changed in kind? If benefits are truly designed to meet the needs of today's employees, benefit plan strategists must realize that programs conceived many years ago will not resonate with the new workforce.

We must move into the *multicultural design and marketing of benefits.* Here's where we look for archetypes without falling into stereotyping. It's important to look for patterns — where the bell curve of behavior is concentrated — because it helps us see where we need to call out differences in order to create true inclusion. Like a moving impressionistic painting, what we initially see may not be what is really going on, but it invites us to peer more deeply into the hidden messages hidden in the bold patterns. We need to discover the deeper meanings of our first impressionistic pass and — with these insights — design and market benefits in ways that mutually benefit employees and corporations.

II

Time Warps and Money Binds: Having Enough for the Future

Let's make this practical by looking at one benefit that is increasingly important to the financial well-being of employees — the 401(k) savings plan. This benefit has become particularly valuable as entitlement programs, such as pensions, go away and Social Security turns into Social *Insecurity.*

Even when members of different racial groups earn the same amount of money, investment practices vary dramatically. The 2008 Black Investor Study (conducted by Charles Schwab and Ariel Capital Management, the largest minority owned investment firm in the United States) reveals a 15 percent gap in savings when comparing Whites and Blacks. Only 65 percent of Blacks in households earning more than $50,000 annually invest in stocks or mutual funds, compared to 80 percent of Whites in the same income bracket. In another study, the *non*participation rate at one Hewitt manufacturing client was 33 percent for

Hispanics/Latinos, compared to 26 percent for African-Americans and 9 percent for Whites.

The differences don't stop there. When we first conducted a 401(k) and diversity analysis for a client, we looked at five different behaviors around retirement savings. We saw discernable differences between Blacks and Whites, as the following table indicates.

DIFFERENCES IN 401(K) BEHAVIORS
BETWEEN BLACKS AND WHITES

Behavior	Black	White
Participation	52%	71%
Average Contribution Rate	2%	5%
Average Percentage in Equities	43%	60%
Internet Usage	45%	72%
Loans Outstanding	14%	5%

Hewitt Associates, analysis of 401(k) usage at a Medical Education Institution, 2005

Compared to Whites, Blacks not only under-participated, but their contribution rates were less than half that of Whites. They also invested more conservatively, were three times more likely to take loans through their 401(k) plans, and were 30 percent less likely to use the Internet to manage their retirement money.

For the next set of clients, we added Latinos/Hispanic and Asians/Asian Americans to the mix and studied what factors were most significant in determining various 401(k) behaviors. We looked at age, tenure, salary, gender, and race/ethnicity. The common wisdom was that salary would be by far the largest determinant of whether people saved, how much, and how.

Again, race/ethnicity emerged as the main determinant for differences in behavior. Depending on the client, gender and income alternated as the second most prevalent factor.

In 2008, we upped the ante. In partnership with Ariel and with funding from The Rockefeller Foundation, we looked at the 401(k) data of 57 Fortune 500 companies across a variety of different industries and sectors. In the process, we studied the patterns in investment behaviors of almost 3 million employees. The findings of this comprehensive study revealed the same pattern: Race was the most influential factor in whether and how people saved. The findings of gaps from that one client showed up across the board. Not only in the aggregate, but in every one of those 57 participating companies.

The table here shows the differences based on race when comparing emploees earning the same amount of money.

OVERALL RESULTS BY ETHNICITY

Regression-Adjusted Comparison of 401(k) Behavior:
Minorities Compared to Whites

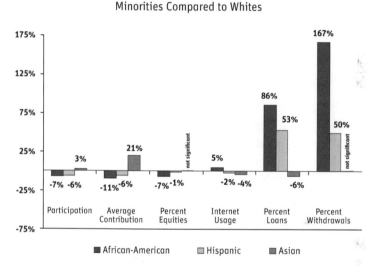

Hewitt Associates analysis, in collaboration with Ariel Capital Management, of 401(k) usage of 57 Fortune 500 companies with nearly 3 million employee records. A 2009 study funded by the Rockefeller Foundation.

These findings were a game changer. Why would color of skin affect savings behaviors? We'll get to this in a moment.

The study was repeated in 2012. This Ariel/Aon Hewitt update on the *401(k) Plans in Living Color* study[1] showed that significant gaps remained among different racial and ethnic groups. Blacks and Latinos continued to save far less for retirement than White employees; participation differences continued to exist; and different racial/ethnic groups borrow against or are cashing out these accounts at significantly different rates.

The 2008 economic slowdown aggravated the racial and ethnic differences seen in 401(k) or 403(b) accounts. More Latinos and Blacks than Whites or Asians tapped into their accounts to deal with short-term financial distress. Whether those hardship withdrawals addressed unexpected emergencies, daily living expenses, or simple debt, they still threatened workers' long-term financial security.

Here is just one example of how delving into the differences among various racial/ethnic groups and developing creative responses to diversity challenges can provide positive results. Opportunities exist to address the gap in remaining areas, such as contribution rates and borrowing/cash out rates. This is exceptionally important to keep our eye on since Black and Latino employees, even when they are in the plan, are still not saving enough to meet their retirement years' needs.

In addition, Black and Latino behaviors around their retirement accounts further undermine their ability to optimize their returns. For example, their lower Internet usage when it came to managing their retirement money raised important questions about how best to communicate to multicultural audiences. For a variety of reasons, certain demographic groups are less inclined to use the Internet. Thus, corporate employee communications that rely too much on the Internet may be inadvertently leaving some employees behind.

According to the Schwab/Ariel Black Investor Study, Blacks also differ from Whites in what they're saving for. While retirement is cited as the number-one reason for the majority of Whites, Blacks tend to prioritize saving for a home and their children's college education. When it came to a preferred vehicle for investment, African-Americans preferred real estate over the stock market (45 percent vs. 40 percent).[2]

The Schwab/Ariel studies over time have shown little change in the opinions between Blacks and Whites, with two exceptions. For the first time since the study began, the 2010 Black Investor Study showed that Blacks felt that stocks or stock mutual funds were better investment vehicles than real estate. However, the investment rate between Blacks and Whites maintains a significant gap. White investment rates remained around 80 percent even during the recession, while the investment rate for Blacks continued its downward trend to about 60 percent.[3]

We can apply the Inclusion Paradox to other differences, such as age and gender. In comparing the retirement savings patterns of men and women, we see the effects of socialization. Women face uncertainties about how to participate — and whether to even participate at all — because they've been less exposed to financial matters and have had more interruptions in their careers. They will also need to save more than men due to lower average salaries, more conservative investing, longer life expectancies, and higher retiree medical needs. In a 2008 study,[4] Hewitt found that 30 percent of women did not contribute to their 401(k) plans and another 24 percent did not contribute at a high enough level to take advantage of the company match. Given these factors, women will need to replace nearly 130 percent of their final pay at retirement, 7 percentage points more than men. Over 30 years, the average woman will need to save 2 percent more of her pay each year than the average man to achieve the same standard of living.[5]

Money Worldviews

What's the cause of these disparities? This question must be answered in order to successfully pursue multicultural marketing of benefits. Only then can we know how to effectively reach different audiences with messages that ring true and lead to action.

In an April 13, 2009 article, "How Obama Is Using the Science of Change," *Time* magazine declared *Nudge: Improving Decisions about Health, Wealth, and Happiness* to be among a handful of books "already shaping dozens of [Obama] Administration policies." Authors Richard Thaler and Cass Sunstein make the case for tapping into the findings of behavioral economics to influence preventive health care and long-term savings choices that address worrisome gaps.[6] They base their arguments on hundreds of experiments, conducted over decades, exploring what shapes the choices we make. Their perspective is that our choices lead us to either good or not-so-good results, depending on the influence. Much of what we accept as truth might not be objectively true, contrary to our shared social assumptions. This work is particularly timely in light of the trend to push health and wealth decision-making away from government and corporations and toward employees.

Seeking the middle ground between government dictating what people should do and unrestrained *laissez faire* capitalism, the authors make the argument for "nudges." These nudges are created by "decision architects" who design policies and programs that are more likely to produce desired results, based on what we know about behavior. Among the many nudges they describe — automatically enrolling employees in their 401(k) and giving them the choice to opt out.

Behaviorally, humans tend toward inertia. The *Time* article references a study in which only 36 percent of women joined a 401(k) plan when they needed to initiate enrollment. Participation jumped to 86 percent when they were automatically enrolled and then given the chance to opt out.[7]

The 2012 Ariel/Aon Hewitt updated study proved this out. The participation gap in 401(k) among the various groups has narrowed when comparing 2012 vs. 2009. And why? Indeed it's the growing numbers of employers automatically enrolling employees into 401(k) or 403(b) plans. By applying the human reality of inertia in reverse they have offered them an opt-out rather than an opt-in choice. The result? The enrollment gap between Black and Latino workers on the one hand and White or Asian employees on the other practically disappears.

The *Nudge* authors focus on American mainstream culture, so they stop short of exploring how behavioral economic theory plays out in different subcultures. But here, as in the following section on health, I will offer crosscultural insights about the behaviors of different racial and ethnic communities. I encourage you to extract principles to apply to the health and wealth behaviors of other demographic groups.

Returning to 401(k) under-participation by Latinos and African-Americans, cultural studies show Latinos have a shorter time horizon than Whites. When asked how they define "the future," Latinos tend to answer, "The next three to five years." Whites tend to say, "The next generation." Asians tend to say, "The next century."

Why is this? Latinos like myself have come from a part of the world and during a time where we've been unsure what our government was going to be like in four years. So this concept of projecting a nest egg over the next 40 years has been a complete abstraction. Whether experienced firsthand, by a parent or grandparent, or delivered by institutions such as churches, cultural worldviews get passed on subconsciously.

For African-Americans the reasons may be different, but the under-saving behavior is the same. According to Mellody Hobson, Ariel's president and a frequent guest financial analyst on *Good Morning America*, there are various sociohistorical factors at work. When you've been marginalized from participating in diversified investment vehicles by the now-outlawed practice of redlining, what viable savings choices remain? African-Americans either turned to mom-and-pop savings institutions in their communities that offered only basic savings vehicles or put their money under the mattress. Making matters worse, recent corporate scandals and the global economic meltdown resulted in many employees losing their jobs and their long-term savings, while unethical corporate leaders were led out in handcuffs or faced Congressional scrutiny. These scandals further undermined an already existing wariness on the part of African-Americans with regard to the financial system. The people being hauled out of gleaming corporate offices in handcuffs or sitting in front of Congressional hearings don't look like them. Given these legacies, it's not unusual to meet African-American millionaires who still use low-interest savings accounts as their primary investment tool.

How about the differences between Whites and Blacks with regard to what they save for? African-American emphasis on saving for college is understandable, given the role of higher education in building a Black middle class. For many African-American families, a college education may still be a first- or second-generation phenomenon. Coupled with uncertainties about financial aid, African-Americans may save more than will actually be needed for college at the expense of their retirement savings.

While these answers provide the *why* for low participation, they don't tell us how to close the gap. The low participation rate of Latinos and African-Americans is worrisome, given the wholesale shift from guaranteed pensions to greater employee responsibility in preparing for retirement through 401(k). If employees don't make good choices along the way over a long period of time, they will be in jeopardy of not being able to take care of themselves and their families when the time comes to retire.

Again, here is where authors of *Nudge* offer help. The Ariel/Aon Hewitt[8] study suggests further changes that can "nudge" employees to prepare for retirement. It recommends upping the penalties for non-hardship withdrawals and fine-tuning contribution rates. With changes like these, it is possible to narrow the disparity gap between how different groups get ready for retirement, which can only strengthen our entire society.

Multicultural Marketing of 401(k) and Retirement Planning

Since long-term investment can create wealth for all, how can employee communications respond to diverse attitudes and beliefs about saving? How can it motivate people of color to more assertively plan for their retirement? The answers to these questions go beyond having more diverse pictures in 401(k) materials or translating those same materials into another language.

Let's take a look at traditional communication and marketing efforts around retirement savings.

Quick! What picture comes to mind when I say "retirement planning brochure?" White audiences anticipate the following: A white-haired couple strolling on the beach, maybe a golden retriever at their side.

Question: How do you make this picture inclusive? Response: Oh, make it a Black couple walking down the beach. Challenge: Diversity in the pictures is a start, but is that all? Response: Let's do a Spanish version!

Even if we replace the couple in the picture with a couple of color and print the words in another language, we still have the wrong image. Why? *Because the whole picture is wrong to begin with for non-White groups.* For many African-Americans, their image of retirement often includes another job, possibly one where they are giving back to their community. Latinos picture an elderly couple surrounded by grandchildren. They look at the White couple on the typical retirement brochure and feel sorry for them. "They are all alone! Why have they been abandoned? No wonder they need the dog."

Regarding lower Web usage, the challenge is not just to recognize there is a gap or even to understand why the gap exists. Rather, what can be done, in a culturally savvy way, to motivate under-participating groups to get more comfortable with the Web? This might entail providing easier access, addressing distrust of corporate Web sites, and making the sites more appealing by speaking directly to their worldviews and preferences. It might require more in-person sessions offering hands-on demonstrations of how to manage one's money through Internet tools. For Latinos, it might mean creating family-oriented events where they can bring their children — who often are digitally proficient — so they can not only enjoy being with *Papá* or *Mamá* at work, but can be included in some of the navigation exercises.

A few years ago, I teamed with one of Hewitt's Communications practice leaders to facilitate a Latino focus group about using the Internet to manage money. Our discussion elicited some unexpected insight into some of the mainstream messages used to motivate money management via the Internet.

Our communications consultants had created materials not only to orient employees to their 401(k) benefit, but also to encourage employees to manage their money via the Web, thus reducing administration costs by reducing traffic to the call center.

As communicators, they were practiced in knowing their audience and tapping behavioral drivers. Instinctively, they knew the message "Save your employer money — use the Web!" would not work. Instead, they chose the motivator of "control." Throughout their materials, they wove messages such as "take control  of your money, take control of your future." In addition, they showcased the 24/7 access of the Web tool, along with color graphs showing asset allocation, and the ability to move one's money as many times as one wanted.

We conducted various segmented focus groups. Not surprisingly, the message of control played very well with White employees. When challenged, one flustered participant responded, "Of course we like the message of control. *What other message could there be?*"

However, the Latino group had a defiant answer to that rhetorical question. When presented with the message of control, seven out of the nine Latinos responded negatively.

When asked why, they responded, "Because it's a take-away of a benefit." The communicators responded, "But it's not. You still have the call center, but now you have the Web as well."

"You don't understand," said one. "The benefit for me was that my employer took care of my money. And now you're telling me I have to take control of that."

"Don't you want to?"

"No."

"Why not?"

"Because I did not grow up with my parents ever talking about it among themselves, much less passing any of that on."

For this group, the taking control message was intimidating and daunting. The thought of managing money via the Web did not offer a greater sense of control — it actually made them feel less in control. For us facilitators, it was an epiphany. The communicators realized they had created communication pieces based on the "traditional" workforce, which, until recently, was mostly White and mostly male.

Companies need to consider not just the message, but the delivery. Hewitt and Ariel studies show that African-Americans and Latinos are more communal and oral cultures, which respond better to face-to-face presentations and workshops. This raises the potential for higher costs. E-mail blasts are more cost effective than workshops. But as the workforce gets more diverse, what happens when these cost-effective measures are not behavior-change effective?

The multicultural marketing of benefits is not just about one-way adaptation on the part of corporations to account for differences among diverse populations. It's also about knowing how to move employees toward behaviors that are good for them and for their employers. Web usage for managing money, for example, reduces administration costs for companies by reducing the number of calls to the 401(k) call center.

But the racial/ethnic digital divide of Web 1.0 has been deep and real, it is disappearing thanks to the social media of Web 2.0. According to a Pew Internet study, "Groups that have traditionally been on the other side of the digital divide in basic Internet access are now using wireless connections to go online." In fact, African-Americans and Latinos are the highest users of social media compared to any other demographic group. Seventy percent of Blacks and 67 percent of Latinos report using social media. Latinos are more likely to have video and Internet enabled cell phone than the general market (44 percent vs. 35 percent).

Smartphones and other mobile devices combined with social media tools are proving to be very adept at linking consumer behavior to technology, and in some instances, changing it.[9] About 88 percent of American adults own a cell phone, 57 percent have a laptop, 19 percent have an e-reader, and 19 percent own a tablet computer. About 63 percent of adults wirelessly go online by using these devices.[10] This evolving technology is narrowing the digital divide. For instance, Latinos lead all ethnic groups in the purchase of tablet computers (15 percent vs. 8 percent for Blacks and 7 percent for Whites). And Latinos are the highest users of text messaging, mobile Internet, e-mail, downloading pictures, and music to mobile devices.

Driving up Minority 401(k) Participation at McDonald's

Shortly after joining McDonald's board, Ariel Investments CEO John Rogers gave a talk in honor of Martin Luther King, Jr.'s birthday to members of one of the company's employee networks — the McDonald's African-American Council known as the Mac2C. *BusinessWeek* reporter Lauren Young described the speech in an online sidebar to her article "McDonald's Supersized Retirement Plan: The fast-food giant is persuading more African-American workers to enroll in 401(k)s. Can McDonald's keep talent by helping families save?"

"[During the talk] John Rogers focused on the plight of Black investors and why they don't save more, using data from the annual survey of Black investors Ariel conducts in conjunction with Charles Schwab. 'If people of color retire with less than half the money saved as Whites, it's a real crisis for our country,' Rogers told the crowd. Rogers didn't know that Andrés Tapia, [then] chief diversity officer at Hewitt Associates, the benefits consulting giant, also was present. After the event ended, the two men clicked as they started comparing notes on the issue, along with possible solutions. 'It was the first time ever in all my public speeches or private meetings that I ran into someone who not only understood what I was saying, but also was thinking about trying to solve the same problem,' Rogers says. It also helped that James Cantalupo, who was McDonald's chairman and chief executive at the time, heard Rogers speak. 'We need to think about the economic health of minority employees and vendors,' he told Rogers."

A Hewitt utilization analysis of 401(k) by racial ethnic groups revealed that gaps existed at McDonald's as well. Given their long-standing commitment to diversity, the fast-food giant decided to do something about it. Most companies won't even match a contribution until an employee puts in at least 3 percent, but McDonald's decided that employees who put just 1 percent of their salary in the plan would get $3 for every $1 they invested. McDonald's then makes a dollar-for-dollar match on the next 4 percent. This could lead to a company match of as much as 11 percent. To ease the pain of automatically deferring 1 percent of pay, the company gave managers a one-time, 1 percent salary increase. And then, to make sure employees took advantage of the program, they made enrollment automatic — with, of course, the option to opt-out if one does not want to participate.

What motivates McDonald's? "In addition to this being a tangible demonstration of our commitment to diversity," explains Richard Floersch, McDonald's chief human resources officer, "this is also about a talent retention strategy in an industry that sees a costly 36 percent turnover."

Other torchbearers are lighting the way in their own companies. Ariel president Mellody Hobson sits on the corporate boards of Starbucks, Estée Lauder, and DreamWorks, where she is advocating an analysis of the retirement savings habits of minorities at those firms. In the second half of 2009, the 57 companies participating in the Ariel/Hewitt 401(k) and diversity study will have on-hand their own data, as well as information on how they compare to other Fortune 500 companies and to others in their industry. Just how should they respond? In addition to approaching this issue with design strategies such as McDonald's there are also some companies beginning to couple incentives with financial education tailored to the worldviews of the different populations in their workforce. (For a more detailed account of how a medical education institution has approached this issue, see "Appendix D: Driving Up Minority 401(k) Participation at a Medical Institution.")

McDonald's is lovin' it™. And so are its employees. Calling out differences and addressing diverse assumptions below the waterline has the potential to create stronger financial health for all.

III

Que Sera, Sera: When It Comes to Health, Can Fate Be Defied?

When it comes to the nation's healthcare system, much has happened since I first penned this book. The passage of healthcare reform and the judicial confirmation of its constitutionality have dominated political debates and public discussions for several years, and promises to continue to do so. Whether it's called by its official moniker, the Patient Protection and Affordable Care Act, or more informal titles like the Affordable Care Act (ACA), healthcare reform, health insurance reform, or even Obamacare, this legislation is a game changer for how the nation provides and pays for health care.

The need for this legislation is predicated on the reality that our healthcare system is sick and needs healing. Even with the ACA and its 2014 launch, the system faces a long recovery process that must include attitude and mindset changes by everyone. The challenges are real and daunting:

- Between 46 – 50 million Americans do not have health insurance, including a sizeable proportion of families with a working adult.[11] And for the millions who are insured, too many are limited in what their insurance covers. This situation leaves them to pay out of pocket for preventive procedures like mammograms or colonoscopies, to tackle practically incomprehensible policy documents on what is covered, and to worry about unexpected insurance price increases or medical denials. Some 45,000 people die every year because they lack access to health care.

- Of the uninsured, more than half (55 percent) are people of color. While only 13 percent of Whites lack healthcare insurance, 32 percent (14.4 million) of Latinos, 21 percent (6.9 million) of Blacks, 19 percent (3.8 million) Asians, and 28 percent (700,000) American Indians are uninsured. Many of the newly insured under the ACA will be people of color making it a massive diversity and inclusion initiative.
- Within five years, national health expenditures will increase by more than $1 trillion over today's nearly $3 trillion.
- The poor health status of many American workers costs the economy about $153 billion in lost productivity.

An even more disconcerting challenge is the shortage of medical personnel. The ACA will transform the insurance standing of about 32 million Americans who now lack health insurance. But our healthcare system is nowhere near ready to accommodate the coming influx of new and diverse consumers. The capacity to handle that number of patients is simply not there and the severe shortage of doctors, nurses, and other medical professionals is critical. By 2020, the nation will face a physician shortage estimated to be about 91,000.

A look at the healthcare system through a diversity lens indicates a need for additional worry. It already falls short of providing quality care to people of color even when they have insurance. Racial health disparities are deep, pervasive, and well documented.

Compared to Whites, African-Americans and Latinos under-participate in preventive health care, even when it's available to them at little or no cost. What's more, they use the emergency room — the most expensive form of medical intervention — at a higher rate than other groups. By contrast, Asians tend to over-insure, paying for more health coverage than they actually need. These patterns not only lead to greater health and/or cost risk for the members of these groups, but can lead to greater health care costs for employers and governments.

Some worldviews, such as Catholic Latino fatalism, create resistance to taking proactive measures to reduce their health risk. Dr. Thomas Fisher, vice president at Health Care Service Corporation and previously at the University of Chicago, who leads efforts on addressing healthcare disparities, explains another variable, "It's about establishing trust and having conversations. If physicians can't establish the type of relationship where trust is central, where patients can feel confident that this is in their own best interest, then patients are unlikely to be motivated to adhere to uncomfortable, costly, or inconvenient recommendations."

But companies need not be fatalistic, believing there's nothing they can do to encourage Latinos or African-Americans to seek preventive care. It is not enough to understand why certain groups don't respond to mainstream messages. By calling out differences, it's possible to find overlooked enablers within a cultural worldview that can motivate members of that culture to engage in preventive care.

Let's look at diversity disconnections throughout the healthcare system that lead to disparities. These are not only detrimental to diverse groups, but also contribute to higher healthcare costs.

Disparities in Disease Prevalence. According to the Centers for Disease Control and Prevention (CDC), racial and ethnic disparities are clearly evident in the incidences of fatal diseases and in other medical areas. A few:

- The African-American death rate from cardiovascular disease is *40 percent higher* than it is for Whites.
- The African-American death rate around all forms of cancer is *30 percent higher* than for Whites.
- The African-American death rate from HIV/AIDS is seven times that of Whites.
- The Latino death rate from diabetes is twice that of Whites.
- When comparing African-American and White women who get regular mammograms, Black women still die from breast cancer at a higher rate than White women.[12]
- Black and Latino teens are three times as likely to be diagnosed with schizophrenia instead of affective disorder, the more common diagnosis for White teens.[13]
- Racial and ethnic minorities are less likely to be treated for pain, and find their pain is underestimated compared to White patients.[14]
- Blacks and Latinos are treated through amputation at a higher rate than Whites, a statistic that suggests interventions that are too little or too late.[15]
- Fear of discrimination and stigma keep many in the LGBT community from seeking care for themselves or their families or from disclosing relevant personal information once in care.[16]

What are the cost implications of such disparities? Just to pick up on one data point, Latinos are not only suffering a higher incidence of diabetes, but diabetic Latinos also are more likely to die from the disease than are diabetic Whites. And with Latinos expected to comprise almost one-third of the United States by July 1, 2050,[17] a costly situation will get exponentially worse. We need ways to call out differences, so we can more effectively arrive at workable solutions.

Disease prevalence is not the only place differences surface in health care. Here are a few more:

Disparities in Communication. When it comes to reliance on corporate-provided communications to help make healthcare decisions, a Hewitt study found it's 31 percent for Whites (a low number to begin with), 24 percent for African-Americans, 11 percent for Asians, and 6 percent for Hispanics. Companies spend millions of dollars communicating their health benefits to employees, but the more diverse the population, the lesser the effect.[18]

So where do minorities go for their information? Instead of print materials, they rely on personal communication, talking with family members, and the amigo around the corner. Of course, friends and family members are not healthcare experts, so Latinos look to their doctor to be the primary disseminator of medical information. Although a doctor is an expert, studies show significant communication breakdowns between physicians and their ethnic patients. Nearly half of non-English-speaking U.S. patients say they have a hard time communicating with a doctor, nurse, or health provider who speaks a different language. In other words, there's a breakdown at the very point where they seek the most authoritative information about health. But it gets worse: Even when they get good advice, they don't follow it. In one survey, 24 percent of Whites, 30 percent of African-Americans, and 40 percent of Hispanics said they did not follow the doctor's advice because it was too costly.[19]

Worldviews at Play

Classic issues of racism and discrimination are at play in many of these disparities. According to Dr. Fisher, other breakdowns result from obvious, yet important, gaps in "in-language" communications. He tells of how medical literature describes cardiac episodes as "crushing or pressure more like an elephant sitting on a chest." Yet older African-Americans often describe cardiac pain as "sharp," which can lead doctors to another diagnosis. "If physicians don't ask some follow-up questions, or describe it more carefully, that sharp chest pain may, in fact, be the type of pressure/crushing that leads to a cardiac diagnosis."

But the more profound differences show up at the level of worldviews.

Think about traditional communication around preventive care. Typical messages are: "Take care of yourself," "You've only got one life to live," "Enjoy your life." These messages are inadvertently based on an *individualistic* European American worldview. Not surprisingly, these messages usually resonate well with the traditional European-American audience.

By contrast, communities of color in the United States often possess a more *communal* worldview. Individualistic messages usually do not strike a familiar chord, and they are less influenced into increasing their health prevention behaviors. Among Latinos, our communal perspective shows up in our language, as we pepper our conversations with *nosotros* (us), *la familia* (the family), *el equipo* (the team).

We must then factor in different cultural beliefs about our ability to manage what happens to us today and tomorrow. Interculturalists Fons Trompenaars and Charles Hampden-Turner refer to these as the *internal* and *external control* dimensions of culture. Those cultures that believe there is something one can do to avoid fate are referred to as having a strong sense of internal control. European-American culture has a strong sense of internal control. This worldview is manifest in sayings such as, "Pull yourself up by your bootstraps," "Tame the wild west," and "God helps those who help themselves." By contrast, other cultures have a sense of external control, believing there is little they can do to make their present or future better or less dangerous. Hispanic culture, influenced by Latin Catholic fatalism, operates within this external control worldview. The Spanish language reveals this worldview in sayings such as *"Dios quiere,"* (God willing), *"Que sera, sera,"* (What will be, will be), or when showing up late to the airport, *"El avión nos dejó"* (The plane left us.)

This plays out in health care. Why do Whites engage in more preventive healthcare than minorities? In part, it is connected to the worldview of internal control that says, "There's something I can do today to minimize the risk of something bad happening tomorrow." Preventive health care presupposes this very worldview. For those who have an external sense of control, governed by fatalism, the worldview manifests itself in beliefs such as, "There is nothing I can do today to prevent something that is going to happen to me tomorrow."

These different worldviews are evident in surveys as well. When asked, "Is your good health a matter of luck?" in a Commonwealth survey, a quarter of Latinos and African-Americans said yes, compared to only half as many Whites.[20]

No wonder those individualistic, internal control messages work for one group but not others.

With the Affordable Care Act, the future of health care now moves from an implied contract between employer and employee to a basic constitutional right. With rights come responsibilities. One duty will be for everyone to take care of his or her health as much as possible. So preventive health behaviors become more than a private issue, but a public one. The ACA goes on the offensive to promote prevention in health matters, and incents health providers to take a more active role in motivating patients toward preventive care. This is where the different healthcare worldviews play out on the national stage. And it's why calling out our differences on prevention messages and behaviors becomes more of a national priority, less of a commercial one.

The Case of the Dehydrated, Vietnamese Women in Labor

Do these worldview differences make a difference in life and death situations? They sure do. Consider this story told to me by intercultural diversity consultant Howard Ross.

A strange phenomenon occurred at a hospital that served a diverse patient population. No one could explain why, but most of the Vietnamese women coming in for delivery became dehydrated as they went through labor. While not always life-threatening, this affected the health of these women as well as the connection between mother and baby because it delayed lactation. It was also more costly to the hospital due to the resulting lengthened hospital stay. It took a professional willing to call out differences to unlock the answer. While knowing nothing about Vietnamese culture, he knew enough about the differences in worldviews to ask the right questions: What was it about how Vietnamese women experienced labor that was different from other cultures? What was the hospital doing that failed to take into account these differences?

The world of medical anthropology yielded this finding: Vietnamese culture sees the world as having hot and cold events. During these events, people need to consume the *opposite*. Labor and delivery are seen as cold times. Therefore, patients should not consume cold foods or liquids. This discovery yielded a eureka moment. How did the hospital keep women hydrated during labor? By giving them ice chips to suck on. The breakthrough was in getting the nurses to ask the patients what temperature water they wanted. This resulted in patients requesting and drinking plenty of warm water, thereby avoiding dehydration.

Other gaps exist that are related to language, culture, and leadership. Many states mandate interpreters for patients whose primary language is other than English. However, access or quality of those interpreters is patchy at best, which can lead to tragic consequences. A paper titled "The Legal Framework for Language Access in Healthcare Settings: Title VI and Beyond, tells of 13-year-old Gricelda Zamora. Like many children of immigrants, Gricelda served as the family's interpreter. This arrangement worked for a while until she developed severe abdominal pain. Her parents took her to the hospital. But Gricelda was too sick to interpret for herself and the hospital failed to provide the family with one. A communication mix up followed with her parents not totally understanding the doctor's direction to return to the emergency room should her symptom worsen, otherwise they should see the family doctor in three days. Two days later with Gricelda's condition rapidly deteriorating, her parents rushed back to the emergency room. Doctors discovered she had a ruptured appendix and airlifted the gravely ill teen to a nearby medical facility. Gricelda died a few hours later.

Addressing some of the cultural gaps that exist will require the skill of cultural competence to effectively treat patients. The gaps show up in practically every aspect of the medical experience. Consider the visiting hours that don't take into account the night and double shift workers who have hospitalized family members. Or the story shared by former Surgeon General Antonia Coello Novello at the 2012 Hispanic Association on Corporate Responsibility National Conference. A Spanish-speaking patient read a prescription and understood the direction that read "take a pill once a day" as "take eleven pills a day" because in Spanish the letters o-n-c-e means eleven. Further, the very concept of westernized medicine can be a cultural mismatch for some. Certain groups prefer the wisdom and treatments from centuries-old traditions of curanderas (female faith healers) and shamans.

These cultural and language gaps are further exacerbated by the lack of diversity in the medical profession, particularly in its upper echelons. Fewer than 12 percent of physicians, speech and language pathologists, and physical therapists and only 15 percent of registered nurses are Black or Latino, even though those two groups represent about 25 percent of the working population – twice the number that is represented in healthcare provider roles. The number gets worse as we go up the levels of leadership. Fewer than 16 percent of medical and health-care managers are Black or Latino. Asians represent less than 5 percent of those managers. And people of color constitute only 9 percent of all healthcare CEOs.[21]

These gaps and disparities in health outcomes, healthcare access, preventive care participation, care quality, and others require a holistic revamp of the entire healthcare landscape. One skillset that can serve as an antidote to the many ills that exist within our healthcare system is crosscultural competence – which as I have shared throughout this book is the ability to recognize, value, and navi-gate through cultures other than one's own. This skill must exist throughout the healthcare supply chain. At the hospital, this ranges from the front desk greeter to the orderly to the person taking vitals to the person managing the waiting room to the nurses, doctors, executives, and board members.

Aside from offering insurance coverage as an employee benefit, health care has not traditionally been the purview of most of corporate America. That is changing as more and more companies are getting involved in the well-being of their employees through a variety of initiatives, which can positively affect a com-pany's healthcare costs. This is happening for good reason. Employees of color are carrying a disproportionately greater burden of having to show up to work with more health problems, more aches and pains, and greater depression. This situa-tion not only affects their work performance, but also their engagement, stamina, and, indirectly, advancement opportunities.

Organizations must play a part of restoring our healthcare system. Compa-nies can support wellness initiatives for employees. Taking diversity into account can help increase the effectiveness of these programs. For instance, Health Care Service Corporation, commonly known as the operator of Blue Cross Blue Shield of Illinois, Texas, Oklahoma, and New Mexico embarked on a weight loss cam-paign for employees. Employees collectively lost 53,000 pounds in 2011.

Linking what we now know about how multicultural audiences are using social networking and digital devices, such as smartphones, can lead to positive changes in employee behavior. For example, the San Francisco-based health and wellness company, Keas, uses an online, interactive game that moves clients' employees to adopt healthier habits. Employees can take quizzes, set goals for exer-cising, eating right, and other healthy habits – all through the use of a Web-based gaming program. Team members cheer each other on and earn financial rewards for meeting health goals. Two companies that have contracted with Keas found that 50 – 80 percent of employees participate in the games and programs.[22] Since Blacks and Latinos are already frequent users of social media, how responsive might they be using this type of 'gamification' to address issues of health and wealth?

Here's another instance where interactive technology and/or social media promotes health and wellness. The American Diabetes Association in Washington State has teamed up with a social media technology company. A Facebook plus mobile application enables the entire community to manage the disease.[23] Given the greater incidence of diabetes among Blacks and Latinos, how effective might this effort be in helping to keep this disease under control?

Cultural competence plays a role by providing insights about the types of messages and incentives that resonate with specific employee populations. Health care is the ultimate work-life issue because it affects employees at work, at home, and in the community.

Corporate Communications That Partners With Community

We need to think about corporate communications that go beyond corporate walls. According to a poll commissioned by New American Media, ethnic — not mainstream — media is the primary and secondary news source for 50 million Americans. Considering the demographic trends, this number is only going to grow.

Many minority groups do not look to the corporation as the primary influencer in their lifestyle decisions. According to one Hewitt poll, Whites are more likely to seek out and trust medical information provided by their employer. Minority groups look to their community leaders — the priest, pastor, imam, alderman — as the voice of authority. In this era of multiculturalism and diverse workforces, corporate communicators could benefit from developing strategies that partner with these channels to get messages across to employees.

According to the May 2007 issue of *Hypertension* magazine, Black men's barbers could help test their clients for high blood pressure.[24] In one study, a group of men receiving standard hypertension care was compared to a group that received enhanced intervention via their barbershop. The proportion of men in the enhanced intervention group that received hypertension treatment increased from 45 percent to 92 percent, while those who successfully managed their condition rose from 19 percent to 58 percent. In another study, barbers were trained to check blood pressure, provide health education, and make medical referrals.

Imagine a diabetes management campaign initiated by a large company employing people from various ethnic communities. Equipped with the messages they want to provide and the know-how to deliver them most effectively to non-White employees, these corporations could enlist the help of community leaders. Maybe ask to do a benefits workshop for employees in the community center, rather than in the corporate offices? Perhaps a community leader would be willing to lend her or his voice to the message? These corporations could then partner with ethnic media to cover the topic. They could buy ads in community and ethnic papers in return for the publisher agreeing to print editorials reinforcing messages on health or retirement savings.

Companies Doing Health Benefits Inclusively

On Location Pharmacies and Health Clinics

Employers like Wal-Mart, Pitney Bowes, and Disney are experimenting with onsite health clinics for their employees. The premise: With their large employee base, they can help clinics manage costs and make a check-up less time-intensive and more accessible for employees. This model is likely to appeal to the worldviews of various minority groups, including Latinos, who represent an ever-increasing percentage of the workforce.

These at-work clinics are bound to be attractive for cultures with communitarian and paternalistic worldviews, particularly Latinos, who have a higher expectation that "my employer will take care of me and my family's needs." And since the clinic is at work, it's a chance for mamá and papá to integrate work and family by bringing the whole family to the workplace for a medical check-up.

What if employers sponsored healthcare fairs for the whole family? Nurses could take blood pressure and draw blood samples for cholesterol and diabetes screening, while HR staff at PC workstations show employees how to use the intranet to access benefits information. Make it a party. Kids walk away with lollipops and balloons, and their parents learn their cholesterol levels.

Finding the Levers that Tap into Minority Worldviews

An individualistic, internal-control message of "take care of yourself" may not be enough to motivate a communal, fatalistic Latino male to get an annual physical. But what if you showed him a picture of his 15-year-old daughter at her *Quinceañera* (coming-of-age fifteenth birthday), and then made your case:

¿Si algo te pasara a tí?
(If something happened to you.)
¿Quién cuidaría a tu hija?
(Who would take care of her?)
Cuídala.
(Take care of her.)
Cuidándote.
(By taking care of yourself.)
De una vez, chequea tu salud.
(Once and for all, get a check up.)

Several Sizes Fit Most

I'm not suggesting organizations adopt a multitude of approaches to address every possible demographic. But we need to get past the one-size-fits-all mentality that's grounded in the views and preferences of the majority group. As Hewitt research reveals, there are overlaps in behavioral drivers between different groups, sometimes surprisingly so. For example, there is a key similarity in 401(k) behavior between older Baby Boomers, low-income European Americans, and African-Americans. They all have less experience with financial literacy, leading to non-participation, tentativeness, and over-conservative behaviors that bring down their investment returns.

By identifying these overlaps, we can develop marketing campaigns to address the needs of a variety of demographic groups. This is accomplished by shaping the campaigns around a handful of behavioral drivers (for example, "inexperienced with investing" and "very experienced with investing") rather than a given demographic group. So while "one size fits all" is not effective and "all sizes fit everyone" would be cost prohibitive, the new approach could be called "several sizes fit most."

Providing flexible programs that meet individual needs is only half the battle. If employees don't use them, it doesn't matter how suitable the programs. Success only occurs when workers understand what is available to them *and* use what best meets their needs. They must become educated consumers. All employees must be empowered to make decisions that personally optimize the effectiveness, financial efficiency, and appreciation of programs.

Targeted communication may be required for various groups so that each is motivated to take the desired action. These are the "nudges" authors Thaler and Sunstein argue for in their book. Granted, some employers already use different, specific messages for younger and older employees when it comes to retirement savings. This sort of specialized communication can inform and then motivate a wide variety of diverse employee segments to take action.

Employers should not aim to have separate communication initiatives for each demographic group, however. It's illegal to target specific employee segments — for example, sending pieces of communication to only one demographic group. What's more, effectiveness would be compromised as over-reliance on archetypes leads to stereotypes.

It's not only the choice of message that's important, but also the medium. Studies have found, for example, that older workers, those without high school diplomas, and employees without broadband access at home are less inclined to use the Internet.[25] By being aware of cultural tendencies, communication campaigns can be shaped with more of a marketing approach to help get individuals more comfortable with using the Web, or other communication channels.

From the beginning of the diversity movement, there has been an underlying premise that a diverse workforce would be beneficial to the enterprise. It would bring more creativity and innovation — and a workforce that could better recognize the needs, wants, and desires of an increasingly diverse marketplace. A diverse workforce offers a communal benefit as well. As we call out differences to better create, communicate, and market health and wealth benefits, something unexpected emerges. By developing alternative ways to meet the needs of diverse groups, we discover new ways of reaching *the majority* as well.

When describing a Latino-oriented, communal, family-focused pitch for preventive care, I've had European-American audience members say, "Hey, that's appealing to me too." I've had White audiences tell me, "That example you pointed out for Latinos and the 15-year-old daughter taps something deep within me — and I'm not Latino. Or maybe I am and I don't know it! Those traditional forms of communication don't move me either." *This* is diversity at work. While we need a handle on broad-based archetypes to assess our communication strategies and benefit plan designs, there are plenty of people in other cultural groups that, for various reasons — personality, income level, part of the country, spiritual beliefs — also need different ways of being reached. Taking into account the mix and how to make it work creates new forms of outreach whose benefits go beyond the minority groups. Diversity enriches us all.

Think about how Latino culture already has enriched mainstream U.S. culture. Salsa has surpassed ketchup as the number one condiment. *Dulce de leche* is the second best selling ice-cream flavor, right after vanilla. And the popular TV show *Ugly Betty* came directly from the Spanish telenovela, *La Fea Betty*.

La Fea Betty  **Ugly Betty**

Cristina Benitez's book, *Latinization: How Latino Culture Is Transforming the U.S.* dedicates 125 pages to this phenomenon.

There is also a long, rich history of how Black and White cultures have influenced each other. Merely by tracing the gospel roots of rock 'n' roll, one can embark on a socio-cultural-historical journey of cross-influences encompassing hairstyles, clothing, expressiveness, and more. Likewise, as women entered the workplace in large numbers, they transformed male culture, both inside the corporation and at home. Meanwhile, Americans have influenced cultures worldwide through the export of values like democracy and free trade, as well as through pop culture flowing from Hollywood and MTV.

Multicultural marketing is built into the Inclusion Paradox. To create true inclusion, we must call out differences. In so doing, not only do we broaden our own outreach to better include diverse workforces in the organization's mainstream culture, but we also create ways for these different groups to influence and enrich the mainstream culture. This is 3-D inclusion: influences that flow every which way for the enrichment of all.

This is the next frontier of true diversity and inclusion. In the Obama Era, long-held assumptions around corporate and governmental benefits are being deeply questioned and made more relevant for today's multicultural workforce.

If done right, employees and citizens — from the minority to the majority — and their organizations and nations will be the winners.

Cultural Immersion

Corporate communicators must steep themselves in the iconography of different demographic groups. The whole marketing piece needs to work — not just through the substitution of diverse images, a different language, or even the appropriate worldview levers. The feel of the entire piece — from font to colors to images — needs to appeal to different demographic groups, while still meeting corporate branding guidelines, of course.

For example, here are some images that may appeal to Latinos. Keep in mind that some may appeal to middle-class Latinos and others to low-income Latinos. Also, some country-of-origin differences may work with one group of Latinos and not another.

Illustrated soap operas called *fotonovelas* are popular. Latino Health Care Solutions, owned by United Healthcare, uses this form to create storylines in which a father and his two daughters talk about the dangers of untreated diabetes.

For Mexican migrants to the United States, *lucha libre* (wrestling) superheroes are players in morality dramas. Super Amigos is a documentary of four men in Mexico City, who have taken on different causes using the *lucha libre* art form. Super Barrio (Super Neighborhood) fights against people being evicted through gentrification. Super Gay fights for homosexual rights. Ecologista Universal fights against global warming and contamination, and Super Animal dons his mask to protest bullfighting. Could any of these superheroes be recruited to put on a cape and fight heart disease or diabetes?

Soap operas on primetime, with all their taboo topics, are a typical form of family entertainment. For Latino culture, where family issues can be hard to talk about, telenovelas provide an acceptable, albeit somewhat sensationalized, outlet to broach difficult subjects. One Latino public relations firm inserted a story line dealing with alcoholism into one of the more popular telenovelas showing in the United States.

SUMMARY POINTS

- Inadvertent exclusion may determine whether minority employees take advantage of company benefits and how they go about doing so.
- Compared to White Americans, African-Americans and Latinos tend to under-save in 401(k) plans and under-participate in preventive health care programs. Meanwhile, women are more conservative in their investments than men.
- Employers must start viewing employees as consumers, not passive recipients, of company benefit packages.
- When it comes to health and other company benefits, one size does not fit all. Such an approach can be both cost-prohibitive and ineffective.
- In an increasingly diverse workforce, the 'average employee' no longer applies, and company benefits designed for that fading paradigm will not resonate with today's emerging workforce.
- We must move to multicultural design and marketing of benefits. This entails much more than translating words and changing pictures. It means taking into account the differing

worldviews of multicultural constituencies.
- Crosscultural competence and understanding the existence of different worldviews helps companies find motivators within cultural contexts that encourage employees to participate in various corporate benefit offerings.
- Calling out differences in employee behavior may uncover common behaviors across different groups. Instead of developing different approaches for each demographic group, companies can look at what behavior drivers are shared by these constituencies.
- Employee health status economically affects company performance.
- The Affordable Health Care Act will add about 32 million currently uninsured Americans to the current healthcare system.
- Societal trends affect an organization's employee healthcare coverage.
- Diversity and inclusion strategies that are well-known in the corporate world can be used in the healthcare system to improve patient outcomes and increase cost savings.

SHAPING YOUR STRATEGY

- Has your organization experienced differences in the utilization of benefits based on demographic characteristics? If you don't know, how can you convince key stakeholders it's worth their while to find out?
- How successful is your organization at designing and marketing multicultural ben-

efits packages? What can it do to change the way these packages are created to make them more inclusive of different cultural worldviews?
- What motivators can your organization tap into to encourage employees to participate in preventive care and save more for retirement?

THE MOTHER
OF ALL BATTLES

Chapter 14

Work-Life Flexibility:
The Mother of All Battles

The imaginary work-life camera slowly pans out to reveal Mom and Dad both working. A nursery is available on-site, and older children are welcome in the workplace. There's no commute, and homestyle breakfasts and lunches are served daily. A progressive 21st Century Best Company for work-life balance? Perhaps. But I was actually describing how things looked for most people working on the family farm before the Industrial Revolution. Since coal-based energy technology changed all that two centuries ago, workers and their families have had to toil within an economic model that violently cleaved home and work into completely separate spheres.

This split resulted in irreconcilable parental, spousal, community, and workplace responsibility dilemmas. Until recently, it was simply understood that individuals had to solve their dilemma by choosing one sphere over the other. "You can't have it all!" was the message to angst-filled female employees. The work-life balance movement, led by the first modern-age working moms, counterpunched. Propelled by the flagship publication of the movement, *Working Mother* magazine, women challenged detrimental workplace and career assumptions. Taking the retort and remaking it, the working moms' battle cry became, "We *can* have it all!"

Boomer women launched the powerful archetype of the Super Woman who worked a fulfilling career; had a satisfying, intimate relationship with her husband; stayed in shape; and tended expertly and lovingly to her children's emotional, developmental, and practical needs. Rising to the challenge, millions of women strived to live balanced lives. In the first decade of the 21st Century, 55 percent of first-time mothers returned to work within six months of giving birth, compared to 14 percent in the early 1960s.[1] But they struggled against a Category 1 headwind of inflexible structures — not only those related to the office, but also school schedules, store hours, doctors' appointments and traffic-clogged commutes, to name just a few.

The women at the forefront of this movement made demands: more flexible office hours, on-site child care, and paid-time-off (PTO) banks that allowed workers to care for runny noses and fevers. Not wanting to lose this newfound talent pool, corporations slowly, reluctantly, responded. Today, PTO banks exist in about 30 percent of companies.[2] And arriving a little late due to a sick child or leaving a little early for a day care pickup is tolerated, for white collar workers anyway. But only a handful of truly progressive companies have tried to bridge the home-office gulf by providing on-site day care and fitness centers.

While generally helpful, these accommodations worked around the edges, rather than yielding transformational changes that could resolve the home-office split. Balance remained elusive. As long as office and home and "standard work hours" remained in place, this artificial dichotomy kept the ideal of work-life balance out of reach.

These systemic barriers didn't stop other demographic groups from jumping on the work-life bandwagon. Working fathers, singles, near-retirees, and Millennials *all* want it. "Moms' requirements for flexibility have opened this up to others who didn't even realize they wanted it too or were too afraid to ask," says Kristin Slavish, an HR vice president at Aon Hewitt.

As more women worked, they had less time for housework and child care. Dishes stacked up; diapers needed to be changed; and deadlines loomed. Men had to take up the housework slack. While imbalances still exist, the trend is toward housework equity. According to the Council on Contemporary Families, men's contribution to housework doubled — from 15 percent to 30 percent[3] — between the 1960s and the first decade of the 21st Century. Men are now increasingly expected to contribute equally to the functioning of the household as well as succeed at work.[4] Meanwhile, something profound and inherently human happened as fathers spent more time with their kids — they discovered the joy of parenthood, just as they came to realize how much they had missed from their own fathers' deficit of time with them. What started as an imposition to accommodate their partners' job aspirations became, for many, a personal desire. Suddenly, fathers were demanding their own work-life balance so they could coach their kids' 4 o'clock soccer practice or attend a late-afternoon kindergarten recital.

As these parents broadened the demand for work-life balance, singles began to make their voices heard as well. Parenthood, they argued, should not be the only argument for honoring a request for balance. They, too, had other priorities they wanted to tend to — church, synagogue, and mosque commitments; serving as a Big Brother or Big Sister to a neighborhood kid; taking care of aging parents; preparing for a marathon.

Next in line were near-retirees who, feeling healthy and intellectually alert, did not want to retire altogether. Some did not feel economically ready. Either they hadn't saved enough for their post-work years or they discovered they were going to live much longer than the actuaries had anticipated. To top it off, here come the Millennials, the And Generation, for whom nano second technology means there are no trade-offs. For them, the divide between personal and work has shrunk along with the size of their smartphones.

The good news: This congruence is accelerating debates about the next generation of work-life balance. The bad news: In a 24/7 global economy, Americans, Canadians, and Western Europeans compete with Indian, Chinese, Filipino, Eastern European, and Central American talent located *anywhere* in the world. And where G7 developed nation wages have gone stagnant and health and retirement benefits have been curtailed, most individuals have to work harder than ever.

Still, few want to go back to sacrificing family, community service, and other pursuits at the altar of work and career success. We want to cling to that aspiration to be more than our work. Yet, the increasingly competitive marketplace and this quest for a more holistic life are careening down a collision course with each other. The pioneering working mothers freed the genie from the bottle, and there's no stuffing it back in. It is shaping up to be the Mother of All Battles. Which will yield to the other? Or is there another way?

Work-life Balance is Dead! Long Live Work-life Flexibility!

There is a battle being waged *within* the work-life movement. The original clarion cry had been all about balance between work and everything else. But given the rush of life, the expectation that we manage our own tech support, retirement savings, health management, learning, and career planning; the increased load on our personal lives as we manage children's complex schedules and care for aging parents, and ubiquitous access to *all* information *all* the time; the quest for balance has yielded little but frustration. Is balance even possible? In clamoring and longing for it, we and progressive companies have inadvertently made both spheres larger — making the elusive Holy Grail of work-life balance even more out of reach.

When I describe this to audiences, they ruefully connect with this realization. "But if balance is out of reach, how about flexibility?" I ask. "Yes!" they respond. "That's what it is." They elaborate: "We need the flexibility to manage the competing priorities in our whole lives — flexibility to move in and out of being a worker, boss, parent, partner, sibling, son, daughter, volunteer, community organizer, athlete, arts lover, friend, camper, dreamer. We've surrendered to the faster, more complex pace of life and thus tempered our quest for balance. At any one time, something will be out of balance in our lives, as family emergencies, client deadlines, an upcoming competition, or vacation consume a greater share of our collective moments. But we won't surrender to inflexible structures. Flexibility is the currency we need to survive and thrive.

Even our first lady, Michelle Obama, has come out in support of greater work-life flexibility. At a women's economic roundtable in Pontiac, Michigan, on July 9, 2009, she said, "As we all know, our country is in the midst of a major economic crisis. And we're all feeling the effects. ... And folks are feeling it at the workplace. Because right now, thousands of women across the country don't have family leave at their jobs. And those who do can't afford to take it because it's not paid. And 22 million working women don't have a single paid sick day. That's just unacceptable. Families shouldn't be punished because someone gets sick or has an emergency."[5]

In the Obama Era, an increasing number of employers are offering flex-time in lieu of higher salaries, raises, or the traditional end-of-year bonus. As Michelle Obama alluded, companies simply cannot afford to increase salaries in these tough economic times. But they *can* offer greater flexibility in exchange for high productivity, loyalty, and a decrease in turnover.

As long as we were tethered to offices and desks, bound by 9-to-5 rhythms, we faced a dead end in our ability to help workers balance their work and home loads. Limited by time and space, corporate equations could not yield different answers. Accommodations were made through an either/or equation. Part-time or flex-time assumed that time away from the physical workplace meant work did not get done. While many working mothers got what they asked for — more time with their kids — it came at the cost of their long-term career advancement. The preeminent career advancement equation became: Strong Performance + Time = Advancement. High-performing women who chose to take time off simply fell behind.[6] No matter how good they were, most would never be able to make up for the lost work time.

To accommodate this conundrum, Ellen Galinsky suggests, "Employers need to think of career flexibility, not just flex-time and flex-place, so that there is an understanding that there are times where you move in and out of the workforce. Think about the irony: flexibility *can't* be a rigid flexible work arrangement!"

But now, technology — the culprit responsible for creating the work-home split in the first place — is saving the day by enabling flexibility.

The pivotal tool was the Internet, which offered employees a platform on which they could share their work with colleagues in Mumbai, London, and Chicago or with team members at their kitchen tables. The Internet made a new equation possible, driving a wedge into the concept of workplace. With *work* and *place* no longer inexorably connected, alternate possibilities emerged.

Still, one more structural equation remained to reconfigure: Work From Home + Slow Connectivity = Diminished Productivity. Along came broadband wireless, which toppled the final vestiges of structural limitations. For knowledge workers, work can now happen anyplace, anytime, with instant connectivity to anyone and any content.

We have reached the tipping point in the Mother of All Workplace Battles. Full work-life flexibility is now structurally possible. The next battlefront is policy.

The Resistance — Trapped in 20th Century Thinking

Many leaders and managers are busy spray painting over the "Long Live Flexibility!" graffiti on figurative corporate walls. The rigid structures of the modern corporation made sense in the workplace era. But the emerging work/place shift runs smack into long-held assumptions of how, where, and when work gets done. How does one manage by walking around if there's no one in the office? And how can you raise productivity if there's a fear of "out of sight, out of mind"?

"Most senior leaders and middle managers in organizations today are still operating in a 'time card' mentality," says Carol Sladek, at the time Hewitt's work-life consulting leader. "They can't get past measuring productivity in hours and the number of hours an employee's car is in the office parking lot."

Managers are not getting much support from the organization when it comes to managing this complexity. While a third of companies offer flexibility at manager discretion, nearly two-thirds provide no training for managers on how to go about doing this.[7]

Leaders and managers may resist making way for work-life flexibility. Understanding why requires a short philosophical conversation. *Modernism*, the worldview that believes reality is fixed and determined by those in authority, is being challenged by *postmodernism*, a worldview that believes reality is based on each individual's interpretation. This philosophy first emerged in literature: the story doesn't necessarily mean what the writer intended but rather what the reader understands it to mean. Soon, postmodernism infiltrated multiple arenas. It has influenced new interpretations of history,[8] the creation of alternative curricula — from Montessori to African-American and Women's Studies — and the emergence of New Age and "The Secret" spirituality.

This postmodernist worldview has also made the diversity movement possible. Modernism accepts how things are — including the dominance of White males in leadership — because there can be only one reality and that is the one we live in. Postmodernist thinking allowed the deconstruction of assigned roles. This led organizations to question the lack of diversity in leadership roles. The key to inclusion — making the mix work — lies in understanding the varying interpretations of the workplace experience by diverse constituencies.

This takes us to work-life flexibility. Different constituencies, for different reasons, want to redefine what "work" looks like, and when and where it gets done. This postmodern view triggers conflict with the modernist view of many leaders and managers. The battle lines manifest mostly along generational lines (Boomers, disciples of modernism, on the one hand and Gen Xers and Millennials, the children of postmodernism, on the other), though individuals of all ages are lining up on either side.

Diffusing Backlash

As the established worldview clashes with the emerging one, a backlash occurs. The forces of culture change move according to the laws of physics: As the new worldview begins making inroads, it invites an equal reaction of resistance.

With work-life, the resistance comes from multiple fronts. It's not just managers who resist loosening the structures to allow more flexibility for working mothers, for example. According to Carol Evans, CEO of Working Mother Media, it also happens among women themselves as they wrestle with what the changes imply about their own identity. "We see one wave of the backlash against working mothers come from other women who have staked their position as a stay-at-home mom," she says. "Not all stay-at-home moms, of course, but a vocal minority of them who may resent the lifestyle choices that working mothers have made." She goes on to explain that another wave of backlash comes from other women — those first glass-ceiling-crashers who chose not to have children in order to move up the corporate ladder. Even more backlash comes from White men who feel women in the workplace are being granted special privileges. Then there's the inevitable backlash from singles, who feel people with children are allowed work schedule freedoms that they themselves should also receive. "These bands of resistance then go up against family-friendly company programs," says Evans.[9] The shock waves of debate reverberate throughout the corporation.

The Inclusion Paradox requires solutions that break the *zero sum game* mindset and instead get into what Dr. Michael Broom refers to as an *infinite game* mindset.[10] In a zero sum game mindset, your gain is my loss. In an infinite game, your gain triggers gains for me as well. It goes beyond the 1 + 1 = 2 of win-win to 1 + 1 = 3 or more. The challenge lies in discovering how *all* constituents — including managers and leaders — can win in the quest for true work-life flexibility.

When we constructively call out the differences of traditionally marginalized groups in order to better understand what they need, we get new answers for other groups as well.

Let's look at how this works. Addressing working moms' need for maternity leave leads to the realization that new fathers need time off as well to bond with their new child and support their partner. In addressing the architectural needs of those with physical disabilities, we discover an overlap between what they need and the desire to make our buildings greener. And in rethinking the subconscious bias toward a White male style of leadership, we create new possibilities for introverts.

"This is one of the reasons why, in all the work that we do at *Working Mother*," Evans explains, "whether we are working on behalf of women of color, diversity in general, or working mothers, we always emphasize the benefit to all employees for any gains that any one group makes. Because if I have never had a child but now my mother needs elder care, I can take advantage of the same flex-time a working mother gets to take care of her children." Young, healthy men and women are now using flexibility to train for marathons. Millennial singles can more easily volunteer in a political campaign. Near-retirees can take off mid-afternoon to hang out with their grandchildren. "Any progress we make we can apply to other groups," concludes Evans.

Candi Castleberry-Singleton mentions her own experience creating workplace flexibility programs at Motorola and UPMC, emphasizing the benefits these programs ultimately provide to a wide range of employees, not just working mothers: "Flexible work programs get traction when people are able to see how they personally benefit from them. Because people tend to mentally associate flexible work programs with female employees, I never use the term 'working mothers' or 'working parent' to sell them. Instead I present the programs as inclusion initiatives — meaning they're available to everyone — so that both women and men see the personal advantages of flexible work, whether for reasons related to parenting or something entirely different, such as going back to school to get an MBA."

Such programs gain greater traction when managers and leaders see that they win as well. Employees are dealing with ever-longer commutes, made even more cumbersome by rising gas prices and heightened concern about reducing our carbon footprint. Productivity suffers when employees arrive at the office stressed even before the workday begins. Settling in at their desk, their minds may wander to their 2-year-old's ear infection or the need to get home in time to make dinner for a frail, aging parent, or their 6 p.m. physical trainer session or their desire to finish a painting in time for an upcoming art exhibit.

Some managers think they've put boundaries in place to keep "the rest of life" at bay by demanding their workers be seen. However, such restrictions are breached right under their noses through a digital sieve called the Internet. They may appear to be busily working on a new marketing campaign or drafting the white paper that will unveil the firm's revolutionary thought leadership to the world, but in reality, workers are webcamming into their doggie day care to see how their schnauzer is doing, scheduling immunizations for their kids, planning their next vacation, and monitoring highway backups on Traffic.com.

Ironically, many studies show that those out-of-sight workers tucked away in their home offices are actually more engaged with their employers, more productive, and more satisfied with the ability to manage their work and their life responsibilities.[11]

Virtual, telecommuting workers deconstruct their workdays. Rather than dedicating large chunks of time to specific things — 9 to 5 for work, 6 to 9 for family — they chunk work into productivity modules that are then interspersed with child care, fitness, artistic expression, socializing, and personal planning modules. They may go offline from work at 3 p.m., but they're back online at 9 p.m. after the kids have gone to bed and the workout clothes are in the washer. This arrangement, by happy coincidence, helps move the work forward in a global economy: Now, managers have workers who can take calls from ten time zones away in India, without those calls intruding too much into their lives.

There are still more benefits for businesses. In the quest for reducing costs, having virtual workers enables a game-changing reduction in the real estate footprint. This means not only less office space but also less furniture, fewer coffee stations, lower energy costs, reduced security costs, and so on. In addition, a mobile, flexible workforce will no longer need to ask for flex-time to meet home demands. Flex is built in.

Maria Awilda Quintana is a Gen X executive at Banco Popular in San Juan, Puerto Rico whom I met at a conference for financial advisors where I was giving a workshop on Millennials. In the conservative environment of the banking industry, Quintana breaks with conventional wisdom to get the highest productivity from her employees. "At five o'clock, I send anyone who is still in the office home. 'Go take care of your kids, go work out, go volunteer,' I tell them. And they can't believe that their manager is telling them to stop working when there is so much work to do." In a hierarchical, communal Latino culture, this directive has a powerful, positive effect. And guess what? At 9 p.m., after the kids have gone to bed and the dishes are done, they're all logging in from home. "I never set that up as an expectation," she says. "But they do it because in my helping them with meeting their multiple life demands, they flex in return to help the bank meet its multiple demands." This not only means a more engaged workforce, it also translates into business results. Quintana's team's client satisfaction scores are over 86 percent.

This, then, is the quid pro quo — the employment contract of what gets offered in exchange. Flexibility begets flexibility. Zero sum game capitulates to infinite game.

The Postmodern 21st Century Workplace

So in this flex world, where exactly is the office? It's in the home den, at the Starbucks, or the neighborhood park. It's wherever one can take an Android or a laptop with a broadband wireless card. It does not mean the end of the traditional office, but rather, its redefinition. Instead of the workplace being *the* place where work gets done, it becomes a place where a *certain* type of work gets done.

There are still plenty of reasons to maintain the workplace. Virtual workers need face time for relationship building, certain types of creative brainstorming, and production, among other activities.[12] Clearly, there are plenty of customer facing businesses that must have personnel on-site. Also, the traditional office is an option for the type of employee who can focus better away from home or is energized by working in the presence of colleagues. But even here, the office moves with the worker. He or she may not have a fixed desk. And as they move around the building from meeting to water fountain to boss's office, they can stay in constant touch with colleagues in and out of the office. "Walking down the hall" can be literal or virtual, as colleagues available for a quick visit show up in an online chat tool and you ping them, "R U there?"

While cube farms signaled an end of sorts to the hierarchy of job title and experience based on the size and position of one's office, they still demarked boundaries. Broadband wireless enabled through pocket-sized devices now supports a less restricted and contained workplace, as the office goes mobile even within the building. At the same time, acute cost pressures and the push to reduce their carbon footprint are heightening corporations' appetites to shed costly real estate. "They still want the quality and the performance, but they don't want to pay for workspace that's occupied less than half the time," says Tom Vecchione, the workplace leader for Gensler, one of the top global workplace design organizations.[13]

As flexible work-life trends create a new paradigm for how work happens, a new office design becomes a necessity. In a recent workplace survey, Gensler discovered that "today's office workers spend less time at their desks [alone]. Instead they're collaborating, learning, and socializing with their peers."[14] The workspace needs to be redesigned to accommodate these preferred styles. At one media company, Gensler designed bench-style desks for print reporters, bullpens for Internet reporters, and dog-bone-shaped workstations for broadcast teams. It's the postmodern workplace, where deciding how to use the space is up to the users. The top financially and innovatively ranked companies already are seizing these issues — and reaping the rewards. At these companies, 82 percent of workers expressed satisfaction with their physical workplace, versus 49 percent of workers from average-performing companies. Why does this matter? In their survey, Gensler validated a high correlation between workplace design and multiple business measures, such as productivity, business competitiveness, job performance, and worker satisfaction.[15]

The "green imperative" dovetails into this. With greenhouse gas emissions from all buildings accounting for almost half of the U.S. total, new flex buildings must open up to natural sunlight and enable more efficient heating and cooling. Meanwhile, from a disability perspective, we need to move from a compliance driven "Americans with disabilities" approach to true, inclusive flex buildings that are holistically user-friendly to people of different sizes, mobility, and light and noise sensitivities.[16]

The Inclusion Paradox is at play here as well — more open spaces facilitate the inclusive collaboration of people with diverse skills and approaches. When it comes to the evolving workplace, Chris Sullivan, former editor of *Architecture* magazine, writes, "one-size-fits-all standardization is history."[17]

Uber-Flexibility — Diversity of One

Clearly, work-life flexibility is about time and space. But it's even more profound than that. Work-life flexibility is about a state of mind. If we can bend and twist where and when we work — and concepts like 9-to-5 and "the office" start to feel anachronistic — then what other givens of "how things work" can be challenged? Galinsky sees even greater challenge to work and advancement: "We ought to not assume that workers will get on a track and stay on that track, and there are on-ramps and off-ramps. Instead, we ought to think of career lattices. You just can't think about careers as linear ladders that we're climbing or if we move we fall off into the abyss. That's just not reality and we are losing huge talent when we think that way." Diverse workers from different perspectives are challenging assumptions about the rigid structures around paid time off, career progression, the definition of what a job is, and what kind of health care coverage, retirement savings, and other benefits are desirable.

It is a call for uber-flexibility.

In the chapter on Millennials, I laid out some specific ways in which the twenty-something uber-flexible worldview is forcing new and urgent conversations in corporations. Here I want to explore the implications of uber-flexibility to diversity.

The diversity movement has established the need to create different approaches for attracting, engaging, and advancing groups of employees, such as women, LGBT, and people of color. Mentoring, affinity groups, and affinity job fairs are a few ways this has been tackled. Given the continued presence of glass, concrete, bamboo, tortilla, and rainbow ceilings, strategies and best practices for *diversity of groups* are needed.

In the end, we are multidimensional people who can't neatly be defined by one diversity category. I am a 50-something, able-bodied Peruvian male in a mixed marriage with one adult daughter. I describe my faith as Catholic Evangelical Afro Baptist New Age Pentecostal. My passions include soccer, dancing, the beach, world music and food, and reading and writing. Yes, I do have several archetypical ways of being, doing, and thinking that correlate with being Latino and a guy. I believe these archetypes are helpful in crafting diversity strategy for addressing group needs and wants. This is evident in how I approach different diversity topics in my writing and work. A natural extension of uber-flexibility is the concept of *diversity of one*.

But uber-flexibility doesn't just challenge the one-size-fits-all mentality. It also challenges the updated response that several sizes fit most. Uber-flexibility demands that we address the multidimensional needs and wants of individuals — The African-American Millennial female IT engineer who's a marathon runner. The wheelchair-using actuary who's an extreme sports athlete. The gay doctor who seeks to do volunteerism in Africa with Doctors Without Frontiers. The passionate fifty-something Boomer human resources executive who's running for a local political office. The variations are infinite!

At first, this kind of talk seems costly in the eyes of business folks. On 20th Century technology platforms, the ability to customize corporate responses to the individual was, indeed, cost-prohibitive. But early 21st Century technology has dramatically driven that cost down. Remember when cell phones passed the tipping point from being a luxury item to a mass-market product? We are at the same type of tipping point. Online magazines provide content at a fraction of the cost of print magazines. Services such as iTunes distribute music to millions every day without any postage costs. We are on the verge of learning how to tailor corporate experiences and employee benefits in cost-effective ways that address individual wants and needs. We need creative souls to design the programs and delivery systems.

Best Buy's Results-Only Work Environment (ROWE) means they have no formal work schedule. Hours worked are set by the employee. Best Buy then measures employee performance solely on output, not hours. According to the company, productivity has increased 35 percent, engagement has increased, and voluntary turnover has declined for those on ROWE.[18]

Why should other companies take this kind of approach? Despite the tough economic climate, we still are in a fierce fight for skilled talent. But wages are rising slowly and will remain under pressures due to global labor competition. Subsidies for health and retirement are declining, meaning employees have to pay more out-of-pocket for less. Companies can't really compete on salary and traditional benefits anymore. The new competitive benefit will be uber-flexibility, in all its forms.

Why Work-life Flexibility Will Drive High-Performance Work Cultures and Strong Business Results

In business, the bottom line is always the bottom line. What impact will work-life flexibility have on financial measures? In addition to the cost savings that come by reducing turnover, a more flexible workforce can contribute directly to higher revenues and improved margins. According to Hewitt's 2008 Timely Topic Survey "About Flexible Work Arrangements," two-thirds of employers said flexibility increases engagement; nearly two-thirds said it improves retention; and nearly half said it enhances recruiting. In the 2012 poll by the National Partnership for Women and Families 86 percent of respondents wanted Congress to work on family friendly policies like paid family leave and paid sick leave for employees.[19]

Given these stories and stats, *Working Mother* magazine's Carol Evans says — half-jokingly at first before she makes it a statement of conviction: "We have developed a theory at *Working Mother* that flexibility is the answer to every problem. It's the answer to the gas crises and high rent and environmental pollution, family time, engagement, boredom with our jobs and careers, access for those with disability, cost management in an age of margin squeezes, staffing in a 24/7 global world, to mention a few."

President Obama seems to agree. At a 2010 White House Forum on Workplace Flexibility, which was hosted by Michelle Obama, the President encouraged businesses to think about flexibility in the workplace as more than a women's issue, but an economic imperative. He cited a report by the White House Council of Economic Advisers that found companies with flexible work arrangements have lower turnover and absenteeism, and higher productivity, and healthier workers. Obama said, "This disconnect between the needs of our families and the demands of our workplace also reflects a broader problem, that today, we as a society still see workplace flexibility policies as a special perk for women rather than a critical part of a workplace that can help all of us. ... Workplace flexibility isn't just a women's issue. It's an issue that affects the well-being of our families and the success of our businesses. It affects the strength of our economy—whether we'll create the workplaces and jobs of the future we need to compete in today's global economy."[20]

The push for greater flexibility is the current goal of *Working Mother* magazine and National Partnership for Women and Families in its petition drive to Congress instituting a paid family leave insurance program for new parents. By 2015, *Working Mother* wants every employee to have the flexibility to take paid parental leave on the birth or adoption of a child. This would broaden the impact of the current Family Medical Leave Act and bring U.S. employers and workers in line with the rest of the industrialized world where the United States is the only nation in this group without paid parental leave. In fact, only 16 percent of U.S. companies offer paid family leave.[21] More than just a women's or family concern, Working Mother Media President Carol Evans sees this as a business issue. She explains, "It's also critical to the economic health of our companies and our nation. Our ability to compete in the global marketplace depends upon the energy, intelligence and commitment our mothers and fathers bring to the workplace every day—qualities that are built on a strong family foundation."

Flexibility makes managing by objective more critical than ever. What matters is delivering results. The how and where become much less relevant. So, how to manage this uber-flexibility? Managers focus on ensuring results. Objectives, targets, and goals become the new boundaries, replacing physical walls, desks, and chairs, and employees being within a manager's line of sight. And as companies are flexible, workers are flexible in return. Flexibility begets flexibility. It is both a worker and manager currency that both can use with each other. In the mother of all workplace battles, flexibility means everyone wins. ♀

SUMMARY POINTS

- Women were instrumental in pushing for work-life balance. Corporations slowly responded with more flexible office hours, on-site day care, and PTO banks instead of rigid vacation or sick time allotments. Yet traditional structures stayed intact and balance remained elusive.

- Women's push for work-life balance encouraged others — fathers, singles, near-retirees, and Millennials — to request the same consideration.

- Work-life flexibility is a more attainable goal than work-life balance.

- Work-life flexibility represents more than merely revising our traditional views on space and time. It is a profound reworking of a state of mind. It is uber-flexibility.

- Uber-flexibility rejects the one-size-fits-all or the one-size-fits-most paradigm, recognizing we are multidimensional people who resist category-limiting labels.

- In addition to the cost savings that come about by reducing turnover, a more flexible workforce contributes directly to higher revenues and improved margins.

- As companies become more flexible, workers are more flexible in return. Flexibility begets flexibility and everyone wins.

- Workplace flexibility is more than a business benefit, but also strengthens our national economy.

- Paid family leave for new parents will bring the United States in line with other industrialized nations.

SHAPING YOUR STRATEGY

- How flexible is your organization? What flex benefits do you offer and what percentage of your staff takes advantage of them?

- If your organization is not flexible, what are some of the reasons given for adhering to a 20th Century work model? What can

you do to alleviate manager resistance in ways that are reassuring to them?

- How does your company's workspace reflect the trend toward a more open, flexible work environment? How can you provide a more streamlined office design?

the broken, leaking, plugged up reservid

es r ,

e

talent

15

The Toughest Challenge

pipeline

Chapter 15

The Toughest Challenge:
The Broken, Leaking, Plugged-Up
Diverse Talent Pipeline

Are companies ready for the Talent War? In most cases, the answer is a resounding "No!" The pipeline is cracked; it's leaking; it's clogged up. In some places, it's connected to talent pools that are drying up, and in other places, it's not connected to the talent pools whose tides are rising. If not addressed, the very sustainability of our organizations could be at stake.

- It's well known there will be ten to 20 million jobs that will go unfilled in the coming decade due in large part to the Baby Boomer retirement bubble, yet two-thirds of CEOs haven't taken any steps to address the aging workforce.[1]
- Starting in 2012 women and minorities make up about 70 percent of the workforce,[2] yet HR leaders spend less than 25 percent of their time dealing with the implications of this shift.[3]
- Minorities comprise more than 30 percent of the United States workforce, according to the Bureau of Labor Statistics. That number is expected to hit nearly 40 percent by 2020. Yet 95 percent of all executive-level positions in the United States are still held by White males, according to authors David A. Thomas and John J. Gabarro in *Breaking Through: The Making of Minority Executives in Corporate America.*[4]

- In many companies, there are now at least four generations working together, yet only 16 percent have made any changes to address these and other profound demographic shifts.[5]
- Among Fortune 500 companies, 50 percent expect to lose half of their senior management team over the next five to six years, according to RHR International. These corporations also anticipate a shortfall in the number of middle management candidates prepared to take on greater responsibility.

When the spotlight is directed at the advancement of multicultural leadership talent, the outlook gets even worse. In the 2008 Chicago United Corporate Diversity Profile 2008, which assessed leadership representation among people of color in the Windy City, the organization found that the number of minority directors hadn't increased since the 2006 report, but the number of director seats had increased by ten. The report observed that if organizations maintained that current pace, it would take nearly 90 years for boards of directors to be representationally diverse.

Little has changed since then. The 2012 Profile found that minorities accounted for only 12 percent of the boards of directors at Chicago's 50 largest firms, compared to 15 percent at the 200 largest S&P 500 firms. Nine of those 50 firms have no diversity in their boardrooms and only three companies have boards with 25 percent people of color. Across the top levels of leadership, there is a dearth of representation by people of color, particularly among CEOs, chief financial officers, and other C-level positions, as well as other top executives.[6]

Making matters worse, 47 percent of senior executives expect to see an increase in culture and gender diversity in the CEO's office, while 48 percent expect continuation of the status quo, according to Korn Ferry's survey, *Diversity in the Executive Suite.* Not only does this indicate little hope for progress, but also a disconnect between the expectations for corporate diversity initiatives and their impact on the workplace.

This is bad news in terms of our ability to address the broader talent shortage. If our companies are going to continue to be viable, we're going to have to nurture and find talent in *all* labor pools.

As has often been said, what gets measured gets done. Well, here's one case where we are measuring and we are still not getting it done! Many companies deliberately don't track certain demographics because once they identify a gap in their corporate culture, they are forced to deal with it. The perception is that this could lead to added expense which, in turn, detracts from the bottom line. What's missing here is accountability — which is really no different than the challenge businesses face when they try to drive any kind of improvement.

Seriously compounding the problem is the fact that too few people of color are finishing high school and going on to college. According to the National Center for Education Statistics, high school graduation rates for Latinos and African-Americans hover around 60 percent.[7] Of these, only *half* go to college. Of those that go on to college, only 40 percent actually graduate. That gets us to a 10 percent college graduation rate.[8]

This is no longer merely a social service issue. This is a bottom-line business issue. Our collective talent lifeblood is retiring at one end of the pipeline and getting siphoned off at the other. Nothing less than our economic sustainability is at stake.

A 2009 study by management consulting firm McKinsey & Company illustrates just how devastating this broken, leaking, clogged-up pipeline has become. According to the report, "The Economic Impact of the Achievement Gap in America's Schools," if the United States had closed the educational achievement gap between the United States and better-educated countries (such as Finland and Korea), the 2008 Gross Domestic Product (GDP) could have been $1.3 trillion to $2.3 trillion higher — that's 9 to 16 percent of GDP. Noteworthy gains also could have been achieved by closing the gap between Whites and Blacks and Latinos or by closing the gap between low-income students and the rest. As the report dramatically asserts, these ongoing achievement gaps result in an economic equivalent of a permanent national recession for the United States.[9]

The situation does not appear to be improving. McKinsey followed that 2009 report with a 2012 blueprint, "Education to Employment: Designing a System that Works," that looks at the gap between employers, youth, and educational institutions. The study found:

- Globally 75 million young people are unemployed and three times less likely than their parents to have a job
- Roughly half of young people don't see the connection between jobs and education, even those with some college experience
- Only 43 percent of employers can find enough entry level workers with the necessary skills

• By 2020 there will a shortage of 85 million skilled workers across the globe

This shortage of skills and shortage of jobs is further exacerbated by the different interpretations of the situation by employers, educational institutions, and students. It's as if these three key players exist in parallel universes. Such circumstances distress the global economy and present national security threats to countries around the world.[10]

Insights

After two decades of explicitly addressing issues of diversity, the United States isn't advancing at the required pace. Good intentions are not enough! And we just can't will "talent of color" into positions of leadership. We have to discover new ways of finding and nurturing that talent. And we need to look within the pipeline to identify top-performing multicultural talent that may contribute in ways that aren't yet recognized as valuable *because of the limitations of our own experiences.*

As we've seen, the number of people of color entering the corporate talent pipeline is too low, according to findings from the Chicago United report. At the same time, other studies reveal that the attrition rate of this very same talent is too high. In effect, we compete intensely with each other for this coveted yet limited in numbers talent, creating a revolving door of multicultural employees. The reports also point out that top talent of color serves on an average of almost four boards compared to the norm of three. We appear to be overtaxing this talent by asking the same people to meet our board diversity representation goals.

The weaknesses in the multicultural talent pipeline also reflect the weakness of overall leadership development. If we don't have strong leadership development programs, it doesn't matter what kind of focus we have on filling the pipeline with diverse talent. Progress will be hampered. The reverse is also true: by focusing development resources on multicultural leadership, companies will benefit by building bench strength in an increasingly global and competitive marketplace.

The shortage of multicultural talent is a business issue that must be tackled like any other business issue — with a keen focus on specific objectives. As business leaders, we must put a relentless focus on repairing the pipeline. Today's global marketplace is very different from the one many of us grew up in, requiring new approaches and a diverse leadership team in terms of worldviews, experiences, and thought processes.

As we think about solutions to our most pressing challenges, it's important to be clear about the outcomes we're trying to achieve:

- Will we have a competitive workforce in our various geographic markets globally?
- Will we have a workforce that mirrors the marketplace to help us produce relevant and profitable products and services?
- Will we have the leadership we need to sustain our growth?
- Do we have leaders who can lead diverse, multicultural, and global teams?

Now, let's turn our attention to some of the ways we can address these challenges.

THE SOLUTIONS

Cultivating the talent and leadership necessary to fuel our futures cannot be resolved by just one or two interventions. The required solutions are not all that complex — but they require deliberate action and that we hold ourselves accountable for the results.

Clearly we must find ways to increase the flow of talent going into the pipeline in the first place, remove clogs that are blocking the advancement of talent of color, and plug leaks where we're losing talent to competitors or to fields outside the corporate world. Here are three strategies I suggest for doing this.

1. We Must Widen the Entrance to the Pipeline

Admittedly, this recommendation is one that will not yield results in the short term, but if we don't find a way to *begin* widening the entrance to the pipeline, we're going to face a talent shortage in the next decade that we might have difficulty recovering from. IBM's diversity leader Ron Glover explains, "There are some skills that in any industry or any society are in overabundance. The real question for us is, will we take this downturn as an opportunity as a nation and across the globe to begin to re-skill people for the coming opportunities?" As a society, we must find a way to increase the number of students of all backgrounds graduating from high school and college.

There are several highly successful school programs that, if replicated nationwide, could significantly boost the amount of talent entering the pipeline. In his 2008 book, *Outliers: The Story of Success*, Malcolm Gladwell tells the story of the KIPP Academy, an experimental public middle school in the South Bronx, one of the poorest neighborhoods in New York City. Roughly half of the students are African-American, the rest Latino. Ninety percent are below, at, or just hovering above the poverty level. And yet, writes Gladwell, "By the end of eighth grade, 84 percent of the students are performing at or above their grade level in math ... as well ... as the privileged eighth graders in America's wealthy suburbs."[11]

To find out why, I highly recommend you read the chapter, "Marita's Bargain," in Gladwell's book. It's an uplifting, yet practical read. You'll see why there are now 125 KIPP Academies across the United States and more on the way. The KIPP methodology is well-thought-out and backed by organizational, parental, and student willpower and discipline. The underlying message is: *Despite well worn arguments about why it can't happen — poverty, single-parent households, crime, ineffective infrastructure — solutions do exist.*

New York Times columnist David Brooks wrote about another innovative program, the charter schools operated by the Harlem Children's Zone.[12] Like KIPP, these schools have a specific philosophy and methodology for dramatically — not just incrementally — improving the academic scores of low-income minority students. Again, major breakthrough is possible. A Harvard economist who assessed the program wrote, "[This] study has changed my life as a scientist." Bottom line: Promise Academy eliminated the achievement gap in math between its Black students and the city average for White students.

Closing that math gap is crucial, not only for Promise Academy students, but for our nation as a whole. A report by the Brookings Institution stated, "American companies urgently need professionals trained in science, technology, engineering, and mathematics (STEM) fields, but there are not enough workers with the necessary skills and too few Americans earn post-secondary STEM credentials."[13] STEM jobs represent the lifeblood of innovation and economic expansion for the United States and the world. Yet only about 16 percent of all U.S. undergraduates major in science or engineering, compared with 25 percent in Europe, 38 percent in South Korea, and 47 percent in China.[14] And according to a Commerce Department report, "Although women fill close to half of all jobs in the U.S. economy, they hold less than 25 percent of STEM jobs. This has been the case throughout the past decade, even as college-educated women have increased their share of the overall workforce."[15]

The situation is just as dire for students of color. For instance, African-Americans received just 7 percent of bachelor's degrees in STEM fields, 4 percent of master's degrees, and a paltry 2 percent of PhDs. In 2009, slightly more than 5,000 doctoral degrees were awarded in chemistry, physics, and other physical sciences, but Blacks received 89 or less than 2 percent.[16]

But it's not just rocket scientists or biochemists that populate STEM jobs. The reason STEM is so important is because it represents the next phase of middle class jobs in this country. A 2012 conference that focused on the "State of STEM" and was hosted by U.S. News and World Report, observed, "The sweep of industries affected by the STEM skills shortage was revealing, from healthcare, energy production and distribution, and autos to the whole slowly renewing domestic manufacturing area, transportation, and agriculture. 'There are no more jobs that require a strong back,' said Tom Luce, the force behind the successful National Math and Science Initiative. 'We have to explain to parents and kids that 30 years ago you could have a living wage job and not be STEM capable. Today that is not possible.'"[17]

In the Obama Era, educating our youth will be a priority. But implementing successful programs at every school that needs help will require funding. While this is largely the responsibility of school districts, local, and federal government, there is a place for corporations to partner with schools and not-for-profits to help build tomorrow's diverse workforce. This would mean providing grants through foundations and volunteer hours through employees. While this type of giving has been beneficial, I believe there is opportunity for more coordinated efforts to drive greater returns on our philanthropic investments. IBM's Glover suggests making it a question of business sustainability. "It's a simple answer. It says you find a problem, you recognize that no company can fix it on its own, and reach out to others across government, industry, and the public sector to really help you to figure out how to manage this challenge."

A growing number of companies have started to recognize the seriousness of the situation and are doing exactly what Glover advises — reaching out to school systems, community groups, and others to address it. IBM, for one, is putting significant resources where its sentiments are. Big Blue is partnering with schools in New York and Chicago to increase student understanding of the STEM field. Selected schools adopt an innovative 9th through 14th grade curriculum that graduates students with an associate's degree, and the skills (and option) to get an information technology job or to continue toward a bachelor's degree. Students are paired with mentors and other industry professionals who provide a real-world view of the field.[18]

Here's another example. Microsoft targets girls for STEM careers across the globe and sponsors DigiGirlz High Tech Camp and DigiGirlz Day. The camp, for girls 13 years and up, is a three-day hands-on experience with technology, meeting tech rock stars, and networking with industry leaders. The DigiGirlz Day is a one-day event held at Microsoft offices around the world and uses fun-filled technology exercises to entice middle school and high school girls to think about career paths in the field.[19]

Another example of corporate involvement is an initiative sponsored by the Mexican American Legal Defense and Educational Fund (MALDEF) and Sodexo that seeks to educate Chicago Public School students and parents about healthy eating and wellness. According to Sodexo's CDO Rohini Anand, "We have a chef and a dietician working with us on four sessions a year. In the process, we are exposing the kids and parents to who Sodexo is and careers at Sodexo." While not a direct recruitment initiative, this program certainly raises awareness of Sodexo among kids and parents, and may indirectly influence these students to apply at Sodexo when they enter the workforce.

Twenty-First Century Core Skills

What kind of employees, with what kinds of competencies, do our companies need? And how can we influence the educational institutions, so they are adequately preparing today's youth for the kinds of jobs and work environment that will be waiting for them?

We need a generation of employees who possess the technical skills required in our respective industries. They must also have developed **crosscultural** competencies, along with **adaptability, learning agility,** and **creative problem solving.** The marketplace is changing so rapidly that technical skills become obsolete every five years. Good companies and smart employees find ways to ensure that talent remains current with the emerging technical skills.

But what's harder to learn on the job is the mindset, emotional intelligence, and personal mastery skills required to flex, bob, and weave with the constantly evolving marketplace. Our companies will continue to restructure, reengineer, de-layer, off- and on-shore work. The talent supply chain now extends across the globe and we're inventing new ways to deploy resources and work around the world.

If the emerging workforce is not equipped with flexibility and adaptation skills, they will not be successful. Technological breakthroughs are creating new products at warp speed, while local politics and economics affect everything from the price of oil, the Dow Jones index, and immunization plans. The competency of problem solving is more critical than ever. We'll continue to face unprecedented challenges for which there are no guidebooks, no benchmarks, no best practices. The most valuable talent will be the ones who can come up with solutions to never-before-seen problems.

Sure, we need to see a higher percentage of tomorrow's diverse workforce graduate. But we also need them to graduate with the required competencies. Admittedly, this raises the bar for the kinds of skills we need. This only heightens the urgency for the various stakeholders — including government, educational institutions, and business leaders — to address the issue of widening the entrance into the pipeline.

2. We must unclog the pipeline by rethinking how we assess and advance those who are different.

To have the leadership we need to sustain our growth, we must accelerate the advancement of talent of color by unclogging the barriers which slow down their advancement. Already, there are some best practices that have yielded good results in encouraging the advancement of multicultural talent:

- Many companies make it a requirement that all succession plan boxes include people of color and female talent. This is a start, but we need to go beyond this practice and find new ways to address the unintended barriers.
- Often, we find talent one or two jobs away from a coveted open role, with too little experience to take a risk. By implementing a rotational assignment program, top talent of color can gain exposure and experience under the watchful eye of an experienced leader that accelerates their advancement.

Leadership studies by various HR consultancies have declared that great companies for leadership clearly differentiate their high-potential talent. However, we may be overlooking some high-performing talent within the multicultural talent pipeline due to the lack of crosscultural competence in our leadership assessments.[20]

In an increasingly multicultural and global economy, we need diverse styles of leadership. If we continue to only recognize potential new leadership through behaviors that are familiar to us, we'll never accelerate the advancement of talent of color. Instead that talent will remain stuck and frustrated. Thus, we must begin valuing experiences that we traditionally have not valued.

When leadership teams are not diverse, they often don't realize their assessment of what makes a good leader can be culturally biased. Strong leadership can look very different in U.S. subcultures and in national cultures. We're familiar with the European-American leadership model of assertiveness, speaking one's mind and challenging others openly. But there are other strong leadership models (such as in some Asian cultures) that more heavily emphasize consensus-building and face-saving with less public confrontation.

This kind of development is what's required to positively answer the fourth question: Do we have leaders who can lead diverse, multicultural, and global teams? Without crosscultural competence, our leaders will not be successful at leading these increasingly diverse teams. "And if they get good at this," adds Aon Hewitt principal Mollie Kohn, "leaders with this type of competence will also be more effective across the board because they will be better able to effectively manage other types of individual differences such as in personality, style, thinking patterns that may not be attributable to a particular cultural group."

It's also beneficial to require global experience as a prerequisite for senior positions. This requires the investment to create a "tour of duty" for high potential talent. The employee excited by these opportunities probably already possesses a natural openness to experiencing and mastering a more diverse work environment.

3. We must seal the leaks by recognizing our high-performing talent of color

In Chapter 12, I made the case about the importance of recognition. Recognition is one of the four pillars for the engagement and retention of people of color, and is an essential tool for repairing the broken pipeline. I encourage you to revisit that chapter as you develop your own case for strengthening your organization's pipeline.

The key point to internalize is that, for racial/ethnic groups that traditionally have been marginalized, the deep significance of public recognition should not be underestimated. A powerful affirming message can run counter to generations of destructive messages. Given the communal nature of various minority groups, recognizing an individual within that group also speaks to that individual's broader community. This can generate additional good will and positive public branding for the organization.

Companies that understand the power of public recognition and that actively advance technically skilled talent of color will be better able to keep their top diverse talent from leaving. These companies will also become more attractive to new talent of color outside the organization and provide a compelling reason for them wanting to join the company … and to stay.

By identifying and recognizing minority talent that exhibit adaptability, agility, and problem-solving competencies, we can get to know those who may be often overlooked in our organizations.

Green shoots of hope

If we don't take steps now to repair the shaky pipeline of multicultural talent, it will mean waiting 40-plus years to see true parity in leadership representation. The three key strategies I've just outlined can help create a pipeline with a stronger influx of qualified talent at the front end, remove hindrances to career progress, and seal the leaks of our most promising talent along the way. Only by taking both immediate and systemic actions will we accelerate the advancement of top talent of color.

So what does this all mean within the context of the Obama Era? Does a President who reflects the diversity of our culture automatically mean that we will see an increase in diversity and inclusion initiatives throughout corporate America? Not necessarily.

According to an article published in the February 2009 issue of *Workforce Management,* within days of his first Inauguration, critics of affirmative action were telling HR managers that the fact the United States has a Black president meant there was no longer a need for diversity practices because the country had fully embraced diversity.[21] According to this same article, however, companies with long-standing affirmative action programs could expect the Equal Employment Opportunity Commission (EEOC) and the Office of Federal Contract Compliance Programs (OFCC) to be granted more resources under Obama. And this indeed has been so as there was an upturn in the enforcement of these types of programs with greater emphasis placed on how companies compensate minorities as opposed to non-minorities. Mark Bendick, a partner at Bendick and Egan

Economic Consultants, says, "HR staffs within companies that have affirmative action will now have more ammunition with which to go to the CEO and make their case because enforcement is going to be more stringent."

Another green shoot in the Obama Era is the expected emphasis on education — in both policy and funding — with particular emphasis on significantly increasing graduation rates and equipping students with the right skills to thrive in a global economy.

Whether the issue is early childhood education or higher education and worker retraining, President Obama has been leading one of the most aggressive education reform efforts in our nation's recent history. President Obama said, "If we want America to lead in the 21st Century, nothing is more important than giving everyone the best education possible — from the day they start preschool to the day they start their career."

For the youngest students, the Administration has targeted $600 million for the Race to the Top-Early Learning Challenge, which incents states to transform their childcare and pre-K school systems (public and private); expanded Head Start; and boosted the quality of childcare while increasing the number of children served. Once students reach elementary and high school, the groundbreaking Race to the Top (RTT) initiative, with its $4.2 billion federal backing, comes into play. RTT represents a bold initiative to improve standards, teaching, and prepare students for education beyond high school. And to recognize and encourage teachers in STEM subjects, the STEM Master Teacher Corps will recognize 10,000 of the nation's best STEM classroom teachers.[22]

While those and other important Pre-K through 12th grade initiatives address the long-term education challenges faced by school-aged students, it's the Administration's efforts on behalf of higher education and worker retraining that promises more immediate progress. Just a few examples of Obama Era initiatives:

- Raising the maximum Pell Grant award to $5,500 and helping 9.5 million students in the 2012-13 school year
- Providing families with up to $10,000 for college tuition assistance through the American Opportunity Tax Credit
- Fostering partnerships between industry, business, and community colleges through the Skills for America's Future, which plans to provide 500,000 Americans with the skills needed for the new workplace[23]

Along with his commitment to education, the President has set the goal for the United States to have the highest proportion of college graduates by 2020, which includes an additional 5 million community college graduates.

It's only fitting that such resources be targeted to higher education and worker retraining. In a speech before the Hispanic Chamber of Commerce, the President said, "We know that economic progress and educational achievement have always gone hand-in-hand in America. ... The source of America's prosperity has never been merely how ably we accumulate wealth, but how well we educate our people. This has never been more true than it is today. ... Education is no longer just a pathway to opportunity and success, it's a prerequisite for success."

This focus on education targets all Americans, but as the data shows, some of the greatest dividends from these initiatives will go to women and students of color, who lag far behind on too many national and international academic and economic indictors. And it's those same women and racial/ethnic minorities who are desperately needed in the talent pipeline by today's companies.

There is yet another sign of hope. *New York Times* columnist Thomas Friedman wrote about a call he received in April of 2009 from Wendy Kopp, founder of Teach for America. Kopp "shared the following statistics about college graduates signing up to join her organization to teach in some of our neediest schools in the coming school year: 'Our total applications are up 40 percent. Eleven percent of all Ivy League seniors applied, 16 percent of Yale's senior class, 15 percent of Princeton's, 25 percent of Spelman's and 35 percent of the African-American seniors at Harvard. In 130 colleges, between 5 and 15 percent of the senior class applied.' In part, said Kopp, this could be attributed to a lack of jobs elsewhere. But part of it is 'students responding to the call that this is a problem our generation can solve.'"[24]

What would be possible if today's CEOs and their companies also rose to the challenge?

President Obama has said the country needs to look beyond race when evaluating its policies on diversity. Either way, greater diversity in our leadership ranks means greater economic strength throughout the pipeline. A strong and healthy multicultural pipeline, armed with education and skills, means prosperity for all. ♀

SUMMARY POINTS

- The talent pipeline is cracked, leaking, and broken. In some places, it's connected to talent pools that are drying up. In other places, it's not connected to the talent pools whose tides are rising. Compounding the problem, too few people of color are finishing high school and going on to college.
- We just can't will talent of color into positions of leadership. We have to discover new ways of finding and nurturing that talent.
- We must identify top performing, multicultural talent that makes its contributions in ways that we don't recognize as valuable because of the limitations of our own experiences.
- We need a generation of employees who have developed the competencies of adaptability, learning agility, and creative problem solving.
- Corporations need to partner with schools and not-for-profits to help build tomorrow's diverse workforce.
- More than ever, students skilled in STEM subjects are needed by companies and the national economy.
- STEM jobs represent the next phase of middle class jobs.

SHAPING YOUR STRATEGY

- How healthy is your organization's talent pool? How do you recruit new employees? What percentage of those employees are people of color or from minority backgrounds?
- How well does your organization identify top performing, multicultural talent? Can you relate experiences where you may have missed out on some of these top-performers due to the limitations of preferences within your worldview?
- How can you influence your company and others within your industry to partner together to contribute to the strengthening of the talent pipeline in primary schools and high schools?

The Broken, Leaking, Plugged-Up Diverse Talent Pipeline

CONCLUSION:
BE THE CHANGE
YOU WANT TO SEE
IN THE WORLD

Be the Change
You Want to See
in the World

From the top of Inspiration Mountain, vision and purpose seem very clear. But change in *any* era is a pretty tall order. And change in the Obama Era will require no less courage, smarts, perseverance, and passion than have other transformational times. To land right-side up in an upside-down world demands much more than quoting our favorite orators. The acid test is whether we have the fortitude and skills to change our *own* preconceptions, habits, and preferences so we can, in turn, influence other individuals and entire organizations to make the transformational changes required to survive and thrive in the new world order.

Up to this point, the Inclusion Paradox has focused on the transformative and positive power of constructively calling out our differences to build greater inclusion. But I would be remiss if I didn't acknowledge that which psychologist Carl Jung explored in depth — that every psychological archetype has a potential "shadow side." It is almost like a flip side — or the potential negative element — of an archetype.

Some Jungian psychologists allege that the shadow sides of the competitive male and the collaborative female archetypes are aggression and passivity, respectively. This same potential for a shadow side exists for *any* philosophy, ideology, theology, or business model. One could argue that the shadow side of Christianity's quest for truth was the Inquisition. The shadow side of liberty could be licentiousness. And the shadow side of national security, restricted civil rights. Being aware of the potential pitfalls of one's own beliefs, or worldview, is essential for creating sustainable change without dampening one's passion. When we encounter people who don't share our worldview, we should remember those people may harbor a fear of the shadow side of that particular worldview deep down inside. Consider, for example, interpretation of time: Those who are clock oriented may secretly fear that an event-oriented approach would lead to chaos and inefficiency. Similarly, event-oriented people may secretly believe a clock-oriented approach is insensitive and dehumanizing.

We must ask, then: What could be the shadow side of the Inclusion Paradox? It could be that we end up focusing too much on how we differ, in the process forgetting to nurture what we have in common. In other words, greater fragmentation, isolation, and insulation. In effect, *exclusion*.

How can we avoid falling into this shadow side? By keeping our focus on *bridging* the differences between ourselves and others, rather than *defending* them. The first approach leads to connection, the latter to polarization

As we call out differences constructively, we must embrace the legacy paradigm of tolerance and sensitivity. No, this is not coming "full circle." Rather, it's embracing a paradoxical "both/and" approach. Calling out differences requires seeking out our similarities differently. Rather than merely "understanding" each other, we must discover and embrace our similarities so that we can find a common ground on which to constructively call out our differences. Thus, the melting pot becomes a *paella* instead — where the wild variety of ingredients both retain their unique character in terms of flavor, texture, and shape and, yet at the same time, the *combination* of flavors yield something superlatively tasty, attractive, differentiated, and memorable.

What I've sought to offer in *The Inclusion Paradox* is a way to evolve beyond merely focusing on our similarities at the expense of getting to know each other more truthfully. It involves our ability to interact with each other, and with groups and organizations in ways that take into account the fact that our differences help us better achieve our goals, wants, and desires. As we've seen, constructively calling out differences affects everything — from interpersonal relationships to healthcare policy to retirement benefits to talent assessment to product design to operational strategies to marketing and much more.

True, the shadow side of the Inclusion Paradox, if not accounted for, could result in greater division and, therefore, destruction. But the promise of the Inclusion Paradox is one of creation — of innovating new responses to address brand new challenges by making our differences work together. The seeds of creation lay in finding our commonality in the midst of difference.

The central premise for the Inclusion Paradox is not simply, "I do my thing and you do yours." This leads to fragmentation and isolation. Rather, it's about, "I'm different, you're different — how can we connect?"

Coming Back to the Eight Cultural Implications of the Obama Era

We started this conversation looking at the cultural implications of the Obama Era. I intended these to be headlights for the rest of the book, illuminating how to apply the Inclusion Paradox to a variety of different dimensions. As we bring this book to a close, let's now see these implications through the rearview mirror.

Inclusion Is a Transformative Force. Inclusion represents a positive value and goal — one everyone must continually work toward. Instead of a perfect storm that threatens to derail us, the Obama Era and the convergence of global trends offer a chance to create new opportunities for inclusion, for making the mix work, in individual and corporate environments. Plenty of bytes have been expended highlighting the negatives of corporate influence on issues such as work environments, habits, and labor practices. But here I want to focus on the positive impact corporations are having at a more profound level in helping address one of the most destructive and intractable human issues: the polarizing effect of differences. Despite having a long way to go in achieving true diversity and inclusion, many large corporations have confronted the challenge of inclusion head on and invested heavily in financial, leadership, and personnel resources to bridge the gap. And those who have made the investments have not only improved the lives of their talent, but improved their own bottom line. Compare the scene at the National Black MBA Association's national conference — with its 10,000 Black MBAs courted by the largest multinationals in the world — with what labor conditions were for Blacks just a generation ago, and you'll know we are not in Kansas anymore.

Whatever We Do Has Global Impact. While corporations still have a long way to go in fully advancing those different from the mainstream, ironically, multinationals have managed to be an accelerating force for their advancement. Corporations, particularly those rooted in American and European contexts, come from a worldview of meritocracy, where the best performers reap the greatest rewards. Granted, the dearth of minorities and women in top leadership positions proves the meritocracy value has not been lived out fully. Yet, around the world, multinationals have played a significant role in economically lifting diverse groups. Consider women, for example. Fully aware of the dominant corporate male paradigm of both recent and ongoing history, multinationals have been a change agent for advancing women globally first in the economic powers that arose out of World War II and now in the emerging markets of Brazil, India, and China.

Diversity and Inclusion Requires Intentionality. Workplace power struggles will not be resolved solely by White males or even by the organizational power structure. As I said at the beginning of this book, we must address both power and crosscultural issues. Granted, my focus has mostly been on crosscultural issues. But as we wrap up our journey together, let us reconsider the issue of power and how it is inherent in the various ceilings hindering advancement. Women and minorities need to face their own power issues. Rather than waiting for the dominant group to change this requires looking within themselves for how they can act and behave more powerfully *right now*. The decisive role that these groups had in the 2012 presidential elections is evidence of this starting to happen in the public square. Women are starting to really breakthrough in the corporate realm while people of color still are treading water too far downstream.

And, as these traditionally marginalized groups press forward to their rightful place to the fullness of their abilities, these emerging workplace groups must also be ready to acknowledge and address the difference between selling out versus supporting authentic adaptation for their members. Constructively facing these issues helps build the necessary environment for the work of crosscultural competence, which aims at not just cracking, but shattering, the ceiling.

We Will Experience a Renaissance of Values-Driven Decision Making. Organizations need to help workers take care of themselves in ways that benefit both employee and employer. At Aon Hewitt, for example, an on-site health clinic helps address today's challenging medical environment. "It's in the company's best interest to care for its associates, who, in turn, care for our clients," says Tom Sondergeld, the founding director of health and clinics at Aon Hewitt. "And Aon Hewitt's clinic further benefits the company by lowering healthcare costs. At the same time, it benefits associates by providing easy access, flexibility, and quality health care." The clinic not only demonstrates a unique, functional solution for bringing down healthcare costs, but also offers an example of *values-driven* decision making. This includes both economic- and values-based inputs. It's aligned with Millennial thinking and has appeal for those who rely on religious values to order their lives. Values-based decision making might offer the right antidote to the world's current economic situation, which has discredited "consumerism" and forced a deeper examination of "unrestrained capitalism."

We Must Have a Heightened Focus on Results. Well-developed diversity and inclusion efforts can lead to profitability. Accommodating differences and honoring archetypal preferences is not only good diversity practice, it's also in a company's best interests. For example, inclusive health care that accommodates individual differences is good for the community and is good cost management. Seeking out diverse talent expands the talent pool and makes an organization stronger. Knowing how to manage differences leads to less workplace friction, which leads to greater efficiency. Knowing how to help members of all groups to save more for retirement is good for individuals, and financially prepared retirees are good for society. Looking forward, we have to find more ways like this to address the many challenges that confront us while still ensuring economic viability.

The Bottom-Up Is as Important as the Top-Down. Barack Obama rose to the presidency in part because he surrounded himself with a highly efficient, top-down team that was motivated and well-organized. This team was critical to his success, but it represents only half of the story. Equally critical was a powerful grassroots set of individuals who were hungry for change and just waiting to be tapped. It was a process that gave voice to the voiceless. It was true in 2008 and even more so in 2012 where these grassroots had available to them the most effective and efficient, as well as easy-to-plug into-and-contribute, electoral ground game ever.

Corporations need to begin using the same combination of top-down/bottom-up to be effective, particularly in sustaining inclusion efforts. Infrastructures for government, labor, corporations, and work in general are changing and require mutual support or rediscovering of commonalities. Affinity groups need to connect with each other, as well as with the larger organization. By connecting with each other, they increase the size and scope of their grassroots activities. The survival and thriving of affinity groups depends on each group finding common ground with other affinity groups no matter how different they are from one another. The most disheartening issue in this work is the "crabs in the barrel" syndrome, which can be seen when one group pulls another one down, or when individuals from *within* an affinity group pull others down, for their own short-term benefit.

"Both/And" Trumps "Either/Or." The Inclusion Paradox leads to our human need for community and connection. It resembles the paradox of marriage or community. We need to be individuals, yet we need to be connected. We form groups for a variety of reasons. Our groups need to be unified and connected to other groups. If we don't form these vital connections, we can end up with Balkanization — where two or more communities or societies fail to recognize their common concern and subsequently try to destroy each other. The Inclusion Paradox invites us to honor our differences while rediscovering our commonality. It calls us to refute "either/or," "win/lose solutions," and instead uncover "and/and," "win/win" ones — to find a third, new way for relationships, groups, organizations, and perhaps even nations. Take multinational corporate culture, for example. It tends to reflect the culture of the country of origin. Yet today corporate cultures forged from inclusion will not be American or Indian or German or Brazilian, but something richer, deeper, and more inclusive than the current model. And may our politicians take heed as well!

True Diversity and Inclusion Requires Calling Out Our Differences, Not Minimizing Them. 'Nuff said!

We've Been to the Mountaintop

The complexity, high stakes, and myriad possibilities of diversity and inclusion remind me of a passage in one of the Judeo-Christian scriptures that says, "We are perplexed, but not in despair."[1] The work of diversity and inclusion is about finding profitable answers to today's difficult issues. *"Se hace el camino al andar,"* goes the Spanish saying. "We make our path as we walk it."

A reporter once asked me, "If diversity were a climb of a mountain, how close to the top would you say you are?" The images of the Inca trail on the majestic Andes mountain range in Peru immediately came to mind. I could look back and see several passes in the distance, including a 10,000-foot-high one we had climbed after many days of hiking. Our progress through the sleet, scorching sun, and thin air was exhilarating. But then I looked ahead and saw several more passes shimmering in the distance, including one at 15,000 feet. We celebrated our progress so far with trail mix and coca tea. Then we slipped our backpacks on and continued the journey forward. Step by step.

That's where we are on Diversity Mountain. After many years working to diversify and engage a wide variety of people in the workplace, we can indeed enjoy new views from higher up. And while we've advanced in the journey, there is so much more to be done to ensure we have a true representative mix — and that the mix is working.

It won't be without struggle. It never has been. But strategy by strategy, leader by leader, conversation by conversation, succession plan by succession plan, hire by hire, we're eroding and dismantling exclusionary processes, structures, and systems. As the Japanese saying goes, "Fall down seven times. Get up eight." The challenges are formidable, our quest audacious, the problems complex. We need to look at each other and say, "I need your difference. And you need mine." It's the only way we can achieve our unity of purpose to make the world a better place to work — for *everyone*.

People often ask me, "So when is this Diversity thing over? When do we 'get there?'" Interculturalist Dianne Hofner Saphiere offers this answer: "Intercultural effectiveness is an ongoing process. It's not like you ever get there and you're done. It's always going to be something else. You never stop discovering, like in any partnership or marriage, that you never totally get the other person or for that matter, yourself." In other words, by touching the core issues of who we are — gender, race, ethnicity, sexual orientation, nationality, physical ability, thinking styles, you name it — the answer of when we get there, of course, is "never." Given that this is a life-long journey, we must note that the Inclusion Paradox applies to many other topics and issues that we haven't covered in this book — such as faith, aging, size/weight, personality, thinking styles, and on.

We can take this further by applying this discussion to product and home design, school curriculum, and classroom management, among other things. "We have to be able to argue about workplace and marketplace and the plethora of other issues," says diversity pioneer Ted Childs. "We can't be one-subject leaders in the diversity movement. We've got to be able to package and debate multiple issues." The purpose of this book has indeed been to contribute to the conversation about creating the next generation of diversity work.

"The greatest danger of all is to allow new walls to divide us from one another," then candidate Obama told more than 200,000 at the Victory Column in Berlin on July 24, 2008. "The walls between old allies on either side of the Atlantic cannot stand. The walls between the countries with the most and those with the least cannot stand. The walls between races and tribes, natives and immigrants, Christian and Muslim and Jew cannot stand. These now are the walls we must tear down."

Let's tear down the walls that separate us — not only in the workplace, but in our homes, families, and communities — wherever we have the power to influence change in other people, as well as in ourselves. This is the message of the Obama Era. It's the message of the Inclusion Paradox.

Share this message, implement what you can, and, most importantly, as Gandhi said, "Be the change you want to see in the world." ☺

An Invitation

This is an ongoing conversation. As you read this book, you probably found yourself asking "Well, what about this?" or, "No way!" or, "I've got a story, too." No book on this topic could ever be complete in terms of answers and issues. This is why we've created the blog, www.InclusionParadox.com. I will be updating it continuously with links, observations, and other discussions based on the topics covered here and more. I invite you to check it out and post your own questions, comments, stories, and challenges. Add your two cents, two pesos, two yuan, two rupees, two euros. We'll take any idea currency!

And there's always Twitter @AndresTTapia or LinkedIn at LinkedIn.com/in/andrestapia1

Appendix A

Figuring Out How
Crossculturally Competent You Are

Answering the question "Am I crossculturally competent?" requires more than a yes/no answer. Dr. Milton Bennett lays out a more complete answer in his Developmental Model of Intercultural Sensitivity (DMIS), a framework to explain the way in which people commonly develop crosscultural competence (which Dr. Bennett prefers to call "intercultural" competence).

Because I have found it simple to grasp, relevant around the world, and practical in its application, the DMIS is one of the underlying frameworks on which I have constructed the concept of the Inclusion Paradox.

As Dr. Bennett explains it, the DMIS can be used to explain the reactions of people to cultural differences.[1] The underlying assumption of the model is that as one's experience of cultural differences becomes more complex, one's potential competence in intercultural interactions increases. Dr. Bennett has identified a set of fundamental cognitive structures he refers to as "worldviews" that act as orientations to cultural difference. The worldviews vary from more ethnocentric to more ethnorelative. In the DMIS model there are three stages of development within each worldview.

Ethnocentrism means that we tend to view others from our own perspective, through our own lens. It's our own experiences that shape what we see, how we feel about, and understand how we and others behave. It is our conditioned response to our upbringing by parents or others, the society we grew up in, the messages we hear in the media, the things we learn in school. Given how formative this perspective is, ethnocentrism is a natural human response to the world around us.

The three stages within ethnocentrism are Denial, Defense, and Minimization. Those in *Denial* ignore cultural differences and focus instead on the familiar. Those in *Defense* see differences in stereotyped ways and find them threatening and believe theirs is the "true" culture. And those in *Minimization* reduce the importance of differences by emphasizing common humanity and values.

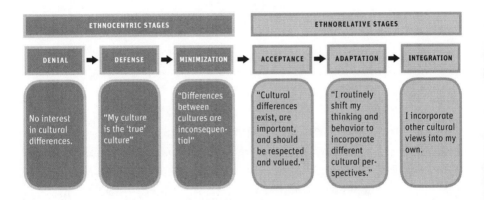

Ethnorelativism means that a person has developed the ability to imagine events or empathize with experiences from another perspective. As children, we saw the world as revolving around us. As we mature into adulthood, we develop the ability to step back and put ourselves into others' shoes. This ability is reflective of an ethnorelative worldview. There are three stages within ethnorelativism: Acceptance, Adaptation, and Integration. Those in *Acceptance* acknowledge and believe that cultural differences exist in addition to similarities and they are significant. Those in *Adaptation* are able to navigate effectively between the differences, and those in *Integration* have in effect internalized the worldviews of others into their own.

According to the DMIS theory, more ethnorelative worldviews have more potential to generate the attitudes, knowledge, and behavior that constitute intercultural competence. In this DMIS model, ethnorelative competencies can take a lifetime of experience and purposeful reflection to fully develop.

Intercultural Development Inventory (IDI)

The Intercultural Development Inventory (IDI) is a way of measuring where individuals and groups are in their cultural competence as conceptualized by the DMIS. The IDI, developed by Dr. Milton Bennett and Dr. Mitch Hammer, measures an individual's or group's fundamental worldview orientation to cultural difference, and thus the individual's or group's capacity for intercultural competence.

The IDI is a 50-item, theory-based instrument that can be taken either in paper and pencil form or online. The instrument is easy to complete and generates an in-depth graphic profile of an individual's worldview orientation. The IDI is currently in twelve languages (Bahasa Indonesian, English, French, German, Italian, Portuguese, Spanish, Russian, Korean, French, Japanese, and Chinese). Translations from the English-language version were completed using rigorous "back translation" scientific protocols to ensure both linguistic and conceptual equivalency.*

Administering and debriefing the instrument and coaching individuals on the best way to develop requires people certified in the IDI. During my tenure Hewitt had over two dozen IDI certified associates who had conducted debriefs with individuals around the world. Certification is available from IDI, LLC led by Dr. Hammer (www.idiinventory.com).

The DMIS and the Next Generation of Diversity Learning

In Chapter 4, I made the case for moving from the paradigm of tolerance and sensitivity to one of crosscultural competence. Using DMIS language, tolerance and sensitivity helped individuals, organizations, and societies move from the intercultural competency stage of Defense (quite prevalent during the time of Civil Rights and early Affirmative Action) and into Minimization. It was a successful strategy in that it helped create more tolerant environments. However, by

---

* Full details about the design of the IDI are available in, *International Journal of Intercultural Relations, Special Issue on Intercultural Development*, Volume 27, Number 4, July 2003. The entire issue is dedicated to DMIS and IDI.

reinforcing Minimization, diversity work has been struggling to break out of a legacy approach of addressing differences and shaping a new way that effectively addresses the explosion in diversity among workers.

Moving to the paradigm of crosscultural competence, using DMIS language, is to move from Minimization to Acceptance and Adaptation. I have made the claim throughout *The Inclusion Paradox* that this worldview can be more conducive toward achieving true inclusion. I don't make the case, however, that it is necessary to develop into the Integration phase. Whether one internalizes others' worldviews into one's own is not necessary to create inclusion. But being able to accept and adapt to those differences behaviorally and in action and mindset is.

Appendix B

Without trying to precisely map a three-staged competency framework to the DMIS, we have defined a starting point in our work within Diversity Best Practices and with our clients on what three stages of crosscultural competence could look like when converted into organizational behavior. This is intended for global application and is a journey that requires learning, reflection, and personal experience.

Stage	Description
Stage I	**Individual Contributor:** Demonstrates an understanding of the definition and aspects of culture. Seeks to understand own culture and perspective, how it differs from others, and how culture and perspective can impact interactions with coworkers, customers, clients, and others. Demonstrates an awareness of other cultures, diverse perspectives, styles, backgrounds, and worldviews in order to enhance contribution.

Stage II	**Leveraged Contributor:** Manages own biases and stereotypes and accepts cultural differences in styles, behaviors, beliefs, and worldviews. Reaches out to others with different backgrounds, perspectives, styles, and/or opinions to achieve optimal business results. Incorporates the diverse perspectives and talents of others to accomplish objectives, and constructively addresses situations in which cultural differences are overlooked or not respected. Coaches others to be crossculturally competent in questioning their assumptions about differences and shifting their thought processes and behaviors to culturally relevant perspectives.
Stage III	**Leader:** Shapes organizational solutions that are crossculturally competent in their philosophy, design, implementation, and communications. Builds a crossculturally competent organization by developing and supporting systems and processes that optimize the value of diverse cultures, backgrounds, skills, perspectives, and ideas. Shares crosscultural competency innovations with thought leaders outside the organization. Leads entire organization so that other leaders are able to do the same in their areas of influence and authority.

In my work with my teams throughout the years we have developed groundbreaking crosscultural competence curriculum and training courses and strategic learning experiences that moves individuals, groups — and more profoundly — organizations, into crossculturally competent behaviors, systems, processes, and structures for managing people, innovating new products and services, and going to market.

Over 100,000 employees at client companies that I have worked with have gone through one or more of these courses, sessions, experiences, tools, and solutions.

Appendix C

An Excerpt from "401(k) Plans in Living Color: The Ariel/Hewitt Study" published in June 2009. The study also had input from the Chicago Urban League, the Joint Center for Political and Economic Studies, the National Council of La Raza, the National Urban League, and The Raben Group.

In describing the savings gaps between African-Americans and Hispanics on the one hand and Asians and Whites on the other, the report summarized its findings this way:

[The gaps] are alarming and require swift and corrective action. Employers, government, and individuals all have a role to play if there is to be real change.

- **Savings and participation rates:** While age and salary play a clear role in driving retirement savings, the meaningful role race and ethnicity also play has been obscured until now. Regardless of age and income, African-American and Hispanic workers are less likely to participate in their company 401(k) plans, and when they do contribute, they save at much lower rates than Whites. Asian employees have the highest participation and savings rates of all ethnic groups studied.

- **Stock exposure:** African-American workers are less likely than other workers to invest in equities, a behavior that may limit the long-term growth potential of their accounts, since historically, equities have been the highest yielding investment over the long term.
- **Loans and hardship withdrawals:** African-Americans are more likely to take a loan and more than twice as likely to take a hardship withdrawal as the study population overall. Hispanics also borrow from their retirement accounts at a higher rate than Whites, but not to the same degree as African-Americans. By contrast, Asian employees are the least likely to take early distributions from their 401(k) plan accounts.
- **Account balances:** Lower participation, contribution rates, and equity exposure, coupled with higher withdrawal rates, lead to smaller average account balances. Consider, for instance, individuals who earn between $30,000 and $59,999. Employees with a similar range of income show a significant difference in account balances: African-Americans ($21,224), Hispanics ($22,017), Asians ($32,590), and Whites ($35,551). Naturally, these results are influenced by other factors, such as age, job tenure, and pay within the range, but variations exist, even after adjusting for these factors.

Later in the study, the following scenario is painted:

When the data are controlled for factors such as salary, job tenure, and age, they show that African-Americans contribute 11 percent less and Hispanics 6 percent less as a portion of pay than do Whites. Imagine four employees working side by side, doing the same job, making the same amount of money, contributing to their 401(k) plans, and expecting to retire at the same time. Chances are that the African-American and Hispanic employees are saving somewhat less per month than the White employee, and the Asian employee is saving somewhat more. Now, let that difference in today's dollars grow through compounding, and the difference at retirement is significant. These four employees will find themselves experiencing considerably different comfort levels in their retirements.

The report then goes on to make the following recommendations:

Recognizing the Problem and Finding Solutions

When 401(k) account balances are so quantifiably different by race and ethnicity, it is highly likely that financial comfort levels during retirement will be decidedly unequal for different groups. This phenomenon prompts a call to action to ensure that all employees have both the knowledge and opportunity to secure a financially sound retirement for themselves. This phenomenon prompts a call to action to ensure that all employees have both the knowledge and opportunity to secure a financially sound retirement for themselves.

The answer is not a simple, singular action. We need to balance the remedies with reality. Some easier solutions may be costly to implement or could put an undue burden on employers — an unrealistic outcome, especially in the current economic climate. However, failure to act could create a future in which whole categories of workers will be financially insecure, which ultimately affects society as a whole. We encourage policymakers and employers to act on the following recommendations.

Recommendation #1: Design 401(k) plans in a way that benefits a broad, diverse employee base. Employers should consider making the following changes to plan design:

- Implement automatic 401(k) plan enrollment for new employees. Additionally, do a one-time sweep to add nonparticipants into the 401(k) plan, unless they have previously opted out.
- Set a default contribution rate for employees automatically enrolled in a 401(k) plan so that employees get the full company match, and contribution rates are automatically increased over time to exceed the match threshold.
- Offer investment advice and various tools for investing to meet the needs of all participants. Investment advice can be effective at providing guidance for people with different needs, and possible tools for investing can range from simple suggestions to detailed recommendations to turning over a portfolio to an investment professional.

Recommendation #2: Provide necessary communication, education, and resources to help individuals make wise choices. For example, employers can:

- Promote greater awareness of the costs and consequences of taking loans from 401(k) plans, including strong and compelling education at the point of loan initiation.
- Provide retirement planning resources such as workshops (and company time to attend these), call centers, and online tools and education to enable individuals to make more effective use of their 401(k) plans.
- Create user-friendly and easily understood communication, enabling workers to learn more about how to effectively manage and grow their savings. Information should be made available in multiple forms, recognizing differences in the population. Effective communication that targets specific behaviors (loan usage, the need to save, and so on) should be used when gaps between categories of employees are identified in the data analysis.
- Incorporate different cultural perspectives in broad-based employer communications about 401(k) plans that resonate with diverse groups of employees. The information could be promoted via employer affinity groups.

Recommendation #3: Encourage employers to voluntarily collect and report their 401(k) plan data by race and ethnicity of participants. The federal government could:

- Encourage voluntary collecting and reporting of data about 401(k) plan participants that would enable employers to know where gaps exist among their employees. The types of data to be collected could include account balance, contribution rate, equity exposure, percentage with loans, and percentage taking hardship withdrawals.
- Provide guidelines for the data collection process, such as what measures to use, how to collect data, and the frequency for collecting data. Additionally, if these data were compiled across participating companies, they could be used for benchmarking purposes, and employers could compare their own results with others in their industry and beyond. The resulting information would enable employers to take steps to improve overall outcomes and close any gaps that may exist.

Recommendation #4: Modify loan requirements in 401(k) plans to decrease the likelihood of default when an employee terminates employment.

Though the availability of loans from 401(k) account balances makes investing in these plans attractive, taking loans is likely to reduce account balances. In challenging economic times such as these, employee terminations and loans against 401(k) accounts that are not repaid are both likely to increase.

Most 401(k) plans currently require that employees who terminate with an outstanding loan must repay the loan (often within 60 days*) or default. For a person who has just been laid off during a time when unemployment is high and new jobs are scarce, and who is worried about paying the mortgage and other day-to-day bills, it is virtually impossible to pay off a 401(k) loan on time. When a default occurs, the loan is considered a distribution from the plan and is thus taxable. If the employee is not yet retirement age, an additional penalty may apply. In this way, a distribution permanently reduces an employee's retirement savings.

Extending the amount of time a terminating employee has to pay off a loan may improve overall retirement savings. Modifying the current loan rules could help African-American and Hispanic employees in particular retain assets in their 401(k) accounts.

Rules could be changed (which may require legislation) to the following:

- Provide a longer period for repayments. Instead of requiring departing employees to pay off a loan within 60 days of termination, they could be given a longer period of time, perhaps up to six months. At the end of this period, if the loan has not been repaid, it would become a distribution. Or, more narrowly, consider suspending the loan repayment requirement for a given period of time for employees who involuntarily lose their job.
- Allow loan repayments after termination. A second way to decrease defaults on loans is to allow periodic loan repayments that follow the initial timetable even after termination. Currently, most employers do not accept loan repayments after employee termination, largely because payments can no longer

---

* The rules regarding loans are complex but do include limits on the time period a person has to repay before default occurs. Many employers simplify the process by establishing a 60-day repayment requirement.

be made via payroll deduction. Instead, employees could be allowed to repay a loan by regular payments from their personal accounts at financial institutions.

- Make loans portable. If a 401(k) account balance, plus the outstanding loan against it, could be easily rolled over from one corporate employer to another, employees could be encouraged to roll over their 401(k) and continue loan repayments. This option would be much better than cashing out the account altogether.

Recommendation #5: Provide financial education as a mandated component of both public and private school curricula at all levels, from kindergarten through secondary school.

- Improve financial literacy by providing financial education at younger ages. While this recommendation takes a longer-term perspective, it may ultimately be more successful than other approaches, especially when it comes to closing the sizable racial and ethnic gaps in 401(k) account balances. This is a key component for long-term success.
- Implement financial literacy curriculum in schools to provide future generations with a comprehensive understanding of both the mechanics and importance of sound money management, saving, and investment. Although some schools include financial and investment education throughout their K–12 curricula, most do not. Furthermore, state school systems that offer financial and investment curricula do not uniformly mandate that students enroll in or complete these courses.

Appendix D

Driving Up Minority 401(k)
Participation at a Medical Institution

To increase the 401(k) retirement savings plan participation rate on the part of African-American employees at a large medical center Hewitt, in collaboration with Ariel Investments President Mellody Hobson, designed and implemented the following five-pronged approach:

1. Selected Black History Month as the timing for the education and enrollment campaign so it could be coupled with other messages appealing to African-American employees.
2. Emphasized face-to-face workshops that would appeal to the more oral (versus written) preference of African-American culture. This also leaned on a communal approach to a call to action. A parallel can be drawn to the communal power of the African-American church experience in influencing behavior. Call it *communal peer pressure*.
3. Set up financial education workshops co-led by African-American leaders. In this case it was the diversity leader at the medical center and one of Hewitt's consultants with deep expertise in financial education. The idea was to help

overcome Black skepticism about the value of long-term investing which has been documented in more than 10 years of research in the Ariel/Schwab Black Investor study. The premise was that the trust gap could be narrowed by having members of their own community serve as the advocates as well as the subject matter experts.

4.   Tailored the messages in the workshop to address both the opportunities and reticence the African-American worldview may pose toward greater 401(k) participation. For example, when the audience was presented with the data that Blacks tend to put saving for college education over retirement, the question posed was, "Who are you looking to take care of you when you retire?" The answer often came back: "My children." This then led to an eye-opening conversation about how putting that burden on their children may be undermining the very economic advancement they were banking on by sending them to college. Further, it was pointed out that while there are multiple sources to pay for college (many types of scholarships, low-interest loans, etc.), there are very few additional sources for retirement other than one's ability to have saved for it over a period of time.

5.   Applied techniques that have worked in general regardless of multicultural demographics. These have to do with making it logistically easy for employees to enroll right at the workshop itself. So, participants were allowed to fill out enrollment cards at the end of the workshop.

Results

In this project 42 percent of attendees who had been nonparticipants before the workshop enrolled during the workshop.

Bibliography

Ariel Investments and Charles Schwab Corporation. *The Ariel/Schwab Black Investor Survey: Saving and Investing Among Higher Income African-American and White Americans.* Black Investor Survey, 2008.

Bennett, Milton J., editor. *Basic Concepts of Intercultural Communication.* Yarmouth, ME: Intercultural Press, 1998.

Benitez, Cristina. *Latinization: How Latino Culture Is Transforming the US.* Ithaca, NY: Paramount Market Publishing, 2007.

Broom, Michael F., and Donald C. Klein. Power: *The Infinite Game.* Ellicott City, MD: Sea Otter Press, 1999.

Catalyst. *The Bottom Line: Connecting Corporate Performance and Gender Diversity.* Research study. January, 2004.

Cohen, Adam, and Elizabeth Taylor. *American Pharaoh: Mayor Richard J. Daley – His Battle for Chicago and the Nation.* London: Little, Brown, May, 2000.

de Tocqueville, Alexis. *Democracy in America.* 1835.

Gladwell, Malcolm. *Blink: The Power of Thinking without Thinking.* New York: Little, Brown and Company, 2005.

Gladwell, Malcolm. *Outliers: The Story of Success.* New York: Little, Brown and Company, 2008.

Hewlett, Sylvia Ann. *Off-ramps and On-Ramps: Keeping Talented Women on the Road to Success.* Boston: Harvard Business School Publishing, 2007.

Hewlett, Sylvia, Carolyn Buck Luce, Peggy Shiller, and Sandra Southwell. "The Hidden Brain Drain: Off-Ramps and On-Ramps in Women's Careers." *Harvard Business Review.* February 24, 2005.

Johansson, Frans. *The Medici Effect.* Boston: Harvard Business School Publishing, 2006.

Kochman, Thomas. *Black and White Styles in Conflict.* Chicago: University of Chicago Press, 1981.

Korn Ferry International. *Diversity in the Executive Suite: Good News and Bad News.* Research study. N.d.

Lee, Malcolm D., director. *Undercover Brother.* DVD. Universal City, CA: Universal Pictures, 2002.

Libert, Barry, Jon Spector, Don Tapscott and thousands of contributors. *We Are Smarter than Me: How to Unleash the Power of Crowds in Your Business.* Upper Saddle River, NJ: Wharton School Publishing, 2007.

Macintosh, Peggy. "White Privilege: Unpacking the Invisible Knapsack." Excerpted from Working Paper 189. "White Privilege and Male Privilege: A Personal Account of Coming To See Correspondences through Work in Women's Studies." Wellesley, MA: Wellesley College Center for Research on Women, 1988.

McKinsey & Company. *The Economic Impact of the Achievement Gap in American's Schools.* Social Sector Office Report. April 2009.

Obama, Barack. "A Perfect Union" speech, Constitution Center, Philadelphia, Pennsylvania, March 18, 2008.

Obama, Barack. *Dreams from My Father: A Story of Race and Inheritance.* New York: Three Rivers Press, 2004.

Obama, Barack. "The Impact of the Obama Economic Plan for America's Working Women." Report. Obama for America. www.barackobama.com, 2008.

Obama, Barack. *The Audacity of Hope: Thoughts on Reclaiming the American Dream.* New York: Crown Publishers, 2006.

Obama, Barack. "Second Inaugural Address," White House, Washington, DC, January 21, 2013.

Obama, Barack. "Second Term Acceptance," speech, McCormick Place, Chicago, Illinois, November 7, 2013.

Porter, Kira. "Women Leaders: Strategic Yet Invisible Assets." *Link & Learn.* May, 2003.

Rubin, Henry Alex, and Dana Adam Shapiro, directors. *Murderball.* DVD. Hollywood, CA: Paramount Pictures, 2005.

Shelton, Chuck. *Leadership 101 for White Men: How to Work Successfully with Black Colleagues and Customers.* Garden City, NJ: Morgan James Publishing, 2008.

Tammet, Daniel. *Born on a Blue Day: Inside the Extraordinary Mind of an Autistic Savant.* New York: Free Press, 2006.

Tapscott, Don, and Anthony Williams. *Wikinomics: How Mass Collaboration Changes Everything.* New York: Portfolio, 2008.

Thaler, Richard H., and Cass R. Sunstein. *Nudge: Improving Decisions about Health, Wealth, and Happiness.* New York: Penguin Books, 2008.

Thomas, Roosevelt. *Beyond Race and Gender: Unleashing the Power of Your Total Work Force by Managing Diversity.* N.p.: AMACOM, 1992.

Thomas, David A., and John J. Gabarro in *Breaking Through: The Making of Minority Executives in Corporate America.* Boston: Harvard Business School Publishing, 1999.

Trompenaars, Fons, and Charles Hampden-Turner. *Riding the Waves of Culture: Understanding Diversity in Global Business.* 2nd ed. New York: McGraw Hill, 1998.

Winters, Mary-Frances, and Andrés Tapia. "Crosscultural Learning Partners Program." Proprietary program of Winters Consulting Group and Hewitt Associates. Lincolnshire, IL: N.d.

Endnotes

Introduction

[1] http://www.whitehouse.gov/the-press-office/2012/09/25/remarks-president-un-general-assembly.

[2] http://sustainability.baxter.com/sustainability_at_baxter/index.html.

Chapter 1

[1] "$1.9 Trillion Seen Flowing to Oil Producing Nations in '08," *Asia Pulse, International News,* June 30, 2008.

[2] "The Coming Oil Windfall in the Gulf," A Report, McKinsey Global Institute, McKinsey & Company, January 2009 http://www.mckinsey.com/insights/mgi/research/financial_markets/the_coming_oil_windfall_in_the_gulf

[3] David Gardner, "The Age of America ends in 2016: IMF predicts the year China's economy will surpass U.S.," *Mail Online,* 25 April 2011. http://www.dailymail.co.uk/news/article-1380486/The-Age-America-ends-2016-IMF-predicts-year-Chinas-economy-surpass-US.html

[4] Leslie H. Gelb, "Joe Biden On Iraq, Iran, China and the Taliban," *Newsweek,* December 19, 2011

[5] Thomas Fisher, The Contingent Workforce And Public Decision Making, *Public Sector Digest,* Spring 2012 http://blog.lib.umn.edu/cdescomm/cdes_memo/Thomas_Fisher_Public_Sector_Spring2012.pdf

6   Giampaolo Lanzier, *Population and Social Conditions*, Statistics in Focus, Eurostat, August 2008.

Nadja Milewski, (INED), *"Immigrant Fertility in West Germany: Socialization Effects in Transition to 2nd and 3rd Births,"* *[PowerPoint Presentation]*, Conference on Effects of Migration on Population Structures in Europe, Vienna Institute of Demography, December 2008.

Luke Harding, *"German birth rate falls to lowest in Europe,"* The Guardian on the web, March 15, 2006.

7   "The Future of the Global Muslim Population: Projections for 2010-2030," *Pew Forum on Religion & Public Life*, January 27, 2011. http://www.pewforum.org/the-future-of-the-global-muslim-population.aspx

8   U.S. Census Bureau, "An Older and More Diverse Nation by Midcentury," Press Release, August 14, 2008.

9   Mitra Toossi, "Labor Force Projections to 2012: The Graying of the U.S. Workforce," *Monthly Labor Review,* www.bls.gov, February 2004.

10 "A Global Platform for Diversity–Organizational Crosscultural Conference," Hewitt Presentation at the Intercultural Development Conference, Minneapolis, MN, October 3, 2008.

11 Steven Erlanger, "After US Breakthrough, Europe Looks in Mirror," *New York Times*, November 11, 2008.

12 Abul Taher, "UK's First Official Sharia Courts," *The Sunday Times*, September 14, 2008.

13 United Nations Committee on the Elimination of Discrimination Against Women; and www.WomenCount.com.

14 New Mexico last voted Democratic in 2004, but has voted Republican 4 out of 5 times since 1992; Nevada last voted Democratic in 1996; and Colorado last voted Democratic in 1992. *New York Times 2008 Election Results*, www.nytimes.com, January 6, 2009.

15 Mark Hugo Lopez and Paul Taylor, "Latino Voters in the 2012 Election," Pew Research Hispanic Center, November 7, 2012. http://www.pewhispanic.org/2012/11/07/latino-voters-in-the-2012-election/

16 Ryan Lizza, "The Party Next Time," The New Yorker, November 19, 2012. http://www.newyorker.com/reporting/2012/11/19/121119fa_fact_lizza?currentPage=all

17 Geoffrey Colvin, "The End of a Dream," *FORTUNE*, June 20, 2006.

18 Shawn Pogatchnik, "Airline Pay Toilets? Ignore That Beverage Cart," *The Associated Press*, February, 27, 2009.

19 "Total Retirement Income at Large Companies: The Real Deal," Study by Hewitt Associates, 2008.

20 "How Obama Tapped Into Social Networks' Power," *New York Times*, November 9, 2008.

21 Tim Mullaney, "U.S. energy independence is no longer just a pipe dream," *USA TODAY*, 05/15/2012. http://usatoday30.usatoday.com/money/industries/energy/story/2012-05-15/1A-COV-ENERGY-INDEPENDENCE/54977254/1

22   Alan S. Binder, "How Many US Jobs Might be Offshorable?" *World Economics: The Journal of Current Economic Analysis and Policy*, November 2, 2009

23   "World Employment Report 2001: Life at Work in the Information Economy," International Labour Organization, 2001.

24   U.S. Manufacturing Nears the Tipping Point, Boston Consulting Group, March 2012 https://www.bcgperspectives.com/content/articles/manufacturing_supply_chain_management_us_manufacturing_nears_the_tipping_point/

25   "Future of Work Overview," New Zealand Department of Labour, 2002.

26   "The American Workplace," Employment Policy Foundation, 2003.

27   "2008 National Science and Engineering Indicators," National Science Foundation, www.nsf.gov.

28   "Research Reveals Competing Agendas of Employers and Jobseekers, With 37% of Individuals Willing to Relocate Anywhere in the World for a Better Career, While 31% of Employers Are Worried About Talent Migrating Abroad," PR Newswire, June 24, 2008; and "Call to Bring Talent Home: Most Employers Say Too Little is Done to Tempt Expats to Return," *The Star (South Africa)*, June 30, 2008.

29   "No Llegarán a Ejecutarse Millones en Inversión," El Comercio, December 25, 2012.

30   Susan F. Martin, "Heavy Traffic," *The Brookings Review*, Fall 2001.

31   Justin A. Heet , "Beyond Workforce 2020: The Coming (and Present) International Market for Labor," Hudson Institute, 2004.

32   "Employer Perspectives on Global Sourcing," Hewitt Associates, 2004.

33   "Employer Perspectives on Global Sourcing," Hewitt Associates, 2004; and Robert Gandossy and Tina Kao, "Overseas Connections," *Across the Board*, Hewitt Associates, November/December 2004.

34   "Employer Perspectives on Global Sourcing," Hewitt Associates, 2004; and Robert Gandossy and Tina Kao, "Overseas Connections," *Across the Board*, Hewitt Associates, November/December 2004.

35   Linda Levine, "Offshoring (or Offshore Outsourcing) and Job Loss Among U.S. Workers", Congressional Research Service, January 21, 2011 http://assets.opencrs.com/rpts/RL32292_20110121.pdf

36   Patrick Thibodeau, "Workers Losing Jobs at IBM Get Overseas Option," *Computerworld*, February 16, 2009.

37   www.ibm.com.

38   Robert Gandossy and Tina Kao, "Channels to Anywhere," Hewitt Associates, 2004.

39   Dan Bilefsky, "In Romania, Children Left Behind Suffer the Strains of Migration," *New York Times*, February 15, 2009; and John Tagliabue, "Eastern Europe Becomes a Center for Outsourcing," *New York Times*, April 17, 2007.

40   Louise Story, "Some Jobs Move Abroad as Banks Chase Growth and Aim to Keep Talent," *New York Times*, August 12, 2008.

41 Joerg Dietz, "Firms Doomed if They Fail to Tap Diverse Talent Pool," *Toronto Star*, July 27, 2007.

42 "Innovation: Remote Working in the Net-Centric Company," The Economist Intelligence Unit Executive Briefing, July 15, 2003.

43 Rachel Emma Silverman, "Your Next Office: At Home?" *Wall Street Journal Online*, June 20, 2012 http://blogs.wsj.com/atwork/2012/06/20/working-from-home-numbers-jump/

44 James Sunshine, "Workers Spend One-Fourth Of Workday Reading, Responding To Email: Survey," *The Huffington Post* 08/01/2012. http://www.huffingtonpost.com/2012/08/01/email-workday_n_1725728.html

45 Keith H. Hammonds, "You Can Do Anything, But Not Everything," *Fast Company*, May 2000.

46 Chuck Salter "Solving the Real Productivity Crisis," *Fast Company*, January 2004.

47 Paula Rayman, "Life's Work: Generational Attitudes Toward Work and Life Integration," Radcliffe Public Policy Center; Lynn Miller, "Upper-Level Workers Say Time Is Better Than Money," Radcliffe Public Policy Center; Gary Challenger and Cornell Christmas; and "University surveys," *HR Magazine*, 2000.

48 Barry Libert, Jon Spector, Don Tapscott, and thousands of contributors, *We Are Smarter than Me: How to Unleash the Power of Crowds in Your Business*, Wharton School Publishing, 2007.

49 Employment and unemployment of youth summary, Bureau of Labor Statistics, August 2012 http://www.bls.gov/news.release/youth.nr0.htm

50 Catherine Loughlin and Julian Barling, "Young Workers' Work Values, Attitudes, and Behaviours," *Journal of Occupational and Organizational Psychology*, November 2001.

51 Peter Schwartz, Inevitable Surprises, Gotham Books, 2003.

52 Karen Schwartz, "Some Finding Retirement is Only a Temporary State," *Chicago Tribune*, March 17, 2004.

53 "Baby Boomers Envision Retirement II — Key Findings," prepared for AARP by Roper-ASW, May 2004.

54 "Age Discrimination in Employment Act: FY 1997 - FY 2011," Equal Employment Opportunity Commission website, last accessed March 26, 2012

55 "Facts on Women at Work," International Labour Organization, 2003.

56 Meeting the Challenges of Tomorrow's Workforce," supplement to *Chief Executive*, August/September 2002.

57 The thirty members of the Organization of Economic Co-operations and Development (OECD) are: Australia, Austria, Belgium, Canada, Czech Republic, Denmark, Finland, France, Germany, Greece, Hungary, Iceland, Ireland, Italy, Japan, Korea, Luxembourg, Mexico, the Netherlands, New Zealand, Norway, Poland, Portugal, Slovak Republic, Spain, Sweden, Switzerland, Turkey, United Kingdom, United States.

58   Stephanie Armour, "More Men Train to Be Nurses, Midwives, Secretaries," *USA Today*, July 10, 2003.

59   Mark Dolliver, "Just Think How Cheery They'd Be If They Weren't Discriminated Against," *Adweek*, December 1, 2003.

60   Lynn A. Karoly and Constantijn W. A. Panis, *The 21st Century at Work*, Rand Corporation, 2004.

61   "Census Releases Immigrant Numbers for Year 2000," Center for Immigration Studies, June 4, 2002.

62   Demetrious G. Papademetriou, Madeline Sumption, and Aaron Terrazas, et all, "Migration and Immigrants Two Years after the Financial Collapse: Where Do We Stand?" Migration Policy Institute, 2010. http://www.migrationpolicy.org/pubs/mpi-bbcreport-2010.pdf

63   "Migration and Human Rights," Office of the High Commission for Human Rights, United Nations, (last accessed January 4, 2013). http://www.ohchr.org/EN/Issues/Migration/Pages/MigrationAndHumanRightsIndex.aspx

64   David McNeil, "Japan: The grey planet's ticking timebomb," *The Independent*, October 1, 2012. http://www.independent.co.uk/news/world/asia/japan-the-grey-planets-ticking-timebomb-8191524.html

65   Chad Steinberg , "Can Women Save Japan (and Asia Too)?" International Monetary Fund, October 2012. http://www.imf.org/external/pubs/ft/fandd/2012/09/steinberg.htm

66   CIA World Fact Book (page update 12/19/2012) https://www.cia.gov/library/publications/the-world-factbook/geos/ch.html

67   Tom Whitehead, "Migrants to send Britain's population soaring to largest in EU," The Telegraph, October 26, 2011. http://www.telegraph.co.uk/news/uknews/immigration/8851902/Migrants-to-send-Britains-population-soaring-to-largest-in-EU.html

68   "OECD Better Life Index," Organization for Economic Cooperation and Development, (last accessed January 5, 2013) http://www.oecdbetterlifeindex.org/countries/chile/

69   "Work and Family: Latin American and Caribbean Women in Search of a New Balance," The World Bank LAC, 2011. http://siteresources.worldbank.org/LACEXT/Resources/informe_genero_LACDEF.pdf

70   Latin American statistics gathered by Andrés Tapia from a variety of formal and informal sources including journalists, human resources professionals, and marketers in trip to Peru, Chile, Argentina, and Brazil in February 2007.

71   Maddy Dychtwald, "Cycles," *The Free Press*, 2003.

72   "Job Recovery Survey," Report by Society for Human Resource Management and *Wall Street Journal*, December 2003.

Chapter 2

1   "The View From the Front Lines," 2008 CEO Diversity Leadership, Diversity Best Practices.

2   The Safe Space program started at AT&T more than a decade ago and has been adopted by other companies and universities. It promotes a way for organizations to indicate areas where it's 'safe' to be out as LGBT. The Safe Space logo is a registered trademark of EQUAL! www.equal.org.

3   Bank of America, "Hispanic-Related Checking and Savings Products Increased 67 Percent in the First Half of 2004," Press Release, www.bankofamerica.com, August 17, 2004.

4   Witeck Communications, "America's LGBT 2012 Buying Power Projected at $790 Billion," 2012.

5   US Department of Labor, "Business Strategies that Work," 2012. http://www.dol.gov/odep/pdf/BusinessStrategiesThatWork.pdf.

6   Phred Dvorak, "A Firm's Culture Can Get Lost in Translation When It's Exported," *Wall Street Journal*, April 5, 2006.

7   Laurel Wentz, Ad Age Hispanic, "Walmart's Tony Rogers: 100% of Growth Is Multicultural," October 31, 2012 http://adage.com/article/hispanic-marketing/walmart-s-tony-rogers-100-growth-multicultural/238051/.

8   1997 Diversity Conference, Conference Board, March 1997.

9   1997 Diversity Conference, Conference Board, March 1997.

10   Data from various Aon Hewitt studies.

11   www.Xerox.com.

12   www.ml.com.

13   Society for Human Resource Management, " Human Resource Standards: Active Standards Projects," (last accessed December 22, 2012) http://www.shrm.org/HRStandards/ActiveStandardsProjects/Pages/default.aspx.

Chapter 3

1   "2012 CWDI Report on Women Board Directors of Latin America's Largest Companies," Corporate Women's Directors International, June 30, 2012. http://www.globewomen.org/cwdi/CWDI%20Latin%20America%20Charts%20for%20web.pdf and "Women in senior management: still not enough," Grant Thornton International Business Report, 2012. http://www.gti.org/files/ibr2012%20-%20women%20in%20senior%20management%20master.pdf.

2   Catalyst "2010 Catalyst Census: Financial Post 500 Women Senior Officers and Top Earners," March 2011. http://catalyst.org/knowledge/2010-catalyst-census-financial-post-500-women-senior-officers-and-top-earners, and Catalyst, "Women Still Largely Shut Out From Senior Ranks of FP500 Companies," Press Release, www.catalyst.org, March 2009.

[3] Catalyst, "Catalyst Quick Take: Visible Minorities," Catalyst, 2012. http://catalyst.org/knowledge/visible-minorities, and "Career Advancement in Corporate Canada: A Focus on Visible Minorities," Report by Catalyst, www.catalyst.org, February 2007.

[4] Human Resources and Skills Development Canada, last accessed January 2013, http://www.hrsdc.gc.ca/eng/labour/equality/employment_equity/tools/eedr/2006/data_reports/page11.shtml.

[5] "Report on Equality Rights of People with Disabilities," Canadian Human Rights Commission, 2012. http://www.chrc-ccdp.gc.ca/pdf/reports/rerpd_rdepad-eng.pdf; "More disabled people in Canada: report" The Canadian Press, December 28, 2009. http://www.cbc.ca/news/health/story/2009/12/28/disabled-reportcanada.html Canadian, and Human Rights Commission, www.chrc-ccdp.ca.

[6] Gayle Johnson, "Where Will You Find Your Future Workforce?" The Canadian Institute Conference, Winning HR Practices of the Best Employers in Canada, Toronto, April 22, 2008.

[7] Neil Crawford and Andrés Tapia, "Diving Deeper into the Talent Pool," Hewitt Associates, Benefits Canada, January 2008.

[8] Tavia Grant, "Diversity: Easier Said Than Done, But, With Tenacity, It Can Be Done," *The Globe and Mail*, April 25, 2008.

[9] Chad Steinberg , "Can Women Save Japan (and Asia Too)?" International Monetary Fund, October 2012. http://www.imf.org/external/pubs/ft/fandd/2012/09/steinberg.htm; Martin Fackler, "Career Women in Japan Find a Blocked Path," New York Times, Aug. 6, 2007. Oscar Johnson, "Job to Increase Women Managers;" and www.focusjapan.com.

[10] "Japan: Portfolio Strategy Womenomics 3.0: The Time Is Now," Goldman Sachs, October 1, 2010. http://www.goldmansachs.com/our-thinking/topics/women-and-economics/womenomics-2011/womenomics3-the-time-is-now.pdf .

[11] Brazilian labor law 8.213/91, *Lex Mundi Labor and Employment Desk Book*, Lex Mundi Ltd, 2008.

[12] Paul Taylor and D'Vera Cohn, "A Milestone En Route to a Majority Minority Nation," Pew Research Social & Demographic Trends, November 7, 2012. http://www.pewsocial-trends.org/2012/11/07/a-milestone-en-route-to-a-majority-minority-nation/, and U.S. Census Bureau, "An Older and More Diverse Nation by Midcentury," Press Release, August 14, 2008.

[13] Best Employers Latin America 2006, Hewitt Associates, 2006.

Chapter 4

[1] Fay Hansen, "Diversity's Business Case: Doesn't Add Up," Workforce, www.workforce.com, April 23, 2003; and Rohini Anand and Mary-Frances Winters, "A Retrospective View of Corporate Diversity Training From 1964 to the Present," *Academy of Management Learning & Education, 2008.*

[2] Fon Trompenaars and Charles Hampden-Turner, *Riding the Waves of Culture: Understanding Diversity in Global Business, 2nd ed*, McGraw-Hill, 1998.

[3] Fon Trompenaars and Charles Hampden-Turner, *Riding the Waves of Culture: Understanding Diversity in Global Business, 2nd ed*, McGraw-Hill, 1998.

[4] Michelle Hunt, former vice president of Herman Miller Inc, interview, March 2006; and "If the Chair Fits: All Shapes and Sizes," *Herman Miller Newsletter*, Herman Miller Inc, 2001.

[5] "The Cost of Employee Turnover Due to Failed Diversity Initiatives in the Workplace — The Corporate Leavers Survey 2007," Study by Korn/Ferry International and Level Playing Field Institute, 2007.

[6] Thomas Kochman, *Black and White Styles in Conflict*, University of Chicago Press, 1983.

Chapter 5

[1] The Myers-Briggs Type Indicator is an assessment tool used to determine 16 different personality types. The MBTI is used in the workplace, schools, and other organizations, www.myersbriggs.org.

Intro to Part 3

[1] Mark Langler and David Sanger, "World Leaders Pledge $1.1 Trillion for Crisis," *New York Times*, April 2, 2009.

Chapter 6

[1] U.S. Census Bureau, "Older and More Diverse Nation by Midcentury," Press Release, www.census.gov, August 14, 2008.

[2] http://inamerica.blogs.cnn.com/2012/05/17/census-2011-data-confirm-trend-of-population-diversity/.

[3] Eric Schmitt, "Whites in Minority in Largest Cities, Census Shows," *NY Times*, April 30, 2001.

[4] Michael Broom and Donald Klein, *Power: The Infinite Game*, Sea Otter Press, 1999.

[5] Malcolm D. Lee, director, *Undercover Brother*, Universal Pictures, 2002.

[6] Adam Cohen and Elizabeth Taylor, *American Pharaoh: Mayor Richard J. Daley — His Battle for Chicago and the Nation*, Little, Brown, May, May 2000.

[7] Walter Rucker and James Nathaniel, *Encyclopedia of American Race Riots*, Greenwood Press, November 2006.

[8] www.cdc.gov; www.census.gov; www.congress.org; and www.diversityinc.com.

[9] There is much support for this view. An examination of Aon Hewitt's focus group studies that cross multiple industries and multiple regions in the United States, and the works of Norma Carr-Rufino's book, *Diversity Success Strategies*; Dr. Daniel Landis, Dr. Milton Bennett, and Dr. Janet Bennett's book, *Handbook for Intercultural Training*; and the work of the diversity consulting group, White Men as Full Diversity Partners, reveals an overlapping description of European-American worldviews. Here's how White Men as Full Diversity Partners describes on their Web site the values and their interpretation of this culture:

• Rugged individualism as compared to collectivism

• Low tolerance for uncertainty and ambiguity

• Focus on action over reflection (doing as compared to being)

• Rationality over emotionality

• Time is linear and future focused

Norma Carr-Rufinao, *Diversity Success Strategies*, Butterworth-Heinemann, 1999; Dr. Daniel Landis, Dr. Janet Bennett and Dr. Milton J. Bennett, *The Handbook for Intercultural Training, 3rd ed*, Sage Publications, Inc., December 2003; and White Men As Full Diversity Partners, www.wmfdp.com.

10   Winters' research is based on a compilation of focus group research and proprietary studies conducted over several years, with many companies and across multiple industries

11   "Aon Hewitt Engagement Survey Data," Aon Hewitt. Aon Hewitt regularly conducts engagement studies for its clients.

12   Chuck Shelton, *"Leadership 101 for White Men: How to Work Successfully with Black Colleagues and Customers,"* Morgan-James Publishing, 2008.

13   The Chicago Dream Dinner is one of many fundraisers designed to raise funds for the Washington, DC, Martin Luther King, Jr. National Memorial, which will be built on the National Mall, www.mlkmemorial.org.

14   Peggy McIntosh, "White Privilege: Unpacking the Invisible Knapsack," Wellesley College Center for Research on Women, 1988.

15   Dr. Peggy McIntosh, email exchange with author, May 2009.

16   Dr. Peggy McIntosh, "White Privilege: Unpacking the Invisible Knapsack," Wellesley College Center for Research on Women, 1988. For all 50 questions in Peggy McIntosh's "White Privilege," see http://www.mdcbowen.org/p2/rm/mcintosh.html.

17   Yuqing Feng, "Why Black Girls Still Prefer White Dolls," *DiversityInc*, www.diversityinc. com., February 9, 2007.

18   Economic Mobility Project, Pew Charitable Trust, 2012. Link: http://www.pewtrusts.org/uploadedFiles/wwwpewtrustsorg/Reports/Economic_Mobility/Pew-Economic-Mobility-Race.pdf.

19   Economic Mobility Project, Pew Charitable Trust, 2012. Link: http://www.pewtrusts.org/uploadedFiles/wwwpewtrustsorg/Reports/Economic_Mobility/Pew-Economic-Mobility-Race.pdf.

20   Barack Obama, "A More Perfect Union," speech transcript, Philadelphia, Pennsylvania, March 18, 2008. Link: http://articles.cnn.com/2008-03-18/politics/obama.transcript_1_perfect-union-constitution-slavery?_s=PM:POLITICS

21   Jann S. Wenner, "Ready for the Fight: Rolling Stone Inteview with Barack Obama," *Rolling Stone Magazine*, April 25, 2012. Link: http://www.rollingstone.com/politics/news/ready-for-the-fight-rolling-stone-interview-with-barack-obama-20120425#ixzz1t9JA0THw.

22   http://www.csmonitor.com/USA/DC-Decoder/2012/0827/Obama-vs.-Romney-101-5-differences-on-education/K-12-spending. Chapter 6

Chapter 7

1　"Global Employment Trends for Women 2008," International Labour Organisation, www.ilo.org, March 2008.

2　Remarks by World Bank Group President Jim Yong Kim at "Evidence and Impact: Closing the Gender Gap" U.S. State Department/Gallup event on "Evidence and Impact: Closing the Gender Gap" Washington, DC, July 19, 2012. http://www.worldbank.org/en/news/2012/07/19/remarks-world-bank-group-president-jim-yong-kim-evidence-impact-closing-gender-gap, and http://www.ilo.org/wcmsp5/groups/public/---dgreports/---dcomm/documents/publication/wcms_103456.pdf

3　http://www.internationalbusinessreport.com/files/ibr2012%20-%20women%20in%20senior%20management%20master.pdf

4　http://voices.washingtonpost.com/44/2009/01/29/obama_signs_lilly_ledbetter_ac.html

5　"Commission on Status of Women," United Nations, www.un.org, March 11, 2005.

6　Comparison of Gross National Product per capita measured by purchasing power (from the Atlas of Global Inequality, 2000) and UN Gender Development Index (from the UN Development Programme 2003). Corroborated by "Engendering Development," a World Bank report documenting that societies that discriminate by gender tend to experience slower economic growth and greater poverty.

7　Martin Fackler, "Career Women in Japan Find a Blocked Path," *New York Times*, Aug. 6, 2007.

8　"Gender Equality in Mexico," www.wikigender.org.

9　"On Equality Between Men and Women," Second Annual Report, European Commission, http://www.guidance-europe.org, February 14, 2005.

10　http://www.catalyst.org/publication/271/women-ceos-of-the-fortune-1000

11　"Women Entrepreneurs: Why Companies Lose Female Talent and What They Can Do About It," Report by Catalyst, www.catalyst.org, 1998.

12　U.S. Department of Education, National Center for Education Statistics, 2011.

13　U.S. Department of Education, National Center for Education Statistisc, 2006. http://nces.ed.gov/pubs2006/2006084_2.pdf

14　"Women Entrepreneurs: Why Companies Lose Female Talent and What They Can Do About It," Report by Catalyst, www.catalyst.org, 1998

15　In particular, see the revised Bem Sex Role Inventory (BSRI).

16　There are many articles on this topic, including: Anna Fels, "Do Women Lack Ambition" *Harvard Business Review*, April 2004; and "Women 'Take Care,' Men 'Take Charge': Stereotyping of U.S. Business Leaders Exposed," Report by Catalyst, www.catalyst.org, October 19, 2005.

17　Boris Groysberg, L. Kevin Kelly, and Bryan MacDonald, "The New Path to the C-Suite," *Harvard Business Review*, March 2011.

18   Rochelle Sharp, "As Leaders, Women Rule," *Business Week*, www.businessweek.com, November 20, 2000.

19   Kira Porter, "Women Leaders: Strategic Yet Invisible Assets," *Link & Learn*, May 2003.

20   Sylvia Ann Hewlett, Carolyn Buck Luce, Peggy Shiller, and Sandra Southwell, "Hidden Brain Drain: Off-Ramps and On-Ramps in Women's Careers," Harvard Business Review, Feb. 24, 2005.

21   http://online.wsj.com/article/0,,SB112129016232185000,00.html

22   Isobel Coleman, "Why Empowering Women is Good for Business," *Foreign Affairs*, May/June 2010.

23   The World's Women 2010, United Nations, 2010. http://unstats.un.org/unsd/demographic/products/Worldswomen/WW2010Report_by%20chapterBW/Work_BW.pdf

24   Ricardo Hausman, Laura D. Tyson, and Saadia Zahidi, "The Global Gender Gap Report 2010," World Economic Forum, 2010. https://members.weforum.org/pdf/gendergap/report2010.pdf

25   Latin American statistics gathered by Andrés Tapia from a variety of formal and informal sources including journalists, human resources professionals, and marketers on trip to Peru, Chile, Argentina, and Brazil in February 2007.

26   "The Supply Problem Myth: Fortune 500 Boards," Report by Catalyst, 2012. http://catalyst.org/knowledge/supply-problem-myth-fortune-500-boards

27   Aparna Banerji and Kate Vernon, "Women on Boards: Hang Seng Index 2012," *Community Business*, March 2012. http://www.communitybusiness.org/images/cb/publications/2012/WOB_Eng_2012.pdf

28   Hong Kong Equal Opportunity Commission, (last accessed January 5, 2013) http://www.eoc.org.hk/EOC/GraphicsFolder/InforCenter/Papers/StatisticContent.aspx?ItemID=10943, and http://www.eoc.org.hk/EOC/GraphicsFolder/ShowContent.aspx?ItemID=11042

29   Chad Steinberg, "Can Women Save Japan (and Asia Too)?" International Monetary Fund, October 2012. http://www.imf.org/external/pubs/ft/fandd/2012/09/steinberg.htm Martin Fackler, "Career Women in Japan Find a Blocked Path," *New York Times*, Aug. 6, 2007.

30   http://edition.cnn.com/2012/12/24/us/malala-cnn-most-intriguing-2012/index.html?utm_source=feedburner&utm_medium=feed&utm_campaign=Feed%3A+rss%2Fcnn_world+(RSS%3A+World)

31   UN Development Fund for Women 2008

32   Women in politics 2012 elections   http://www.huffingtonpost.com/2012/11/07/women-in-politics-break-records-2012-election_n_2088954.html

Chapter 8

1   Michelle Conlin, "Youthquake," *Business Week*, www.businessweek.com, January 9, 2008.

2   Margaret Hoovr, "Opinion: Failure to attract millennials is sinking GOP," November 14, 2012 http://www.cnn.com/2012/11/14/living/millennials-gop-vote/index.html.

3   "Generation in the Workplace in the United States and Canada," Catalyst, May 1, 2012. http://www.catalyst.org/knowledge/generations-workplace-united-states-canada, and "Getting to Know Generation X," *NAS Insights*, NAS Recruitment Communications, www.nasrecruitment.com, 2006.

4   Ken Dychtwald, Tamara J. Erickson, and Robert Morrison, "Workforce Crisis: How to Beat the Coming Shortage of Skills and Talent," *Harvard Business School Press*, April 2006.

5   Conversation with Carol Evans, Founder and CEO, *Working Mother Media*, December 2007.

6   Kenneth M. Johnson and Daniel T. Lichter, "The Changing Faces of America's Children and Youth," Carsey Institute, Spring 2010. http://www.human.cornell.edu/pam/outreach/loader.cfm?csModule=security/getfile&PageID=50050, and Robert Bernstein, "Nation's Population One-Third Minority," Press Release, U.S. Census Bureau, www.census.gov, May 10, 2006.

7   Don E. Sears, "Workers Looking for New Jobs, Especially Generation Y," eWeek online, April 22, 2012. http://www.eweek.com/c/a/IT-Management/Workers-Looking-forNew-Jobs-Especially-Generation-Y-837345/.

8   Dr. John J. Medina, "Brain Rules: Principles of Thriving at Work," Presentation, Diversity and Inclusion Conference, Society for Human Resource Management, October 23, 2012. http://sessionplanner.shrm.org/conference/shrm-2012-diversity-inclusion-conference-exposition/session/brain-rules-principles.

9   Andrés Tapia, "The Multicultural Marketing of Benefits," Hewitt White Paper, 2007.

10   Interview with proud but perplexed father in Norwalk, Connecticut, December 2007; and email exchange with Leah Campbell, February 2008.

11   Don Tapscott, Anthony D. Williams, *Wikinomics: The Expanded Edition*, Portfolio, April 2008.

12   Sanjay Dholakia, "The Intersection of Web 2.0 and Talent Management," *Talent Management* magazine, January 2008.

13   "Generation in the Workplace in the United States and Canada," Catalyst, May 1, 2012. http://www.catalyst.org/knowledge/generations-workplace-united-states-canada, and "Getting to Know Generation X," *NAS Insights*, NAS Recruitment Communications, www.nasrecruitment.com, 2006.

14   RUUP4IT?: Are you up for it?

Chapter 9

1   "20th Anniversary of Americans with Disabilities Act: July 26," Facts for Features, U.S. Census, May 26, 2010. http://www.census.gov/newsroom/releases/archives/facts_for_features_special_editions/cb10-ff13.html

2   IPS Insights: Emerging Giant – Big is Not Enough: The Global Economics of Disability, www.odenetwork.com/library/global-economics-of-disability-the-april-20-2010, April 2010.

3   "The Business Case for Workers Age 50+: Planning for Tomorrow's Talent Needs in Today's Competitive Environment," A report for AARP prepared by Towers Perrin, December 2005.

⁴ Matthew W. Brault, "Americans with Disabilities: 2005 — Household Economic Studies," *Current Population Reports*, www.census.gov, December 2008.

⁵ http://usatoday30.usatoday.com/news/health/story/2012-05-28/veteran-disability/55250092/1

⁶ "Veterans Day 2012: November 11," Facts for Features, U.S. Census, October 11, 2012. http://www.census.gov/newsroom/releases/pdf/cb12ff-21_veteran.pdf

⁷ Matthew W. Brault, "Americans with Disabilities: 2005 — Household Economic Studies," *Current Population Reports*, www.census.gov, December 2008.

⁸ http://www.census.gov/newsroom/releases/archives/facts_for_features_special_editions/cb12-ff16.html.

⁹ Matthew W. Brault, "Americans with Disabilities: 2005 — Household Economic Studies," *Current Population Reports*, www.census.gov, December 2008.

¹⁰ "U.S. Census Bureau, American Community Survey," November 2006 as quoted by Jonathan J. Kaufman, "The Search for Talent: Why Hiring and Retaining People with Disabilities is Good for Business," *CDO Insights*, Diversity Best Practices, www.consultspringboard.com, December 2007.

¹¹ World Report on Disability 2011, World Health Organization and The World Bank, Chapter 8 "Work and Employment."

¹² U.S. Census Bureau Current Population Report: Americans With Disabilities: 2002 (p70-107) by Erika Steinmetz.

¹³ H. G. Gallagher, *FDR's Splendid Deception*, Vandamere Press, 1994.

¹⁴ "2007 Statistical Abstract: National Data Book," US Census Bureau, www.census.gov, December 2007.

¹⁵ Jonathan J. Kaufman, "The Search for Talent: Why Hiring and Retaining People with Disabilities is Good for Business," *CDO Insights*, Diversity Best Practices.

¹⁶ Yoji Cole, "Corporate America in a Post-ADA World," *DiversityInc Magazine*, November/December 2007.

¹⁷ Yoji Cole, "Corporate America in a Post-ADA World," *DiversityInc Magazine*, November/December 2007.

¹⁸ Jeré Longman, "Embracing the Equality of Opportunity," *New York Times*, August 17, 2008.

¹⁹ Carol Pogash, "A Personal Call to Invention: Amputee's Prosthetic Design IS Helping Pistorius and Others" *New York Times*, July 2, 2008.

²⁰ Jonathan J. Kaufman, "The Search for Talent: Why Hiring and Retaining People with Disabilities is Good for Business," *CDO Insights*, Diversity Best Practices, www.consultspringboard.com, December 2007.

²¹ Bonnie Kavoussi, "Drexel Hamilton, Wall Street Firm, Trains And Hires Disabled Veterans" *The Huffington Post*, 06/18/2012. http://www.huffingtonpost.com/2012/06/18/drexel-hamilton-veterans_n_1605619.html?utm_hp_ref=business.

²² "A 25-Year History of the IDEA (archived)," US Department of Education, www.ed.gov, July 2007.

23   US Census, US Department of Labor, Statistics Canada, European Central Bank, IPS. IPS Insights: Emerging Giant – Big is Not Enough: The Global Economics of Disability, www. odenetwork.com/library/global-economics-of-disability-the-april-20-2010, April 2010.

24   Remarks By The President On Signing Of U.N. Convention On The Rights Of Persons With Disabilities Proclamation, July 24, 2009 http://www.whitehouse.gov/the_press_office/Remarks-by-the-President-on-Rights-of-Persons-with-Disabilities-Proclamation-Signing.

25   Melanie Trottman, "U.S. Pushes Target for Hiring the Disabled," *Wall Street Journal online*, February 29, 2012. http://online.wsj.com/article/SB10001424052970204520204577251303726662194.html.

Chapter 10

1   Inaugural invocations by Pastor Rick Warren of Saddleback Church in California (January 20, 2009) and The Right Rev. V. Gene Robinson, bishop of the U.S. Episcopal Church in the diocese of New Hampshire (January 19, 2009).

2   Hewitt presentation to Talent & Organization Consulting (TOC) North America meeting, May 31, 2007, states: "Hewitt research demonstrates that a 10% increase in attracting and retaining pivotal employees adds approximately $70 to $160 million to a company's bottom line." This research was conducted by Hewitt's Human Capital Foresight team.

3   Shanker, Thom and Patrick Healy, "A New Push to Roll Back 'Don't Ask, Don't Tell,'" *The New York Times*, November 30, 2007. Link: http://www. nytimes.com/2007/11/30/us/30military.html?_r=1.

4   "Defining Marriage: Defense of Marriage Acts and Same-Sex Marriage Laws," National Conference of State Legislatures, (last accessed 01/02/2013) http://www.ncsl.org/issues-research/human-services/same-sex-marriage-overview.aspx.

5   "Mobilizing: The Road to Equality," Annual Report, Human Rights Campaign, 2011. http://www.hrc.org/files/assets/resources/AnnualReport_2011.pdf, and 2013 Corporate Equality Index http://www.hrc.org/files/assets/resources/CEI_2013_Final_low.pdf.pdf.

6   McVeigh, Karen, "Gay rights must be criterion for US aid allocation, instructs Obama," *The Guardian online*, December 6, 2011. Link: http://www.guardian.co.uk/world/2011/dec/07/gayrights-us-aid-criteria.

7   Timmons, Heather, "India Court Overturns Gay Sex Ban," *The New York Times online*, July 2, 2009. Link: http://www.nytimes.com/2009/07/03/world/ asia/03india.html?_r=1.

8   James, Susan Donaldson, "'Gayby Boom' Fueld by Same-Sex Parents," ABCNews.com, August 3, 2009. Link: http://abcnews.go.com/Health/ ReproductiveHealth/story?id=8232392&page=1& singlePage=true#.T8ZUs91q81B.

9   James, Susan Donaldson, "'Gayby Boom' Fueld by Same-Sex Parents," ABCNews.com, August 3, 2009. Link: http://abcnews.go.com/Health/ ReproductiveHealth/story?id=8232392&page=1& singlePage=true#.T8ZUs91q81B.

10 Brodzinksy, David M., Expanding Resources for Children III: Research-Based Best Practices in Adoption by Gays and Lesbians, Evan B. Donaldson Adoption Institute, October 2011. Link: http://www.adoptioninstitute.org/ publications/2011_10_Expanding_Resources_ BestPractices.pdf.

11 Out & Equal, "Seven Out of Ten Heterosexuals Today Know Someone Gay," Press Release, www.outandequal.org, October 10, 2006.

12 Human Rights Campaign, Pass ENDA Now: End Workplace Discrimination, 2011. Link: http://sites.hrc.org/sites/passendanow/index.aspgIQAlAYRjU_story.html?hpid=z3.

13 "Hate Crime Statistics 2011," Uniform Crime Reports, Federal Bureau of Investigations, (last accessed 12/30/2012) http://www.fbi.gov/about-us/cjis/ucr/hate-crime/2011/narratives/incidents-and-offenses, and "New FBI Data Shows Hate Crimes Based on Sexual Orientation on the Rise" Press Release, Human Rights Coalition, December 10, 2012. http://www.hrc.org/press-releases/entry/new-fbi-data-shows-hate-crimes-based-on-sexual-orientation-on-the-rise.*Initially, 2,500 participants were expected to attend the 2012 Out & Equal Summit. However, attendance was affected by Hurricane Sandy, which caused massive East Coast disruptions.

14 "1,400 LGBT Executives and 118 Sponsors Gathered for the 14th Annual Out & Equal Workplace Summit: Baltimore, October 29-November," Press Release, Out & Equal, November 5, 2012. http://outandequal.org/node/514.

15 Samir Luther, "Domestic Partner Benefits: Employer Trends and Benefits Equivalency for the GLBT Family," Report by the Human Rights Campaign Foundation, www.hrc.org, March 2006.

16 Katherine Bindley, "Domestic Partner Health Insurance Benefits Grow For Heterosexual Couples, Too" *Huffington Post*, 6/01/2012. http://www.huffingtonpost.com/2012/06/01/domestic-partner-health-insurance-unmarried-heterosexual-couples_n_1532584.html.

17 Corporate Equality Index 2002," Study by the Human Rights Campaign Foundation, www.hrc.org, August 2002

18 "Mobilizing: The Road to Equality," Annual Report, Human Rights Campaign, 2011. http://www.hrc.org/files/assets/resources/AnnualReport_2011.pdf, and 2013 Corporate Equality Index http://www.hrc.org/files/assets/resources/CEI_2013_Final_low.pdf.pdf.

19 "Mobilizing: The Road to Equality," Annual Report, Human Rights Campaign, 2011. http://www.hrc.org/files/assets/resources/AnnualReport_2011.pdf, and 2013 Corporate Equality Index http://www.hrc.org/files/assets/resources/CEI_2013_Final_low.pdf.pdf.

20 "Witeck-Combs Communications, "Buying Power of Gay Men and Lesbians in 2008," *Gay Market Report 2009*, Market Research Report, www.pinkbananamedia.com, 2009.

21 Witeck Communications, "America's LGBT 2012 Buying Power Projected at $790 Billion," 2012.

22 Humphreys, Jeffrey M., The Multicultural Economy 2012, Selig Center for Economic Growth, Terry College of Business, University of Georgia, 2012.

23   "A look at household income and discretionary spend of lesbian, gay and heterosexual Americans," 2012 LGBT Demographic Report, Experian Simmons, July 20, 2012. http://www.experian.com/blogs/marketing-forward/2012/07/20/sim-a-look-at-household-income-and-discretionary-spend-of-lesbian-gay-and-heterosexual-americans/.

24   Harris Interactive and Witeck-Combs Communications, "LGBT Adults Strongly Prefer Brands That Support Causes Important to Them and That Also Offer Equal Workplace Benefits."

25   Michael Wilke, "IBM: Beyond Gay Vague," *The Gully Online Magazine*, January 5, 2004.

26   "Smoother Transitions" by Lisa Belkin, *New York Times*, Sept 3, 2008.

27   2013 Corporate Equality Index http://www.hrc.org/files/assets/resources/CEI_2013_Final_low.pdf.pdf.

Chapter 11

1   "Bway in Chicago Study Reveals Health of Chicago Theater," Broadwayworld.com, January 16, 2007.

2   John Von Rhein, "Sphinx Looks to Change Makeup of U.S. Orchestras," *Chicago Tribune*, October 3, 2008; John Von Rhein, "Latino Composers Pull the Right Strings, Horns in Seven Free Shows," *Chicago Tribune*, October 26, 2008; and John Von Rhein, "Latino Composers Pull the Right Strings, Horns Percussion," *Newsday*, March 18, 2007.

3   Robert Bernstein, Tom Edwards, "An Older and More Diverse Nation by Midcentury," Press Release, U.S. Census Bureau, www.census.gov, August 14, 2008.

4   John Von Rhein, "Sphinx Looks to Change Makeup of U.S. Orchestras," *Chicago Tribune*, October 3, 2008; John Von Rhein, "Latino Composers Pull the Right Strings," *Chicago Tribune*, October 27, 2007; and John Von Rhein, "Latino Composers Pull the Right Strings, Horns, Percussion," Newsday, March 18, 2007.

5   Josh Getlin, "Tony-Contending Musicals Bring New Audiences to Broadway," *Los Angeles Times*, June 11, 2008.

Intro to Part 4

1   R. Roosevelt Thomas, Jr., "Diversity Management and Affirmative Action: Past, Present and Future," Diversity Symposium, October 7, 2004.

2   Joseph Schumpeter, *Capitalism, Socialism, and Democracy*, Harper & Row, 1942.

Chapter 12

1   "Preparing for the Workforce of Tomorrow," Hewitt Timely Topic Survey, February 2004.

2   Mitra Toossi, "Labor Force Projections to 2012: The Graying of the U.S. Workforce," *Monthly Labor Review*, www.bls.gov, February 2004.

3 Conversation with Dr. Jeff Howard, April 2009. Dr. Howard is the founder and CEO of J. Howard & Associates, a diversity consulting firm that became a part of the Novations Group.

4 2 Corinthians 4:8 (New International Version).

Chapter 13

1 401(k) Plans in Living Color: A Study of 401(k) Savings Disparities Across Racial and Ethnic Groups, Ariel/Aon Hewitt, 2012 http://www.arielinvestments.com/401k-Study-2012/.

2 "2007 Ariel-Schwab Black Investor Survey," Ariel Investments, www.arielinvestments.com, October 2007.

3 http://www.arielinvestments.com/content/view/1774/1173/.

4 "Longer Life Spans, Lower Salaries and Conservative Saving Habits Key Factors in Gap Between How Much Women Need for Retirement and Their Actual Saving Behaviors," Study by Hewitt, July 9, 2008. Study of nearly 2 million employees at 72 large U.S. companies.

5 Excerpts from study in endnote 2:
Some Reasons for the Retirement Savings Gap Between Women and Men

- Make less and live longer. Despite the fact that women's income has increased 63 percent in the past 30 years, their salaries still trail men's, with the average woman earning just $57,000 a year compared to $84,000 for the average man in Hewitt's study. In addition, women are expected to live almost three years longer than men — an average of 22 years after retirement at age 65 compared to just 19 years post-retirement for men. As a result, most women will need to save more to make their retirement savings last over a longer stretch of time. In addition, because medical costs after retirement are a flat dollar amount for all employees, those costs will consume a higher percentage of women's retirement assets than men's.

- Invest less assertively. 2009 Hewitt research reveals that most women have less money saved in their 401(k) plans than men. The average plan balance for women is $56,320 — nearly $47,000 less than men. In addition, women tend to contribute less (7.3 percent of pay versus 8.1 percent for men) to their 401(k) plan, and they are less likely to take advantage of the employer match. Thirty percent of women did not contribute to their 401(k) plans in 2007 and another quarter (24 percent) did not contribute at a level high enough to take advantage of the company match, which, according to Hewitt research, is typically $0.50 for every dollar up to 6 percent of pay per year. Hewitt research also shows that women are less aggressive than men with respect to saving and investing in their 401(k) plans. Women invest less in riskier equity investments (65 percent for women compared to 71 percent for men), and are about half as likely as men to make a trade (13 percent versus 24 percent). Additionally, women tend to choose investments and let them stick more often than men. Just over a quarter (26 percent) make changes to their contribution rate each year compared to 30 percent of men.

- Delay retirement saving and have spotty saving patterns. Not surprisingly, Hewitt's study reveals that the earlier and more consistently employees save for retirement, the greater the impact on increasing overall income replacement rates. Unfortunately, Hewitt's research also shows that women wait 2 to 4 years longer than men to start saving for retirement. In addition, they are more likely to be in and out of the workforce for family reasons, which can result in hundreds of thousands of dollars in missed earnings, promotions, raises, and benefits over the course of a career, including larger deficiencies in retirement savings.

How Can Women Close the Gap?

Despite the challenges they face, it is possible for women to get to a more comfortable place in retirement. In fact, making a few easy changes to their saving and investing behaviors can have a significant impact in helping women shrink the retirement income gap and get to more appropriate retirement levels.

- Invest earlier and at a more vigorous rate. Hewitt research shows that the age at which employees start saving has a significant impact on their retirement balances. Women could potentially increase their nest egg by 18 percent simply by investing two years earlier than they do now, or 23 percent by investing just four years earlier. In addition, women can increase their projected retirement income rates an average of 7 percent simply by investing just 2 percent of pay more a year in their 401(k)s. A woman who makes an average salary of $57,000 and who increases her annual 401(k) contribution from 2 percent to 4 percent — an increase of just $95 per month — will have accumulated an extra $81,000 by the time she reaches retirement age. What's more, she will tack on an extra $40,500 by having contributed at a rate high enough to take advantage of her employer's company match program.

- Put off retirement for a few years. While most employees, including women, estimate they will retire by age 65, working just 2 years longer to age 67 can increase projected retirement replacement income levels by 13.5 percent for women who contribute to their 401(k) plans. And because women will have more money to live on during their years in retirement, their retiree medical costs — typically a flat dollar amount on an annual basis — won't eat up as large a percentage of their savings had they retired at age 65 or earlier.

For more details go to: http://www.hewittassociates.com/Intl/NA/en-US/AboutHewitt/Newsroom/PressReleaseDetail.aspx?cid=5346.

[6] Michael Grunwald, "How Obama Is Using the Science of Change," *Time*, April 6, 2009.

[7] Michael Grunwald, "How Obama Is Using the Science of Change," *Time*, April 6, 2009.

[8] 401(k) Plans in Living Color: A Study of 401(k) Savings Disparities Across Racial and Ethnic Groups, Ariel/Aon Hewitt, 2012.

[9] Amy Gahran, "Why one in five U.S. adults doesn't use the Internet," Special to CNN, April 16, 2012 Link: http://edition.cnn.com/2012/04/13/tech/web/pew-not-using-internet/#.

[10] Kathryn Zickuhr and Aaron Smith, "Digital Differences," Pew Internet and American Life Project, Pew Research Center, Apr 13, 2012 Link: http://pewinternet.org/Reports/2012/Digital-differences.aspx.

Endnotes

11   http://www.statehealthfacts.org/comparebar.jsp?ind=135&cat=3.

12   "About Minority Health," Centers for Disease Control and Prevention, www.cdc.gov.

13   Moyer, Paula, "AACAP: Ethnicity Linked to Schizophrenia Diagnosis for Black and Latino Teens," Medpage Today website, October 25, 2005. Link: http://www.medpageto-day.com/Neurology/Seizures/1994.

14   Demesmen, Didier, "Recognizing and Addressing Healthcare Disparities in Medica-tion…" Medscape.org website, December 30, 2009. Link: http://www.medscape.org/viewarticle/713641.

15   http://works.bepress.com/cgi/viewcontent.cgi?article=1024&context=metraux.

16   The GLBT Health Access Project: A State-Funded Effort to Improve Access to Care http://www.ncbi.nlm.nih.gov/pmc/articles/PMC1446464/pdf/11392930.pdf.

17   Robert Bernstein, Tom Edwards, "An Older and More Diverse Nation by Midcentury," Press Release, U.S. Census Bureau, www.census.gov, August 14, 2008.

18   "[2006] Hewitt Annual Healthcare Survey," Hewitt Associates, www.hewitt.com, 2006.

19   "2001 Health Care Quality Survey," The Commonwealth Fund, www.commonwealth-fund.org, November 2001.

20   "2001 Health Care Quality Survey," The Commonwealth Fund, www.commonwealth-fund.org, November 2001.

21   Dreachslin, Dr. Janet L., and Hobby, Fred, "Racial and Ethnic Disparities: Why Diversity Leadership Matters," *Journal of Healthcare Management*.

22   Lisa Beyer, "Companies are Turning to Technology to Help Keep Workers Well," *Work-force Management*, October 1, 2011.

23   "American Diabetes Association Partners with Numera to Manage Diabetes Using Social Media," Benzina.com, March 2, 2012.http://www.diabetes.org/in-my-community/local-offices/seattle-tacoma-washington/.

24   "Barbershops as Hypertension Detection, Referral, and Follow-Up Centers for Black Men," *Hypertension Magazine*, American Heart Association, 2007.

25   http://edition.cnn.com/2012/04/13/tech/web/pew-not-using-internet/#.

Additional Sources

• "Obama: I Never Thought My Election Meant America Was Post-Racial," *Huffington Post*, April 26, 2012. Link: http://www.huffingtonpost.com/2012/04/26/obama-on-race-in-america_n_1455275.html.

• Seth A. Forman, "Obama's America in Black & White," *National Review Online*, June 23, 2011. Link: http://www.nationalreview.com/articles/270291/obama-s-america-black-white-seth-forman#.

Chapter 14

[1] Julia Overturf Johnson and Barbara Downs, "Maternity Leave and Employment Patterns of First-Time Mothers: 1961-2000 — Household Economic Studies," *Current Population Reports*, U.S. Census Bureau, www.census.gov, October 2005.

[2] Yearly Hewitt benefits surveys.

[3] Oriel Sullivan and Scott Coltrane, "Men's Changing Contribution to Housework and Child Care," prepared for the 11th Annual Conference of the Council on Contemporary Families, April 25-26, 2008.

[4] Kerstin Aumann, Ellen Galinsky, and Kenneth Matos, "The New Male Mystique." Families and Work Institute, 2011. http://familiesandwork.org/site/research/reports/newmalemystique.pdf.

[5] Remarks by Michelle Obama, as prepared for delivery. Women's Economic Roundtable, Pontiac, Michigan, July 9, 2008.

[6] Sylvia Ann Hewlett, *Off-ramps and On-Ramps: Keeping Talented Women on the Road to Success*, Harvard Business School Press, 2007.

[7] "About Flexible Work Arrangements," Hewitt Timely Topics Survey, 2008.

[8] James W. Loewen, *Lies My Teacher Told Me: Everything Your American History Textbook Got Wrong*, New Press, 2008.

[9] Interview with Carol Evans, CEO of *Working Mother Media*, August 2008.

[10] Michael F. Broom and Donald C. Klein, *Power: The Infinite Game*, Sea Otter Press, October 1999.

[11] Tory Johnson, "Flexibility Equals Productivity," ABC News, www.abcnews.go.com, April 13, 2006; Gregory P. Smith, "Flexible Work Arrangements Promote Productivity" Business Know-How (an online magazine) www.businessknowhow.com; and "Survey: Working from Home Boosts Productivity," *Inc Magazine*, www.inc.com, February 2007.

[12] Jennifer Robison, "Workplace Socializing is Productive; An MIT Researcher Talks About the Usefulness of Water Cooler Chatter," *Gallup Management Journal*, December 24, 2008.

[13] Chris Sullivan, "The Next Workplace Revolution," *Dialogue*, Gensler Publication, 2008.

[14] "2008 US Workplace Survey," Report by Gensler, www.gensler.com, October 2008.

[15] "2008 US Workplace Survey," Report by Gensler, www.gensler.com, October 2008.

[16] Blair Kamin, "Come See the Silver Sides of the Sears Tower?" *Chicago Tribune*, March 11, 2009.

[17] Chris Sullivan, "The Next Workplace Revolution," *Dialogue*, Gensler Publication, 2008; and Helen Kirwan-Taylor, "The Time We Waste," *Management Today*, www.managementtoday.co.uk, September 4, 2007.

[18] Helen Kirwan-Taylor, "The Time We Waste," *Management Today*, www.managementtoday.co.uk, September 4, 2007.

[19] http://video.msnbc.msn.com/the-cycle/50075927#50075927.

20   http://www.whitehouse.gov/photos-and-video/video/forum-workplace-flexibility-closing-session#transcript.

21   Carol Evans interview on MSNBC, December 4, 2012. http://video.msnbc.msn.com/the-cycle/50075927#50075927.

Chapter 15

1   Deb Perelman, "Study: Businesses Unprepared for Aging Workforce," *eweek.com*, March 16, 2007.

2   http://www.hirestrategy.com/job_market/feature_content.aspx?article_id=1141.

3   Mitra Toossi, "Labor Force Projections to 2012: The Graying of the U.S. Workforce," *Monthly Labor Review*, www.bls.gov, February 2004.

4   Mitra Toosi, "Labor Force Change, 1950 – 2050," *Monthly Labor Review*, www.bls.gov, May 2002.

5   "The Multi-Generational Workplace — Fact Sheet 09," *The Center on Aging & Work*, Workplace Flexibility at Boston College, July 2007.

6   Paul Merrion, "Chicago Boardrooms Lag Nation in Diversity," Workforce.com, November 15, 2012. http://www.workforce.com/article/20121115/NEWS01/121119971/chicago-boardrooms-lag-nation-in-diversity#.

7   "Status and Trends in the Education of Racial and Ethnic Minorities," National Center for Education Statistics, www.nces.ed.gov, September 2007.

8   "U.S. College Drop-Out Rate Sparks Concern," *MSNBC*, www.msnbc.msn.com, November 15, 2005; and Jay P. Greene, Ph.D and Marcus A. Winters, "Public High School Graduation and College-Readiness Rates: 1991–2002," Education Working Paper, Manhattan Institute for Policy Research, February 2005.

9   "The Economic Impact of the Achievement Gap in America's Schools," Report by McKinsey & Company, www.mckinsey.com, April 2009.

10   "Education to Employment: Designing a System that Works," McKinsey & Company, 2012. http://mckinseyonsociety.com/downloads/reports/Education/Education-to-Employment-exec-summary_FINAL.pdf

11   Malcolm Gladwell, *Outliers: The Story of Success*, Little, Brown and Company, 2008.

12   David Brooks, "The Harlem Miracle," *New York Times*, May 7, 2009.

13   Lisa Quast, "Women And STEM Careers: How Microsoft Is Building A Bridge To Future Innovation — One Girl At A Time" Forbes.com, October 10, 2012. http://www.forbes.com/sites/lisaquast/2012/10/22/women-and-stem-careers-how-microsoft-is-building-a-bridge-to-future-innovation-one-girl-at-a-time/.

14   Jesse Washington, "STEM Education And Jobs: Declining Numbers Of Blacks Seen In Math, Science" *Huffington Post*, October 24, 2011. http://www.huffingtonpost.com/2011/10/24/stem-education-and-jobs-d_n_1028998.html.

15   Lisa Quast, "Women And STEM Careers: How Microsoft Is Building A Bridge To Future Innovation — One Girl At A Time" Forbes.com, October 10, 2012. http://www. forbes.com/sites/lisaquast/2012/10/22/women-and-stem-careers-how-microsoft-is-building-a-bridge-to-future-innovation-one-girl-at-a-time/.

16   Jesse Washington, "STEM Education And Jobs: Declining Numbers Of Blacks Seen In Math, Science" *Huffington Post*, October 24, 2011. http://www.huffingtonpost.com/ 2011/10/24/stem-education-and-jobs-d_n_1028998.html.

17   Brian Kelly, "The State of STEM and Jobs," USNews.com, September 21, 2012. http:// www.usnews.com/news/articles/2012/09/21/the-state-of-stem-and-jobs?page=2.

18   Rodney C. Adkins, "America Desperately Needs More STEM Students. Here's How to Get Them," Forbes.com, July 9, 2012. http://www.forbes.com/sites/forbesleadershipforum 2012/07/09/america-desperately-needs-more-stem-students-heres-how-to-get-them/.

19   Lisa Quast, "Women And STEM Careers: How Microsoft Is Building A Bridge To Future Innovation — One Girl At A Time" Forbes.com, October 10, 2012. http://www. forbes.com/sites/lisaquast/2012/10/22/women-and-stem-careers-how-microsoft-is-building-a-bridge-to-future-innovation-one-girl-at-a-time/.

20   "Top Companies for Leaders 2007," Hewitt Associates, 2007.

21   Jessica Marquez, "Diversity: The Obama Effect," *Workforce Management*, www.workforce. com, February 5, 2009.

22   http://www.whitehouse.gov/issues/education.

23   http://www.whitehouse.gov/issues/education.

24   Thomas Friedman, "Swimming without a Suit," *New York Times*, April 22, 2009.

Conclusion

1   2 Corinthians 4:8 (New International Version).

Appendix A

1   Dr. Milton Bennett, *Basic Concepts of Intercultural Communication*, Intercultural Press, 1998.

Endnotes

Acknowledgements

It not only takes a village to raise a child, as the African proverb says, but it also takes one to create a book. Not just for the actual editorial process of researching, interviewing, reviewing, editing, proofreading, designing, marketing, and project managing, but to also actually create something to write about. Here I want to acknowledge those who played a part either in creating the story to tell or in the telling of the story.

Those who partnered in doing the work:
For your commitment, passion, knowledge, and skills: Tyronne Stoudemire, Elina Rodriguez, Susan McCuistion, Linda DeLavallade, Chuck Adams, Nancy Sedin, Cathy Gallagher-Louisy, Patti Meessmann, Bo Young Lee, Diane Krieman, Carol Sladek, Elaine Masterson, and Kristin Slavish.

Those who believed and were partners in the early pioneering efforts:
For my colleagues, mentors, and leaders where all this got started: Steve King for the opportunity offered for me to become a CDO. Dale Gifford for the deep and broad sponsorship of the early work. Jack Bruner for the opening into the business. Helen Mills, Brandon Bennett, Gino Pinto, Andy Hiles, John Bomba,

Linda Schievelbein, and Sandy Miller for creating marketplace openings. Tracy Keogh and Russ Fradin for sponsoring the first edition of this book. Mary-Frances Winters for that foundation-setting beginning we partnered on.

My editors throughout my career:
David Neff for inculcating the discipline of precision. To Verne Becker for teaching me how to tell a story. To Sandy Close, CEO and executive editor of the New America Media, for providing a platform for finding my author voice.

The ones who kept me together and those around me sane:
My executive assistants, Barbara Grala and Katie Reardon.

The many who agreed to be interviewed for the book and have been quoted throughout.

Our Hewitt and Diversity Best Practices clients who invited us into their community to partner with them and learn from one another.

And finally there were many who in one way or another moved the work forward internally at Hewitt and with our clients when I served there as CDO and now at Diversity Best Practices with our members and clients, or who played a key role in the process of putting this book together in terms of editorial help, graphic design, marketing, and subject matter expert review. Their names along with those mentioned above show up in the roll call that follows.

Gracias to all for the work you do every day,
every moment, around the globe, to make the world
a better place to work — for everyone.

Acknowledgements

Alison Borland, Amanda Wuest,
ANDY HILES, *Artell Smith*,
Barbara Grala, *Barb Hogg,*
BECKY KEEN, ***Bob Campbell,***
Bo Young Lee, *Brandon Bennett,*
Carol Sladek, Cathy Gallagher-
Louisy, *Christi Rager-Wise,*
Chuck Adams, Cindy Dayney,
Cosette Yisrael, **DALE GIFFORD,**
Dana Holmes, *David Neff,*
Dawne Simmons, Diane Krieman,
Don Minner, **ELINA RODRIGUEZ,**
ERIN PETERSON, **Gino Pinto,**
Helen Mills, Jack Bruner,

JD Piro, Jeff Shovlin, Jennifer Hoffman, *Jill Sherer Murray,* Jim Konieczny, JOANNE DAHM, *Jon Leatherbury,* Jon Malysiak, *Julie Cook Ramirez,* *JULIE MACDONALD,* Kelley McDonald, *Kelly Salek,* Kerry LaCoste, KRISTIN SLAVISH, *Linda Mateja,* Linda DeLavallade, Lisa Horuczi Markus, Lori Miller, *MARK BOCIANSKI,* Mary-Frances Winters, MARY KELLEY, *Maurissa Kanter,* Melissa

Giovagnoli, MOLLIE KOHN, *Monica Francois Marcel,* **Nancy Sedin,** Pam Harris, **PAMAY BASSEY,** *PATTI MEESSMANN,* Rajeev Jain, ***Ray Baumruk,*** *Robert Lundin,* Ron Dayney, RUSS FRADIN, **SANDY CLOSE,** Sandy Miller, Steve Bright, Steve King, **SUSAN MCCUISTION, Susan Welch,** SUZANNE KENNEY, *Tanya McKeel,* Tracy Keogh, **TYRONNE STOUDEMIRE,** *Verne Becker,* WENDY RHODES

About the Author

Andrés Tapia is President of Diversity Best Practices, the preeminent diversity and inclusion thinktank and consultancy. Previously he served as the Chief Diversity Officer and Emerging Workforce Solutions Leader for Hewitt Associates.

Andrés is a published writer and prominent speaker. As a journalist, he covered social trends in the U.S. and Latin America via articles appearing in publications such as the *Baltimore Sun*, the *Chicago Tribune*, the *San Francisco Chronicle*, *VOCÊ* (Brazil), *Benefits Quarterly*, and *Hemispheres* magazine. He has been interviewed by major media outlets such as the *Wall Street Journal*, the *New York Times*, *BusinessWeek*, *CNN en Español*, and *FORTUNE* magazine in the United States, *La Nación* and *El Clarín* in Argentina, *El Mercurio* in Chile, *VOCÊ*, *Valor*, and *Revista Amanhã* in Brazil, and HR industry publications such as *HR Magazine*, *Benefit News*, and *Benefits Canada Magazine*.

His experiences in the U.S., Canada, the UK, Spain, India, Kenya, and throughout Latin America and his native Perú have equipped him with a true global perspective. By working with dozens of Diversity Best Practices Consulting's Fortune 500 multinational clients, as well as with public schools, arts organizations, and law enforcement agencies, Andrés is grounded in the cross-industry implications of achieving a diverse, high-performing workforce. He has developed actionable insights into how varying worldviews can impact health, wealth, learning, safety, and workplace performance.

Andrés' innovative approach to foster an inclusive work environment includes shifting paradigms such as: from tolerance and sensitivity to cross-cultural competence, and from programmatic to sustainable diversity. He has created several groundbreaking and high-impact diversity learning and multicultural marketing programs. Andrés was the catalyst for a groundbreaking study on retirement savings that found that race/ethnicity is a greater determinant of differences in savings behaviors than income.

Andrés has received the following recognitions: He is a Leadership Greater Chicago Fellow (Class of 2008), Hispanic Alliance for Career Enhancement Éxito Award (2008), Chicago United's Business Leader of Color Award (2007), CDO Exemplary List published by Diversity Best Practices in *FORTUNE* magazine (2006), the Corporate Diversity Program and Diversity Ad Campaign of the Year granted by the Minorities in Advertising Foundation (2006), and the Hewitt Exemplary Leader Award (2005). He is also on the Board of Luna Negra Dance Theatre.

Andrés holds a B.A. in History with an emphasis in journalism and political science from Northwestern University. He is married to Lori, a musician, and they have an adult daughter, Marisela, who is a flamenco dancer.

About Diversity
Best Practices

Diversity Best Practices, a division of Working Mother Media, is the preeminent membership organization for diversity thought leaders to share best practices and develop innovative solutions for culture change. Through research, benchmarking, publications, and events, Diversity Best Practices offers members information and strategies on how to create, implement, grow, and measure first-in-class diversity programs.

Diversity Best Practices services help companies clarify opportunities and implications of their current diversity strategy, identify and enhance critical diversity leadership competencies, create and implement a system-wide focus on diversity and inclusion and gain the executive-level support needed to ensure the company is successful.

Diversity Best Practices' team includes an impressive group of relationship managers, researchers, senior practitioners, consultants, council members, and committees from a wide range of cultural backgrounds and professional experience. Our research-based benchmarking content builds the knowledge and offers the tools needed to provide diversity solutions that meet the unique needs of our member companies.

In today's information-driven economy, diversity leaders need access to the most relevant knowledge available to execute successful diversity initiatives. Diversity Best Practices provides that knowledge. For more information, visit www.DiversityBestPractices.com.

Made in the USA
San Bernardino, CA
17 December 2013